Inside CorelDRAW!,
4th Edition

Daniel Gray

with Steve Shubitz

D0507396

Inside CorelDRAW!, 4th Edition

By Daniel Gray with Steve Shubitz

Published by:
New Riders Publishing
11711 N. College Ave., Suite 140
Carmel, IN 46032 USA

Printed in the United States of America 1 2 3 4 5 6 7 8 9 0

Library of Congress Cataloging-in-Publication Data

Gray, Daniel, 1961-
Inside CorelDRAW!/Daniel Gray, Steve Shubitz.--4th ed.
        p.   cm.
Includes index.
ISBN 1-56205-106-7: $34.95
1. Computer graphics. I. Shubitz, Steve. II. Title.
T385.G738   1992b
006.6'869—dc20

NEW RIDERS
PUBLISHING

Publisher
David P. Ewing

Associate Publisher
Tim Huddleston

Managing Editor
Cheri Robinson

Acquisitions Editors
Brad Koch
John W. Pont

Production Editor
Geneil Breeze

Editors
JoAnna Arnott
Margaret Berson
Rob Lawson
Rich Limacher
Nora Loechel
Alice Martina Smith

Editorial Assistant
Karen Opal

Technical Editors
Jeff Koch
Dennis Sanner

Book Design
Scott Cook

Book Layout and Production
Scott Boucher
Christine Cook
Dennis Clay Hager
Susan M. Shepard
Allan Wimmer
Alyssa Yesh

Proofreaders
Mark Enochs
Phil Kitchel
Linda Quigley
Julie Walker

Indexed by
Jeanne Clark

Composed in Poster Bodoni and Palatino by
Prentice Hall Computer Publishing

About the Authors

Daniel Gray is a journeyman artist who has been involved in both traditional and electronic publishing for more than ten years. Dan's electronic publishing experience includes stints at the drawing board, in the darkroom, in systems management, and with personal computers. Dan has worked on dozens of publications including *The Princeton Packet* and *Women's Wear Daily*. He founded and publishes Banzai Wire, America's only independent journal for Suzuki automobile owners.

Dan is currently a Graphic Systems Analyst for the Continental Corporation and uses both MS-DOS and Macintosh platforms to publish a wide range of periodicals, from simple newsletters to four-color magazines.

Readers are invited to contact Daniel Gray through CompuServe. His CIS number is 71210,667.

Steve Shubitz is President of Published Perfection!, a La Jolla, California electronic publishing and consulting company that provides production, training, and integration for the Windows and Macintosh platforms. Steve began his graphic arts career as a designer in 1980. Steve is a Permanent Contributing Editor for *Electronic Composition and Imaging Magazine* for which he authors the "Publishing in Windows" column. Steve is a faculty member at The Advertising Arts College where he teaches Desktop Publishing. He has lectured extensively throughout the United States. In 1986 PageMaker for Windows was released, and Steve began using Windows. Steve has been an avid user of CorelDRAW! since its initial release and has trained numerous Fortune 1000 firms in his two-day courses.

Steve's expert knowledge of both PC and Macintosh platforms in a real-world production environment provides his clients with a unique perspective of electronics publishing technology. Readers are invited to contact Steve by phone at (619) 546-9309 or through CompuServe. His CIS number is 72047,3402.

Acknowledgments

In the past two years, we have produced four editions of "Inside CorelDRAW!". This latest edition was our most ambitious effort to date, and would not have been possible without the dedicated efforts of many members of the New Riders family. There are far too many people to thank individually, but you wouldn't be reading this if Rusty Gesner hadn't taken that initial chance on me. In kind, many thanks to Christine Steel for her guidance on the first and second editions, and to Steve Shubitz for penning chapters 13, 14, and 15, and compiling the two disks included with the book.

At Corel Corporation, many thanks for an incredible suite of programs, along with the best software support in the industry. Many thanks to Vivi Nichol for reviewing the first edition and for her (along with her dedicated and talented crew's) continued assistance. In particular, Kim Connerty, Shawn Greenburg, Donna Hogan, Krista Martens, and Rus Miller were of great help. And without Fiona Rochester's and Janie Sullivan's support, we would have never made it to press on time. Merci beaucoup.

My deepest gratitude to Gary Cartwright for his insight, and to ArtRight's talented electronic artists, most notably George Matatko. There is a right way and a wrong way to put a drawing together. If you are curious, just take a look at any of ArtRight's cars.

Debbie and Allie, you deserve the most thanks of all.

Trademark Acknowledgments

New Riders Publishing has made every attempt to supply trademark information about company names, products, and services mentioned in this book. Trademarks indicated below were derived from various sources. New Riders Publishing cannot attest to the accuracy of this information.

Adobe, Adobe Illustrator, and PostScript are a registered trademarks of Adobe Systems, Inc.; Ami Professional is a trademark of SAMNA Corporation; Apple, and Microsoft TrueType are a registered trademarks of Apple Computer, Inc.; CorelDRAW! and CorelTRACE! are registered copyrights of Corel Systems Corporation.; CompuServe is a registered trademark of CompuServe, Inc.; FontMonger is a trademark of Ares Software Corporation; FreeHand and Pagemaker are a registered trademarks of Aldus Corporation; IBM/PC/XT/AT, IBM PS/2, and PC DOS are registered trademarks of the International Business Machines Corporation; Linotype is a registered trademark of Liontype-Hell Company; Lotus is a registered trademark of Lotus Development Corporation; Macintosh is a registered trademark of Apple Computer, Inc.; Microsoft is a registered trademark and Word for Windows is a trademark of Microsoft Corporation; MS and MS-DOS are registered trademarks, and Windows and Windows/386 are trademarks of Microsoft Corporation; Pantone, Inc. is the copyright owner of PANTONE Color Computer Graphics and Software, which is licensed to Corel Systems Corporation to distribute for use only in combination with CorelDRAW!. PANTONE Computer Video Simulations used in this publication may not match PANTONE-identified solid color standards. Use current PANTONE Color Reference Manuals for accurate color; QuarkXPress is a registered trademark of Quark, Inc.; Ventura Publisher is a trademark of Ventura Software, Inc.; Trademarks of other products mentioned in this book are held by the companies producing them.

Warning and Disclaimer

This book is designed to provide information about the CorelDRAW! program. Every effort has been made to make this book as complete and as accurate as possible, but no warranty or fitness is implied.

The information is provided on an "as is" basis. The author and New Riders Publishing shall have neither liability nor responsibility to any person or entity with respect to any loss or damages arising from the information contained in this book or from the use of the disks or programs that may accompany it.

Contents at a Glance

Contents

Part Two: Putting CorelDRAW! To Work

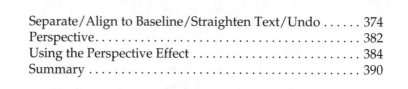

Part Three: Past Your Own PC

11 The Windows DTP Arsenal 461

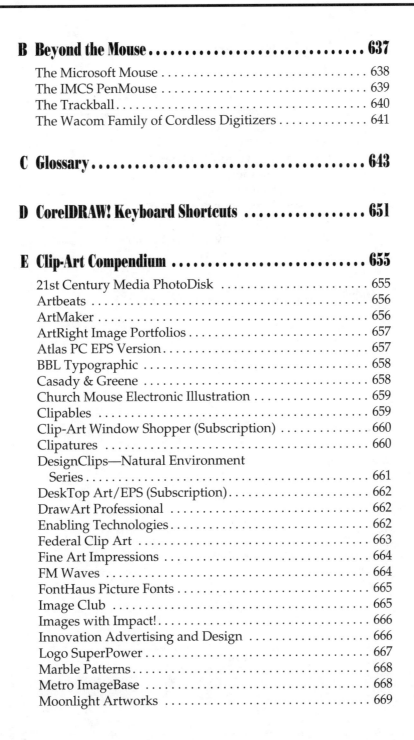

Introduction

orelDRAW! is the premier graphics software package for the MS-DOS environment. The program has an intuitive interface that makes it easy to learn but tricky to master. When you master CorelDRAW!, however, you can use your DOS-based computer to create publication-quality artwork—a domain formerly ruled exclusively by the Apple Macintosh.

CorelDRAW! Version 3.0 is a quantum leap beyond previous versions. The package includes three new modules: CorelPHOTO-PAINT!, CorelCHART!, and CorelSHOW! This trio of new programs—along with the latest editions of CorelDRAW!, CorelMOSAIC!, and CorelTRACE!—form a powerful toolkit that meets the demands of both graphic artists and business people.

CorelDRAW!, the cornerstone program in the package, is an object-oriented drawing program. In many ways, it is more similar to computer-aided design (CAD) programs—such as AutoCAD—than it is to many PC-based graphics programs. CorelDRAW! may seem akin to paint programs such as CorelPHOTO-PAINT!, PC Paintbrush or Windows Paint, but the differences are clear. Paint programs use bit-mapped graphics and give the illusion of painting on canvas or working with pencils. Although you "draw" in both genres, the process of producing an image in CorelDRAW! is more like building a collage.

The Theory behind Object-Oriented Drawing Programs

Vector-based (rather than bit-mapped) programs such as CorelDRAW! are the electronic artist's tool of choice for print media. The two major benefits of an object-oriented drawing program are precision and flexibility. Because you define objects with vector coordinates—think of it as working with mathematical equations—you can operate with output-device and resolution independence. Bezier curves are infinitely scalable in size, giving you the flexibility to reduce or enlarge artwork with no loss of quality.

Where CorelDRAW! Fits into the DTP Arsenal

CorelDRAW! 3.0 is the most full-featured graphics program that a PC-based artist can use, and it is the perfect complement to such programs as Aldus PageMaker, Ventura Publisher, or Quark Xpress. The program's combination of powerful features and ease-of-use put it ahead of the pack, PC or Macintosh. CorelDRAW! also fits well in a workgroup environment.

About This Book

To make the most of this book, both you and your computer need to be properly set up. To run CorelDRAW!, you need a DOS-based personal computer equipped with the minimum of an 80386 processor, a hard disk, a printer, a high-resolution monitor (VGA or better), and a Windows-supported pointing device such as the Microsoft Mouse. Microsoft Windows must be installed on the computer, and you should be familiar with its interface. It is suggested that you have Windows 3.1

Using this Book

Inside CorelDRAW! is a tutorial and is meant for you to use while you are sitting at the computer. You will find that the immediate visual feedback of trying commands as you read about them provides a most effective means of learning.

This book is neither a substitute for, nor a restatement of, the program's documentation. It was written as a learning tool—a doorway into the program, if you will. The CorelDRAW! reference manual and on-line help, along with the other material you received in your CorelDRAW! 3.0 package, are necessary as reference material.

Exercise Syntax and Conventions

You also need to understand how the exercises are presented. When you use CorelDRAW!, you are, in fact, creating PostScript programs that run on your laser printer. You will not find any IFs, THENs, or GO TOs in this book or in your drawings, but your drawings are uncompiled programs. If they are not properly composed, you will have problems when you try to print them.

To this end, the exercises are organized in a straightforward manner, so they are easy to follow and to use as a reference. The exercises are set apart from the text with horizontal rules, and are set up in a two-column format. You will find commands and instructions in the left-hand column. Letters that are underlined on the screen are shown in bold text. Characters that you must enter also appear in bold text. Each exercise's right-hand column contains comments that correspond to the operations.

Here is a short example of an exercise:

Opening a File

Click **File**	The File menu appears.
Click **Open**	The Open File dialogue box appears.

continues

Click BOXKITE.CDR	This specifies the drawing file you want to open.
Click OK	The drawing opens on the screen.

To complete an exercise, follow the commands and instructions in the left-hand column and watch the right column for commentary. In the text, function keys are identified as F1, F2, F3, and so on. Combination keystrokes appear as Ctrl-D, Alt-Tab, and so on.

The book repeatedly uses terms that refer to mouse techniques. These terms are: *click, double-click, shift-click,* and *marquee-select. Clicking* on an object or menu item selects the object or item. *Double-clicking* usually performs a function, without the need to click an OK button. *Shift-clicking* is used to select more than one object. By holding down Shift, objects are added to the number of selected objects. *Dragging a marquee* is like throwing a lasso around a number of objects to select them in one swoop.

Finally, note that this book often refers to the CorelDRAW! program by its popularly used nick-name, "Draw."

What Lies Ahead

Inside CorelDRAW! is divided into five parts, which present a logical progression of information for inexperienced as well as seasoned CorelDRAW! users. Each chapter builds on previously covered topics. This approach is intended to shorten your learning curve and to help you enjoy using the program from the first time you boot up.

Part One: The Basics

In Part One, you start with the simplest of maneuvers and progress through the essentials of creating artwork. Chapter 1, "Getting Up and Running," covers the basics of image manipulation. You open an existing CorelDRAW! clip-art file and stretch, scale, and rotate it. You learn how to save files by using the Page Setup dialogue box to adjust page size and other parameters. You also learn how to use the zoom tool to take a closer look at your image. You finish the chapter by printing the modified clip-art image.

Chapter 2, "Creating and Drawing," gets into the specifics of Draw's tools and guides you through the completion of your first drawing. You learn how to use the pencil tool to draw straight and curved lines and to understand the difference between open and closed path objects. The secrets behind the precise use of the ellipse and rectangle tools, as well as the skew function, are revealed when you turn on the grid to build a box kite.

As you move on to Chapter 3, "Editing and Manipulation," your work begins to get more complex. You begin by learning how CorelDRAW! implements Bezier curves, using the shape tool to tweak the nodes and control points of different node types. The exercise covers the concepts of layering work by building groups as you construct some simple playing cards. Along the way, you learn how to round corners on a rectangle, set up and use the Duplicate command, and create special characters such as hearts, spades, and clubs.

Part Two: Putting CorelDRAW! to Work

Once you get into Part Two, you are ready to roll up your sleeves and put yourself to the task of creating some "real-world" graphics. This book's emphasis is to make you proficient with Draw, so that you can use the program to help pay the rent, rather than merely to entertain.

Chapter 4, "Basic Typography," explains the concepts behind Draw's typographic conventions while you build a quick-and-dirty flyer for the proprietor of an imaginary used car lot. In the process, this chapter covers the basics of Draw's text tool, and you pick up tips about bringing in text from other programs.

Chapter 5, "Advanced Typography," picks up where Chapter 4 ends and gets into a more complex typographical project. It deals with the aesthetic aspects of typesetting while designing an intricately formed logo design. The type is kerned and converted to curves, enabling you to work on the actual character outlines as objects rather than as text. You learn how to use nonprinting guidelines to help objects align properly. You also investigate two of CorelDRAW!'s most powerful effects, Envelope and Extrude.

Chapter 6, "Outline, Fill, and Color," ambitiously covers the theories behind Draw's outline and fill tools. You learn about spot and process (the two different types of printed color) and about Draw's powerful fountain-fill capabilities. To illustrate these concepts, you build a 35mm slide image, importing and colorizing a piece of black-and-white art along the way.

While Draw itself is primarily object-oriented, Chapter 7, "Bit Maps and Draw," shows how the program can work with bit-mapped artwork from a variety of sources. You learn that bit maps can be created with Windows Paintbrush or CorelPHOTO-PAINT!, brought into a PC through an optical scanner, or imported as existing BMP, PCX, or TIFF files. You create a bit map by using Paintbrush, import it into Draw, and use it with a mask to create some pleasantly filled logotype. CorelTRACE! and autotracing also are discussed as you use the process to convert a bit-mapped clip-art file into a vector image.

Building on many of the concepts presented throughout the book, Chapter 8, "Assembling Complex Images," shows you how to create an intricately engineered monarch butterfly. Your object here is to create a lean, mean, working drawing that is complex yet compact. You will see the powerful nature of Draw's Combine command as you craft the drawing for reduced redraw time and imaging. Blend and Perspective, two of Draw's fabulous effects (first introduced in version 2.0), are used in hands-on exercises. Draw's streamlined file format is explored, and you also learn file management and screen preview strategies.

Want to wow your boss and amaze your friends? Chapter 9, "Special Type Effects," consists of a series of step-by-step procedures for creating distinctive drawings and typographical illustrations. Everything from the plain-vanilla drop shadow through chromed and beveled effects is thoroughly detailed. This is the chapter you will turn to when you get stuck for a new idea or design solution.

Members of the Draw community get to show some of their stuff in Chapter 10, "The Galleries." A beautiful four-color process section shows samples of what can be done with images created with CorelDRAW! From printed images to three-dimensional objects, you will learn how some of the guest artists used Draw as a springboard to bring their projects to life.

Part Three: "Past Your Own PC"

Part Three focuses on what you need besides your PC and CorelDRAW! to get your electronic art projects done. Chapter 11, "The Windows DTP Arsenal," contains exercises that delve into exporting and interfacing your images with other programs. It also presents a number of sources for acquiring everything from actual fonts to typographic information and inspiration. CorelMOSAIC!, Corel's visual file manager, also is discussed.

Chapter 12, "Printing Considerations," is where you finally get all your images into print—whether on paper, slides, or vinyl. This chapter covers the intricacies of Draw's Print command and discusses how you can use CorelDRAW! to trap artwork.

Part Four: "OLE, Fighting the Bull"

Part Four dives into the newest additions to the Corel family. In this section, you learn how to use Windows' object linking and embedding (OLE) capabilities to supercharge your work.

Chapter 13, "CorelPHOTO-PAINT!," covers Corel's new bit-mapped paint program. You may already be familiar with Photo-Paint, since this module is really just a rebadged version of ZSoft's PHOTO-FINISH. This chapter sheds light on many aspects of the program, including setup, filters, conversion, and image retouching.

Chapter 14, "CorelCHART!," checks into the second of CorelDRAW!'s new program modules, a powerful charting application. Chart offers a wide array of stunning three dimensional charts, and makes heavy use of Object Linking and Embedding. You will create Pie, 3D-Riser, and Pictograph charts, using the Data Manager.

Chapter 15, "CorelSHOW!," buys you a ticket to the hottest show in town. Show is an OLE-aware multimedia application that enables you to use sound and graphics for everything from tradeshow exhibits to boardroom presentations. In this chapter, you complete a presentation for Rippin' Surfboards, using files created in the two previous chapters, along with an animation supplied on the CorelDRAW! distribution disks.

Part Five: Appendixes

Part 5 includes five appendixes—including a glossary—which provide you with a wealth of practical information about CorelDRAW!. System integration is covered in Appendix A, "Working With Windows." You learn how to fine-tune your system, including information in the CORELDRW.INI file. Relatively unknown features are placed in a new light, and you find out what Windows files you can remove if you are running with little disk space to spare.

More information is contained in Appendixes B, D, and E, which cover a variety of subjects, from drawing tablets to clip-art vendors, along with a list of keyboard shortcuts. Appendix C is a glossary of electronic and conventional graphic art terms.

Meet Joe DeLook and Design by the Sea

The book's imaginary hero is Joe DeLook, proprietor of DeLook Design, a small design firm in a seaside resort town. Joe is an experienced graphic designer, but a fledgling electronic artist. He has just purchased CorelDRAW! for the same reason everybody did—it is the best PC-based illustration package on the market.

Throughout this book, you learn CorelDRAW! alongside Joe DeLook—a novel idea in a tutorial! This may provide a unique perspective and help you grasp the bigger picture of how CorelDRAW! can enable you to do your job in the real world. If you are ready, get yourself a glass or mug of your favorite beverage and get comfortable. You are about to take a trip *Inside CorelDRAW!*

Part One

The Basics

Getting Up and Running

Creating and Drawing

Editing and Manipulating

Getting Up and Running

To function efficiently within the CorelDRAW! environment, you need to know how to handle all the basics. Even if you already are familiar with the program's basic operation, you still should look through this chapter, rather than skipping it altogether. You are bound to pick up a hint or two along the way.

This chapter lays a foundation on which you build in the following chapters. To begin, you learn how to start CorelDRAW! and to open an existing CDR file. (Throughout this book, you will see the name *CorelDRAW!* shortened to just *Draw*.) Once the file is opened, you learn how to use the program's select, move, size and stretch, rotate, and zoom features. Finally, you learn how to save your file, open a new file, adjust the page setup, and import some clip art.

As you move through the exercises, you learn the ways in which CorelDRAW! clusters multiple functions within a single tool. This organization runs throughout the program and is crucial to Draw's uncluttered appearance and functionality.

The tutorial exercises in this book are written with the assumption that your hard disk is drive C and your floppy disk is inserted into drive A. If your computer is set up differently, substitute your own drive letters where appropriate. The book assumes that you are using CorelDRAW! version 3.0 (or newer).

You should have a basic knowledge of Microsoft Windows and be familiar with windows, buttons, scroll bars, and so on. If not, check the documentation that came with the Windows program, or read Appendix A.

Getting Rolling with DeLook Design

In the imaginary village of Seaside, Joe DeLook has loaded Draw on his PC's hard disk, and he is ready to make the plunge into the world of electronic art.

It is well past closing time on Friday afternoon, and everyone has left except for Joe. Rather than sitting with his friends at the bar, he is sitting at his PC. He is intent on learning to use CorelDRAW!

Joe has little experience with personal computers, but he has a solid background in graphic design. Although the PC has been in the studio for a few months, it has been used mostly for book-keeping, not design work. Sitting at the PC, Joe has been aimlessly flipping through the book of symbol and clip-art libraries that came with the CorelDRAW! package. Leafing through the trans-portation section, he pauses at a picture of a Porsche 911—his dream car, and a far cry from the junker he drives now. Joe notes that the file is called CAR366.CDR, and he decides to see if he can load it into Draw.

Before getting started, you need to be sure that CorelDRAW! is properly installed. The installation process is easy to follow and includes options that enable you to install the program and its associated files according to your preferences. For instance, you may or may not choose to install the clip-art files. To perform many of the exercises in this book, you need to have the clip art handy.

It is wisest to load pre-existing artwork (such as existing clip art or a file you have created and saved on floppy disk) onto your computer's hard disk while you are outside of the CorelDRAW! program. A good idea is to load the clip-art libraries into a subdirectory within the CORELDRW directory. This book refers to that subdirectory as C:\CORELDRW\DRAW\CLIPART.

If you have plenty of room on your hard disk, go ahead and load all the clip-art libraries to that directory. If, however, you do not have the disk space to spare, you can copy individual libraries. For the exercises in this first chapter, you need to load the MISC library.

If you did not load the clip art when you installed CorelDRAW!, you need to run Draw's Setup program. Setup can be found on disk 1 of the CorelDRAW! distribution disks.

Before you begin image manipulation, you first must get Draw up and running, which is an easy task. Start this first exercise at the Windows Program Manager. The CorelDRAW! icon should be located in the Corel Graphics window. If this icon is not present on your screen, you can start by double-clicking on CORELDRW.EXE at the File Manager.

NOTE

If you install Draw's clip-art files from the floppy disks, they will take up almost two megabytes of hard disk space. If space is at a premium on your system, you may want to install only the clip art you need.

Booting Draw

Double-click the CorelDRAW! icon

Your computer loads CorelDRAW!. The opening screen greets you, and a clean page appears.

Manipulating Images

Now that you have the program running, see about getting that Porsche 911 image to work with. If you have had the chance to look at Draw's Symbol and Clip Art Libraries booklet, you know that CorelDRAW! comes with a bounty of clip-art files from a variety of manufacturers. These files offer a good sampling of what is available in the commercial clip-art marketplace.

Opening a File

The Open Drawing dialogue box provides a powerful interface for searching, previewing, and loading artwork. When you work through the following steps and load the Porsche file that came with Draw, you will see that it is easy to choose files, either by name, or by "face." As you scroll through the clip art files, click once on the file name; the preview window displays a color thumbnail view of contents of the file.

Like many other dialogue boxes, the Open Drawing dialogue box expands with a click of a button. When you click the Options button, the dialogue box nearly doubles in size. Experienced users will notice that CorelDRAW! version 3.0 has added great functionality to the Open Drawing dialogue box. The Sort by feature enables you to sort files by file name or by file creation date. It is now possible to do keyword searches and review notes without using the Mosaic utility program. However, access to Mosaic is only a button click away.

As you open the Porsche file in the following exercise, take note of the features hidden behind the Options button.

Opening a Clip-Art File

Click **File**	The File menu appears.
Click **O**pen	The Open Drawing dialogue box appears (see figure 1.1).

Most likely, the directory that first appears will not be the one you want. The Open Drawing dialogue box, like other Corel dialogue boxes, remembers where it was left. You need to switch to the correct directory, library, and file type.

Change the directory to
C:\CORELDRW\DRAW\CLIPART\MISC

Click Options	The dialogue box expands.
Click CAR366.CDR	A red Porsche appears in the preview window.
Click OK	The file CAR366.CDR opens.

SPEED TIP: If you like, you can forgo clicking OK, and simply double-click on the file name to open the file.

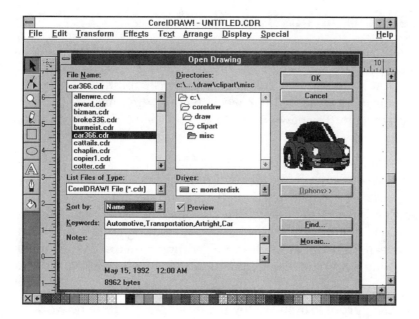

Figure 1.1:
The Open Drawing dialogue box.

The two basic reasons for preloading your clip art are safety and speed. You should try to avoid working with a clip-art file on an original disk; if you ruin the file, you will not have a way to get it back to its original form. Always work with a backup. Loading a file directly into Draw from a floppy is slow and can take more than three times as long as loading from your hard disk. Loading times vary with your computer's speed and the type and size of your hard disk.

Of course, the size of your hard disk is a major factor in deciding where to keep your clip-art files and libraries. If your hard disk has plenty of room to spare, you might want to keep the clip-art

Shortcut

Press Ctrl-O to open a file.

files there. If not, it would be a good idea to back up the files to a second set of floppy disks.

You can load a file directly from a floppy disk into Draw, but if you preload, it safeguards your original disks. Preloading is a good habit to get into. If Draw already is running, you can minimize the program and access the File Manager to load files without using the File Open command.

Full-Color or Wireframe Mode?

When you opened the Porsche file, it appeared on your computer screen in either full-color or wireframe mode. CorelDRAW! version 3.0 introduced full-color editing capabilities; before this version, users could edit artwork in only wireframe mode, although Color Preview was just a keystroke (or a couple of mouse-clicks) away.

Full-color mode editing is preferred by many electronic artists— but the convenience of full-color editing can extract a toll on system performance, particularly on complex images. Wireframe editing is faster—in many cases, dramatically so. For this reason, you will find yourself working in both editing modes. To switch between full-color and wireframe editing, you can change modes by using either the display menu or the Shift-F9 keyboard short-cut.

Shortcut

Press Shift-F9 to toggle between full-color and wireframe editing.

For the purposes of the following exercises, you will be working in full-color mode. A check mark next to the words Edit Wireframe on the Display menu indicates that Draw is in wireframe mode (see figure 1.2). If a check mark appears, click the Edit Wireframe selection to get into full-color mode.

Selecting an Object

Now that the Porsche file is loaded, start exploring Draw. When you place your pointer on the Porsche and click, you see eight black boxes surrounding the car. These boxes are called *handles*. They let you know that the Porsche is selected. The black box handles designate that the object is in the stretch/scale mode. An object must be selected in order to be manipulated.

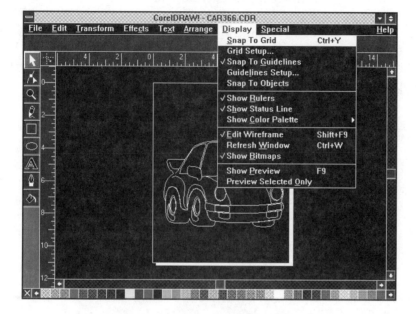

Figure 1.2:

The Display menu with Edit Wireframe selected.

Start out by moving the Porsche around the page. When you click and drag, be sure to position the cursor on the selected object. In wireframe mode, the pick tool's tip should be touching one of the lines in the selected object. If you don't click directly on a selected line, you will deselect the object, and you will have to reselect it. In full-color mode, simply click anywhere on an object to select it.

As you drag the mouse up, you notice that a blue dashed outline box appears (see fig. 1.3). The cursor turns into a four-headed arrow, indicating that you are in the move mode. Don't be surprised when the image of the Porsche does not appear to move while you are dragging. Once you release the mouse button, the original Porsche disappears and reassembles itself in its new position.

Moving an Object

As you move the image around, watch the numbers change on the *status line* at the top of the window. If you do not see a status line, it has been toggled off. You can toggle the status line on and off by a selection on the Display menu. A check mark next to the words Show Status Line indicates that it is operational. If no check mark appears, click the Show Status Line selection now.

Selecting and Moving the Porsche

Click on the Porsche	The eight handles appear.
Drag the Porsche upward	The handles disappear and a dashed outline box appears.
Drag the box to top of the page	
Release the mouse button	The image reassembles itself in its new position.

It may take a few moments for your computer to reassemble the image. You will notice that it redraws object by object. Once you get more familiar with Draw, you may want to dissect the Porsche to learn how it was built.

Simple images redisplay much faster than complex images. As with loading files, the type of your hard disk affects the speed at which Draw operates. A fast hard disk, an accelerated graphics card, and a fast computer—one with a speedy 80386 or 80486 processor—greatly improve Draw's operating speed. If you never wanted a faster computer, you may, after spending a few hours working on complex graphics.

During the process of moving an object, the status line shows you four things: cursor coordinates, object position, distance, and angle. The cursor coordinates (shown in parentheses) tell you the exact position of the cursor relative to the horizontal and vertical rulers. The numbers denoted by *dx:* and *dy:* refer to the amount of horizontal and vertical distance that you have moved the object from its original position. *Distance* also is a linear measurement, denoting the amount of diagonal movement. *Angle* refers to the number of degrees of movement.

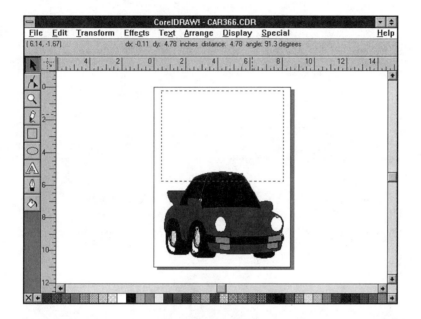

Figure 1.3:

Moving the Porsche with status line.

As you see in subsequent exercises, the status line has different gauges to record different functions. As you perform your own screen maneuvers, keep an eye on the status line.

Stretching an Object

The little black boxes that surround a selected object are called *stretch/scale handles*. To stretch an object, you must pull on the correct handle. Stretching is controlled by any one of the four center handles at an object's top, sides, or bottom.

The top or bottom handles make the object taller or shorter. The side handles make the object wider or thinner. As you stretch an object, it is anchored to the side opposite the one you are dragging.

Stretching the Porsche

Watch the status line as you stretch the Porsche. The status line reports the percentage of stretch.

Click on the Porsche	The eight handles appear.
Put the cursor on the bottom center handle	The cursor arrow becomes a +.
Drag the bottom center handle down	The handles are replaced by a blue box.
Release the mouse button at the bottom of the page	A tall sports car appears (see fig. 1.4).

Figure 1.4:

A tall Porsche.

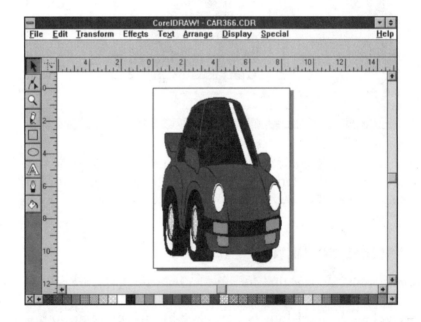

Fixing a Mistake

Shortcut

Press Alt-Backspace to invoke the Undo command.

Every artist needs an eraser to fix those occasional "Oops!" situations. Draw's eraser is the Undo command found on the Edit menu. Before you do anything else to your graphic, give Undo a try.

Using Undo and Redo

The eight handles should still be around the Porsche graphic. If not, you may not be able to undo the last change.

Click **Edit**, *Click* **Undo**	The car returns to its original proportions.
Click **Edit**, *Click* **Undo**	Returns the graphic to its pre-undo state.
Click **Edit**, *Click* **Undo**	The car is restored to its original proportions.

If you want, try stretching the car with its top and side handles. Return the car to its original state with Undo after each experiment. For Undo to work, you should use the command immediately after making a mistake. Do not perform any other actions. Undo can perform its magic on only the last action made. Currently, Draw has only one level of Undo.

Shortcut

Press Alt and Enter to invoke the Redo command.

Stretching Versus Scaling

In most cases, you may want to scale the picture proportionally, rather than anamorphically. If you are working with realistically rendered, finished graphics, you may need to scale (enlarge or reduce in size) proportionally.

When you scale *proportionally*, the width and length of an object enlarge or reduce in direct symmetry to each other, maintaining their width-to-length aspect ratio.

When you pulled on the bottom handle of the Porsche, the image was scaled *anamorphically*. This means that you enlarged (or reduced) the vertical (or horizontal) length (or width) without altering the other axis. This is asymmetrical or anamorphic scaling. Draw simply refers to this as *stretching*.

Enlarge the Porsche by scaling it proportionally. When you do, watch the status line. It tells you how large you are making the graphic on a percentage basis.

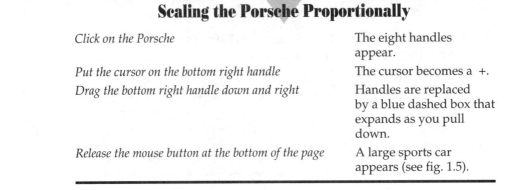

Scaling the Porsche Proportionally

Click on the Porsche	The eight handles appear.
Put the cursor on the bottom right handle	The cursor becomes a +.
Drag the bottom right handle down and right	Handles are replaced by a blue dashed box that expands as you pull down.
Release the mouse button at the bottom of the page	A large sports car appears (see fig. 1.5).

In figure 1.5, the drawing is enlarged beyond the CorelDRAW! page. If you try to print right now, only the part of the drawing that is actually in the page area (defined by the shadowed box) would print.

Figure 1.5:

A big proportional Porsche.

Leaving an Original

Draw has options that can make your sizing and scaling more efficient. In three cases, these options involve pressing a key while dragging the selected object's handles. The fourth option uses a simple dragging procedure. All four options can be used in combination or in unison.

The first option provides a means to build a new, stretched object without altering the original. If you press and release + during the stretching or scaling operation, Draw creates a new object and leaves the original object untouched. You also can use + to duplicate an object while dragging. Clicking the right mouse button yields the same results.

If you press + as you pull on any of the handles, the status line reports the scaling percentage and includes the words Leave Original. You must use the + key on the numeric keypad, not on the top line of the standard keyboard.

The second option enables you to scale objects exponentially. By holding down Ctrl, you can scale in 100-percent increments. This makes it easy to make an object exactly twice as big.

You may have noticed that until now, the selected object has been stretched or scaled from its sides or corners. The third option makes it possible to stretch or scale from an object's center point. By holding down Shift, you can stretch or scale from the middle of a selected object.

Mirroring an Object

The fourth and final option enables you to reverse, or flip over, an object. Draw refers to this as *mirroring*. By pulling the bottom handles over the top handles or the left side handles over the right side handles (or vice versa in both cases), you can create a mirrored version of the original object. In addition to simply changing orientation, the mirroring process can be extremely useful for creating cast shadows and similar effects.

Shortcut

Click the right mouse button or press + while dragging, scaling, stretching, or mirroring to create a new object, leaving the original untouched.

Shortcut

Press Ctrl while scaling, stretching, or mirroring to scale, stretch, or mirror in 100-percent increments.

Shortcut

Press Shift while scaling or stretching to scale or stretch from an object's center point.

Try out the stretching, scaling, and mirroring options on the Porsche. Start by leaving an original, stretch, proceed to a twice-as-big scale, and finish up with a mirrored Porsche.

Using the Stretch/Scale Options

Press + while dragging the bottom right handle down and right	The new car is scaled, with the original left untouched.

Note: Press and release the + key quickly, or you will create more than one copy.

Press Del	Removes the new Porsche.

Now, scale the Porsche in 100-percent increments:

Press Ctrl while dragging the bottom right handle down and right	
Release the mouse button and then Ctrl	The image is scaled in 100-percent increments.
Press Del	Removes the new Porsche.

Next, combine the commands and leave the original while scaling in 100- percent increments:

Hold down Ctrl, press and release the + key while dragging the bottom right handle down and right	
Release the mouse button, then Ctrl	
Press Del	Removes the new Porsche.

Finish this exercise with a mirror and leave the original.

Press and release + while dragging the top left handle down	A mirrored Porsche is drawn.
Release the mouse button, and then +	Removes the new Porsche.
Press Del	

Remember that if you press and release + while moving, stretching, scaling, or mirroring, Draw creates a new object and leaves the original untouched. If you hold down Ctrl, Draw enables you to stretch, scale, or mirror in 100-percent increments. If you hold down Shift, Draw stretches, scales, or mirrors from an object's center point. You can mirror the object by dragging a handle across the opposite side of an object. You can mirror in any direction, but you must drag the handle over the opposite side.

The modifiers Ctrl, Shift, and + commonly are used in combination. Take the time to try a few maneuvers on your own.

Rotating an Object

You can rotate objects as well as size them. To rotate an object, you must select an object twice to display the rotate/skew handles. If the object already is selected, just click on it again.

The black box handles will turn to double-headed arrows. The object is ready to be rotated or skewed. Each time you click on an already selected object, you toggle between the two types of handles.

As you begin to rotate the Porsche, you notice that the cursor turns into a rotation symbol. When you rotate the Porsche, remember to watch the status line. It will tell you the amount of rotation in degrees. This is important, because you will see only the blue dashed box.

To rotate an object precisely, it helps to specify the number of degrees of rotation. A protractor might serve as a handy guide.

Rotating the Porsche

Click on the Porsche	The eight handles appear.
Click on the Porsche again	Arrows replace the handles.
Position the cursor over the bottom right handle	The cursor arrow becomes a +.
Drag the bottom right handle up and left	Arrow handles are replaced by a blue dashed box. The status line shows the amount of rotation in degrees.

continues

Release the mouse button at the top of the page	A rotated sports car appears.
Click **Undo**	Back on all four wheels.

☉ Look at the center of the selected Porsche. There should be a small circle with a dot in the center of it. This is the *center of rotation* marker; it controls the point around which the object rotates. The first time you invoke the rotate/skew handles on an object, the center of rotation is horizontally and vertically centered on the object. You can change the center of rotation by moving the marker (see fig. 1.6).

The center of rotation may be hard to see if the screen is not zoomed up. However, the program will let you select and move it, even if you cannot see it! The center of rotation's default position is the absolute center of the selected object. In this case, it is located just above the car's passenger side headlight. As you move the cursor over the center of rotation, the pointer tool turns into a + symbol, letting you know that the center of rotation is selectable. You can then click and drag it to a new location. Unlike previous versions of Draw, once you have moved an object's center of rotation, Draw 3.0 "remembers" where you left it.

Changing the Rotation Point

Click on the Porsche	The eight handles appear.
Click on the Porsche again	Arrows replace the handles.
Position the cursor over the center of rotation	
Drag the center of rotation to the tip of the "whaletail" rear spoiler	The rotation point is moved.

Now rotate the Porsche again. The sports car rotates on its whaletail spoiler, rather than its center.

Position the cursor over the bottom right handle	The cursor's pointer becomes a +.

Drag the bottom right handle up and left	Arrow handles are replaced by a blue dashed box. The status line shows the amount of rotation in degrees.
Release the mouse button at the top of the page	A rotated sports car appears.
Click **Undo**	Back on all four wheels.

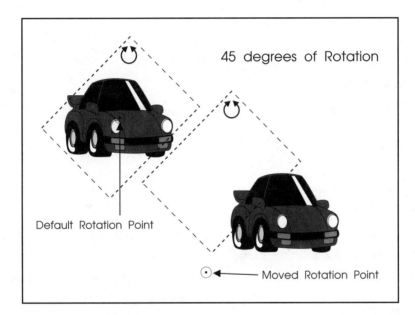

45 degrees of Rotation

Default Rotation Point

Moved Rotation Point

Figure 1.6:

The default and moved rotation point.

In addition to having control over the rotation point, you also can use + and Ctrl while rotating objects. The + key works as it does when scaling—it leaves an untouched original behind. This can be very useful for building things such as spokes on a wheel or blades on a propeller.

Using Ctrl while rotating offers even more advantages. Rotating with Ctrl pressed constrains movement to 15-degree increments with Draw's default setting (the increment can be changed via the Preferences Lines/Curves dialogue box). Once again, this function can be useful for building objects that spiral from a given point.

Shortcut

Press **+** while rotating to rotate the object, to leave the original untouched.

Shortcut

Press Ctrl while rotating to limit movement to 15-degree increments.

Zooming Up with the Zoom Tool

Use the zoom tool to get a good look at the precision work involved in the Porsche drawing.

This feature enables you to magnify your view (hence the magnifying glass icon), giving you ultimate control over your precision work. Zoom works in typical Draw fashion; its features are clustered in a single tool.

Using Zoom

Take the following steps to zoom in:

Click the zoom tool	The Zoom fly-out menu appears (see fig. 1.7).
Click +	The cursor is now a zoom tool.
Click the mouse button and drag across the driver's side headlight	The blue dashed marquee appears.
Release the mouse button	The screen displays a zoomed view of the front of the car.

Take the following steps to zoom out:

Click the zoom tool	The Zoom fly-out menu appears.
Click -	The view returns to its prior state.

Shortcut

Press F2 to access the zoom up tool.

The other functions available on the Zoom menu are 1:1, which provides a close-to-real-size view; ALL (denoted by a peculiar group of polygons), which displays every item on the page and surrounding pasteboard; and a page view (represented by a page icon), which enables you to view everything on the page itself.

Shortcut

Press F3 to zoom out.

There also are two convenient shortcuts for use with the zoom tool. If you want to zoom up in a hurry, just press F2; the cursor changes to the zoom up tool, enabling you to immediately marquee a selected area. To zoom out with haste, use F3; the screen zooms out in a flash.

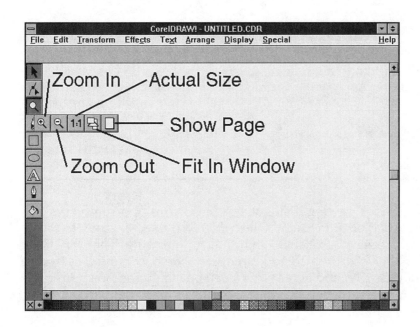

Figure 1.7:
An annotated Zoom
fly-out menu.

Saving Files

Although the process of saving files may seem obvious, there are two ways to save files: Save and Save As. Using the wrong one at the wrong time could wipe out a file.

If you look at the title bar at the top of your screen, you will notice that it reads COREL DRAW - CAR366.CDR. This tells you that you are running the CorelDRAW! program and your current file is CAR366.CDR. If you were to use the Save command to save the current screen, you would immediately overwrite the original file that you loaded at the beginning of the session.

To maintain the originally loaded file, save the current version with the Save As command. The program then enables you to name the new file. If you enter the same name as a file already stored on your computer, the program asks whether you want the old file overwritten.

To save your current version with a new name while maintaining the previous version, you must use Save As.

Saving a File with the Save As Command

Click **File**	The File menu appears.
Click Save **As**	The Save Drawing dialogue box appears (see fig. 1.8).
Type **MY911** *and press Enter*	A new file is saved as MY911.CDR. The title bar reads MY911.CDR.

Shortcut

Press Ctrl-S to save a file.

The Save Drawing dialogue box offers the opportunity to save information along with a file, which can make it easier to organize, retrieve, exchange, and catalog your work. There are fields for keywords (which you can use to search through files by client, for example) and notes (which can be handy for job-specific reminders, such as production information, print-runs, or even phone numbers).

The Image Header option gives you a number of choices for preview thumbnails. You have your choice of: None, 1K (monochrome), 2K (monochrome), 4K (color), and 8K (color). The higher the Image Header option, the larger the file will grow.

If you are working with someone who has an earlier version of Draw, you have the option of saving files as a version 2.x format. You must choose this option for backwards compatibility. When saving files as 2.x format files, the File Header can be None, 1K (monochrome), or 2K (monochrome). There is no color File Header option for 2.x files.

When you are in the process of constructing a drawing, you should get into the habit of saving your files frequently. You can do this very simply by pressing Ctrl-S to save the file, without using the mouse or menus. If you want to save with the mouse, you can access the Save command from the File menu.

If you are working with an unsaved file, Ctrl-S will access the Save As dialogue box.

Saving your files frequently is a good habit to get into. Try to save after every involved maneuver. This will limit your exposure to disaster. The longer you go between saves, the more time it may take for you to re-create your work in case of a computer crash or power failure.

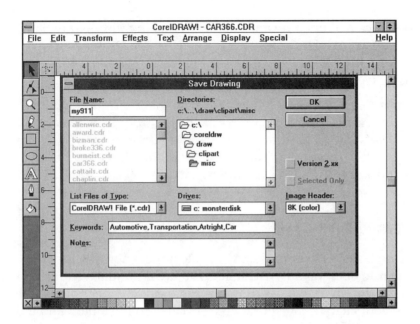

CorelDRAW! version 2.0 introduced Timed AutoBackup. This convenient feature saves files without any intervention on your part. The program is shipped with a default Save File setting of every 10 minutes. However, by editing the WIN.INI file, it is possible to change the AutoBackup frequency to your liking. A setting of 0 disables Timed AutoBackup.

As added insurance, Draw has another backup feature. Each time you save a file, the program saves the current version with a CDR extension, and automatically saves the previous version with a BAK file extension. Should you overwrite a file, you can easily go back to the BAK file. Simply rename the BAK file with the CDR extension, and you will be back in business.

Setting Up a New File

In this section, you learn how to open a new file, work with the Page Setup dialogue box, and import files in different formats. Once again, these are basic program functions that you should be familiar with before proceeding to more complex subjects.

The process of opening and saving an existing file already has been described. Draw uses the file extension CDR when it saves drawing files. Each Draw file must use the CDR extension; otherwise the program will not recognize the file as a CorelDRAW! file.

To use a clip-art file stored in a format other than CDR, you must import the file. Importing converts the file from its native format to Draw's internal format. CorelDRAW! supports many popular image file formats. (See Table 1.2 later in this chapter for a list of file formats that Draw will import.)

Opening a New File

Shortcut

Press Ctrl-N to create a new file.

The next step is to open a new file. Opening a new file is very similar to opening an existing file. If there is an unsaved file on the screen, the Save Changes dialogue box asks whether you want to save your changes. Respond appropriately to this query and the subsequent Save Drawing dialogue box (if you are actually saving a file).

Opening a New File

Click File	The File menu appears.
Click New	A blank file, UNTITLED.CDR, appears.

You now have a blank page on your screen. It may or may not be the proper size page for your drawing. To change the page specifications, you must use the Page Setup dialogue box.

It is a good idea to get into the habit of changing the page setup (if needed) before you start composing your images. Otherwise, you may need to make changes to your image in mid-stream to accommodate a new page size or orientation.

Using Page Setup

Draw's default mode presents you with an 8 1/2 × 11-inch page in portrait orientation each time you open a new file. This arrangement suits most people most of the time. However, certain projects will require paper sizes other than 8 1/2 inches × 11 inches. They also may require a different orientation. To do this, you must use the Page Setup dialogue box (see fig. 1.9) to set the page size and orientation to suit the situation.

Page size is variable. Page orientation is an either/or choice, offering a portrait or a landscape orientation.

Portrait is often called *tall*, and landscape is often called *wide*. This refers to the way a page is laid out, both on your screen, and as it is output from your printer. Portrait is vertical; landscape is horizontal. Think of a page with portrait orientation as standing up and a page with landscape orientation as lying on its side. Call up the Page Setup dialogue box and see what all this means. To start, change the orientation from portrait to landscape.

Shortcut

Double-click on a page border to access the Page Setup dialogue box.

Changing the Page Orientation

Click File	The File menu appears.
Click Page Setup	The Page Setup dialogue box appears.

The portrait and letter buttons are lit. The horizontal and vertical entries are dimmed, but read 8.50 and 11.00, respectively.

Click Landscape	The horizontal and vertical entries are still dimmed, but have reversed themselves, and now read 11.00 and 8.50, respectively.
Click OK	

Look at the page on your screen. You have changed it from a letter-sized (8 1/2 × 11 inches) portrait page to a letter-sized landscape page.

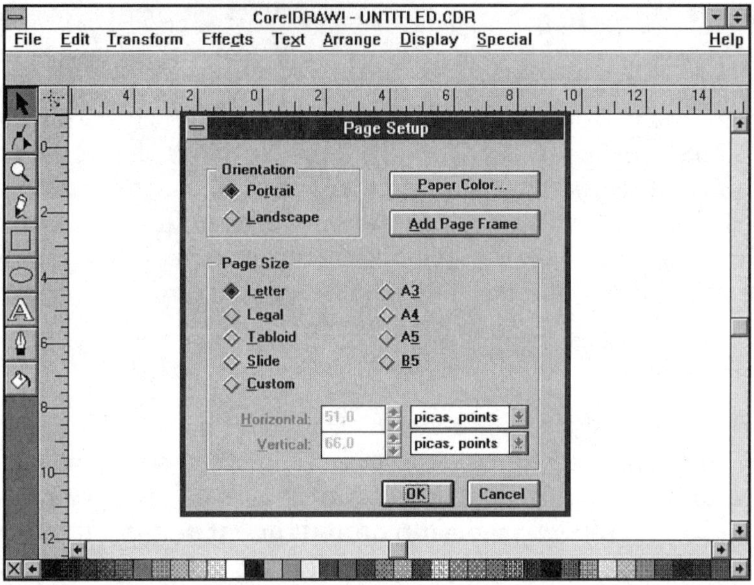

Figure 1.9:

The Page Setup dialogue box.

When you are done flipping the page back and forth between portrait and landscape, investigate the other feature of the Page Setup dialogue box, Page Size.

Although the majority of work you do in Draw might be accomplished with the standard letter page size, there will be times when you need something larger or smaller.

The Page Setup dialogue box offers eight predefined page sizes. In addition, you can choose the Custom option to specify page size up to a maximum of 30 × 30 inches, and to change the measurement units from inches to centimeters or picas and points. You can probably get away with using the letter, legal, and tabloid sizes for most of your work. On certain occasions, however, you will need the flexibility that the Custom option provides.

Changing the Page Size to Legal

Click File	The File menu appears.
Click Page Setup	The Page Setup dialogue box appears. The portrait and letter buttons should be lit.

Click Legal	The horizontal and vertical entries are still dimmed, but now read 8.50 and 14.00, respectively.
Click OK	

The page on your screen should now be a legal-sized (8 1/2 × 14 inches) portrait page. Try changing back to different page sizes by calling up the Page Setup dialogue box and clicking the various predefined choices.

The predefined page sizes (in inches) are as shown in Table 1.1.

Table 1.1
Predefined Page Sizes

Page Setup Choices	*Horizontal*	*Vertical*
Letter	8.50	11.00
Legal	8.50	14.00
Tabloid	11.00	17.00
A3	11.70	16.50
A4	8.27	11.70
A5	5.83	8.27
B5	6.90	9.80
Slide	7.33	11.00

There may be times when you want to use Page Setup's Custom option, rather than the predefined page sizes. For example, imagine that you are designing a wedding invitation with a finished size of 4.25 × 5.50 inches. You could lay out the piece on any of the predefined pages, but that would not be the smartest or fastest way to go. Instead, choose the Custom option. When Custom is selected, the horizontal and vertical value boxes become black instead of gray. This enables you to enter values for the custom size you want.

Check out the Custom page setup option and see how it works. When you call up the Page Setup dialogue box and any of the predefined page sizes are lit, the horizontal and vertical selections will be dimmed. To gain access to those selections, you must select Custom.

To change the horizontal entries, you can either highlight the current entry and type in your new size, or use the entry window up/down buttons to roll through the sizes.

After clicking Custom, press Tab to move your cursor to the horizontal size window. The current size will be highlighted, enabling you to type in the new size immediately. After you enter the new size, another tab will bring you to the vertical size window.

Changing to a Custom Page Size

Click **File**	The File menu appears.
Click **Page Setup**	The Page Setup dialogue box appears.

The portrait and letter buttons should be lit. The horizontal and vertical entries are dimmed. (If they are not, do not worry—you are changing to a custom size anyway.)

Click **Custom**	The horizontal and vertical entries are now active.
Tab to the Horizontal entry	A black bar appears over the entry.
Type **4.25**	Changes the width of the page.
Tab to the Vertical entry	A black bar appears over the entry.
Type **5.5**	Changes the height of the page.
Click OK	

The page on your screen should now be 4 1/2 inches wide and 5 1/2 inches tall. Go ahead and experiment with different page sizes by using the Custom page size option. When you are done, reset the page size to letter and the orientation to portrait.

Those of you who are familiar with printing terms will understand this next concept. If you are not, pay attention, because this next section could save you time, dollars, and frustration.

Using Crop Marks

Crop marks are the lines used by printers to position artwork on a printing press. At this writing, Draw can generate crop marks for you, but only if you are using a PostScript printer.

Think of a view finder on a camera. When you take a picture, the camera records what is in the frame at the moment you click the shutter button. The view finder controls where things are positioned in your picture.

Crop marks are your view finder. When you bring in your artwork to be printed, your printer assumes that the crop marks have been positioned so that what you placed on the page is exactly where you would like to see it reproduced.

To avoid misplacing the crop marks, let Draw make them for you. Just click on Crop Marks & Crosshairs in the Print dialogue box (see fig. 1.10). Crop marks and cross hairs (or what printers refer to as *registration marks*) will be automatically placed on your PostScript printout. (They cannot be printed on any other type of output device.) Crop marks and cross hairs are not visible on the computer screen.

A section on the basics of printing follows. For an in-depth look at the subject of printing, see Chapter 12.

TIP

If you are using process colors and want to make your own crop marks, simply assign them an outline color of 100 percent cyan, 100 percent yellow, 100 percent magenta, and 100 percent black. That way, a crop mark prints on every color separation.

Importing Art: A Brief Look

As you learned in the opening of this section, Draw uses the CDR file extension to denote drawing files. These are the only files that you can open, either directly or through Mosaic. If you need to use a file that has been stored in a format other than CDR, you have to *import* that file.

Figure 1.10:

The Print Options dialogue box with Crop Marks & Crosshairs selected.

CorelDRAW! can import a wide range of file formats. This is marvelous, because most commercial clip art is not available in CDR format. Draw always is adding to the list and may have more options by the time you read this than are listed here. If you need to import a file in other than one of the following formats, contact Draw's technical support for more information. Table 1.2 is a list of file formats supported by CorelDRAW!'s import feature, as of this writing.

Table 1.2
File Formats for Importation

Format	Extension
AutoCAD	DXF
CompuServe (Bit Maps)	GIF
CorelDRAW!	CDR
Corel Trace	EPS
PC Paintbrush (Bit Maps)	PCX, PCC
Targa (Bit Maps)	TGA

Format	Extension
TIFF 5.0 (Bit Maps)	TIF
Lotus PIC	PIC
Illustrator '88, 3.0	AI, EPS
IBM PIF (GDF)	PIF
Gem	GEM
Graphics Metafile	CGM
Hewlett-Packard (HPGL)	PLT
Macintosh (PICT)	PCT
Windows 3.0 (Bit Maps)	BMP
Windows Metafiles	WMF

You may notice that Draw's native CDR format is included in the list. Why would you want to import a file that you can open directly? An excellent example comes to mind.

Imagine that you are producing an advertisement. You have finished the layout, and have set all the type. Now you want to place a piece of electronic clip art into the file. Importing artwork enables you to assemble pieces from a number of different files.

Import the same Porsche file that you experimented with earlier in this chapter. Only this time, import the file into the file you already have open.

Importing a CDR File

Click File	The File menu appears.
Click Import	The Import dialogue box appears.
Double-click CorelDRAW .CDR	The Open Drawing dialogue box appears.
Double-click CAR366.CDR	The Porsche assembles itself on the screen.

You have just imported an existing clip-art file into an open file. You can import many files into one file. Be advised, however, that the more complex a file is, the more time it will take to print, and the more room it will take up on your hard disk. A file that has had multiple files imported into it will save as one (large) file.

Importing files from other programs is just as easy. As the chart above shows, Draw provides a healthy cadre of import filters. Just designate the appropriate drive, double-click on the appropriate file format in the Import dialogue box, and follow the same steps as before.

Although all the clip art supplied with CorelDRAW! version 3.0 is in the native CDR format, most commercial clip art is not. One exception is the ArtRight collection. The CAR366.CDR file is an excellent example of ArtRight's craftsmanship. Like all of their work, it was developed in Draw and saved in the CDR format. There are many advantages to using clip-art files that already are in the CDR format. Chief among them are speed of import (files do not have to be converted from one format to another) and retention of grouping functions. Although ArtRight has been producing files in CDR format for some time, other companies are just beginning to offer their clip art in that format.

If you are looking for more clip art, the first place you should look is Corel Systems. Their CorelDRAW! CD Blockbuster offer is a tremendous value—bundling CorelDRAW on CD-ROM with over 12,000 pieces of clip art, 250 fonts, a CD-ROM drive, and SCSI interface kit for a highly competitive price.

Printing

The last subject that is in this chapter is printing. You learn a few printing basics here, then go into more depth in a later chapter.

Producing output is CorelDRAW!'s reason for existing. A pretty screen file does not do you any good if you cannot print it. Furthermore, you cannot really tell what a piece looks like until it rolls out of the printer.

The print function can be accessed in one of two ways. The first is through the File menu. The easiest way is to use the shortcut, Ctrl-P. This shortcut (along with Ctrl-S for save) will become automatic keystrokes for you. Your brain will think "print," and your fingers will press Ctrl-P.

Shortcut

Press Ctrl-P, then press Enter to print a file.

Printing the Porsche

Click File	The File menu appears.
Click Print	The Print File dialogue box appears.
Press Enter (or click OK)	The file is sent to the printer.

Try to get in the habit of saving your file with Ctrl-S before you walk away from your PC. Although the program will always ask whether you want to save your file before quitting, and the program has Timed AutoBackup, it is still a good idea to save as frequently as possible.

Quitting

You have one last thing to do before you take a break. And that is to learn how to quit the Draw program. You can quit in one of two ways, either from the File menu or with a shortcut.

Shortcut

Press Ctrl-X to quit CorelDRAW!.

If you have an unsaved file on your screen when you quit, the program will asks whether you want to save the file before you exit. Always pay attention to this dialogue box—it could save you a lot of work!

Quitting CorelDRAW!

Click File	The File menu appears.
Click Quit	

If you have a file on your screen that you want to save, save it now.

Summary

In this chapter, you learned some important things about CorelDRAW! You started out by getting up and running, and you opened an existing file. After investigating how to select, scale, rotate, and zoom, you opened a new file and adjusted the page size and orientation. After seeing that the Page Setup dialogue box offers predefined page sizes, you set up an odd-sized page (4.25 inches × 5.5 inches) and found out about automatic crop marks. Finally, you learned a little about importing files and printing.

In the next chapter, you start getting into the exciting stuff. Take a break, get some air, or, like Joe, wrap it up and go home for a well-deserved supper. In the next chapter, you will explore creating and drawing, and you will tackle a real project.

Creating and Drawing

n the last chapter, you learned about some of the Draw basics. Chapter 1 covered the essential file functions: opening, importing, saving, and printing. You also learned how to select, move, scale, and rotate an object. Along the way, you found out how to set up a page and learned about zoom and preview. What you did not learn was how to draw with CorelDRAW!. That is what this chapter is all about.

You are going to open up Draw's toolbox (see fig. 2.1) and use it to do your first project, a letterhead.

As you experiment with Draw's various tools, you see that most of them do double duty. First, you use the pen tool, noting how it can be used to draw either straight or curved lines. Next, you use the ellipse tool to produce perfect circles and ovals, and find that the rectangle tool works in much the same way. For more precision, you set up and use the grid. You learn the basics of outline and fill to finish the drawing. Finally, a quick look at the text tool will give you a chance to complete your first project.

Figure 2.1:

The CorelDRAW!
toolbox.

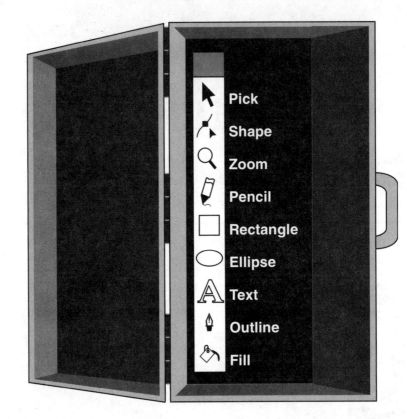

Designing DeLook's First Project

On Saturday morning, Joe DeLook is at it again. Today, he is determined to conquer Draw's design tools. He promised a quick and dirty letterhead to his girlfriend, Katie, for her kite store.

Joe needs a simple drawing of a kite, along with a line or two of type. Nothing fancy, just serviceable. With a fresh pot of coffee in the galley, Joe shoves off into the uncharted waters of electronic design.

Drawing with the Mouse

If you have never drawn anything with a mouse, you are not in
for a treat. Freehand drawing with a mouse is like filleting a fish
with a chain saw. It is not a pretty sight. But there are some excellent alternatives to the mouse; the most notable among them is the
graphics tablet. Appendix B reviews one of the best graphics
tablets, the Wacom SD-420.

Once you have used a graphics tablet, you will not want to go
back to using a mouse. You may have the chance to use a tablet,
but for clarity's sake, this book still refers to it as a mouse.

This new chapter begins with a blank page in CorelDRAW!. It
soon fills up with all kinds of wonderful shapes and doodles.
Your pages may become overly doodle-filled, but you will learn
how easy it is to remove unwanted objects.

Using the Pencil Tool

The drawing tool to start with is the pencil tool. The pencil tool
can draw straight lines or curved objects, depending on how you
use it. Producing an image with CorelDRAW! is akin to building a
collage; you assemble your drawings using different shapes. This
is a helpful philosophy to keep in mind when planning your
drawings.

Remember, too, that Draw is not a bit-mapped paint program. If
you are not sure of the differences between paint and draw programs, re-read the introduction to this book.

The pencil tool has two drawing modes: Freehand and Bezier.
Each mode has its place, but for the purposes of these next exercises, use the Freehand mode. The Bezier mode is explored in the
next chapter, after you understand how Bezier curves work.

Drawing Straight Lines (Open Path)

The pencil tool can draw either straight or curved lines. Begin by drawing some straight lines, and then connect them to build closed-path objects. As you do, watch the status line; it will tell you some important information.

The technique used for drawing straight lines is quite simple. It consists of a position, a click, a second position, and a second click. As you move the cursor around the page, the status line informs you of the dx: and dy: change in position, distance (length), angle of the line segment you are drawing, as well as the line segment's starting and ending points.

Drawing a Straight Line

Click the pencil tool	The cursor becomes a +.
Click the mouse button near the top of the page	A line appears, with a node where you clicked. The status line becomes active.
Move the cursor to bottom of the page	The line pivots around its node.
Click the mouse button	This creates a line with a node at each end (see fig. 2.2).

Try this a few times to get the feel of it.

Shortcut

Press Ctrl-J to access the Preferences dialogue box.

There are two methods you can use to draw a diagonal line. As you have probably seen, you can use the previous technique to draw a diagonal line at any angle. In addition, you can constrain the angle to 15-degree increments by holding down Ctrl while drawing your line. Try drawing a few lines using Ctrl. (You must release the mouse button before releasing Ctrl.) The constrain increment can be adjusted to your liking, via the Constrain Angle option in the Preferences dialogue box. You can access the Preferences dialogue box from the Special menu or with the Ctrl-J shortcut.

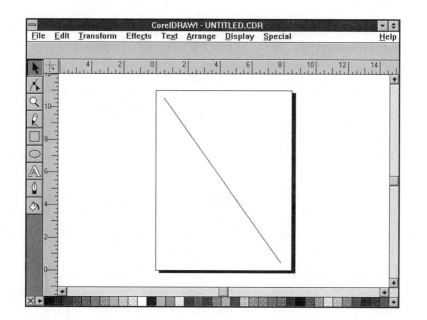

Figure 2.2:
A single line.

The lines you have just drawn are open paths. Although they can be outlined, they cannot be filled with any color or pattern. Closed-path objects are constructed from groups of connected lines and they can be filled (more on this later).

Drawing Straight Lines (Closed Path)

An open path is like a lobster trap with an open lid. To keep the lobsters in the trap, you must close the lid. Closing an open path is like shutting the lid on a lobster trap. How do you go about closing this open path? You play a simple game of connect the dots. The dots are called *nodes*.

There are several ways to connect the dots and close the path. The first method is to draw a line segment from one node to another. The simplest way to do this is by drawing a line with two nodes, and then starting the second line directly from one of the first line's nodes.

Connecting Straight Lines

Draw a single horizontal line segment:

Click on the node	A new line segment is initiated, connected to the node.
Move the cursor up and to the left	
Click the mouse button	A second line segment is drawn, connected to the first line segment.

Now, there are two connected line segments. Objects other than ovals or circles usually consist of at least three segments.

As you do this next exercise, you create a closed path to see a variation on the last exercise. The pencil tool immediately starts a new line segment with the same node by double-clicking, rather than single clicking.

Double-Clicking Connected Straight Lines To Close a Path

Click the pencil tool	The cursor becomes a + with a gap in the center.
Click the mouse button at the bottom left of the page	
Move the cursor to the right	A line appears. Maintain a 0-degree angle.
Double-click the mouse button	Creates a line with nodes at each end, and a new line segment is started.
Move the cursor up and to the left	
Double-click the mouse button	When you reach a 135-degree angle. A connected diagonal line is drawn, and a new line segment is started.
Position the cursor over the initial node	
Click the mouse button	A triangular closed path is created (see fig. 2.3).

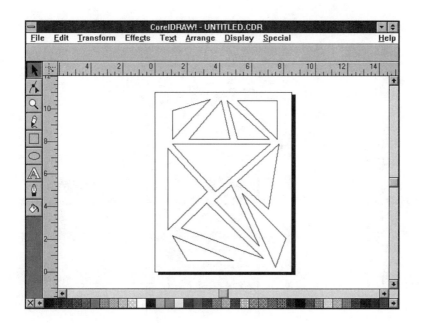

Figure 2.3:
Connected lines.

Snapping to Nodes with AutoJoin

If you cannot seem to get those pesky little lines to connect, try an easier way to get them to snap to each other. A feature called *AutoJoin* controls the pencil tool's "magnetic" node-connection range.

AutoJoin settings are altered through the Curves option in the Preferences dialogue box (see fig. 2.4). This dialogue box is accessed via the Special menu. There, scroll buttons enable you to set AutoJoin in a range from 1 (lowest) to 10 (highest). AutoJoin's default setting is 5. The lower settings make it difficult to connect nodes. Reserve those settings for intricate work where lines need to be close without touching. The maximum setting of 10 greatly facilitates node-connection—you can almost feel the pencil snapping to the node. But be careful; it can do so when you do not intend it to. A high setting may give you haphazard AutoJoining.

Right now, use a few different AutoJoin settings to draw polygons.

Connecting Lines with Different AutoJoin Settings

Click **S**pecial	The Special menu appears.
Click **Pr**eferences	The Preferences dialogue box appears.
Click **C**urves	The Curves dialogue box appears.

Set AutoJoin *to 1*

Click OK

Click OK *again*

With AutoJoin set at 1, you will find it difficult to connect lines, but keep trying.

Click the pencil tool

Draw a single line segment

Click on the last node

Draw a second connected line segment

Draw a few more connected line segments	Close the path.

Now make it easier. Set AutoJoin to an ultra-sticky 10. Feel the cursor's "magnetic" attraction.

Click Special	
Click Preferences	The Preferences dialogue box appears.
Click Curves	The Curves dialogue box appears.
Set AutoJoin *to 10*	
Click OK	
Click OK *again*	
Draw a single line segment	
Click on the last node	
Draw a second connected line segment	
Draw a few more connected line segments	Close the path.

Return AutoJoin to its default setting of 5, and try just a few more.

Click Preferences	The Preferences dialogue box appears.
Click Curves	The Curves dialogue box appears.
Set AutoJoin *to 5*	
Click OK	
Click OK *again*	
Draw a single line segment	
Click on the last node	
Draw a second connected line segment	
Draw a few more connected line segments	Close the path.

In addition to AutoJoin settings, the Preferences dialogue box offers many choices to help make life with Draw a pleasant experience. Shortly, you learn about one of those: freehand tracking.

After all of that, you should understand how to draw a closed path by connecting the nodes. Although you have been working with straight lines, the concept of connecting nodes carries over to curved lines as well.

By now, your screen is probably full of triangles and other assorted polygons. Take some time to clean up the screen by deleting some of the objects. You can do this in a variety of ways.

Deleting Objects

The simplest way to delete an object is to select it with the pick tool, and then delete it. There are at least three other ways to rid your screen of unwanted objects. Take a look at all four procedures.

Four Ways To Delete Objects

CorelDRAW! enables you to delete selected objects by using any of the following four methods:

- Click/Delete
- Shift-Click/Delete
- Marquee/Delete
- Select All/Delete

Deleting a Triangle (Click/Delete)

You should have plenty of lines (open paths) and triangles (closed paths) on the screen from the last exercise. If you do not have any, create a few.

Click the pick tool	This activates the pointer.
Click the triangle you want to delete	The handles appear. The triangle is selected.
Press Del	The triangle is deleted.

If you did not really want to delete the object, you can get it back by choosing Undo from the Edit menu (or by pressing Alt-Backspace).

Shortcut

Press Tab to select the next object.

Shortcut

Press Shift-Tab to select the previous object.

Draw provides a way to select objects without using the mouse at all. With the pick tool selected, you can cycle through objects by pressing Tab. CorelDRAW! refers to this wonderful feature as *select next*. You also can select objects in reverse order by pressing Shift and Tab at the same time.

Try this time-saver right now. There should be plenty of objects on the screen to tab through.

Tabbing through Objects on the Screen

Click the pick tool	Activates the pointer.
Click a polygon	Selects the polygon.
Press Tab	Selects the next object.
Press Tab again	Selects the next object.
Press Tab again	Selects the next object.

If you like, try reversing through the objects by pressing Shift-Tab.

Often, you may want to remove several objects at a time. The next three procedures enable you to delete a number of objects selectively. By shift-clicking (holding down Shift while clicking), you can select several objects at a time. Watch the status line for the number of objects selected.

Selectively Deleting Several Lines (Shift-Click/Delete)

Click the pick tool	Activates the pointer.
Click on the first line you want to delete	The handles appear. The object is selected.
Shift-click on the next line to delete	The handles expand to include both lines. The status line reads 2 objects selected on layer 1.
Shift-click on the other lines to delete	The handles continue to expand to include all selected lines. The status line shows the number of lines selected.
Shift-click on a selected line	This deselects the line. The status line reflects the selection.
Press Del	The lines are deleted.

A variation on the last select/delete is the marquee select/delete. Marquee-selecting is like throwing out a big net.

Deleting with the Marquee (Marquee/Delete)

If you have run out of lines or triangles to delete, draw some more. Then take the following steps to delete them:

Click the pick tool	Activates the pointer.
Position the cursor above and to the left of the lines to be deleted	
Click and drag the cursor below and to the right of the lines to be deleted	A blue dashed box appears around the lines.
Release the mouse button	Handles appear, surrounding all the selected lines. The status line reflects the total number of objects selected.
Shift-click on a selected object	This deselects the object.
Press Del	The objects are deleted.

If you want to erase all the objects on your page, the following exercise shows you the slickest way to do it.

Deleting All Objects (Select All/Delete)

Click the pick tool	Activates the pointer.
Click **Edit**	The Edit menu appears.
Click Select **All**	All objects are selected.
Press Del	All objects are deleted.

Shortcut

Press Alt-E, then A, then Del to delete all objects.

In learning to delete multiple objects, you have learned the principles behind selecting multiple objects. You will soon see that you can use the shift-click, marquee-select, and select-all techniques to apply fills, outlines, and transformations on groups of objects.

Now that you are finished playing search and destroy, start filling up the screen with doodles again. If you are ready, take your mouse in hand and get ready to draw some curves.

Drawing Curves Freehand

The pencil tool can create curved as well as straight lines. Like straight lines, curved lines can be open or closed paths. You can create closed paths composed entirely of curves, or in combination with straight lines. In this section, use the pencil tool to draw curves and create some simple cloud-shaped objects.

The more you work with Draw, the more you will realize that the curves you draw do not always turn out exactly the way you envisioned them. This is largely due to the imprecise drawing capabilities of the common mouse. It can be a difficult tool to use for freehand drawing.

Nevertheless, try drawing some simple curves. Most likely, they will not look all that great at close inspection. Fear not. Through a process known as *tweaking*, you can refine your curves to a more suitable form. The actual process of tweaking is covered in Chapter 3.

The technique to use when drawing curved lines is different from the one to use when drawing straight lines. Drawing curved lines requires a click-and-drag technique. Hold the mouse button down while drawing your curve. When you release the mouse button, CorelDRAW! takes a few seconds to plot your curve. When it is done, nodes appear along the path of the line (see fig. 2.5).

Drawing a Curved Line

Click the pencil tool	The cursor becomes a +.
Drag the mouse in a curving line	A curved line is drawn.
Release the mouse button	After a few moments, nodes are added to the line.

Drawing a curved line is not too difficult. Notice that the status line reads Curve on Layer 1 Open Path. This means that the selected object is not a closed path and cannot be filled.

Figure 2.5:

Clouds.

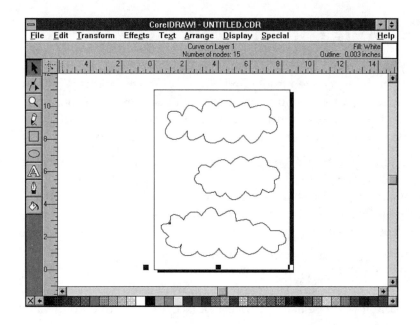

Shortcut

Press Shift to erase while drawing curved lines.

If you do not like the way your object looks while you are in the midst of drawing, you can erase part of it without starting from scratch. Pressing Shift while drawing a curved line enables you to back up and erase the line. When you release Shift, you resume drawing.

Next, draw a curved closed path, following much the same procedure. To close the path, you need to end your line on top of the node where you began the line. This is almost exactly like creating the triangular closed path except this time, you are working with curves. When you are done drawing and the nodes are plotted, the status line should read: Curve on Layer 1.

When working in full-color mode (as opposed to wireframe mode), you will see the immediate results of closing a path—the object will be filled with the default fill. If, however, "no fill" is the default fill, you might not notice the difference. If there is a question in your mind, just remember that the status line will always tell you if it is an open path.

Drawing a Curved Closed Path

Click the pencil tool

Drag the mouse in curving cloud shape   A cloud shape is drawn.

Bring the cursor back where the
line began

Release the mouse button   After a few moments,
                                                nodes are added to the
                                                cloud.

If the status line reads Open Path, you did not close the path. This can be tricky. If you have an open path, try the exercise again. It may take a few tries for you to get your path closed.

What if you have drawn the ultimate cloud, but failed to create a closed path? There is a very simple way to join the nodes and close the path. You are going to use a menu that you have not used before, the Node Edit menu. Chapter 3 covers this feature in more detail.

This next exercise is very similar to the last, except that you should try not to connect the end nodes when you lay down the drawing.

Leave plenty of room between the first and last nodes.

Closing an Open Path

Click the pencil tool

Drag the mouse in a curving cloud shape

Bring the cursor back almost to
where the line began

Release the mouse button   After a few moments,
                                                nodes are added to the
                                                cloud. The status line
                                                should read Curve on
                                                Layer 1 Open Path.
                                                Number of Nodes: X
                                                (where X is the number
                                                of nodes).

continues

Click the node tool	The status line should read Curve: *X* nodes (where *X* is the number of nodes) (see fig. 2.6).
Shift-click the first and last nodes	
Release the mouse button	The first and last nodes turn black. The status line reads 2 selected nodes (see fig. 2.7).
Double-click on a selected node	The Node Edit menu appears.
Click Join	The status line reads First node of a closed curve (see fig. 2.8).
Click pick tool	The status line reads Curve on Layer 1 Number of Nodes: *X* (where *X* is the number of nodes)

You have joined the first and last nodes of an open path with the node edit tool, forming a closed path. If you were not successful in creating a closed path, you may have selected more than two nodes. Only two nodes can be joined. Deselect the nodes, and try again. You also can try marquee-selecting instead of shift-clicking.

Drawing Smooth Lines

Do your lines seem really jagged or, conversely, far too smooth? You can alter the precision that the program uses when converting mouse movements to Bezier curves via another setting in the Preferences dialogue box. CorelDRAW! refers to this function as *Freehand Tracking*.

Like AutoJoin, Freehand Tracking can be set in a range from 1 (lowest) to 10 (highest). The default setting is 5. Lower settings enable the program to follow the line with far more precision. But low settings can render too many nodes and give the line a jagged appearance. High settings will give the line fewer nodes and a smoother curve, with a corresponding loss of precision. Take a

look at what different Freehand Tracking settings do to your
freehand drawings. Try drawing a few more clouds.

Figure 2.6:

A curve (open path).

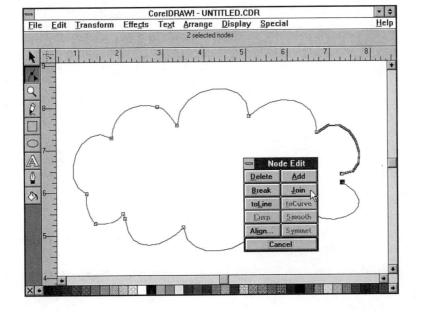

Figure 2.7:

The Node Edit menu.

Figure 2.8:

A curve (closed path).

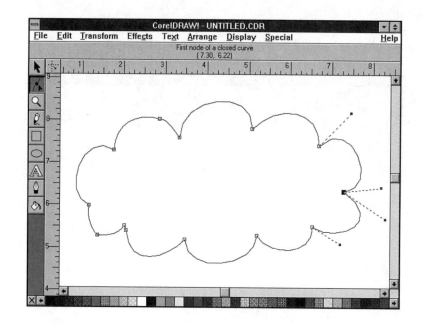

Adjusting Freehand Tracking

Click **S**pecial — The Special menu appears.

Click **Pr**eferences — The Preferences dialogue box appears.

Click **C**urves — The Curves dialogue box appears.

Set Freehand Tracking *to 1*

Click OK

Click OK *again*

With the Freehand Tracking set at 1, you get more precision, more nodes, and more jaggedness.

Click pencil tool

Draw a cloud

That looks pretty rough. Smooth out your technique by setting Freehand Tracking to 10. Notice the loss of precision, as shown in figure 2.9.

Click **Pr**eferences — The Preferences dialogue box appears.

Click **Curves**	The Curves dialogue box appears.

Set **Freehand** Tracking *to 10*
Click OK
Click OK *again*
Draw a cloud

Return Freehand Tracking to its default setting of 5 and try one more setting.

Click **Preferences**	The Preferences dialogue box appears.
Click **Curves**	The Curves dialogue box appears.

Set **Freehand** Tracking *to 5*
Click OK
Click OK *again*
Draw a cloud

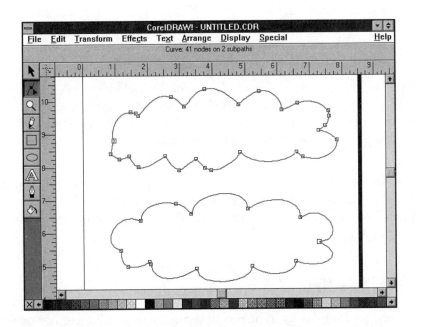

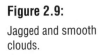

Figure 2.9:

Jagged and smooth clouds.

This is a good time to practice drawing with the pencil tool. You will find it difficult to draw with precision, but have no fear, you will be tweaking those curves soon enough.

Draw several clouds. Imagine that a storm front is moving in, if you will. Delete all the clouds you are less than happy with and save your three favorites. Drag them off to the top of the page—you are going to use them in your first drawing!

At this point, you should save your drawing. Use the file name BOXKITE. If you cannot recall how to save a file, refer to Chapter 1.

Drawing Ellipses and Rectangles

The ellipse and rectangle tools are as straightforward as you could hope a pair of drawing tools to be. Anyone who has ever tangled with a mechanical compass, plastic templates, and technical pens will be ecstatic over the ellipse tool's ease of use. In fact, you probably will hang up your compass, put away your templates, and clean your pens for the last time—abandoning them in favor of working exclusively with CorelDRAW!'s superior electronic versions. There is no need to worry about ink splats or smudge marks. If you draw something the wrong size or shape, there is no heartbreak. Simply undo it and try again!

By using these tools in conjunction with Draw's snap-to grid and guidelines features (both of which are covered shortly), as well as the program's rulers, you can draw ellipses and rectangles of precise proportions. If the rulers are not already showing on your screen, click Show Rulers on the Display menu.

The ellipse and rectangle tools offer flexibility that even the largest collection of templates and technical pens could not hope to match. While you are drawing these objects, look to the status line for immediate feedback.

The Ellipse Tool

The ellipse tool works in one of two modes to produce either ovals or circles. By clicking and dragging, you can draw ovals of infinitely variable proportions. To draw a perfectly symmetrical circle, hold down Ctrl while clicking and dragging. You can draw an ellipse or circle from its center point by holding down Shift. Figure 2.10 shows some samples of what you might draw. Remember to watch the status line as you draw; it shows the exact height and width, as well as the starting, ending, and center points.

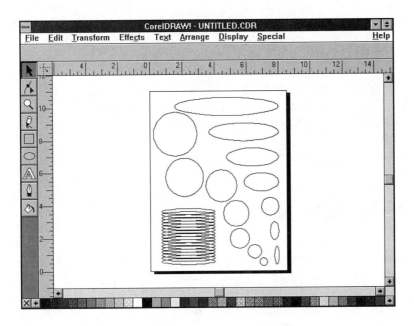

Figure 2.10:

A variety of circles and ellipses.

Drawing Ovals and Circles

Click the ellipse tool	The cursor changes into a +.
Click and drag the cursor diagonally	An oval grows as you move the cursor.
Release the mouse button	An oval is drawn.

That was too easy. Now try a circle. With the ellipse tool still selected, take the following steps:

Press Ctrl while clicking and dragging the cursor	A circle grows as you move the cursor.
Release the mouse button, then Ctrl	A circle is drawn.

continues

Now try an ellipse drawn from its center point:

Press Shift while clicking and dragging the cursor	An ellipse grows from its center point as you move the cursor.
Release the mouse button, and then Shift	An ellipse is drawn.

Try drawing a few more ovals and circles. When you are done, delete them using one of the methods described earlier in this chapter. Try using both Ctrl and Shift to draw a circle from its center point. Attempt to draw to exact proportions, using the status line. Once an object is completed and the mouse button released, the status line displays the dimensions and the page position of its center point.

The Rectangle Tool

The rectangle tool works just like the ellipse tool; it creates either rectangles or squares (see fig. 2.11). By clicking and dragging, you can draw a rectangle of infinitely variable proportions. To draw a perfect square, hold down Ctrl while clicking and dragging. If you want to draw from a center point, hold down Shift.

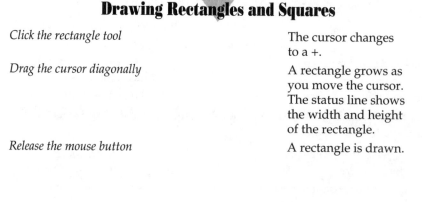

Drawing Rectangles and Squares

Click the rectangle tool	The cursor changes to a +.
Drag the cursor diagonally	A rectangle grows as you move the cursor. The status line shows the width and height of the rectangle.
Release the mouse button	A rectangle is drawn.

Now that you have drawn a rectangle, draw a square. With the rectangle tool still selected, take the following steps:

Press Ctrl while clicking and dragging the cursor	A square grows as you move the cursor.
Release mouse button and Ctrl	A square is drawn.

Next, draw a rectangle from its center point:

Press Shift while clicking and dragging the cursor	A rectangle grows from its center point as you move the cursor.
Release the mouse button and Shift	A rectangle is drawn.

As you have seen, the ellipse and rectangle tools originate (or pull) objects from their corners, or from a center point, depending on whether you have Shift depressed. If you want, try drawing a few more ellipses, circles, rectangles, and squares using different combinations until you are comfortable with the tools. When you are done, delete them to clear the page.

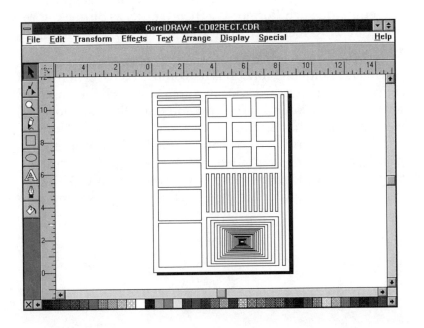

Figure 2.11:

A variety of squares and rectangles.

Using the Grid and Guidelines for Precision

You easily can make your objects fit a particular size by using CorelDRAW!'s grid and guidelines. The grid forces the cursor to "snap" to a pre-defined spacing pattern. Guidelines enable you to draw "bluelines," which exhibit similar magnetic qualities. If you are familiar with Aldus PageMaker, you will find these features similar to PageMaker's snap-to-rulers and snap-to-guidelines options.

Draw's Grid Setup dialogue box (see fig. 2.12) controls the horizontal and vertical grid frequency and the grid origin point. It also gives you the option of displaying the grid. If you have the grid set for a high frequency, the screen display will not show all the grid intersection points unless you are zoomed way up. The tighter you zoom in, the more detailed the grid display becomes.

Shortcut

Double-click on a ruler to access the Grid Setup dialogue box.

The variable options provided by the Grid Setup dialogue box make setting up such (formerly difficult) tasks as business forms that require 1/10-inch horizontal spacing and 1/6-inch vertical spacing a snap!

The grid and guideline functions in CorelDRAW! version 3.0 have been improved (over earlier incarnations) through the implementation of layering controls. The grid and guidelines are now placed on their own individual layers. The Layers Roll-Up window provides control over grid and guideline (non-printing) colors. Both the grid and guidelines can be toggled on or off through either the Display menu or the Layers Roll-Up. The Layers function is covered in depth in both Chapters 3 and 8.

Begin by setting up a simple grid. You will use the guidelines shortly.

Setting Up the Grid

Click Display	The Display menu appears.
Click Grid Setup	The Grid Setup dialogue box appears.

At Grid Frequency, do the following:

Click the unit of measurement box	Click until you reach inches.
Click the grid frequency scroll buttons	Adjust to 6 per inch.
Click Show Grid	The check mark designates that feature is active. If the item is checked, do not re-click or you will turn the feature off.
Click Snap to Grid	The check mark designates that feature is active. If the item is checked, do not re-click or you will turn the feature off.

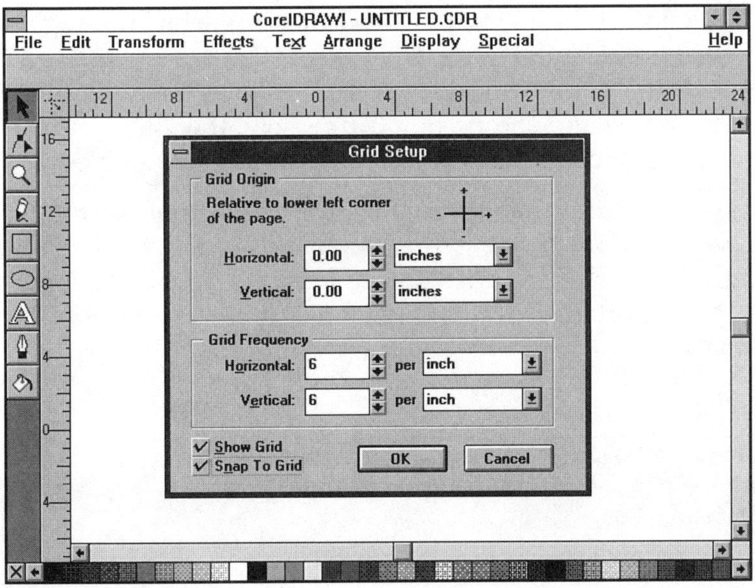

Figure 2.12:

The Grid Setup dialogue box.

Shortcut

Press Ctrl-Y to turn
the grid on and off.

If you do not happen to be in the Grid Setup dialogue box, you can toggle the grid on and off with the Ctrl-Y shortcut.

Now that you have turned on the grid, take a look at what it does. With the grid on, the cursor snaps to the defined grid intersection points like a magnet snaps to a refrigerator. You can set the grid to a maximum of 72 units per inch, conveniently echoing the number of points per inch. Current grid settings are saved with your drawings.

Grid Origin enables you to place the grid's zero point anywhere on your page or pasteboard. You can change this setting with numerical precision via the Grid Setup dialogue box, or change it visually by clicking and dragging from the ruler intersection point. You may want to set the zero point at the upper left-hand corner of the page.

Aligning Objects to the Grid

For the last series of exercises, set up a coarse grid with six grid lines per inch. This translates to one grid line per pica. This size grid helps you develop a simple box kite. You build the box kite at three times its finished size and reduce it later.

Before you start this next section, try drawing a few rectangles with the grid on. Pull the rectangle out to the right, to the left, up, and down. Notice how the grid feature enables you to position your beginning and ending points precisely. It will not let you place a node at anything other than a grid intersection point.

Once you are comfortable with how the grid works, start the exercise. Begin by drawing three connected rectangles, as shown in figure 2.13, which you will use to form the sides of your box kite. It is important to watch the status line when sizing your rectangles.

Building a Box Kite Using the Grid

Click rectangle tool

At the center of the page, do the following:

Drag the mouse down and to the   Make the rectangle
right to form a rectangle   2.00" wide by 1.00" high.

| *Release mouse button* | The status line reads Rectangle on Layer 1. |

That is the back of the box kite. Now draw the sides. Notice that a rectangle can be drawn to the left or the right, and up or down.

Position the cursor on bottom left node of the rectangle	
Drag the cursor up and to the left to form a new rectangle	Make a new rectangle 1.50" wide by 1.00" high.
Release the mouse button	The status line reads Rectangle on Layer 1.
Position the cursor directly on the top right node of the first (largest) rectangle	
Drag the cursor down and to the left to form new rectangle	Make a rectangle 1.50" wide by 1.00" high.
Release the mouse button	The status line reads Rectangle on Layer 1.

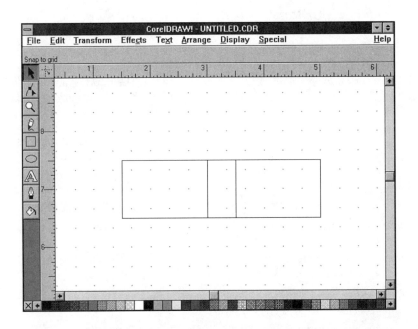

Figure 2.13:

Three connected rectangles.

Are you looking at this collection of three connected rectangles and wondering how you are going to turn this into a box kite? This is where you start to have fun.

Using Skew

You are going to use a feature called *skew* to bend the rectangles into more suitable polygons. When you apply skew to an object, you impart a "leaning" look to it. This tilting can be useful for creating rudimentary cast shadows, or, as in the case of this box kite, a sort of pseudo-perspective.

Skew can be invoked directly from the object. Double-click to display the skew/rotate handles. These are the same handles you used to turn the Porsche on end in the first chapter, and they are yet another example of CorelDRAW!'s tool-clustering philosophy.

This next step gives your box kite some semblance of perspective.

Skewing the Sides of the Box Kite

Click the pick tool	
Double-click the left rectangle	The skew/rotate handles appear.
Position cursor on left vertical two-headed arrow	The cursor becomes a +.
Drag the cursor down	The handles are replaced by a skew symbol and a blue dashed skew box. The status line reports on the number of degrees of horizontal skew.
Position the cursor for approximately 34 degrees of skew	Align the top node with the lower node.
Release the mouse button	The side is skewed.
Double-click the right rectangle	The skew/rotate handles appear.
Position the cursor on the left vertical two-headed arrow	The cursor becomes a +.
Drag the cursor downward	
Position the cursor for 34 degrees of skew	
Release the mouse button	The second side is skewed.

Draw another rectangle

Connect it to the front edges of the skewed sides (see fig. 2.14).

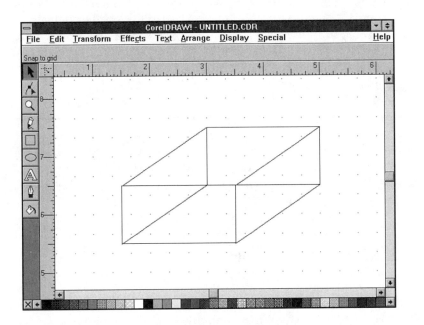

Figure 2.14:

A partially finished box kite.

Skew can be applied to any object. To constrain the angle of skew, use Ctrl. Be careful not to overdo the skew on typography. Just because Draw enables you to make any typeface oblique does not mean that you should.

By now, you should see something that is starting to resemble a box kite. With a few more steps, you add the bottom of the kite by duplicating what you have already drawn. Then you build its frame. You use a shortcut you picked up in the last chapter, drag-duplicate, to clone the top of the kite.

Because the grid is still on, it is easy to place the duplicate precisely. Remember to press + from the numeric keypad to make a duplicate and leave the original object untouched. Use the status line to place the duplicate three inches below, and horizontally centered under, the original.

Finishing the Box Kite

Marquee-select rectangles	
Press + while dragging the rectangles down	Position them 3 inches below the originals.
Draw 4 rectangles to form the frame	Make them 0.17" wide by 4.00" tall.
Marquee-select the box kite	
Rotate the box kite to a more realistic angle	

Now that you have the kite together, it would be a good idea to save your drawing, if you have not already done so. The more often you save, the less work you will have to redo in the event of a power failure or file mishap.

Pulling in the Guidelines

Earlier, Draw's guideline feature was mentioned. Take a moment to draw guidelines to position your artwork on the page. Because Island Printing (Joe DeLook's cousin, actually) usually asks for lots of gripper space and good-sized margins, you will be drawing half-inch horizontal and vertical guidelines.

It is easy to lay down guidelines in CorelDRAW!. If you are familiar with Aldus PageMaker, this will be old hat. Position your cursor over a ruler—horizontal ruler for horizontal guidelines, vertical ruler for vertical guidelines—click, and drag your guideline into position.

Drawing Guidelines

If the rulers are not showing on your screen, activate them by clicking on Show **R**ulers on the Display menu.

Position the cursor over the horizontal ruler

*Click and drag the guideline 0.5
inches from the top of the page*

*Position the cursor over the
vertical ruler*

*Click and drag the guideline 0.5
inches from the left side of the page*

Position the cursor over the vertical ruler

*Click and drag the guideline 0.5
inches from the right side of the page*

You easily can tell whether the guidelines are in the exact position.
Draw provides a convenient dialogue box to handle it (see fig.
2.15). By double-clicking on a guideline, you display the Guidelines dialogue box where you can check on a guideline's position
and change it if necessary.

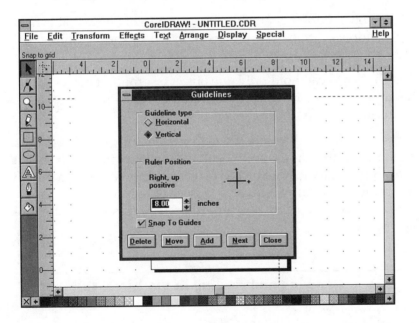

Figure 2.15:

The Guidelines
dialogue box.

The Guidelines dialogue box enables you to move, add, and delete
guidelines with precision. Once the dialogue box is up, you can
use the Next button to pop from guideline to guideline. If you
want, you can try changing the horizontal (gripper) guideline to
three quarters of an inch (0.75).

Shortcut

Double-clicking on a
guideline accesses
the Guidelines
dialogue box.

In the next section, make use of CorelDRAW!'s group and copy functions as you draw the kite's tail.

Forming, Copying, and Pasting a Group

As you learn in the following chapter, CorelDRAW!'s grouping function is a great time-saver and a vital tool. Although this chapter only touches on the subject here, it is imperative that you understand and use the concepts behind grouping. Be sure to work through the "Deck of Cards" exercises in Chapter 3 for a thorough lesson.

Shortcut

Press Ctrl-Ins to copy to the Clipboard.

CorelDRAW! implements the standard Microsoft Windows cut, copy, and paste commands. You can access Copy and Paste from the Edit menu, as well as through keyboard shortcuts.

When you cut or copy an object (or a group of objects), it is held in the Windows clipboard until it is replaced by the next object or until you exit Windows.

Shortcut

Press Shift-Ins to paste current object(s) from the clipboard.

The clipboard can hold only one object or group of objects at a time. When you paste an object from the clipboard, a copy remains in the clipboard.

Draw a tail for the box kite. Even though many box kites do not have tails, Katie has assured Joe that "any box kite worth its salt" can support a long tail. She has even asked for a tail with exactly five segments! You will make good use of the Copy and Paste commands as you carry out her orders. Your results should look like figure 2.16.

Drawing and Pasting in the Kite's Tail

Click the rectangle tool
Draw two squares   Make them 0.50" wide.
Click the pick tool
Click the first square
Rotate the square 45 degrees
Click the second square

Rotate the second square 45 degrees

Drag the square so that its leftmost point is touching the right-most point of its peer. You have drawn the first segment of your kite's tail.

Shift-click or marquee-select tail segment	The handles encompass both objects. The status line reads 2 objects selected.
Click **Arrange**	
Click **Group**	The status line reads Group of 2 objects.
Click **Edit**	
Click **Copy**	
Click **Edit**	
Click **Paste**	New group appears on copied group.
Click and drag the new segment into position	The kite tail has two segments.
Paste in three more tail segments	Drag them into position.
Marquee-select the entire tail	The entire tail is selected.
Click **Arrange**	
Click **Group**	The status line reads Group of 5 objects selected.
Drag the tail into position underneath the kite	
Click **Arrange**	
Click **Ungroup**	
Rotate and place the tail sections as desired	

After the previous exercises, you should be getting a good feel for the grid tool, as well as the rectangle tool. Although Grid is very convenient, it can make things difficult at times. You will find that items drawn without the grid on may not want to snap to the grid once you enable it.

You also can use keyboard shortcuts to group and ungroup objects. To group objects, use Ctrl-G. To ungroup objects, use Ctrl-U.

Shortcut

Press Ctrl-G to group objects.
Press Ctrl-U to ungroup objects.

Figure 2.16:

A box kite with a tail.

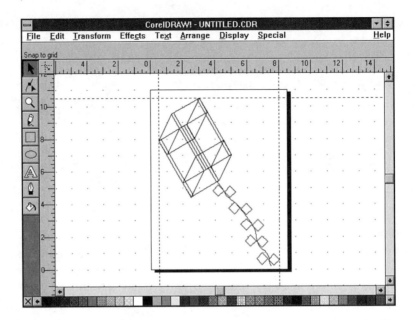

Shortcut

Press Shift-F9 to
toggle between
wireframe and full-
color editing modes.
Press F9 to enable
full-screen preview.

If, up until now, you have been working with CorelDRAW!'s
wireframe, rather than full-color editing mode, turn on the full-
color mode by pressing Shift and F9.

Working in wireframe mode speeds up your computer. It cuts
down on the number of computations that the processor must
perform, and that can make a very large difference in the time it
takes to display a drawing. On complex work, it is a good idea to
work with the wireframes only, popping in and out of full-color
mode only as needed.

Draw also provides a full screen preview; simply press F9. Chapter 8 gives you a closer view at preview strategies. But for now,
just try toggling between full-color and wireframe modes.

Putting Outline and Fill to Work

The outline and fill tools affect the way an object appears, rather
than its shape. Outline refers to the line surrounding an object,
and is invoked by clicking on the outline icon (it looks like an old-
fashioned pen nib). Fill is just that—a tool for filling, in much the

same manner as one might fill a pie crust. Selecting different fills is like choosing different pie fillings. Fill is invoked by clicking on the icon that looks like a paint can.

CorelDRAW! has amazing outline and fill capabilities. The program gives you the power of color, fountain, and PostScript fills. Although this chapter only touches the surface, later chapters of the book go into depth on the subject. You will see that Draw provides three methods for selecting outlines and fills: the fly-out menus, the roll-up menus, and the on-screen color palette (at the bottom of the screen). You use only the fly-out menus for the exercises in this chapter.

In the default mode, new objects have an outline of none and a 100 percent black fill, which explains why the box kite in the preview window is black. You can alter the fill and outline attributes for objects before you create them by clicking on the fill or outline tool while no objects are selected. When you see the New Object Uniform Fill dialogue box, shown in figure 2.17, click OK to change the defaults. Your copy of CorelDRAW! may still be running with the factory defaults, but make sure that you have the same defaults by resetting them now.

The dialogue box offers three options: All Objects, Text Objects, and Other Objects (everything but text). You will be setting the default for All Objects.

TIP

The grid's magnetic effect can be tough to overcome. If you have a rectangle that was drawn with the grid off, there are two ways to make it snap to grid. The first is to convert the rectangle to curves, and then use the node edit tool to drag it onto the grid. The second is to use the Align to Grid option from the Align dialogue box.

Setting New Fill and Outline Defaults

With no objects selected, take the following steps:

Click the fill tool	The Fill fly-out menu appears.
Click **B**lack	A dialogue box appears.
Click **A**ll Objects	
Click OK	The Fill default is reset.
Click the outline tool	The Outline fly-out menu appears (see fig. 2.18).
Click **N**one (X)	The dialogue box appears.

continues

Click **A**ll Objects

Click OK   The Outline default is
                                                        reset.

Figure 2.17:

Setting new fill and
outline defaults.

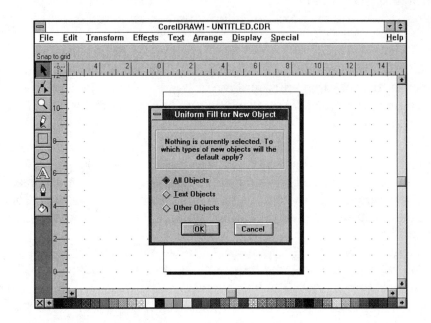

You may have noticed that NONE is now denoted by a simple
"X." The icons can get rather interesting when language is removed! With this next step, you outline every object in your box
kite drawing with a hairline. The hairline icon is unique; it consists of two vertical arrows pointing at a thin rule.

Changing the Outline

Click the pick tool

Click **E**dit   The Edit menu appears.

Click **S**elect **A**ll   Handles appear around
                                                        all objects.

Click the outline tool   The Outline fly-out menu
                                                        appears.

Click the thinnest ruling line (hair)   All objects have a
                                                        hairline outline.

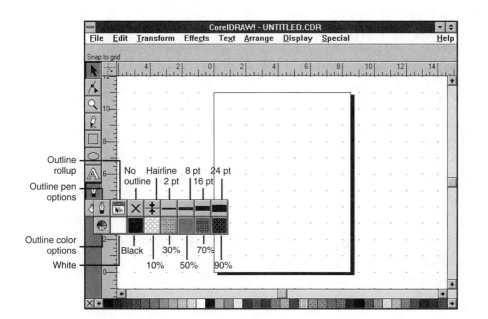

It is hard to tell—all objects are still black—but they are now outlined with a hairline rule. After the next step, you will be able to see the hairline rule. While all objects are still selected, you are going to fill them with white.

Once you have changed the fill to white, the different outline weights become readily visible. You should apply the various rule weights to the drawing to get an idea of how they look.

Changing Fills

With all objects still selected, take the following steps:

Click the fill tool	The Fill fly-out menu appears (see fig. 2.19).
Click White (between none "X" and black)	All objects are filled with white.

Your full-color screen is starting to look like your wireframe screen—you have got a wireframe rendering of a wireframe! Do something about that now.

Figure 2.19:

An annotated Fill fly-out menu.

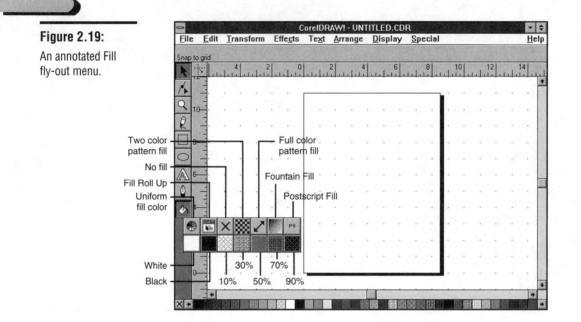

You are going to click off (or deselect) the objects by clicking on an empty place. This enables you to select individual objects or groups of objects. Then, fill the objects with a tint of your choice. The right side of the status line shows each object's fill.

Selectively Changing Fills

Click the screen	Objects are deselected.
Marquee-select the top of the box kite	The top of the box kite is selected.
Click the fill tool	The Fill fly-out menu appears.
Click 50% black	The status line shows top of the kite filled with 50 percent gray.
Click the cloud	The cloud is selected.
Click the fill tool	The Fill fly-out menu appears.
Click 10% black	The status line shows that the cloud is filled with 10 percent gray.

Press Ctrl-S	Get in the habit of saving often.

Continue with all of the individual pieces, until you get the kite looking as you like it. Try using lighter or darker fills on the various sides of the box kite. When you are done with that, try the different outlines.

As mentioned, CorelDRAW! offers far more outline choices and a wealth of fill possibilities. The fly-out menus will take care of your immediate needs. In subsequent chapters, you learn about on-screen palettes, roll-ups, calligraphic pens, fountain fills, pattern fills, and other marvelous features. But for now, the fly-out menus offer a quick and easy way to build your images.

The kite's frame will overprint the kite itself. You can adjust this by arranging the objects in your drawing with the To Front and To Back commands located on the Arrange menu. For more information on arranging your work, refer to the next chapter.

Next, you get a quick preview of the text tool.

Setting Type with the Text Tool

Typography, the craft of setting type, is made possible through one of CorelDRAW!'s most enabling features, the text tool. You learn more about typesetting later on. For now, you set up a simple letterhead and incorporate your box kite and cloud drawings. You will use Draw's text tool, which looks like the letter A.

Setting Up a Letterhead

Click the text tool	The cursor becomes a + (the text tool).
Click the top of the page	The text I bar appears.
Type **Katie's Kite Nook**	The type appears in 24-point Avalon.

continues

Click **Edit**	The Edit menu appears.
Click **Edit Text**	The Artistic Text dialogue box appears.
At Fonts:	
Roll down, Click Banff	The text changes to the Banff typeface.
Click OK	
Click the top of the page	The text I bar appears.
Type **14th and the Boulevard, Seaside**	The type appears in 24-point Banff.
Click **Edit**	The Edit menu appears.
Click Edit Text	The Artistic Text dialogue box appears.
At Fonts:	
Roll down, Click Fujiyama2	The text changes to the Fujiyama2 typeface.
Type **12**	In the size field.
Click OK	
Click the top of the page	The text I bar appears.
Type **800/555-7777**	
Click the pick tool	

There should be three blocks of text: the words *Katie's Kite Nook* in 24-point Banff script, and the address and telephone number in 12-point Fujiyama2.

Select and group all objects in the box kite drawing, and scale them down proportionally to about a third of their original size. Drag the box kite to the upper left-hand corner of the page.

Use the pick tool to drag the clouds into position at the top right side of the page. Add guidelines where needed to aid in aligning the different design elements, and finish up by dropping the type into position within the clouds. Your finished letterhead should look something like figure 2.20.

If you are not quite happy with the way your clouds look, wait until the next chapter—you will be refining their shapes soon enough. In any case, reduce the clouds to fit, and give them a hairline outline and a white fill. Congratulations, you have completed your first project—remember to save your file!

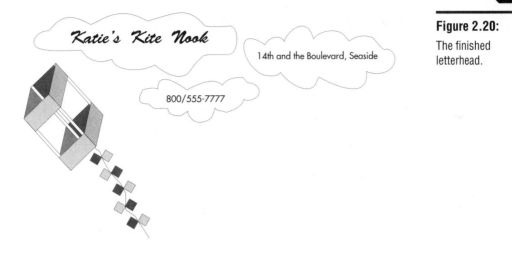

Figure 2.20:
The finished letterhead.

Katie's Kite Nook

14th and the Boulevard, Seaside

800/555-7777

Summary

In this chapter, you learned the basics of CorelDRAW!'s toolbox while creating your first project, a simple letterhead. You used the pencil tool to draw objects consisting of both straight and curved lines. You saw the difference between an open and a closed path, and you learned how to close an open path. The ellipse and rectangle tools were shown to operate in a similar manner. Likewise, the outline and fill commands were compared and explained, and Draw's grid and guidelines features were explored and implemented. Finally, you finished your first project by adding text and scaling the drawing.

Chapter 3 deals with editing and manipulation. You will begin by touching up a few items on your letterhead. The second part of the chapter will show you how to build a set of playing cards to explain the concept of layering and grouping your drawings.

Editing and Manipulating

his chapter has two basic purposes: to enlighten you on the finer points of nodes, and to help you understand the principles of grouping and layering your work. The concepts and practices in this chapter are a bit more complex than what was previously covered, so hang in there. You will end up drawing some playing cards, although not as complex as the one shown in figure 3.1.

In Chapter 2, you learned how to lay down the lines that you will soon be refining. You might think, "But my drawing is perfect—what do I have to change?" Plenty. If you begin to look at your work with a critical eye (and the zoom tool), you will soon see the shortcomings of drawing with a mouse. You are going to use CorelDRAW!'s shape tool to fine-tune your drawing.

As with any creative work, one cannot expect to create excellence in an instant. It may be true that inspiration strikes with speed, but true perfection can only be accomplished through diligent attention to detail. Beauty takes time.

Figure 3.1:

The one-eyed jack.

As you were drawing with the pencil tool, you probably noticed that CorelDRAW! added little boxes to your curved lines. These boxes were positioned at distinct changes in the line's direction. These boxes are what CorelDRAW! refers to as *nodes*, and they are the key to producing high-quality images.

A good portion of this chapter deals with manipulating nodes and their control points. For many people, working with nodes is the most difficult to understand of CorelDRAW!'s functions. Although it is possible to create drawings without ever using the shape tool, its proper use is a clear delineation between the amateur and the expert CorelDRAW! user.

Understanding the concepts behind nodes and control points can help you perform more efficiently and produce work of a higher caliber. It is, therefore, important that you not only sit through this little diatribe but also spend time learning through doing. Consider yourself warned. It may take some practice before you become proficient with the shape tool.

Just as important as grasping the idea of node manipulation is understanding the concepts behind building your work in a series of logical layers and groups. Building structured pieces is, again, the mark of the journeyman electronic artist. Simply looking good does not cut it; your pieces must be functional.

Once you are past the "gee whiz" stage, you soon find that properly assembling your artwork is a key point in achieving success with the CorelDRAW! program. Again, it is a good idea to remember that you are assembling an electronic collage of shapes. Those shapes are of many different tints, colors, and patterns. They have other shapes—filled with other tints, colors, and patterns—"glued" on their surfaces. Planning the construction of your imagery takes time. The more thought you put into building your collage, the easier it is for you to go back in and edit it.

One of the awful truths of commercial art is that the client often asks the artist to alter work that the artist feels is—for all intents and purposes—finished. The artwork could be very difficult, if not impossible, to alter. Conventional artists have been frustrated by this fact for years. Imagine Michelangelo at the Sistine chapel: "It is beautiful, Michelangelo, my son, but maybe the angel should be looking to his left instead of his right, and perhaps you could add a cherub or two in the corner?"

This scenario might have thrown the old master into a fit, but it does illustrate the advantages of creating electronic artwork. Your images are reworkable. You do not have to start a piece over from scratch, should your clients decide that they want a different color scheme or an extra angel.

But in order to accommodate changes, you must plan for them. You must build your collage in a way that accommodates easy editing. You must be able to edit lines and combine and group objects to make yours a "working drawing." CorelDRAW! provides the tools. To be effective, you must learn how best to use them.

Drawing with Bezier Curves

CorelDRAW! uses a device called the *Bezier curve* to generate smooth, resolution-independent objects. Bezier curves are produced by a mathematical formula that governs the shape of a line. Don't worry: you don't have to get out your scientific calculator to complete a drawing—CorelDRAW! does the math for you.

One Bezier curve requires two nodes, each with its own control point(s), to complete the equation. The *node* is the hub from which the control points radiate. *Control points* are the mechanisms that govern the trajectory of a line segment. People have described the on-screen appearance of a node and its control points as looking "like a box with two knitting needles sticking out of it," "a bug with antennae," or even, "the world's smallest voodoo doll." The last is how you might feel about nodes and control points after spending a frustrating session wrestling with them.

Segments are the lines between the nodes. They form the edges of objects and can be either curved or straight. A curved segment requires a control point at each end. Straight lines, however, have no control points. A node has a corresponding control point for each curved segment radiating from it.

If a node is the first node of an open path, it can have only one control point. If it looks as if it has more, you probably have two selected nodes sitting on top of each other.

There are three ways to affect the shape of a line segment without adding a node. The first is to move the node itself. Repositioning the node affects the position at which the control points do their work. Because a line segment is governed by the nodes at either end, as one node is moved, it affects the relationship between both nodes. When you move a node, the shape of the line segments on both sides of that node are altered.

If you do not want to move the node itself, you have two alternatives. A second approach is to change the node type. As you soon see, there are different node types which enable you to create either curved or straight line segments. The node type is specified with the Node Edit menu. The third and final method of altering the shape of a line segment is through control-point positioning. This is the most involved process of the three, and it is where you do the most heavy tweaking.

When you reposition a node's control points, you change the mathematical equation that defines the corresponding line segment. The power of Bezier curves lies in numbers. One Bezier curve is not much use; linking Bezier curves to form paths fully exploits their potential.

In addition to the aforementioned techniques, you have one more option for changing the course of a line segment: adding an additional node. Adding a new node splits one line segment into two, and enables you to make radical changes to that line.

At this point, review the various methods for drawing lines. Chapter 2 covered these techniques in depth, so if you have any questions beyond what is reviewed here, check back a few pages.

Here are a few basics. Click for single straight lines; double-click for connected straight lines. Hold the Ctrl key to constrain straight lines to 15-degree increments (default setting). When drawing curved lines, remember to hold down the left mouse button until you are finished drawing the line. If you want to erase a portion of a curved line (while drawing), hold down the Shift key and "back over" the offending portion of the line.

Choosing Node Types

CorelDRAW! supports three types of curved nodes: smooth, symmetrical, and cusp. When you execute a freehand drawing or import a traced object, CorelDRAW! (or CorelTRACE!) takes its best guess at which type of node is needed. On many occasions, the program does not make the right choice. What do you want, a program that does all the work for you? Since you are the artist, you should make the ultimate decision. Take the information that the program gives you and alter it as you see fit.

Try Drawing Some Curves

Before you get into a formal explanation of the different node types, try drawing some curves. Attempt to draw an octopus—an appropriately curved undersea creature. Try working in wireframe mode to get a better view of the nodes' control points. To toggle between full-color and wireframe modes, press Shift-F9.

You will not need a prompted exercise; just click the pen tool and start drawing. It will probably take a few tries to draw an octopus that you are almost happy with. Do not worry about making it perfect the first time out. You can go back in later to alter the curves and improve its appearance.

Once you have drawn a nice-looking cephalopod, as shown in figure 3.2, select it with the node edit tool. Notice that your octopus has many nodes spread along the path that outlines its body. These are not suckers, or even hooks; they are a means for you to change the shape of your drawing.

Figure 3.2:

An octopus.

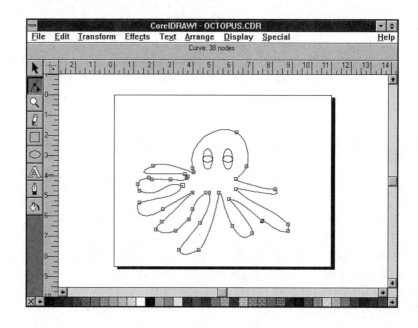

Select a node and try dragging it around. Watch what happens to the curves as you move the node. The node's control points become active once the node is selected. The control points are the squares at the ends of the dashed lines. Try pulling on the different control points, and take note of how the control points alter the shape of the line.

As you select different nodes, you see that they do not all act the same. Also notice that a selected node's type appears in the status line. The next sections discuss CorelDRAW!'s assortment of curved and line nodes.

Smooth Nodes

In a smooth node, both of the control points and the node itself are in a straight line (see fig. 3.3). Pull up on one node, and the other goes down. The control points and the node are linearly linked. Think of a spinning propeller on a seaplane. The blades always spin in the same direction, be it clockwise or counterclockwise. Unlike a propeller, however, the control points in a smooth node do not have to be the same distance from the node. The farther away a control point is from the node, the larger the curve.

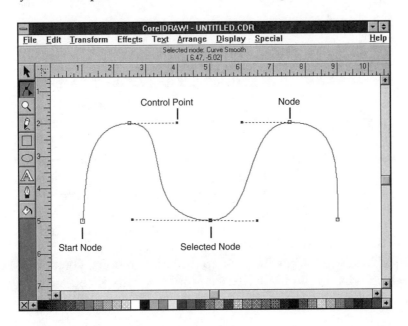

Figure 3.3:

A smooth node.

Symmetrical Nodes

The symmetrical node takes the smooth node's propeller analogy a bit further. Not only are the control points and node linearly linked, the control points are of equal distance from the node. Moving one control point affects the other control point, resulting in exactly the same curve on each side of the node.

Symmetrical nodes are, in effect, smooth nodes with *equidistant* control points (see fig. 3.4).

Figure 3.4:

A symmetrical node.

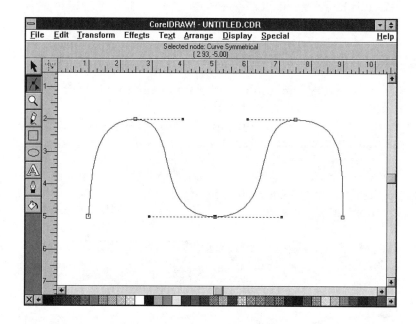

Cusp Nodes

Cusp nodes are very different from smooth and symmetrical nodes. In a cusp node, the control points operate independently of each other (see fig. 3.5). One side of the curve can be affected without altering the other side. A cusp node is used where there is a radical change in direction or a severe angle. You can compare cusp-node control points to a set of rabbit-ear antennae on a portable television set. To pick up different stations, you adjust each antenna individually. To manipulate a curve, you move the control point corresponding to that curve.

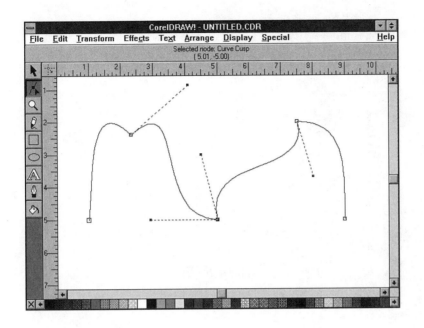

Figure 3.5:
A cusp node.

Line Nodes

Line nodes are not as flexible as curve nodes. Where a line meets a line, you *must* have a cusp node. Two straight lines cannot be connected with a smooth node or a symmetrical node. Actually, you can have a smooth or symmetrical node connecting two straight line segments—but in title only. For all intents and purposes, the node will still act like a cusp node. On the other hand, when a line meets a curve, you can have either a cusp or a smooth node (see fig. 3.6). Because they do not curve, straight line segments do not have control points. You will find that objects are often made up of both curved and straight line segments. A node with a straight line segment on one side and a curved line segment on the other has only one control point.

Now it is time to put you to work. Remember the letterhead you completed in the last chapter? You are going to pull out that drawing and clean up the clouds using the shape tool.

If you have the octopus drawing or another unsaved file on the screen when you attempt to open BOXKITE.CDR, the program asks whether you want to save the file. Respond to this and to the following dialogue boxes accordingly. If you'd like, save the file as Octopus.CDR.

Figure 3.6:

A smooth node where a line meets a curve.

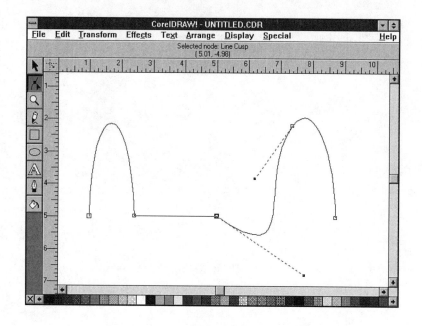

Editing Nodes

Click **File**	The File menu appears.
Click **O**pen	The Open File dialogue box appears.
Click BOXKITE.CDR	To select the letterhead file from Chapter 2.
Click OK	The letterhead appears.
Click the zoom tool	The Zoom fly-out menu appears.
Click +	
Marquee-select the cloud	To zoom up on the cloud.
Click the shape tool	The cursor becomes the shape tool.
Click the cloud	The cloud's nodes appear (see fig. 3.7).

According to the status line, the cloud in figure 3.7 has 24 nodes—far more than necessary for this basic object. Your cloud may have many more (or less) nodes. The first thing you are going to do is remove some of the excess nodes by simply selecting each node and deleting with the Delete key.

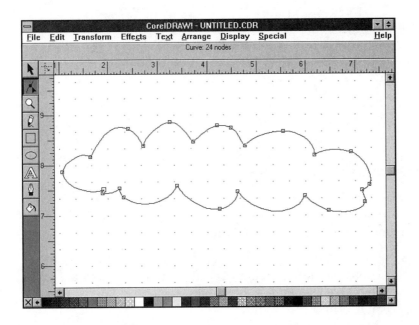

Figure 3.7:
A cloud with the
nodes showing.

Before you continue, however, save this as a new file by clicking Save As (from the File menu). Name the file BOXKITE2. This action prevents you from overwriting the original version.

If you marquee-select your cloud, notice that curved nodes are denoted by small black boxes. Line nodes show as larger outlined boxes. The first node of a closed curve is always a large, black box when selected. Your cloud drawing should consist of mostly curved nodes. Go in and prune a few extra nodes. As you do, watch the status line; it reads: Selected node: Curve Cusp (or Smooth or Symmetrical) depending on what type of node is selected.

Removing an Extra Node

Click File
Click Save **As**
Type **BOXKITE2**
Click OK
Click an extra node   The node turns black.
Press Del   The node is deleted.

You have two other ways to delete a node. After selecting a node, you can click Clear from the Edit menu, or Delete from the Node Edit menu, to accomplish the same thing. There are also ways to add nodes—the next section covers that.

Shortcut

Click the node and press Del to delete a node.

The Draw program enables you to work with more than one node at a time. Go back in and remove a pair of nodes by selecting them with a marquee and then deleting them. Another way to select more than one node at a time is to hold down Shift as you click on the nodes you want to select.

After you finish selecting and deleting nodes, and you have grown tired of cloud pruning, move on to working with (rather than simply deleting) the remaining nodes.

Begin by selecting a node. Click and drag that node to a new location. Watch how the node's control point (or points) move with the node. The curves change, governed by the relationship between neighboring nodes.

When you click a node, the control points for that point—as well as the relevant control points of all related nodes—become active. These "knitting needles" bend and flex their respective curve segments according to the conventions of their node type.

TIP

If a line segment goes whacko after you delete a node, fear not; there is a quick fix. Double-click on the wayward line. Once the Node Edit dialogue box appears, click Line; this changes the whacko curve into a straight line. Double-click on the line again, and click Curve. Finally, tweak the control points until the curve is back in shape.

Before you get into a prompted exercise, you should begin to get the feel of nodes and control points. Just tweak those nodes until it seems familiar. Push and pull on the different control points.

As you get further and further into tweaking your cloud, you will begin to understand the differences between the types of nodes. You will see that the control points in a cusp curve operate independently of each other. And you will see the similarity and differences between smooth and symmetrical curves.

Adding Nodes to an Object

In this next exercise, you build a cloud from scratch. Start by drawing an ellipse and use Convert to Curves to enable access to the object. Then, use Add from the Node Edit menu to add four extra points.

CorelDRAW! does not enable you to manipulate the nodes in an ellipse, rectangle, or in text without first using Convert to Curves. If you try to use the shape tool on a "normal" ellipse or circle, CorelDRAW! turns the object into an arc or pie wedge (this technique is covered in Chapter 6). Using the shape tool on a rectangle renders a rounded-corner rectangle (which you will see in a few pages when you start building your playing cards).

Once an object has been converted to curves, you can perform some amazing maneuvers. By the time you finish with this exercise, you will have more than a hint of what the Convert to Curves command enables you to do.

To get started, set up your grid so that there are six lines per inch. Then, use this setup to build some perfectly cartoony clouds. Convert to Curves adds three nodes to the oval (it starts with one). If you click on each node, you find that they are all symmetrical curves.

Turning the Ellipse into a Cloud

Click Display

Click Grid Setup

At both Horizontal and Vertical   At Grid
Enter 6.00 per inch   Frequency prompt.

Click OK

Click the ellipse tool

Draw an oval   Make it 1.50" high by 5.00" wide.

Click **Arrange**   The Arrange menu appears.

Click Convert to Curves   Three nodes are added to the oval (see fig. 3.8).

Click the shape tool

Marquee-select all four nodes

Double-click on a node   The Node Edit menu appears.

continues

Click **Add**	Four new nodes are added (see fig. 3.9).
Double-click on a node	The Node Edit menu appears.
Click **C**usp	All nodes are now cusp nodes.
Click the screen	The cloud is deselected.
Click on a node	The node is selected.
Pull control points from object at a 90-degree angle	Curves grow out from the object.
Continue pulling out control points	A cloud forms (see fig. 3.10).

Figure 3.8:

An oval with four nodes.

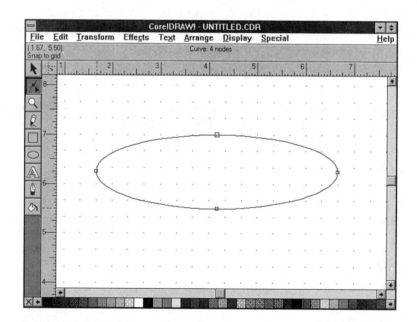

The Node Edit menu provides a simple way to change between node types. To display the menu, double-click on a selected node. In this menu, you can choose between line and curve nodes, the latter in cusp, smooth, or symmetrical variations. In addition, the menu gives you the capability to break or join a path, and add or delete a node.

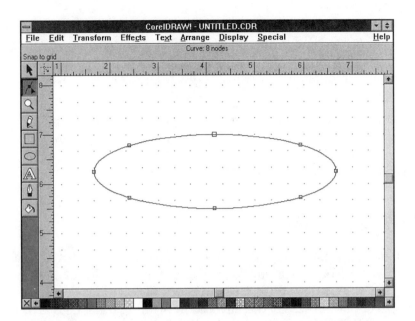

Figure 3.9:

An oval with eight nodes.

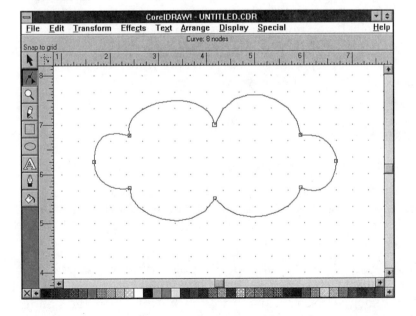

Figure 3.10:

The finished cloud.

As you have seen, cusp nodes enable the severe change in direction needed to render this object. See what happens when you change all the nodes to smooth or symmetrical curves. Remember, you can immediately undo any wayward actions with Alt-Backspace.

If the new cloud looks any better than what you already have, save it. Use the scale function to bring it down to the correct size for your drawing. If the new cloud looks worse than what you already have, go ahead and delete it.

Nodes and Tracing

Generally speaking, you should use as few nodes in your objects as possible. The reason for this is that the more nodes in an object, the larger your files. With the increase in file size also comes a loss of speed, both in screen display and in printing time. Less is more. You will find that an autotraced or freehand-rendered image includes far more points than necessary to portray the object accurately. If you notice an excessive amount of jaggedness, you probably have a bunch of untweaked cusp nodes. For this reason, be careful of cusp nodes—use them only where you must. The time you ultimately save will be your own.

Node Pointers

Here are a few other things you should know about nodes.

When moving a node or control point, you can constrain movement by using the grid. In addition, holding down Ctrl while moving a node or control point restricts the action to either vertical or horizontal movement.

It's easy to add a node at a specific point. With the shape tool, double-click at the spot you want to add the new node. The Node Edit dialogue box appears; simply click Add. The node is added at the exact coordinates at which you double-clicked. To add nodes with pinpoint precision, remember to use Draw's snap-to guidelines. Drag out a set of horizontal and vertical guidelines, adjust them for dead-on accuracy, and go! Take the time to try this technique on one of your clouds.

If a control point is hidden underneath a node, there is a simple way to dig it out. Make sure that the node is deselected. Press and hold Shift, and then click and drag the control point from underneath the node.

Do not worry if you still feel uncomfortable with nodes. It takes time. The best advice is practice, practice, practice. After you are done with your node tweaking, remember to save your work. In the next section, you start with a clean screen. As you get further along in the book, you will see how important it is to create lean, mean objects with a minimum of nodes. An extra node is a wasted node.

Shortcut

Deselect the node, Shift-click, and drag to pull out a hidden control point.

Drawing in Bezier Curve Mode

The 3.0 version of CorelDRAW! enables you to draw directly in Bezier curve mode. This may seem like torture for some, but others may welcome the extreme precision and flexibility that this feature affords.

Learning how to draw in Bezier mode helps you to understand how the curves function. There is no substitute for practice when it comes to working with Bezier curves, and mastering the skill is essential if you want to be successful with object-oriented graphics programs like CorelDRAW!, Adobe Illustrator, or Aldus Freehand.

To draw with Bezier curves, rather than freehand, you select a variant of the pencil tool. When you click on the pencil tool, hold down the left mouse button and drag downward and to the right to access the fly-out menu. Click the icon on the right to get into Bezier mode.

When you click on the pencil tool, the status line reports: Drawing in Bezier Mode.... When drawing straight lines in Bezier mode, you don't notice any differences between it and Draw's freehand modes. However, drawing curves in Bezier mode is quite different from drawing curves in freehand mode.

When drawing curves, consider how the curve exits and enters its starting and ending nodes (respectively). Think of threading a line through a series of fish hooks. The line segments form your fishing line, while the nodes are the hooks. The direction you pull the line through the hook affects the first half of the arc. Likewise, the direction you thread the line into the next hook (node) affects the second half of the arc. Figure 3.11 shows a variety of Bezier curves.

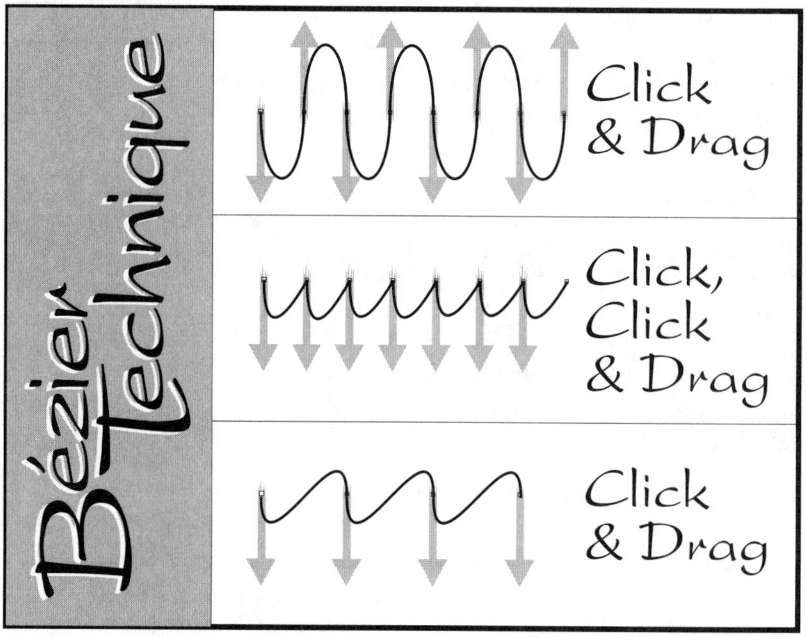

Figure 3.11:

Point and shoot Beziers.

In practice, it goes something like this: If you click-drag away from the first node in one direction, then click-drag (placing the second node) in the opposite direction, a one-bump curve is drawn. However, if you click-drag away from the first node in one direction, then click-drag (placing the second node) in the same direction, a two-bump curve is drawn.

Try working in Bezier mode. Start by laying down a few straight lines to form a triangle. Once you have that down, move on to the curves. For the straight lines, you can turn on the grid for precision, but you may want to turn it off when drawing your curves.

Drawing in Bezier Mode

First, draw a triangle with straight lines:

Click the pencil tool, drag down and to the right	The pencil tool fly-out menu appears.
Click the Bezier icon	The cursor becomes a +.
Click the page	The first node is placed.
Click 2" to the right of first node	A two-inch line is drawn.
Click 1" to the left and 1" above second node	A one-inch line is drawn.
Click the first node	A triangle is formed.

Now try some curves. When you first click, the curve's starting node appears. As you drag, two control points pull away from the node in opposite directions. Remember: the curve is drawn in the direction you pull away from the starting node until the apogee, where it is then drawn in the direction you thread through the ending node.

Place the cursor at the curve's starting point	
Click and drag down	Node and control points appear.
Release the mouse button	Node and control points remain on-screen.

Now, position the end of the curve segment, and draw the curve. Draw a one-bump curve to begin. Watch how the curve is altered as you drag.

Place the cursor at the curve's ending point	
Click and drag upward	The end node, control points, and line segment appear.
Release the mouse button	A line segment is drawn, and the end node and control points remain on-screen.

Shortcut

To begin drawing a new object, press the spacebar twice. (This works in either freehand or Bezier modes.)

Draw a few more connected curves. Then try pulling in the same direction for both the starting and ending nodes. You see the curves change into two-bump segments.

To draw cusp nodes, you need a little more patience, and a bit more skill. The technique here consists of a double-click on each end node and a control-point position for each segment. Double-click, position; double-click, position; double-click, position—it is not quite as tough as learning to waltz in junior high! Try drawing a few clouds this way. Give yourself plenty of time—soon you will be laying down Beziers with precision!

At this point, save your drawing and open up a new file.

Planning a Layering Strategy

Layering and arranging your work is like shuffling a deck of cards. You can stack the deck in your favor by assembling your image so that it may be easily manipulated.

Except for the most rudimentary drawings, all of your drawings should contain groups. Only the most quick-and-dirty scribbles, with a minimum of objects, should not be grouped.

Complex work, however, requires careful planning and execution. Thankfully, CorelDRAW! 3.0 has implemented a sophisticated layering function. In addition to layer control, Draw can arrange the order of objects through the use of five basic commands: To Front, To Back, Forward One, Back One, and Reverse Order. This command set works well, especially when used in conjunction with Draw's layer control.

You can extend the versatility of these commands by using two other commands from the Arrange menu: Group and Combine.

By building groups of objects, you take the first step towards forming an effective layering strategy. A complex work should not consist of hundreds of individual objects. It should be broken down into as few groups/layers as practical.

If you do not arrange your work properly, you will spend far too much time reworking the composition when it is time to make changes to it. And you *will* be making changes, like it or not.

Although it can take more time initially, grouping and layering saves time in the long run. Similar objects should be strategically combined to take advantage of like features such as outline and fill. Likewise, the objects, or combined objects, should be arranged into layer-specific groups.

The spots on a leopard and the stripes on a zebra are excellent examples of objects that might be grouped, if not combined. If they are exactly alike, and on the same layer, combine them. If they are all on the same layer, but not necessarily alike, group them. You can group combined objects with other objects. However, you cannot combine objects and maintain individual attributes.

As you get further on in the book, you will delve into the subject of layering and grouping in depth. In the next exercise, you see that with strategic grouping, you can rearrange your drawings at will.

A Lonely Saturday Night at DeLook Design

What is Joe DeLook doing? It is Saturday night, and he is still sitting at his desk, working with CorelDRAW! That is what owning your own business will do for you. Joe would rather be with his buddies in the back room of the Tiki Bar for the regular Saturday night poker game. He would even settle for playing blackjack in Atlantic City—and donating his money to Donald Trump. But here he is.

Joe has cards on his mind. He has promised himself that he will only work for an hour or so before he cuts out. Determined though he is, Joe is itching to lose some money to his pals. He cannot stop thinking about cards.

Arranging Objects without Using Layer Control

Building a set of cards and shuffling the deck goes a long way toward illustrating the concept of grouping and layering your work. In this exercise, you create a few playing cards in order to learn how to arrange objects without using layer control.

To make your computer respond faster, make sure that you are in wireframe mode. You turn full-color mode back on again at the end of this chapter, for a quick shuffle of the deck.

Drawing a Card

Click Display	The Display menu appears.
Click Grid Setup	The Grid Parameters menu appears.
Enter **6.00** *per inch*	At the Grid Frequency prompt.
Make sure that **Sn**ap to Grid *is checked*	
Click OK	
Click the rectangle tool	The cursor becomes a +.
Click and drag a box	Watch the status line for the size. Make the box 2.50" wide by 3.50" high. The rectangle tool snaps to the grid.
Release the mouse button	A rectangle is drawn.
Click Fill	The Fill fly-out menu appears.
Click White	The rectangle is filled with white.
Click Outline	The Outline fly-out menu appears.
Click 2 point rule	The rectangle is outlined with a two-point rule. You will not see this change until you print or preview.

Rounding Corners

You now have a white rectangle, outlined with a two-point rule, approximately the same size as a playing card (see fig. 3.12).

Although it may be the same size as a playing card and even the same shape, there is still one little adjustment that needs to be made: the corners must be rounded.

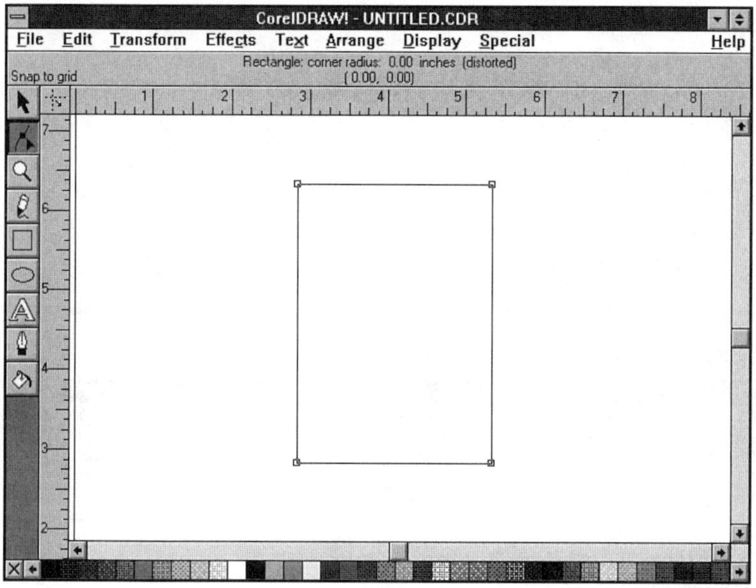

Figure 3.12:

The square-corner playing card.

This modification is easily accomplished with the shape tool. Earlier in the chapter, you manipulated the nodes and control points in your cloud drawings using the same tool. When you use the shape tool on a rectangle, it behaves quite differently.

Rectangles are constructed in a way that enables you to round corners without altering the overall dimensions. This prevents you from radically messing up your original object. There is no chance of you pulling one of the points off its original position.

When you click on a rectangle using the shape tool, the only thing that the tool enables you to do is round the corners. Try that now.

As you begin, notice that the status line reads: Rectangle: corner radius: 0.00 inches. As you drag, the corners become rounded, and the status line reflects the corner radius. Change the corner radius to 0.14 inches.

Cutting the Corners

Click the shape tool	The cursor becomes an arrow.
Click the rectangle	The rectangle is selected.
Click the top left node	The top left node is selected.
Click and drag the selected node to the right	The second set of nodes appears.
When the radius is 0.14 inches, release the mouse button	The rectangle now has 0.14-inch radius rounded corners (see fig. 3.13).

Figure 3.13:

A rounded-corner playing card.

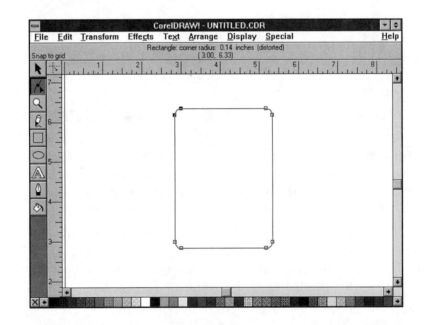

As you were dragging the corners around, you probably noticed that they only work in one direction. If you pull away from the object, rather than towards the center, the corners of the rectangle return to 90-degree angles.

The shape tool also works on ellipses. If you need to draw perfect arcs or pie wedges, using the shape tool on an ellipse is the slickest way to go. This can be a valuable tool for building pie charts, and is covered in Chapter 6.

Setting Special Characters

Now that you have the card drawn, place some suits and numbers on it. Corel has conveniently included a number of different fonts filled with special characters in the font load that comes with the program. There are many symbols in the fonts that you will want to use from time to time. They include stars, arrows, boxes, and musical symbols, to name a few.

Right now, you are building playing cards. Hence, you need symbols for the four different suits: clubs, diamonds, hearts, and spades. You can find these symbols in two of the fonts, either Dixieland or Greek/Math. You use the Dixieland characters for this project.

To use these special characters, you must specify Dixieland in the type dialogue box, and use a special keyboard sequence to access the character. This procedure is necessary for a simple reason: There are more characters in a font than can be directly accessed from the keyboard's standard keys. Use your Alt key and your keyboard's numeric keypad to access the special character sets, using the sequences shown in table 3.1. Make sure that Num Lock is on. This procedure works only with the numeric keypad; using the top row of number keys yields no result.

Until you select the correct font, the symbol portrayed does not necessarily match the symbol you are requesting. Do not worry. Once the proper font is selected, the symbol will be correct. Follow the directions in the next exercise carefully, and you should have no problems. You begin with an easy card: the ace of spades.

Table 3.1
Dixieland Special-Character Entry Sequences

Special Character	Keyboard Sequence
Club	Alt 0168
Diamond	Alt 0169
Heart	Alt 0170
Spade	Alt 0171

Drawing the Ace of Spades

Click the text tool	The + appears.
Click inside the card	The Text I bar appears.
Hold down Alt and type **0171**	This accesses the special character.
Click **Edit**	The Edit menu appears.
Click **Edit Text**	The Artistic Text dialogue box appears.
Scroll down and click Dixieland	Dixieland is now the specified typeface.
In the Point Size window, type **144**	144-point type is specified (see fig. 3.14).
Click OK	A 144-point spade is drawn.

You may have noticed that the character that originally appeared in the text-editing window was not the spade symbol. However, once you changed the font to Dixieland, the character appeared as it should. And once the character was placed on the page, everything looked fine. If you use many special characters, you will eventually become accustomed to this way of "typing" a character. You also may have noticed the little box to the left of the spade—that is the character's node. As you will see in the next chapter, character nodes are invaluable tools for controlling inter-character spacing (kerning) and baseline alignment.

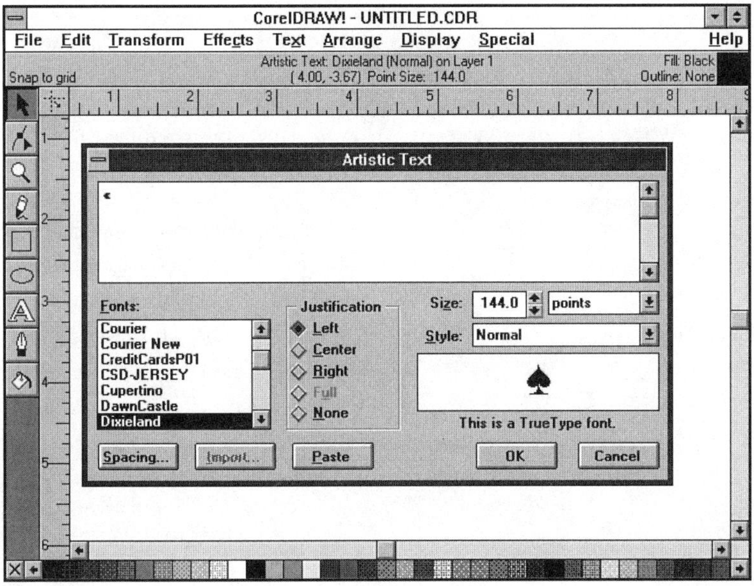

Figure 3.14:

The Artistic Text dialogue box.

CorelDRAW! Version 3.0 includes an extensive symbol library, apart from the special-character fonts. You use these symbol libraries in a different manner than the special-character fonts, although you access both with the text tool. The symbol libraries are covered in Chapter 4. The Windows Character Map utility is a great convenience for setting special characters. If you want, flip forward to Appendix A for more information on Character Map.

Using Align

Now that you have a big symbol on your card, center it. Rather than eyeballing it, use the Align command. You will find that Align is an invaluable tool for positioning objects relative to each other.

In this instance, you are going to center the big spade, both horizontally and vertically, on the card.

Centering Using Align

Click Pick tool	
Marquee-select the card and spade	Draws a blue dashed box.
Release the mouse button	The status line reads: 2 objects selected.
Click **A**rrange	The Arrange menu appears.
Click **A**lign	The Align dialogue box appears (see fig. 3.15).
Click Horizontally **C**enter	
Click Vertically **C**enter	
Click OK	The spade is horizontally and vertically centered within the card (see fig. 3.16).

Figure 3.15:

The Align dialogue box.

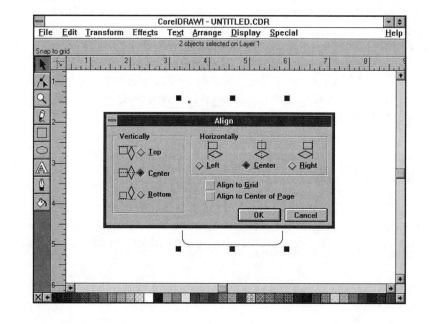

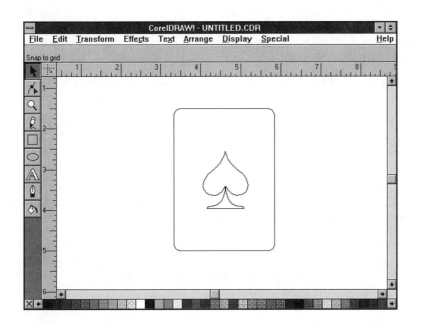

The Align command has a few properties that you should be aware of. When aligning two or more objects to the left, right, top, or bottom, Draw aligns all objects to the *last* object selected. The last object selected does *not* move. When marquee-selecting objects, Draw aligns the selected objects to the first object drawn. This can be confusing. You may find it easier to shift-click the items to be aligned.

The Align dialogue box also provides the options of Align to Grid or Align to Center of Page. Each of these options must be selected *before* selecting horizontal or vertical alignment.

Shortcut

Press Ctrl-A to get to the Align menu.

Soon, you will be using the Align command again. This next time though, you only need to worry about horizontal centering. But before you center anything else, you need to place the objects that you will be centering.

Scaling with Leave Original

Rather than using the procedure for inserting special characters again, you are going to use a technique you tried briefly in

Chapter 1: you will create a new, smaller spade while leaving the old one in place. You do this by pressing and releasing the + key on the numeric keypad as you use the scale function. The + tells CorelDRAW! to leave the original alone and to create a new object.

Remember that you also can click the right mouse button while stretching/scaling/moving/rotating to leave an original.

As you perform this next maneuver, watch the status line. You want to scale down to approximately 43 percent of original size. When you release the left mouse button, a new shrunken spade is drawn, and the original spade remains unscathed.

Using Scale with Leave Original

Click the spade	The spade is selected.
Position the cursor over the bottom right handle	The cursor becomes a +.
Drag the mouse and press + while dragging	Drag toward the spade's upper left corner (see fig 3.17).
Release the mouse button when the status line reads: 43%	A new shrunken spade appears.
Drag the small spade	Drag the spade to the upper left corner of the card.

There are other ways to accomplish the function you just performed. The first is to duplicate the object and scale the duplicate. This takes two steps and can be a waste of time. But it is your time, and you can waste it if you want to.

The second method for simultaneous duplicating and scaling is done with the Transform menu. Although it can also take more time, the Transform menu offers a distinct advantage to eyeballing your scales. The Transform menu lets you access the Rotate & Skew and Stretch & Mirror dialogue boxes (see fig. 3.18). These dialogue boxes let you leave the original behind while creating a new object. More importantly, through these dialogue boxes, you can input precise numbers for your rotations, skews, stretch/ scales, and mirrors. Use the dialogue boxes when creating a scale that needs to be "right on the money."

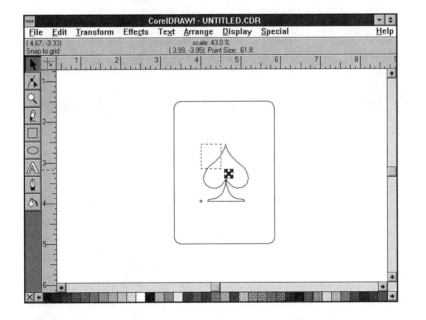

Figure 3.17:

The Scale/Leave original function.

Now that you have a little spade, drop in an *A* for Ace. Then you align the two objects horizontally and group them. This is another quick and easy deal.

As you work through the following exercise, notice that the text tool "remembers" its last settings. You go in and alter the type specifications once the character is on the page.

Figure 3.18:

The Stretch & Mirror dialogue box.

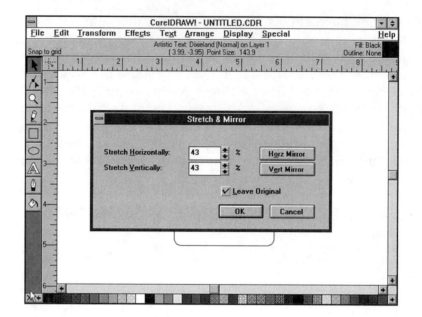

A Is for Ace

Click the text tool	The + appears.
Click the card	The Text I bar appears.
Type **A**	
Click **Edit**	The Edit menu appears.
Click **Edit Text**	The Artistic Text dialogue box appears.
Scroll down and click Bangkok	Bangkok is now the specified typeface.
In the Point Size window, enter **48**	48-point type is specified (refer back to fig. 3.14).
Click OK	A 48-point *A* is drawn.
Click the pick tool	
Drag the A *above the small spade*	
Shift-click the small spade	The status line reads: 2 objects selected.
Click **Arrange**	The Arrange menu appears.
Click **Align**	The Align menu appears.

Click Horizontally **Center**

Click OK

> The small spade and the
> *A* are horizontally
> aligned with each other.

Drag the A *and the small spade
into position at the card's upper left corner*

Click **Arrange**

> The Arrange menu
> appears.

Click **Group**

> The status line reads:
> Group of 2 objects.

The card is really starting to look like the ace of spades. With a few more steps, this card will be complete. You will find this next procedure to be similar to the scale/leave original that you just completed.

Using Stretch & Mirror

In the next sequence, you use Stretch & Mirror with Leave Original to create the upside-down version of the symbols for the bottom of the card. To perform this maneuver, you access the Stretch & Mirror dialogue box from the Transform menu.

Shortcut

Press Ctrl-Q to get to the Stretch & Mirror menu.

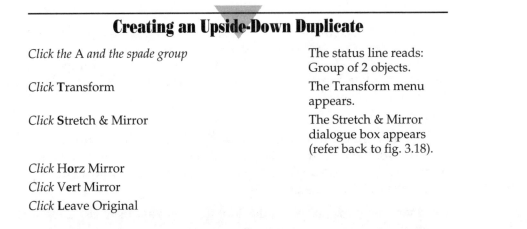

Creating an Upside-Down Duplicate

Click the A *and the spade group*

> The status line reads:
> Group of 2 objects.

Click **Transform**

> The Transform menu
> appears.

Click **Stretch & Mirror**

> The Stretch & Mirror
> dialogue box appears
> (refer back to fig. 3.18).

Click **Horz** Mirror
Click **Vert** Mirror
Click **Leave Original**

Click OK	A new *A* and spade are drawn upside-down. The original pair remains (see fig. 3.19).
Drag the new pair to the card's lower right corner	

Figure 3.19:

A horizontal/vertical mirrored duplicate.

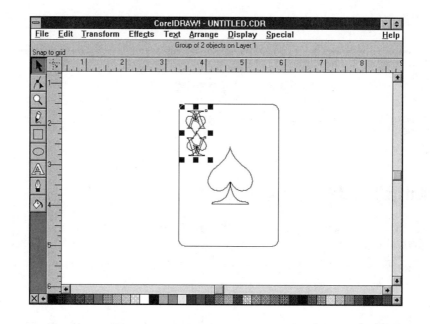

Because of the magnetic pull of the grid, you might not be able to position this second set of symbols exactly. You can wing it, and turn the grid off. This is where the good old art of eyeballing comes into play. Press Ctrl-Y, zoom way up on the card, and place the symbols by eye.

On the other hand, you might want to increase the grid frequency if you are more comfortable with the grid on. Start by doubling the grid frequency to 12 units per inch. This may help you to line up the symbols with a minimum of hassles. The grid allows up to a maximum of 72 units per inch.

Once you have the ace of spades looking the way it should, arrange all the symbols into one group. The results should look like figure 3.20.

Grouping the Ace of Spades

Click the pick tool

*Marquee-select all the objects
in the card*

Release the mouse button   The status line reads: 4
                                              objects selected.

Click **A**rrange   The Arrange menu
                                              appears.

Click **G**roup   The status line reads:
                                              Group of 4 objects.

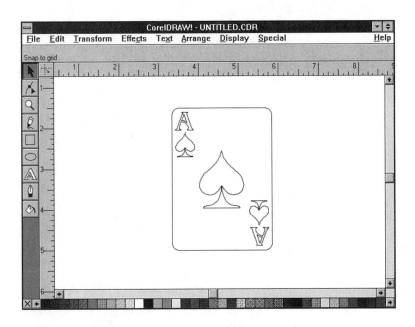

Figure 3.20:

The completed ace
of spades.

The ace of spades is now one group. You can move it around,
rotate it, duplicate it, and generally perform any function you
want. Every item in the group moves in concert.

Shortcut

Press Ctrl-G to
group selected
objects.

Setting Up and Using Duplicate

Copy the ace of spades and make a second card, the three of clubs. Begin by using the Duplicate command. Then, you alter the new card after you ungroup the objects. Grouped objects cannot be individually altered, so they have to be ungrouped.

You will see that Duplicate works in a similar fashion to Copy and Paste, but it does so in a more direct manner. Instead of being a two-step operation, like Copy and Paste, Duplicate works in one step.

Duplicate can be used for creating step-and-repeats. It is great for setting up small labels for gang printing. Unfortunately, the maximum distance you can step is limited to two inches. This makes the feature unusable when stepping larger images, such as business cards; in these cases, you want to use a drag-leave original-repeat approach.

Before you use Duplicate, it would be a good idea to check out the Preferences dialogue box. Among other things, the Preferences dialogue box controls where CorelDRAW! places a duplicate. You can access the Preferences dialogue box with the Special menu.

Shortcut

Press Ctrl-D to duplicate objects. Press + to place a duplicate behind a selected object.

In the next sequence, you set up the Preferences dialogue box (see fig. 3.21) to place duplicates 12 picas (2 inches) from the left side of the original objects. This may seem confusing, but it ensures that the duplicated objects are aligned to the grid. Let us hope that the next version or CorelDRAW! is not hindered by the 2-inch maximum.

Note that Duplicate works differently than simply pressing the + key. When you press +, a duplicate object (or objects) is (are) always placed directly *on top of* the selected object. By using the Duplicate command, you have control over the placement of the duplicate(s).

Setting Up the Duplicate Preferences

Click **S**pecial   The Special menu appears.

Click Preferences	The Preferences dialogue box appears (see fig. 3.21).
Set Place Duplicate **H**orizontal *to 18,0 picas and points; set* Place Duplicate **V**ertical *to 0,0 picas and points* *Click* OK	

Notice that the Preferences dialogue box also includes settings for curves, display, and a host of other selections. These settings do not apply in the present exercise, but you now know where to find them.

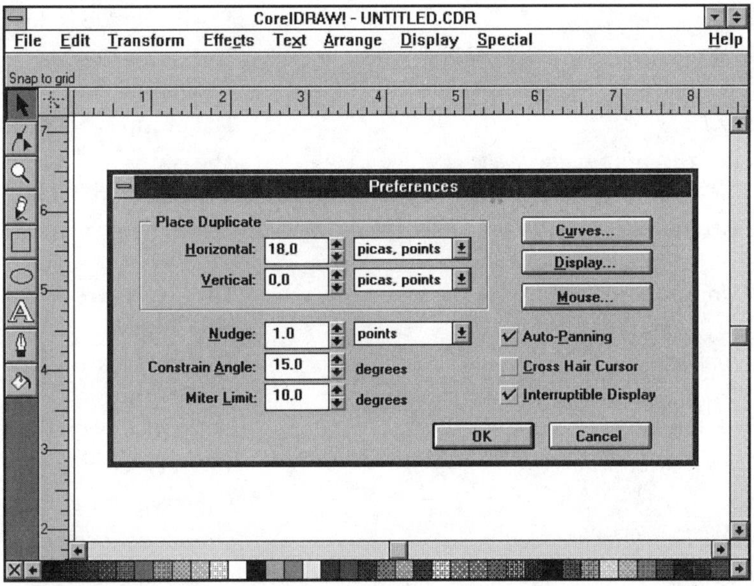

Figure 3.21:
The Preferences dialogue box.

The next step is to duplicate the ace of spades card and turn it into the three of clubs. You use the text tool to alter the text that has already been set. CorelDRAW! Version 3.0 introduced onscreen text-editing capabilities. In previous versions of Draw, you had to access the Edit Text dialogue box to make any text changes. Now, to alter a piece of type already on the screen, all you have to do is click on the text tool and click and drag over the text you want to edit.

Shortcut

Press Ctrl-T to call the Text dialogue box.

Creating the Three of Clubs

Click the ace of spades	The ace of spades is selected.
Press Ctrl-D	The ace of spades is duplicated and placed to the right of the original.
Click **Arrange**	The Arrange menu appears.
Click **Ungroup**	The duplicate ace of spades is ungrouped.
Click the screen	The card is no longer selected.
Click the big spade	The big spade is selected.
Press Del	The big spade is deleted.
Click the upside-down A *and spade*	The status line reads: Group of 2 objects.
Press Del	The group is deleted.
Click the remaining A *and spade*	The status line reads: Group of 2 objects.
Click **Arrange**	The Arrange menu appears.
Click **Ungroup**	The objects are ungrouped.
Click off objects	The objects are no longer selected.
Click the text tool	The cursor becomes a +.
Click and drag over the A	The A is selected.
Type **3**	A 3 replaces the A.
Click and drag over the spade	The spade is selected.
Hold down Alt and type **0168**	A club replaces the spade.
Click the pick tool	
Marquee-select or shift-click the 3 *and the club*	
Release the mouse button	The status line reads: 2 objects selected.
Click **Arrange**	The Arrange menu appears.

Click **Align**	The Align dialogue box appears.
Click Horizontally **Center**	
Click OK	The 3 and the club are horizontally centered.
Click **Arrange**	The Arrange menu appears.
Click **Group**	The 3 and club are grouped. The status line reads: Group of 2 objects.

You have just replaced the *A* and a spade with the *3* and a club. Now use the upside-down duplicate procedure you learned a few pages back to create the second set of objects.

After you have done that, add three smaller clubs to the middle of the card using the text tool. Then, center the three clubs on the card both vertically and horizontally using the Align command. Finally, group the three clubs together using the Group command.

Adding the Three Clubs

Click the text tool	The cursor becomes a +.
Click the center of the card	The Text I bar appears.
Hold down Alt, type **0168,** *and press Enter*	Do it three times to get three clubs.
Click **Edit**	The Edit menu appears.
Click Edit Text	The Artistic Text dialogue box appears.
Click **Center**	To center the clubs.
At Point Size, enter **30**	Creates 30-point type.
Scroll down and click Dixieland	Dixieland is now the specified typeface.
Click **S**pacing	The Spacing dialogue box appears.
At Inter-Line, enter **150**	For 150 percent of point size leading.
Click OK	Three clubs appear.

continues

Shift-click the 3 clubs and the card	The status line reads: 2 objects selected.
Click Arrange	The Arrange menu appears.
Click Align	The Align menu appears.
Click Horizontally Center *and*	Centers the clubs on Vertically Center the card.

Now, go back and check that everything is positioned perfectly. You might have to move a few things around. If you have properly grouped everything, this should be no problem. Once everything is in position, group the entire card as you did with the ace of spades. Congratulations, you have completed your second card!

You will need to build one more card before you proceed to the next phase. To make things simple, why not build a two of hearts? Use the procedures you have just learned to construct this last card. The keyboard sequence you need for the heart symbol is Alt-0170.

Arranging Grouped Objects (or Shuffling the Deck)

You should have three separate playing cards: the ace of spades, the three of clubs, and the two of hearts. Not a winning hand, but good enough to illustrate your point. Drag the three cards into a horizontal row, with space between them. Go ahead and turn full-color editing on (turn off wireframe mode).

You should see three perfectly complete cards in the preview window (see fig. 3.22). If one of the cards seems to be missing objects from its face, have no fear. The wayward object merely needs to be brought forward. Ungroup the card in question, click off, click the unruly object(s), and select To Front from the Arrange menu. When you are done, group the card again.

If you had to mess around with anything in the last paragraph, you got a head start on everyone else. The opening of this chapter promised that you were going to shuffle the deck, and that is what you are just about to do (in an abbreviated manner), using just three commands.

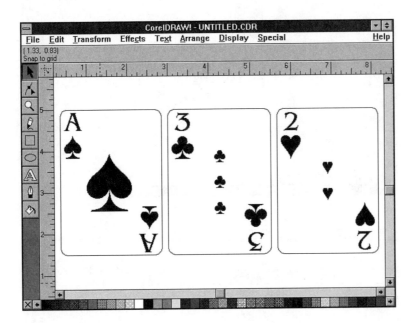

Figure 3.22:

The three cards next to each other.

Start shuffling by dragging all three cards on top of each other. Stack them perfectly by selecting them all, and then using horizontal and vertical align (see fig. 3.23). If you look at them in full-color mode, or in a full-screen preview, only the top card should show, as in figure 3.24. Deselect the deck.

Cutting the Cards

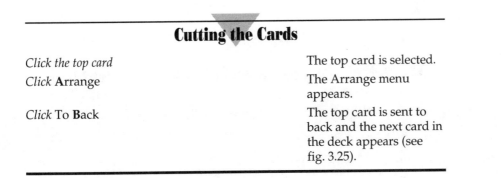

Click the top card	The top card is selected.
Click **Arrange**	The Arrange menu appears.
Click To **B**ack	The top card is sent to back and the next card in the deck appears (see fig. 3.25).

Figure 3.23:

A deck in wire-frame mode.

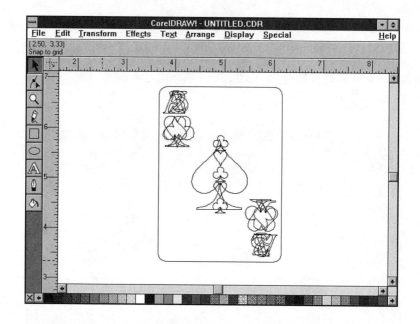

Figure 3.24:

A deck in full-color mode.

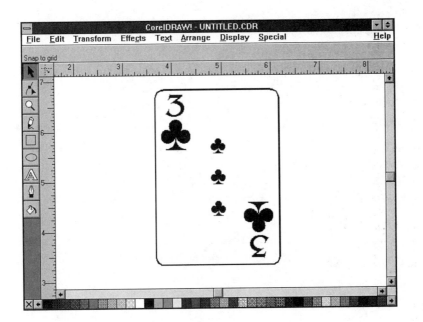

Figure 3.25:
A new card.

As you learned earlier, Draw has five commands in its object-arranging lingo: To Front, To Back, Forward One, Back One, and Reverse Order. Now that you have seen what To Back does, try To Front.

One More Time

Click Arrange	The Arrange menu appears.
Click To Front	The original top card reappears.

That was easy. Try sending the cards to back and front a few times. Using To Front and To Back, an object can either be placed on top of everything or underneath everything.

The in-between layers—ones that are neither at the top nor bottom—can be handled with Forward One and Back One. It is important to reduce your work to as few logical levels as possible. Each level can contain many other levels and sublevels. Try shuffling the deck using Forward One and Back One. You can cycle through the cards by using Tab or Shift-Tab.

The last object-arranging tool, Reverse Order, is the device that you will likely use for between-object work. Reverse Order works with two or more selected objects and transposes the sequence between them.

Start this next exercise by sliding the cards out, as if you were fanning them out on a table. On each card, leave a vertical strip, half-an-inch wide, showing. Make sure that the card numbers and suits are visible (see fig. 3.26).

Switching Cards with Reverse Order

Shift-click the top two cards	The top two cards are selected.
Click Arrange	The Arrange menu appears.
Click Reverse Order	The top two cards swap sequence.

Figure 3.26:

Fanned cards.

This is a simple example of how the object-arranging command set works. Obviously, as you get more proficient with CorelDRAW!, and your illustrations become more complex, it will be increasingly important that you construct and arrange your work logically.

Using Layer Control

In response to many requests from the installed user base, CorelDRAW! Version 3.0 introduced a full-blown layering structure. Layer control is now handled through the Layers Roll-Up menu, which can be summoned either by the keyboard shortcut Ctrl-1, or by selecting Layers Roll-Up from the Arrange menu.

Shortcut

Press Ctrl-1 to get the Layers Roll-Up menu.

If you are accustomed to working with overlays on conventional mechanical artwork, you should feel right at home with the Layers menu. You can think of each layer as residing on its own individual acetate.

Here's an example of why you might want to use layers in a drawing. Let's say you wanted to use the cards you just created in another drawing. This new drawing contains a number of elements, including a glass (filled with scotch on the rocks), a stack of chips, a patterned tablecloth, and perhaps an ashtray (can we add any other vices?). To simplify the composition of a complex drawing, you may want to place each object on its own layer. Furthermore, Draw allows you to name the layers as you want, with up to 32 characters. You can call the tablecloth layer *Tablecloth*, and the ashtray layer *Ashtray*.

As you delve further into more complex projects, you will learn how to handle layers with authority. Once you've completed the project in Chapter 8, "Assembling Complex Images," you should have a thorough understanding of how Draw's layers work. For now, reflect on the project just completed, where you worked on just one layer. You need these skills whether or not your artwork requires the control afforded by the Layers Roll-Up menu.

Summary

This chapter covered some heavy subjects. You took on the shape tool and looked into manipulating the various node types. In a rudimentary exercise, you changed your cloud drawing from a rough to a finished object. You learned about Bezier curves, and used a small deck of cards to illustrate some of the simple concepts behind layering and arranging your work.

These are important foundations on which subsequent chapters build. The more complex your work gets, the more imperative it is to build working drawings. You may work on a drawing for hours, days, or even weeks. To keep from wasting your time, be mindful of how you are constructing your image. The question is not whether you *will* change your drawing; it is *when*.

Perhaps you are working on an illustration for a men's clothing store. You have got the right cut on the suit. The model looks dashing. Everything looks great, except that the store's owner does not like the color of the suit. As the saying goes, "You want a green suit? Turn on the green light." You need to be able to turn only the suit green, not the model's gills, and to do so with a minimum of hassles. By building your illustrations logically, you can effect those changes with just a few clicks.

Part Two

Putting CorelDRAW! to Work

Basic Typography
Advanced Typography
Outline, Fill, and Color
Bit Maps and Draw
Assembling Complex Images
Special Type Effects
The Galleries

Basic Typography

ith the drawing basics out of the way, you can move on to working with type. After the preceding chapters, you should be familiar with the CorelDRAW! interface. You even did a few exercises that briefly involved the text tool. This chapter and following chapters show you how you can use CorelDRAW!'s text tool in the real world, producing flyers, T-shirts, advertisements, 35mm slides, and more.

In this chapter, you use the text tool to produce a simple flyer. It isn't pretty, but it serves its purpose. The flyer is an uncomplicated piece, designed so that you can get the hang of setting type with Draw.

Those of you who bought CorelDRAW! to set fancy type will spend much of your time using the text tool. Therefore, it is important that you have a thorough understanding of the tool and its features. It packs a lot of wallop in a simple guise.

Using CorelDRAW!'s Typographic Conventions

Draw's text tool can operate in one of three modes: artistic (headline) text, paragraph text, or symbol. This chapter touches on all three modes. You see that the text tool operates in a logical manner—like the other implements in Draw's toolbox—and with a consistent look and feel.

The workings of the artistic text and paragraph text tools are analogous. You use the artistic text tool for much of the following exercise, add a bit of embellishment with the symbol tool, and finish up by using the paragraph text tool in a two-column layout.

The text tool's user interface is similar to that of many other drawing packages. Type size and face are specified with scroll bars and text-entry boxes. Type weights (normal, bold, italic, and bold-italic), where available, are selected with the text-entry window's buttons. In addition, you may select ragged left, ragged right, centered, unaligned, and fully justified margins.

Type Sizes

Type point sizes can be freely specified. The Text dialogue box enables you to specify point sizes as large as 1440 points or as small as 0.7 point, in tenth-of-a-point increments. This flexibility is a boon to the typographer whose clients continually ask for type to be set to fit. Once you have set a block of type, you can scale type proportionally or anamorphically, as you can any other object.

Be careful when using a 300 dpi laser printer: the legibility of type smaller than 6 points is severely impaired. However, on a high-resolution imagesetter such as the Lino L/300, you need not worry about this restriction; the L/300 is capable of imaging at 2540 dpi. Newer, high-end imagesetters from Linotype-Hell, Scitex, and other manufacturers can print at even higher resolutions.

Typefaces

You will never run out of typefaces; CorelDRAW! version 3.0 ships with 153 immediately accessible typefaces in TrueType format. The CD-ROM version of Draw features over 256 fonts (in both PostScript and TrueType formats). If you need a font not supplied with the program, it is no more than a phone call—and a credit-card charge— away. With more than 10,000 fonts available in PostScript format, your design choices are governed only by your financial resources.

If you take a look at Draw's font list, you'll notice some rather unfamiliar typeface names. However, the bizarre names refer to many typefaces with which you are probably already familiar. Corel had to name them with those curious names to avoid stepping on anyone's copyright. For some obscure reason, the laws protect typeface names, but not designs. This is an unfair practice, which punishes type designers who spend inordinate amounts of time creating and perfecting new typeface designs. Generally, the CorelDRAW! typefaces are inferior to the original designs. If you are a professional designer or typographer, you may want to purchase the authentic font from its original foundry.

The fonts supplied with CorelDRAW! provide a sound basis for starting a type library, but it is likely that your favorite faces may not be included. Check out Chapter 11 for more information on obtaining fonts.

Other Type Specs

Type specifications other than point size, type face, and alignment are easy to set with the Text Spacing dialogue box. You can access the Text Spacing dialogue box through a button on the bottom of the Text dialogue box. Use the Text Spacing dialogue box to specify inter-character, inter-word, inter-line, and (in paragraph text) inter-paragraph spacing with scroll bar and text-entry boxes. Typographers usually refer to these settings as *tracking, word spacing, leading* (pronounced "ledding"), and *paragraph spacing,* respectively. (It is always interesting to see how programmers name things you have always taken for granted.)

Unfortunately for users, inter-line and inter-paragraph spacing are relative settings, based on a percentage of point size. It would be preferable to have an absolute setting, such as 12-point type on 14-point leading, since different typefaces are set in distinctly different sizes. But alas—maybe in the next version.

These text-spacing settings, along with settings available in the Character Attributes dialogue box, make setting type with CorelDRAW! a breeze; the clients make the job tough.

PostScript or TrueType?

CorelDRAW! version 3.0 and Windows 3.1 introduced a new dilemma for electronic artists and desktop publishers. Earlier versions of Draw used proprietary WFN fonts; the latest version of CorelDRAW! uses the system fonts, which can be either PostScript or TrueType. Now, you have to decide which font format you want to use.

Corel provides fonts in both formats. Although TrueType fonts can be loaded automatically from the CorelDRAW! installation disks, you must use the Adobe Type Manager (ATM) control panel to load the PostScript fonts from the CD-ROM. If you want to use PostScript fonts, and you do not have a CD-ROM drive, contact Corel Systems for information on obtaining the fonts on floppies.

Which font format should you choose? It all depends on who you are, what you do, and where your images are ultimately printed. Because Windows 3.1 integrates TrueType, many offices will likely use TrueType. If your work is printed on a laser printer and run on an office copier, you'll do just fine with TrueType.

Professional graphic designers, typographers, and publishers should stick with PostScript. If your files are printed on a high-resolution imagesetter, your service bureau will probably want nothing but PostScript files and fonts. The same is true for files handed up to a high-end prepress system at a color trade shop or large printer. If your work goes to a Lino or Scitex system, save yourself some hassle and stick with PostScript.

Why Is Every Job a Rush?

If you have been in the graphic arts field for a while, you know that "rush" jobs are the norm—as are last-minute changes. With that in mind, and just for fun (?), hang a deadline over your head when you work through the example in this chapter.

Although you are doing this for kicks, the sample flyer you create in this chapter is an excellent example of the way things are. It seems that clients can never stop in to see the typesetter until the job is already a week late. This chapter should give you an idea of how CorelDRAW! can be put to work in the real world.

Speaking of the (almost) real world, stop in at DeLook Design and see what Joe and the crew are up to. It is Monday morning. Joe has learned some of the essentials of CorelDRAW! over the weekend, and he is anxious to put them to work.

Freddie Needs a Fast Flyer

DeLook Design has just landed a new client—Fast Freddie, proprietor of a local used-car lot specializing in summertime fun vehicles.

Freddie has come up with the idea of distributing flyers on car windshields. It is not the type of work that DeLook Design likes to take in, but Freddie has that wad of bills out, and he is willing to cover Joe's troubles as long as Joe can whip up something in half an hour. Considering that the rent is due, and that Joe is a bit short, it looks as if he will be doing some quick-and-dirty flyers—like it or not!

Freddie hands over a napkin from Thurston's combination bait, tackle, and coffee shop next door. On it, Freddie has scrawled his basic information (see fig. 4.1). The flyer is intended to promote the grand opening of Fast Freddie's Speed-O-Rama Service Center. Freddie is offering a lube and oil change for twenty dollars in twenty minutes flat or your money back.

With a qualifying, "Think you can handle that in half an hour? I'm going over to Thurston's for an early lunch," Freddie heads out the door.

There is no time to roll up his sleeves: Joe has to fire up CorelDRAW! and go to work! Looking at Freddie's napkin layout, it is obvious that there is no time to prepare any intricate graphics. A big, bold, hard-sell approach is what is called for here.

Figure 4.1:

The napkin layout.

Building the Flyer

This advertisement has three basic parts. The first is the introduction, which would be effective in a starburst. Tacky, but Freddie will love it. You need to know your customer and his audience. Secondly, the offer—$20 oil change—has to hit the reader in the face. The hook is "20 Minutes, Or Your Money Back!" Finally, the logo and address have to be big and bold, but not too large.

In this flyer, limit the number of typefaces to three. In practice, you find that the fewer typefaces you use, the less likely you will commit typographic hari-kari. This flyer will not win any awards, but at least it will be readable and do its job. There will not be time to do any kerning, but who ever saw a pretty advertisement from a garage anyway?

One of CorelDRAW!'s greatest features is its excellent typographical screen representation. Although it is not perfect, it is about as good as you are going to get without PostScript display. The screen quality is good enough that you can specify typefaces on the computer itself, rather than on a layout sheet. If a block of type is too big at 60 points, you can see it immediately and reduce the point size before you run a copy out of the printer.

Without wasting any more time, open a new file and get down to work. In the Page Setup dialogue box, specify a portrait letter page. When you choose a letter-sized page (or any of the other predetermined page sizes), the horizontal and vertical settings boxes are grayed out. Custom is the only page-size option that allows you to make changes to the horizontal and vertical dimensions.

Shortcut

Double-click the page outline to get to the Page Setup dialogue box.

Opening a New File

Click **File**	The File menu appears.
Click **New**	A new page appears.
Click **File**	The File menu reappears.
Click **Pa**ge Setup	The Page Setup dialogue box appears.
Click **Portrait**	
Click **Letter**	
Click OK	A new page appears.

Using the Text Tool

You have gotten a taste of the text tool in the previous two chapters. Now it is time to really start setting type. In the next exercise, you use all the settings in the Text Spacing dialogue box (see fig. 4.2). Take a moment to learn about the spacing specifications:

- **Inter-Character Spacing (or tracking).** This specification controls the space between all characters in a text block. Do not confuse inter-character spacing with kerning, which affects only the space between two specific characters. Tracking influences the overall "color," or density, of the type on the page. You will find that a slightly negative number works best in everything but body copy sizes. You should tighten up headlines to maintain readability, but avoid tightening up body copy.

- **Inter-Word Spacing.** This specification governs the space between words. The factory default setting (of 100 percent) may be too wide for display-type purposes. At times, you may find yourself continually adjusting this specification to a value of 70 percent or less.

- **Inter-Line Spacing.** This specification, which is more commonly referred to as *leading*, affects the space between lines of type in a text block. Most type is set with a slightly positive leading (more than 100 percent of the size of the typeface). A value slightly larger than 100 leaves white space between the lines of text. Negative leading (less than 100 percent) is used in special cases, such as when type is set in capital letters. Care must be taken when setting uppercase and lowercase type with negative leading to avoid clipping ascenders and descenders.

- **Inter-Paragraph Spacing.** This specification affects the space between paragraphs, and is only available when using the paragraph text tool. Draw adds inter-paragraph spacing when it encounters a hard return. The first line of each paragraph is given the inter-paragraph spacing value. Paragraph spacing is relevant to the typefaces and layout of any given job; specifications may call for a setting anywhere from 100 percent to 200 percent of point size. This function can be misleading; using an inter-paragraph spacing percentage of less than 100 percent yields negative leading. When you use the artistic text tool, the Inter-Paragraph option is grayed out.

- **Save as Default.** This button is a handy device for applying the same character spacing settings to many blocks of type within a page. When you adjust spacing settings and click the Save as Default button before clicking OK, the spacing settings are stored as defaults. Those settings then apply to each subsequent block of text (until reset or overridden) in the file. If a new file is subsequently opened, the default settings continue to apply. Default settings are not stored along with a file; if an existing file is opened, the current default settings remain in force. Each time you boot up Draw, the default settings from the last on-screen file are used.

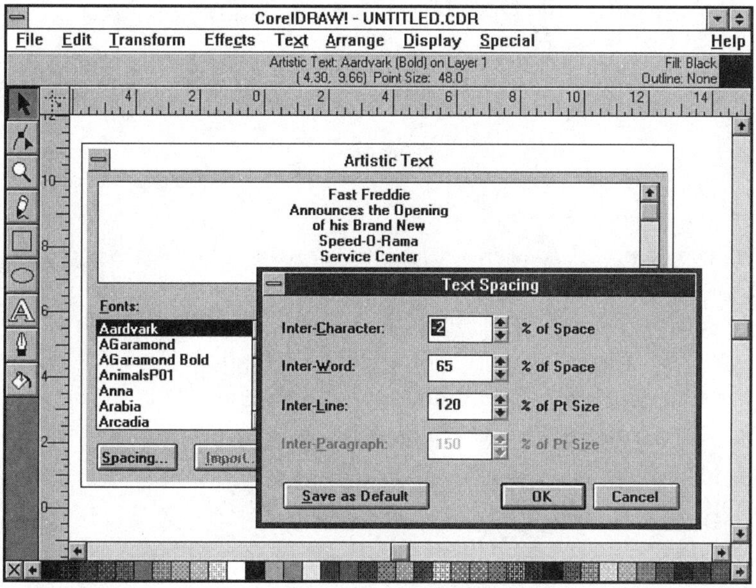

Figure 4.2:

The Text Spacing dialogue box.

You can control tracking and leading interactively, in addition to entering precise measurements in the Text Spacing or Frame dialogue boxes. When you click a text block with the shape tool, inter-character and inter-line spacing control arrows appear to the left of and below the text block, respectively. Although this method is easy to use with artistic text, it is difficult to use with paragraph text.

Shortcut

Press F8 for the Text tool.

Lay down the first text block in 48-point Aardvark (Aachen) Bold, centered in the top third of the page. Take the time to cover all the specs, making sure not to miss any of the dialogue boxes.

Aardvark is about as big, bold, and hard-sell as typefaces come. Fast Freddie will appreciate the flair of this typeface.

Setting the Headline

Click the text tool	The cursor becomes a +.
Click the page	The Text I bar appears.

Type the following and press Enter after every line except the last one:

> **Fast Freddie**
> **Announces the Opening**
> **of his Brand New**
> **Speed-O-Rama**
> **Service Center**

Press Ctrl-T	The Artistic Text dialogue box appears.
At Point Size, enter: **48**	
At Fonts, Roll up, click Aardvark	
Click **C**enter	
Click **S**pacing	The Text Spacing dialogue box appears.
At Inter-Character, enter: **-2**	
At Inter-Word, enter: **65**	
At Inter-Line, enter: **120**	
Click OK	
Click OK *again*	The type is set according to your specifications.

Use the pick tool to drag the block of type to the top of the page and eyeball it into position (see fig. 4.3).

You should have a 48-point Aardvark Bold headline, set centered on (approximately) 58-point leading. The inter-word and inter-character spacing should be moderately tight, but by no means touching. You might have noticed that there was no need to click the Bold button; Aardvark only comes in bold.

On second thought, it looks like 48 points is just a bit too large. Bring the size down to 42 points. Although you can attempt to scale down the text by eye, do it with precision. You go back into the Text dialogue box to adjust the point size accurately.

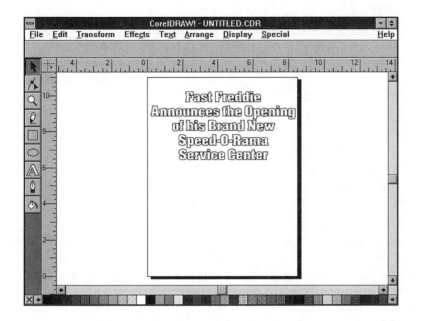

Adjusting the Point Size

With the text still selected, take the following steps:

Press Ctrl-T   The Artistic Text dia-
                                                logue box appears.

At Point Size, enter: **42**
Click OK

When you use the text tool in this next exercise, notice that all of
the earlier specs—except spacing information—are still in effect.
This is yet another of CorelDRAW!'s time-saving features.

Shortcut

Press Ctrl-T for the
Text dialogue box.

Setting the Second Block of Text

Click the text tool   The cursor becomes a +.
Click the page   The Text I bar appears.
Type the following and press Enter after the first line:

continues

20 Minute
OIL CHANGE

Press Ctrl-T	The Artistic Text dialogue box appears.
At Point Size, enter: **60**	
Click **Left**	
Click **S**pacing	The Text Spacing dialogue box appears.
At Inter-Character, enter: **-2**	
At Inter-Word, enter: **50**	
At Inter-Line, enter: **100**	
Click OK	
Click OK *again*	The type is set according to your specifications.

Use the pick tool to drag the block of type to the left side of the page.

Drag this block of type over to the left side and center it vertically on the page. Notice that this last block of type was set with 100 percent inter-line spacing. This style is known as "set solid," or set with no extra leading. You can get away with setting solid when you are setting text in all caps, or when there are no (or very few) descenders. At times, you may even want to use negative leading by setting the inter-line spacing for less than 100 percent.

Setting Superior Characters

The next piece of type you set is the largest type on the page. After you set it, you go back in and make one of the characters a super-script (or superior) figure. To do so, you access the Character Attributes dialogue box.

You can make alterations in this dialogue box that apply only to selected characters in a text string. This feature allows you to use superior and inferior (subscript) characters. It also lets you change the type face, size, and baseline of individual characters. Additionally, the dialogue box provides a precise method for character kerning and rotation.

Remember when you double-clicked on a selected object's node to bring up the Node Edit menu? The Character Attributes dialogue box is accessed in a similar manner by double-clicking on a selected text character's node. Text characters only have one node, positioned directly to their lower left.

If you are only kerning or shifting baselines, you need not use the dialogue box. You can manually kern characters or shift individual baselines by dragging the characters by their nodes. Finish this next exercise by dragging a character baseline down.

Setting Superior Figures

Click the text tool	The cursor becomes a +.
Click the page	The Text I bar appears.
Type: **$20**	Enter this string in the text-entry window.
Press Ctrl-T	The Artistic Text dialogue box appears.
At Point Size, enter: **130**	
Click **Center**	
Click OK	The type is set according to your specifications.
Click the shape tool	
Click $20	Nodes appear for the characters.
Double-click the $ node	The Character Attributes dialogue box appears.
At Placement, click Superscript	
Click OK	The $ is now a superior figure.
Drag the $ node down 0.17 inch	The $ is now properly positioned.

If you set a lot of advertisements that include price information, the superscript option comes in handy. The last step was necessary to precisely align the superscript $ to the imaginary line at the top of the caps.

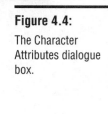

Figure 4.4:

The Character
Attributes dialogue
box.

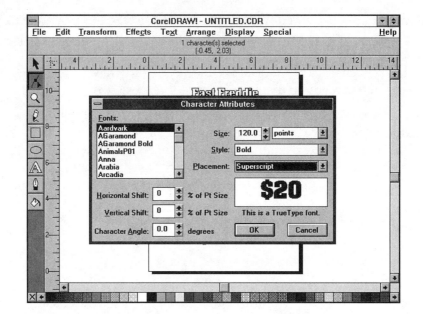

Using Pseudo Base-Alignment

Next, you will drag the *$20* to the right side of the *20 Minute OIL CHANGE* text. Give it even horizontal spacing. Do not worry about the baseline alignment; the program does that for you. Once you have it in position, you use bottom vertical alignment to square up the baseline alignment. Then you use Group to keep the two alignments locked in position with each other.

Bottom vertical alignment is a quick way to pseudo base-align different blocks of text. However, it does not provide true base-alignment. The vertical alignment command does not "look at" character baselines; it looks at the text as an object. Therefore, if you have two different sizes of text, the length of the bottom line's descenders throw off the alignment.

This next exercise cheats a bit. Because there are no descenders in either block of type, you might think that the two blocks of type should base-align regardless of type size, but they do not. You try aligning them with bottom, center, and top alignments. It takes a bit of finesse to align the baselines by eye. Using snap-to guide-lines can reduce your frustration level!

Condensing Type

The two-object group (the *20 Minute OIL CHANGE* and the *$20* objects) is slightly too wide for the page. You finish up the exercise by using the stretch function to anamorphically scale the group to 85 percent of its original width. This action maintains the character heights as it condenses the widths.

The stretch function is a convenient CorelDRAW! feature, but it is often abused. Condensing type beyond a certain percentage reduces the type's legibility. It may fit on the page, but the reader cannot read it.

Be very careful not to "squeeze" type too much. The same goes for extending (or "squashing") type. Use these two tricks with caution. With that warning out of the way, move on to the exercise.

Base-Aligning, Grouping, and Squeezing Text

Click the pick tool	
Drag $20 *to the right side of* 20 Minute OIL CHANGE	
Shift-click 20 Minute OIL CHANGE	The status line reads: 2 objects selected.
Click **Arrange**	The Arrange menu appears.
Click **Align**	The Align dialogue box appears.
Click Vertical **Bottom**	
Click OK	The type is not base-aligned: the $20 is far above the baseline.
Click **Arrange**	The Arrange menu appears.
Click **Align**	The Align dialogue box appears.
Click Vertical Center	
Click OK	The type is not base-aligned: the $20 is still above the baseline.

continues

Click **Arrange**	The Arrange menu appears.
Click **Align**	The Align dialogue box appears.
Click Vertical **Top**	
Click OK	The type is not base-aligned: the *$20* is just below the baseline.
Shift-click 20 Minute OIL CHANGE	*$20* remains selected.
Nudge $20 *up a couple of points*	
Shift-click 20 Minute OIL CHANGE	The status line reads: 2 objects selected.
Click **Arrange**	The Arrange menu appears.
Click **G**roup	The two objects are grouped.
Drag the right-side center handle	Drag toward center of group; watch the status line and release the mouse button when the group is squeezed 85 percent.

Now you need to add the hook, *20 Minutes, or Your Money Back,* to the bottom of this group of text. Use a smaller, condensed sans serif typeface: 36-point Fujiyama (Futura Condensed). Once you set this line of type, center-align it horizontally with the group you just made and group them all together.

When you begin typing, notice that the type appears on the page in huge, 130-point letters. This situation is quickly remedied in the Artistic Text dialogue box.

Adding the Hook

Click the text tool	The cursor becomes a +.
Click the page	The Text dialogue box appears.

Type the following:

20 Minutes, or Your Money Back

Press Ctrl-T	The Artistic Text dialogue box appears.
At Point Size, enter: **36**	
Click Fujiyama	
Click **B**old	
Click **C**enter	
Click OK	The type is set according to your specifications.
Click the pick tool	
Drag 20 Minutes, Or Your Money Back	Drag underneath *20 Minute OIL CHANGE $20.*
Shift-click 20 Minute OIL CHANGE $20	The status line reads: 2 objects selected.
Click **A**rrange	The Arrange menu appears.
Click **A**lign	The Align dialogue box appears.
Click **H**orizontal **C**enter	
Click OK	The type is centered.
Click **A**rrange	The Arrange menu appears.
Click **G**roup	The two objects are grouped (see fig. 4.5).

This exercise is probably starting to feel a lot like the last chapter, where you built the playing cards. By now, you are getting the feel of how to build and use groups.

Changing Face with Character Attributes

You have one more block of type to set before you are done with this grubby little flyer. Although this block has four lines and three different typefaces, you learn how easy it is to use character attributes to alter lines of type.

Figure 4.5:

The half-finished
flyer.

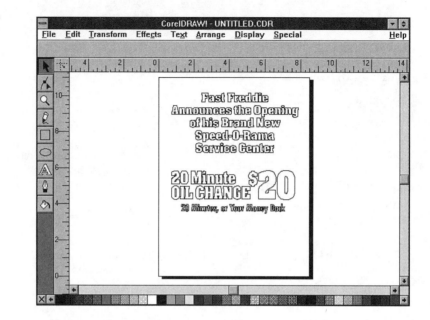

When you accessed the Character Attributes dialogue box a few pages back, you turned the dollar sign into a superior figure. Now you are going to use the dialogue box to change typeface and size.

The capacity to have multiple typefaces and sizes in a single block of type is essential for professional typography. It gives the artist the flexibility to move one block of type around, instead of trying to position, align, and group many individual pieces. If you have ever had the displeasure of building big, nasty supermarket advertisements, you are sure to appreciate the power that the Character Attributes dialogue box provides.

Setting the Logo with Character Attributes

Click the text tool   The cursor becomes a +.

Click the page   The Text I bar appears.

Type the following and press Enter after every line but the last:

> **Fast Freddie's**
> **Speed-O-Rama**
> **Service Center**
> **On the Causeway 555-1234**

Press Ctrl-T	The Artistic Text dialogue box appears.
At Point Size, enter: **48**	
Click Aardvark	
Click **Center**	
Click **S**pacing	The Text Spacing dialogue box appears.
At Inter-Character, enter: **-2**	
At Inter-Word, enter: **65**	
In Inter-Line, enter: **110**	
Click OK	
Click OK *again*	The type is set according to your specifications.
Click the shape tool	
Click Fast Freddie's	Nodes appear for the characters.
Marquee-select Fast Freddie's	Character are selected nodes.
Double-click any selected character's node	The Character Attributes dialogue box appears.
Change typeface to Freeport	
At Point Size, enter: **72**	
Click OK	
Marquee-select On the Causeway 555-1234	Characters are selected nodes.
Double-click the O node	The Character Attributes dialogue box appears.
Change typeface to Fujiyama	
Click Normal	
At Point Size, enter: **42**	
Click OK	

Try to select the middle block of text with the shape tool: you can't do it! That is because it is part of a group of objects and cannot be manipulated with the shape tool until it is first ungrouped.

As you have seen, the shape tool is a valuable instrument for adding typographic versatility. In the next chapter, you use the shape tool to do some kerning. And you get into setting some aesthetic and tricky type.

Centering Objects to the Page

You are almost done. You need to use a nifty little option to horizontally center all the items on the page (see fig. 4.6). Normally, when you use the Align command to center objects, they center against each other, not the page. To center objects to the page, you must click Align to Center of Page in the Align dialogue box. This option—introduced in Draw version 2.0—is a great convenience. After clicking Align to Center of Page, you click Vertical Center to deselect that option. If you do not deselect Vertical Center, all three selected objects are placed on top of each other—in the center of the page, of course!

Centering Objects to the Page

Click **Edit**	The Edit menu appears.
Click Select **All**	Three objects are selected.
Click **Arrange**	The Arrange menu appears.
Click **Align**	The Align dialogue box appears.
Click Align to Center of **Page**	
Click Vertical C**enter**	To deselect this option.
Click OK	All items are centered horizontally on the page (see fig. 4.7).

Quick Changes with the Text Roll-Up Menu

CorelDRAW! version 3.0 introduced a great little device known as the Roll-Up menu. This little time-saver is a wonderful convenience. To access the Text Roll-Up menu, select the Text Roll-Up option from the Text menu, or use the Ctrl-2 keyboard shortcut. Once a Roll-Up menu is on your screen, you can move it around at will (see fig. 4.8). Why is it called a Roll-Up menu? Simply because a click on its up arrow makes the menu spring up and closed like a roller shade. Another click drops the menu down again.

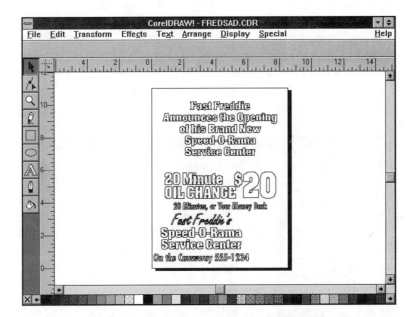

Figure 4.6:
The flyer text, unaligned.

Figure 4.7:
The flyer text, aligned.

Shortcut

Press Ctrl-2 for the Text Roll-Up menu.

The Text Roll-Up menu offers instant access to a number of text attributes, including typeface, size, and justification. You can set type in bold, italics, superscript, or subscript with one click. You can summon the Character Attributes dialogue box and make changes to horizontal and vertical shift, as well as character angle. Clicking the Frame button brings up the Frame dialogue box, which offers complete control over paragraph text. Although you cannot access the Frame dialogue box from the Text Roll-Up menu when you are using artistic text, you can always select Frame from the "normal" Text menu.

Figure 4.8:

The Text roll-up menu.

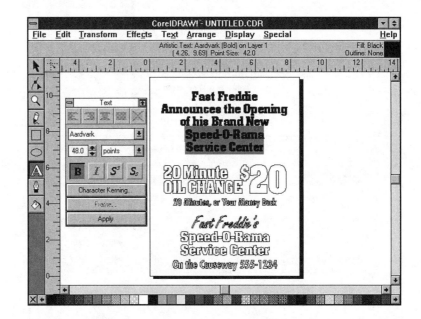

There are two ways to use the Text Roll-Up menu to make changes to text already on the screen. The first is to select a block of text with the pick tool, and then use the Text Roll-Up menu to make changes to the entire block. The second method is to use the text tool to click and drag over a range of text, and then make changes in much the same way that you make changes with the Character Attributes dialogue box, affecting only a selected range. Remember that you can access character kerning only if text has been selected with the text tool, rather than the pick tool.

Use the Text Roll-Up menu to set the flyer text in a variety of typefaces. It is easy to select a block of type, choose a typeface, and click Apply to make the changes. When you are done, set the type back to its original specs.

Starburst Effects

Now you have all the flyer text, but something is still missing. Remembering the scribbled starburst on Freddie's napkin, Joe whacks himself in the head for inspiration.

Try building your own starburst instead of searching for one in Draw's Balloon symbol font or your electronic or conventional clip-art files. You do not have time to look (you have a deadline, remember?) and certainly no time to scan and trace. By drawing straight lines, connected with double-clicks, you can weave a custom starburst into the page in under two minutes (with luck).

Once the starburst is drawn and selected, choose a fill of 20 percent and a two-point outline rule from the fly-out menus. You do not have time to mess with all the dialogue boxes. The defaults are good enough for this job. When you are done, go to the Arrange menu and send the starburst To Back.

Building a Starburst

Click the pencil tool
Double-click around the headline   Draw lines to form a
                                                   starburst.

When you are done drawing the starburst, you can go back in and tweak the individual nodes to make the starburst look just right.

Click the shape tool
Tweak the nodes
Click the pick tool
Click the fill tool   The Fill fly-out menu
                                                   appears.

Click 20% fill

continues

Click the outline tool	The Outline fly-out menu appears.
Click 2 Point	
Click **Arrange**	The Arrange menu appears.
Click **To Back**	

Switch your display to full-color mode (it has been in wireframe mode) with Shift F9. Looks like this baby is done (see figure 4.9)!

Figure 4.9:

A starburst.

Freddie Wants More

Joe sends the file to the PostScript printer with little time to spare. Phew! Five minutes to go, and here comes Freddie through the door. Just as he reaches the desk, the page emerges from the laser printer. Good thing there were no time-consuming fills or intricate graphics! Freddie is wide-eyed as he takes the camera-ready laser print in hand. "Hey, this is pretty good." he says. "Yeah," he continues, "This is exactly what I wanted, except..." Freddie pauses as he thinks. "Maybe I could add something else. Just look at all that space at the bottom of the page."

Bringing in Clip Art

Realizing that Freddie has no appreciation for the aesthetic use of white space, Joe immediately reaches for CorelDRAW!'s clip-art book. "Freddie," Joe says with confidence, "I know exactly what you want."

CorelDRAW! 3.0 comes with an abundance of clip art: over 12,000 pieces of art come on the CD-ROM, where you can find the checkered flag that should finish off the flyer. If you do not have a CD-ROM drive yet, consider getting one in the near future. Prices have been dropping, and CD-ROM is currently the best method for distributing large programs, clip art, and typeface collections.

Do not fret if you do not have access to a CD-ROM drive. You can easily create your own flags with the rectangle tool and the snap-to-grid!

Adding Clip Art to the Flyer

Click File	The File menu appears.
Click Import	The Import window appears.
Click CorelDRAW! CDR	The Import window configures for CDR import.
Maneuver to your CD drive	
At Directories, double-click Clipart	The Clipart Directory is selected.
Roll down, double-click Flag	The Flag Directory is selected.
Double-click Other	The other directory file names appear.
Roll down, double-click WAVING.CDR	The WAVING.CDR file is imported.

The checkered flag clip-art is too big to fit on the flyer, so you have to size, rotate, and finally, mirror-duplicate it. To do this with precision, use the dialogue boxes.

Scaling, Rotating, and Mirroring the Flag

With the flag selected, take the following steps:

Click **T**ransform	The Transform menu appears.
Click **S**tretch & Mirror	The Stretch & Mirror dialogue box appears.
At Stretch Horizontally, enter: **25**	
At Stretch Vertically, enter: **25**	
Click **OK**	The flag is scaled 25 percent.
Click **T**ransform	The Transform menu appears.
Click **R**otate & Skew	The Rotate & Skew dialogue box appears.
At Rotation Angle, enter: **-15**	
Click **OK**	The flag is rotated -15 degrees.
Click **T**ransform	The Transform menu appears.
Click **S**tretch & Mirror	The Stretch & Mirror dialogue box appears.
Click **H**orz Mirror	
Click **L**eave Original	
Click OK	The flag is horizontally mirrored, and the original is left alone.

Drag the flags, one to either side of the *Speed-O-Rama Service Center* text at the bottom of the page. Align and group the flags and text. Be sure to save your page with the filename: FREDSAD.

Uh-oh. Fast Freddie's taken a look at the flyer and he is still not satisfied with it. "Too much wasted space," he says with a sigh. Joe is rapidly losing what little respect he had for this client, but he knows exactly what to do.

Using Symbols

As mentioned in the beginning of this chapter, Draw's text tool does triple-duty. Until now, you have set all the flyer type using only the artistic text tool. Now, finish it off by adding a pair of symbols with the symbol text tool.

The symbol tool is a fast way to place rudimentary art—objects that are more icon-like than life-like—into a file. Amazingly, CorelDRAW! comes with approximately 3000 black-and-white symbols at no additional cost. The program also enables you to export images and create your own personal symbol library. You soon see the advantages of using and creating symbols. If you want more information on exporting symbols and characters, check out Chapter 11.

The symbol text tool is easy to access: click the text tool, drag down and to the right, and the text tool fly-out menu appears. The symbol tool is denoted by a star. Select it, click the page, and the Symbols dialogue box appears. You now have over four dozen symbol libraries from which you can choose.

The Symbols dialogue box asks you to make three choices. First, you must select the library you want to use. Then, you select a symbol (as soon as you click a library, one of the symbols available in that library appears in the sample window; click it and a pop-up menu of symbols available in the selected library appears). The libraries that come with CorelDRAW! are listed in table 4.1. You can select a symbol either by clicking on it or by entering its symbol number in the text box. Finally, select the size of the symbol you are placing. Now click OK, and the symbol is brought into the page. Once the symbol is on the page, you can scale, stretch, rotate, skew, or mutate it as you would any other object. Symbols can be assigned different fills and can be extruded, blended, and enveloped—or manipulated in whatever other manner you can dream up.

Table 4.1
Corel's Symbol Library

Animals	Landmarks
Arrows1	Medicine
Arrows2	Military
Awards	MilitaryID
Balloons	Music
Borders1	MusicalSymbols
Borders2	NauticalFlags
Boxes	People
Buildings	Plants
Bullets1	Science
Bullets2	Shapes1
Bullets3	Shapes2
Business&Government	Signs
CommonBullets	Space
Computers	Sports&Hobbies
Dixieland	SportsFigures
Electronics	Stars1
Festive	Stars2
Floorplan	Symbol
Food	Technology
Furniture	Tools
GeographicSymbols	Tracks
GreekMathSymbols	Transportation
Household	Weather
Hygiene	

Placing Symbols

Click the text tool, drag down and to the right	The text tool fly-out menu appears.
Select the symbol tool (denoted by a star)	
Click the page	The Symbols dialogue box appears.
Roll down, click Transportation	A transportation symbol appears in the sample window.

Remember, you can select a symbol in one of two ways: either click the symbol in the sample window to access the pop-up menu, or type the symbol number directly into the text box.

At Symbol #, type **50**	The ragtop sports car is highlighted in the sample window.
At Size, type **1.50 inches**	
Click OK	A 1.5-inch ragtop sports car is drawn.

Now you are going to add another ragtop, this one a 4x4 sport utility vehicle. Its symbol number is 58. Use the preceding steps to place it on the page. This time, try using the pop-up window to select the symbol (see fig. 4.10).

Once you have the symbols on the page, position them below the starburst. Put the sports car on the right side, and the 4x4 on the left side. Use the mirror tool to make the 4x4 face into the middle of the page. Finish up by giving both a 50-percent tint.

Fast Freddie has cracked a grin. Joe's stomach is churning, but the page looks pretty good (considering). Now Joe runs out a print (see fig. 4.11).

"That's it!" exclaims Freddie, as the page rolls out of the laser printer. "Just in time to get it to the Seaside Print Shop before they close for lunch!" A big grin washes over his face as he reaches for his wad of bills. "Say, we're gonna do right well together, you keep up that kind of work!"

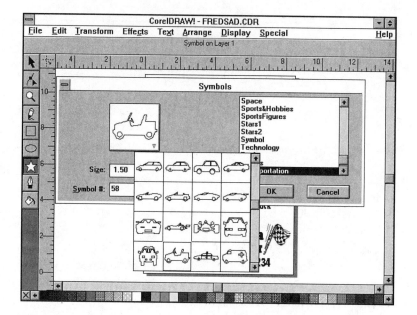

Joe grins back sheepishly, shakes his hand, takes his money, and laughs like hell as soon as Freddie is up the block and out of earshot. The rent is paid. It is time to take a break before tackling the next section on importing text.

Importing Text

Luckily for Joe, Freddie's flyer had only a small amount of text on it. Joe is a two-finger typist; he could never have made Freddie's half-hour deadline if he had had to type a lot of characters. However, there are a couple of ways to import big blocks of text into Draw.

Why import text? Two simple reasons: to save time and trouble. By importing text, you eliminate the need to retype text that may already exist electronically. Unless you really enjoy typing, it makes good sense to import text, especially large amounts of text. If you type, rewrite, and proofread large blocks of text before bringing them into Draw, you save time in the long run.

Figure 4.11:
The final flyer.

With your word processor, you can spell-check text and run it through a thesaurus. (Even though CorelDRAW! now contains both a spell checker and thesaurus, it is not a tool for wordsmiths.) Text also can be scanned in, captured from electronic mail or even from PC-Fax. You can bring in files from across the office network or across the world. Importing text enables you to concentrate on design, not keyboard skills. You can even do yourself a favor and let your clients do the typing on larger jobs.

This method encourages workgroup computing. The designer designs. The writer writes. The proofreader proofreads. This is how it should be.

If you have been using desktop publishing for a while, you have probably had the occasion to import text from a word processing program into a desktop publishing program like PageMaker. PageMaker has a large variety of text (and graphics) import filters, which are similar in purpose to CorelDRAW!'s selection of graphics import filters.

Unfortunately, CorelDRAW! has no fancy text import filters. But fear not—this does not mean that you cannot import text. It does mean, however, that you are limited to importing unformatted ASCII text using one of two methods. The first method works for either headline or paragraph text, and consists of using the clipboard and those old friends, the Cut, Copy, and Paste commands. The second method can only be used with paragraph text; it enables you to import ASCII files with the TXT extension. The clipboard method is presented first.

The Clipboard

One of the most functional features of the Windows environment is the capability to move items between two concurrently running programs with the clipboard. Never heard of the clipboard? Whether you are aware of it or not, you have been using the clipboard since you first booted up CorelDRAW!—or any other Windows program for that matter.

Each time you use the Cut, Copy, or Paste command, you access the clipboard. When you cut or copy an object, it is placed onto the clipboard. When you paste an object, it is pasted from the clipboard.

The clipboard is like a shallow bucket; it can only hold one object or group of objects at a time. If you copy something to the clipboard, it dumps itself out before allowing a new item (or group of items) to be poured in. Although the clipboard can only be full or empty—whether with a block of text or a graphic—you can store clipboard files. Check out your copy of the Windows documentation for more information on saving CLP files.

Text Importation and the Clipboard

Windows comes with its own word processor, Windows Write, which is a bit limited in function. Write has no built-in spell-checker or thesaurus although you can always use Draw's built-in spell checker and thesaurus. However, it does provide a couple of ways to key text ultimately intended for inclusion in a CorelDRAW! file.

It is best to use a Windows-based word processing program such as Microsoft Word for Windows, or Lotus Ami Professional. These programs allow a direct link to the clipboard. Simply copy the block of text you need, switch to Draw, open up the Text dialogue box, and paste the block.

Non-Windows word processing programs do not work as easily. You must save a copy in plain-vanilla ASCII without any format-ting (proprietary file formats do not work). If you are setting headline text, you have to open the file in Windows Write and copy the text to the clipboard. If you are setting paragraph text, you have the luxury of importing ASCII files with a TXT extension directly into CorelDRAW!.

For the purposes of the following exercise, assume that Windows Write is your only word processing program. First, you type the text into Windows Write (which you should have), copy it to the clipboard, and paste it into Draw. Then you try saving a Write file as a text-only file and naming it with the TXT file extension.

If Draw is already running, minimize it by clicking on the down arrow in the upper right corner of the screen. You must bring up the Program Manager to start Windows Write. For the sake of an uncluttered screen, minimize the Program Manager after bringing up Write.

Running Write and Draw Next to Each Other

Click minimize arrow	CorelDRAW! is minimized.

In the Windows Program Manager, take the following steps:

Double-click the Accessories icon	The Accessories folder opens.
Double-click the Write icon	Windows Write launches.
Drag the Write window's left side to the middle of the screen	Write is in a half-screen window.

Type the following. (Press enter after each line except the last, and add an extra line after the fourth.)

> **USE THE CLIPBOARD!**
> **You can save time and trouble**
> **by using the Windows clipboard**
> **to import text into CorelDRAW!**
>
> **Simply use the Copy and Paste**
> **commands to capture text that**
> **has already been keyboarded.**

Double-click the CorelDRAW! icon	CorelDRAW! is maximized.
Drag the Draw window's right side to the middle of the screen	Draw is in a half-screen window.

Shortcut

Press Ctrl-Esc to summon the Windows Task Manager.

Shortcut

Press Alt-Tab to cycle between running programs.

You should now have Draw running on the left side of the screen and Write running on the right side. The text you typed into Write is sitting there waiting for you to do something wonderful with it.

If you like to work with full-screen windows, there are a couple of easy ways to switch between programs. By pressing Ctrl-Esc, you summon the Windows Task Manager. You can then pop between programs by selecting the one you want from a dialogue box. It is even easier to use Alt-Tab to move between programs. Each time you press the Tab key, you have instant access to another (already running) program.

Text Importation from Windows Write

Copy the text from Write and paste it into Draw. A simple click
and drag in Write, followed either by pressing Ctrl-Insert or
selecting a couple of menu options, copies the text to the clipboard. Then switch over to Draw, select the text tool, click the
page, and paste the copied text.

Copying and Pasting Text

In the Write window, drag the cursor over the text	The text is reversed, white on black.
Click **Edit**	The Edit menu appears.
Click **C**opy	The text is copied to the clipboard.
In the CorelDRAW! window, click the text tool	The cursor becomes a +.
Click the page	The Text I bar appears.
Press Shift-Insert	The text is pasted onto the page (see fig. 4.12). Change any type settings you want.

Pretty slick. You can use the Copy-and-Paste method to import
text from almost any word processor. The stipulation is that the
text might first need to be saved in ASCII format in order for it to
be opened by Write. The only file formats that Write can open are:
WRI, DOC, and TXT. The upcoming section "Using Paragraph
Text" teaches you how to import text files directly into
CorelDRAW!

Some Provisos

Did you get a warning box or two? According to Corel's specifications, the program enables you to paste a maximum of approximately 256 characters into its artistic text-entry window. However,

this may not add up in the manner you expect. Each carriage return counts as two characters: the carriage return and the line feed. The limitation is in Draw, not in the clipboard itself.

Figure 4.12:

CorelDRAW! and Write running simultaneously.

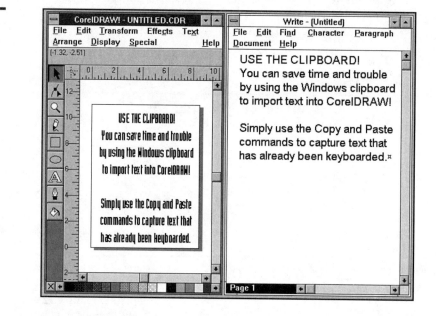

This character-limit handicap is not specific to imported text. It applies only to any artistic text entry. CorelDRAW! treats all artistic text as objects, whether the text has been converted to curves or not. While the "per object" character count can be restrictive, it does not limit the number of characters in a page. It simply means that if you have a text-heavy page, you must either use multiple text entries or paragraph text.

To get back to a full-screen Draw window, click the maximize (up) arrow at the Draw window's upper right corner.

Using Paragraph Text

This chapter has made repeated references to paragraph text. "Exactly what is paragraph text?" you wonder. Simply put, paragraph text is body (or columnar) text. Think of a newspaper; artistic text is for headlines, and paragraph text is for body copy.

Although it is highly unlikely that you would put yourself through the agony of publishing a newspaper with CorelDRAW! (although it would do quite well in the advertising department), the newspaper is a good analogy to remember.

The paragraph text tool adds a new dimension to CorelDRAW! If you produce brochures and other similar documents, you will welcome the flexibility that the paragraph tool offers.

The paragraph text tool builds on the basics of the artistic text tool, embellishing it with the additional capabilities of columnar text, full justification, and ASCII-text import capabilities up to a maximum of 4000 characters per text block.

Even though you can fully justify paragraph text, the results may be disappointing with narrow columns. If you have narrow columns, you will be much happier with the flush left/ragged right setting. Wider column measures allow the program more room for inter-word spacing.

You can use the paragraph text feature for many projects. Although Draw may seem slow to process paragraph text, it may still be faster than shuttling between two separate programs. If your job contains one or two simple colors and is more text-based than design-based, you are probably better off using PageMaker or Quark Xpress for the text-heavy pages.

But if your project involves multiple colors, it may be better to do the whole job within Draw. Page layout programs may not be able to fully color-separate the placed graphics, which can lead to increased prepress charges for film stripping. The idea behind CorelDRAW! is to generate plate-ready film, complete with traps. Although this is a lofty goal, it can save the experienced graphic artist money. For more information on Trapping see Chapter 12.

The Paragraph Text Tool

The paragraph text tool is just as easy to use as most other Draw tools. If you understand how the artistic text tool works, then you have all the basics. The only important extras you need to know are how to access the tool, how to set up columns, and how to import text files.

Over at DeLook Design, Fast Freddie has shown up again. This time, he needs a disclaimer for the flyer that you just finished. It is an easy job, and one that is well-suited for the paragraph text tool.

Freddie has the text on a disk—his secretary typed it on their old XT clone—and he claims that it is in ASCII format (as if he knew what that meant).

The text reads something like this:

DISCLAIMER

We are not responsible for anything. If your oil is not changed within 20 minutes, you do not have to pay. However, if there is no oil in your car at the time, you'll have to pay a $50 towing charge to get your car out of our garage. This may seem harsh, but what do we care? We own the tow truck anyway.

If we actually get your oil changed in 20 minutes, please note that the oil we use isn't fit for a greasy pizza parlor, much less your car's crankcase. If you want real oil, you have to pay for it, at an additional charge, of course. Nor will we replace your oil filter, so all that new cheap oil will just get dirty, real fast. What do you expect for $20? If you want a new filter, that'll be an extra $15.

If our grubby mechanics smear sludge over your beautiful velour uphol-stery, you're out of luck. We're not covered (and neither were your seats). If you happen to drop your car off for a few hours while you're shopping, don't be surprised if one of the mechanics takes your car for a test drive (using up all of your gas). Hey, at least we didn't charge you for that.

If all of this seems rather frightening, so what? There's no other garage for 15 miles, and besides, you're on vacation. What do you care?

Of course, only Joe DeLook can use Freddie's floppy disk. You have to type the disclaimer text using Windows Write. Then save the file as a text-only file, and give it a file name with a TXT extension. You should be familiar with Write after the last exercise, so get to work.

Before you start this next exercise, be sure to store the most recent version of FREDSAD.CDR. Then you can open a brand new Draw file, and (if it is not already open) open up Windows Write as you did in the last exercise. Type in the paragraphs of the disclaimer. When you are done, proceed with the following exercise.

Saving an ASCII TXT File in Windows Write

Click File
The File menu appears.

Click Save **As**
The File Save As dialogue box appears.

At Save File As Type, Click **Text** files (*.TXT)

Take note of where the file is to be stored. Most likely, it is in the Windows directory.

At Filename, type **FREDDIE.TXT**

Click OK
The file is stored in the Windows directory as FREDDIE.TXT.

The file is now stored as an ASCII text file.

The Paragraph Text Dialogue Box

Now you must bring the ASCII text file into the Paragraph Text dialogue box. The paragraph text tool works in the same click-and-drag fashion as the rectangle tool (see fig. 4.13). Used in conjunction with snap-to-grid or guidelines, you can lay down a text box of exact proportions. The status line reports the size of the paragraph text box as you draw it. But beware: once paragraph text is on the page, the status line does not report any dimensions.

You can resize a paragraph text box once it is on the page; it can be stretched or scaled to fit. The concept of paragraph text boxes will be very familiar to Quark Xpress users. You "pour" your text into the box once it is drawn. Unlike Xpress, however, if a box is too small for the text file you have imported, Draw will not "tell" you that there is more text.

The Paragraph Text dialogue box looks almost exactly like the Artistic Text dialogue box. Take note of the Import button at the bottom of the dialogue box. You soon see what this button does, because you use it in the next exercise to import the text you just typed in Windows Write.

The Text Import function is a bit clunky. In addition to the limitation of ASCII-only files, tab and indent settings are not supported. Furthermore, you must have at least one character in a block of paragraph text before you are allowed to access the Paragraph Text dialogue box. No character, no access. Follow the next exercise closely.

Figure 4.13:

Dragging out a paragraph text block.

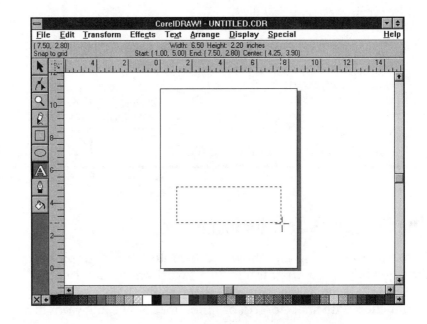

Laying Down a Paragraph Text Box with Imported Text

Remember that you must have at least one character in the paragraph text to access the Paragraph Text dialogue box. In the following exercise, you type a dummy *X*, then access the dialogue box, highlight the dummy character, and import the text.

Click the text tool

Click and drag a text box on the Draw screen; make it 6.50" wide and 2.20" high

Release the mouse button

The paragraph-box outline appears (see fig. 4.13).

Type **X**

Press Ctrl-T

The Paragraph Text dialogue box appears.

Highlight the X

Click Import

The Import Text dialogue box appears.

Change to the Windows directory in preparation for bringing in the FREDDIE.TXT file you just created. Once the file is imported, you set up a two-column format with a two-pica gutter. If the settings are not specified for picas and points, change them.

Double-click FREDDIE.TXT

FREDDIE.TXT is imported. The *X* is replaced by the imported text (see fig. 4.14).

At Point Size, enter: **8**

Click Switzerland

Click Normal

Click Full

Click OK

The Frame Attributes Dialogue Box

CorelDRAW! splits paragraph text specifications over two different dialogue boxes. You just used the first of the two, the Paragraph Text dialogue box. The second is the Frame Attributes dialogue box. In this second dialogue box, you alter a number of settings, including the number of columns, column width, justifications, spacing, and hyphenation. The Frame Attributes dialogue box is accessed from either the Text menu, or the Text Roll-Up menu.

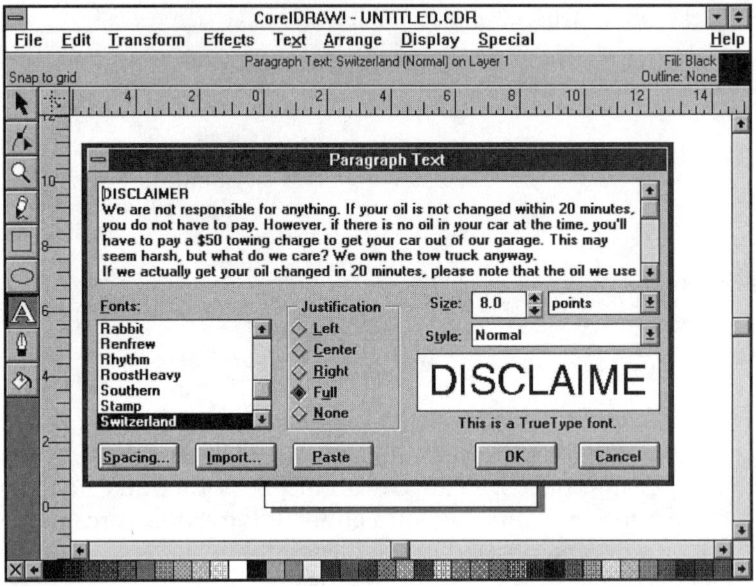

Figure 4.14:

The Paragraph Text
dialogue box with
imported disclaimer
text.

The Frame Attributes dialogue box provides powerful control over the hyphenation hot zone. The *hot zone* is a user-definable hyphenation range, giving you the power to govern where words hyphenate and lines break, and allowing for tight or loose rag settings. Draw is rather unique in offering hot-zone control; you would expect this power in a page layout package, but not in a drawing program!

Now you are going to finish up the paragraph-text specifications for Freddie's disclaimer with the Frame Attributes dialogue box.

Finessing Paragraph Text with the Frame Attributes Dialogue Box

Click **Text**	The Text menu appears.
Click **Frame**	The Frame Attributes dialogue box appears.
At Character, enter: **0**	
At Word, enter: **60**	
At Line, enter: **120**	

At Paragraph, enter: **150**

At Units, click picas, points

At Number, enter **2**

At Gutter Width, enter **2**

Click Automatic **H**yphenation

Click OK

The settings specified in the Frame Attributes dialogue box are accepted (see fig. 4.15).

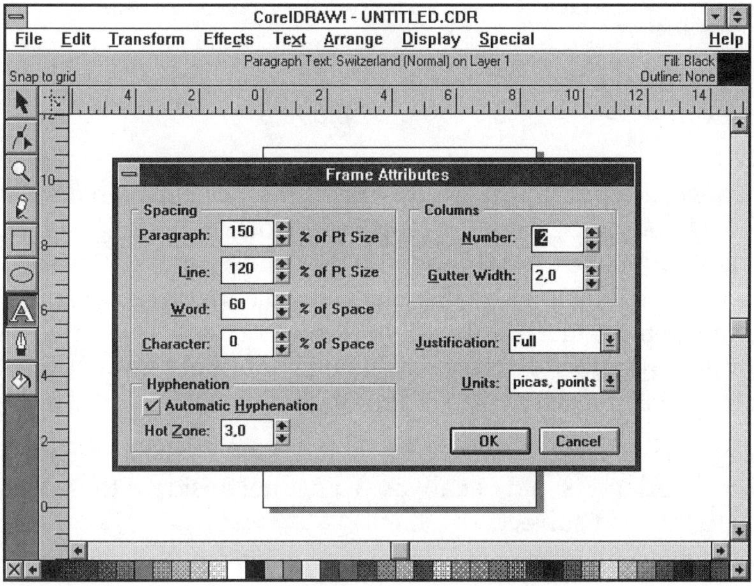

CorelDRAW! - UNTITLED.CDR

Figure 4.15:

The Frame Attributes dialogue box.

As you have seen, the paragraph text tool enables you to import your text—a powerful, time-saving feature. Of course, you can always type your text directly into CorelDRAW!. All text within a paragraph text block must be of the same typeface and size; you cannot alter individual characters within a paragraph.

Now that you have a block of paragraph text on your page, you can start fooling around with it. Try different numbers of columns, gutter widths, point sizes, and so on (see fig. 4.16). You can change the size and shape of the text box as you would any other object in CorelDRAW!. Like objects, the text block can be scaled, stretched, skewed, and rotated.

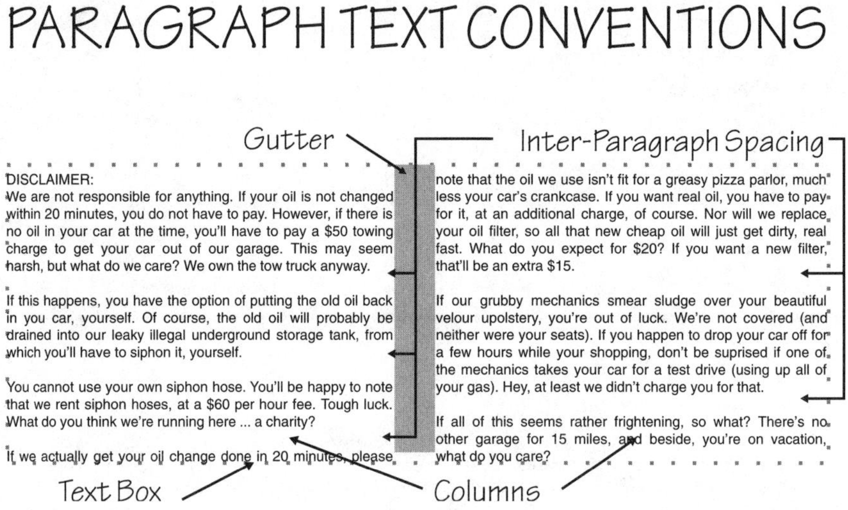

Figure 4.16:

The paragraph text conventions.

PARAGRAPH TEXT CONVENTIONS

Gutter · · · · · · · · · · · · Inter-Paragraph Spacing

DISCLAIMER:
We are not responsible for anything. If your oil is not changed within 20 minutes, you do not have to pay. However, if there is no oil in your car at the time, you'll have to pay a $50 towing charge to get your car out of our garage. This may seem harsh, but what do we care? We own the tow truck anyway.

If this happens, you have the option of putting the old oil back in you car, yourself. Of course, the old oil will probably be drained into our leaky illegal underground storage tank, from which you'll have to siphon it, yourself.

You cannot use your own siphon hose. You'll be happy to note that we rent siphon hoses, at a $60 per hour fee. Tough luck. What do you think we're running here ... a charity?

If we actually get your oil change done in 20 minutes, please

note that the oil we use isn't fit for a greasy pizza parlor, much less your car's crankcase. If you want real oil, you have to pay for it, at an additional charge, of course. Nor will we replace your oil filter, so all that new cheap oil will just get dirty, real fast. What do you expect for $20? If you want a new filter, that'll be an extra $15.

If our grubby mechanics smear sludge over your beautiful velour upolstery, you're out of luck. We're not covered (and neither were your seats). If you happen to drop your car off for a few hours while your shopping, don't be surprised if one of the mechanics takes your car for a test drive (using up all of your gas). Hey, at least we didn't charge you for that.

If all of this seems rather frightening, so what? There's no other garage for 15 miles, and beside, you're on vacation, what do you care?

Text Box · · · · · · · Columns

Experienced typographers know the difference between display type and body type. Fancy typefaces are lots of fun for headlines, but they can make lousy body type. For body copy, stick with faces that are legible at smaller sizes, like Switzerland (Helvetica). Do not use faces like Frankenstein (Fette Fraktur). These two examples are rather extreme—and you should not limit yourself. Just try to keep it within the realm of good taste!

One of the reasons for specifying Switzerland in the last exercise is that Switzerland is (almost always) a printer-resident font. This leads to the next subject...

Print Time with Paragraph Text

When you use paragraph text, it soon becomes apparent that Draw's font-description scheme has drawbacks relative to print file sizes and printing times. However, there is a simple solution to the problem: either use resident fonts or download your fonts beforehand, then click All Fonts Resident in the Print dialogue box when you are ready to print.

When Draw sends a file to a PostScript output device, it assumes that the fonts are not printer-resident unless the fonts "came with the printer." Consequently, print files can grow in alarming proportions as the program downloads font-outline information for each and every character in your file.

Once again, the way to get around this is to download the needed fonts before sending the file to the printer. By using this trick, print files shrink, and print times are reduced. If you revise your proofs repeatedly along the way, downloading fonts to the printer can save hours a day in print time alone. Of course, if you enjoy waiting for your printer, keep doing what you are doing—there is no reason to become more productive!

For more information on printing, refer to Chapter 12.

Editing with Spell Check, Thesaurus, and Hyphenation

CorelDRAW! 3.0 added three powerful new text-editing functions: a spell checker, a thesaurus, and a hyphenation option. This trio of features helps you do an even better job creating text-intensive artwork. Although you may have used a spell checker and thesaurus in a word processing program, hyphenation may be new to you. Even if you have never used any of these features, you have little to fear. They are all easy to use, and you should be power-editing with the pros in no time flat.

Get It Right with the Spell Checker

The CorelDRAW! Spell Checker is easy to use. Simply highlight a word or range of text with the text tool. Then select Spell Checker from the Text menu. Click Check Text to begin checking. If there are no errors in the selected text, a dialogue box pops up and lets you know that everything checks out. If the Spell Checker finds a questionable word, a dialogue box shows you the first unknown or misspelled word. Clicking on the Suggest button displays alternative spellings. Double-click the desired word in the Alternative box (or select the desired word and click Replace) to replace the misspelled word with the alternative. The Spell Checker then moves on to the next anomaly.

If you click the Always Suggest button, alternative spellings automatically pop up. If you repeatedly spell the same word incorrectly in a selected range of text, click the Replace All button to immediately change all instances. Conversely, you can click the Ignore All button to leave all instances of an unknown word alone (see fig. 4.17).

Figure 4.17:

The Spell Checker.

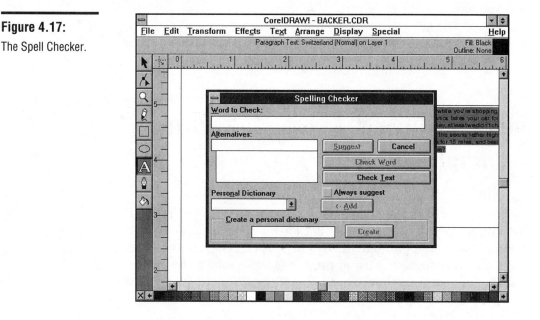

The use of a spell checker should be an adjunct to, and not a replacement for, good proofreading. In many cases, however, you may not have the luxury of a "real" proofreader. Considering that it is difficult for many people to proof their own work, Draw's Spell Checker can be a great help. Use it, but do not rely on it. Spell checking cannot pick up a number of typographical errors, including: outsets (missed sections), transposed words, the "wrong" (although spelled correctly) word, and bad grammar.

Make the effort to get someone else to take a look at your files before you "send them out to print." You can save yourself untold grief (and reprints).

Want to try out the Spell Checker? If you'd like, select Fast Freddie's disclaimer text with the text tool, and let the Spell Checker go to work!

Try the Thesaurus When You Can't Think of a Word

Perhaps you have needed a synonym for a word, but have not had
a thesaurus at hand. With CorelDRAW! 3.0, it is easy to use the
built-in Thesaurus to change a word with a few clicks. Just use the
text tool to highlight the word you want to replace, and select the
Thesaurus from the Text menu. The Thesaurus dialogue box pops
up with the selected word in the Synonym for field. Depending on
whether or not the selected word is in the dictionary, its definition
and any synonyms (and their definitions) may or may not appear
(see fig. 4.18).

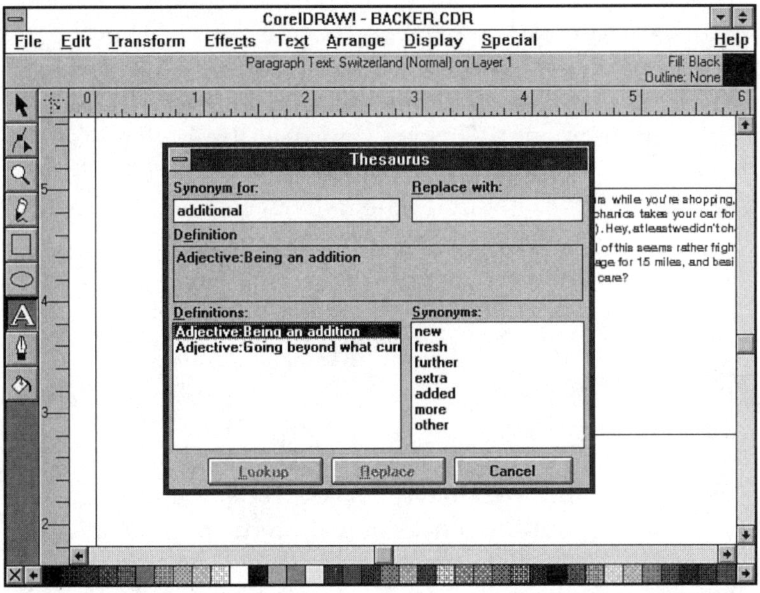

Figure 4.18:
The Thesaurus.

If no definition or synonyms appear, enter a new word in the
Synonym for field and click Lookup. Once you find a synonym
that fits your needs, double click the synonym (or select the
synonym and click Replace), and the synonym replaces the word
you originally selected in your text.

Cut Yourself a Break with Hyphenation

Have you ever had to consult a dictionary to decide where to hyphenate (break) a word? Now you can check your hyphenation options in CorelDRAW! without leaving your seat for the bookshelf. The Hyphenation option enables you to select a word with the text tool, and review and choose your breaks according to the Houghton Mifflin Dictionary.

When you select a word or range of text and click Hyphenate on the Text menu, the Hyphenate Word dialogue box appears (assuming that the word can be hyphenated). The first "hyphenatable" word in your selected text is shown. Next to it is a down-arrow button. Click the button, and a list of the hyphenation options appear. Click your choice, and then click Go to accept the change (and move to the next word, if you selected more than one). Clicking Cancel at this point closes the dialogue box without making a change. If you made multiple changes, Cancel does not undo them. In fact, the Undo feature has no effect on changes made with the Hyphenate option. If you want to fix things, you must do it manually.

Summary

This chapter took you through the production of DeLook Design's first "real" job with CorelDRAW!. It covered placing, aligning, modifying, and grouping blocks of text on the page. You used the Character Attributes dialogue box to modify type, and you delved into the use of symbol text. In the second section of the chapter, you learned how to import text with the Windows clipboard, and used the paragraph text tool to import an ASCII text file.

As you continue to see, much of Draw's strength is in its text handling and links to other programs. After producing that first simple flyer, the program's typographical power should begin to become apparent. The exercise on importing text gives you an idea of how the program can be used in a workgroup environment.

Building an effective system comprised of both computer and human factors is the key to success in electronic arts. For more information on putting together a selection of software and hardware, refer to Chapter 11.

In contrast to the preceding chapters where Joe uncovered the basic functions of the program, the following chapters include more advanced hands-on projects. First up is a project in the next chapter that delves into some involved typographical maneuvers.

Advanced Typography

ith chapters 1-4, you have already learned most of the basics of setting type. This chapter explores the many typographical possibilities that CorelDRAW! offers the designer. The program has few equals for composing exquisite display typography at the desktop—and at desktop prices. This chapter discusses some of Draw's more advanced typographical, special effect, outline, and fill features. You will find that simplicity in design carries through to all aspects of the program.

You will begin by setting some text and proceed to kerning that text while it is still in its native state. Then, using Convert To Curves, you will gain access to the text's character outlines. This feature gives you an incredible amount of control over character shapes. Even more amazing are Draw's Envelope and Extrude effects. The exercise you begin here will be finished up in Chapter 12 with a study of CorelDRAW!'s trapping capabilities.

This book does not atempt to teach typography. Teaching typography is not an easy task; becoming a master of typography takes years of study and practice. This book can, however, teach you how to use the tools of typography incorporated within CorelDRAW!; what you do with these tools is your decision.

The purpose of this chapter is to show you how to use CorelDRAW! to produce type with various effects. Like kids on the beach with pails and shovels, one builds a beautiful sand castle while another digs a hole. And yet both begin with the same tools and foundation. Remember, it is important to establish a solid foundation—by learning to use your tools properly—before laying the bricks of good design.

Using the Right Tool for the Job

To be most efficient, an electronic artist has to know each program's limitations. CorelDRAW! offers superb typographical control, although it does have its restrictions. Certain projects should be done elsewhere.

CorelDRAW! is at its best when it does not have huge amounts of type to set. Some examples of typographical projects for which CorelDRAW! is best suited include: advertisements with tightly kerned headlines, company logos, newsletter mastheads, and standing heads. Try not to use the program for setting text-heavy projects such as formatted columns of text, lengthy brochures, or tabular column work.

Due to the overall restrictions of the program's text editing feature, and the artistic text tool's 256-character text string limit, be sure to think a project through before deciding to use CorelDRAW! or getting too heavily involved in production. You will need to decide whether to use the artistic or paragraph text tools. Non-formatted text pages will work with the paragraph text tool. Or, if it is a text-heavy page with formatting, tabs, and indents, begin looking for the PageMaker (or Xpress) icon. Use the right tool for the right job.

In the imaginary town of Seaside, it is lunch time at DeLook Design. Joe and the crew have taken their lunch break at Thurston's Bait and Tackle (and coffee shop). Sam Thurston, the proprietor and namesake, appears eager to see Joe DeLook. It seems that Fast Freddie dropped in on his way to the printer to show off his new flyer.

Sam wants DeLook Design to create a T-shirt that would convey some of the history and ambiance of Seaside's oldest bait-and-tackle shop. After a few thumbnail sketches, Joe decides that the shirt's emblem should look similar to the sign that hangs over Thurston's front door (see fig. 5.1). The sign is rendered in classic sign painter's style and has hung there for over six decades.

Figure 5.1:

Thurston's sign.

Joe knows what he wants. Now he has to figure out how to use CorelDRAW! to create what he needs.

Treating Text as an Object

The last chapter mentioned that Draw treats all text as objects. It does this in two ways. The first is to treat text as normal, editable text. The second is to convert text to curves.

While text is in its "native"—or unconverted—state, you can use CorelDRAW!'s tools to perform any number of transformations. Text can be filled, outlined, rotated, stretched, mirrored, and fit to a path. In addition, individual characters can be kerned, rotated, pulled above or below the baseline, and sized. Most of the time, you will apply these modifications to text that is still in its original, non-converted state.

There is one basic reason to convert text to curves—to alter individual character shapes. Once text has been converted to curves, you can make some amazing modifications. It is possible to bend, pull, stretch, twist, and mutate individual character outlines at will. This is strong stuff, but exactly the thing that makes CorelDRAW! so powerful.

Once a block of text has been converted to curves, there is no going back. Text that has been converted is no longer editable in the normal sense. It becomes pure object and cannot be reconverted to text. While it may still look like text, it will not act like text. It cannot be accessed via the Text dialogue box, nor through the Text roll-up menu. In the next exercise, you will see the control afforded by text that has been converted to curves. As you stretch out the letters in the design, the advantages (and disadvantages) of manipulating a character's individual nodes will become obvious. This is a time-consuming, though superb, feature.

Text in a "converted-to-curves" state can be a challenge to work with. Get in the habit of saving multiple versions of your files. If a foul-up occurs, you can simply recall the last version stored.

Using Special Effects on Text

CorelDRAW! version 2.0 introduced a trio of effects that greatly enhance your ability to produce customized type in a tight time frame. Designs that previously took hours to accomplish can now be done in a fraction of the time, using the following effects:

- **Envelope.** This effect enables you to place a boundary around a piece of text (or other object) and apply different arcing styles with a few clicks and drags. The Thurston's sign that you will duplicate in this chapter is a prime example of this effect.

- **Extrude.** This effect applies depth to text (or other objects). With extrude, you can easily create block type with a three-dimensional effect. The direction and amount of depth, as well as the percentage of perspective, is unrestricted. The Extrude effect was greatly enhanced in version 3.0.

- **Perspective.** This effect is a snazzy tool for altering the line of sight by varying degrees. You can make a line of text appear to run down the side of a building or package. This can be a fabulous instrument for package design and conceptualization. Chapter 8 will cover this effect.

When you use these effects, text remains in an editable state. However, you may find that to fine-tune things, you need to convert the text to curves. It all depends on your professional perspective. High-end advertising typography, for example, has far different standards from a relatively unsophisticated in-house newsletter.

You are going to use the good old manual method to begin this next project. Along the way, you will save a copy of the file, so that you can go back in and try a more automated method later. You will be amazed at the possibilities once you have gained an understanding of what can be accomplished with these powerful tools.

Tackling the Bait-and-Tackle T-Shirt Project

This group of exercises begins with setting the type for the Thurston's Bait-and-Tackle T-shirt project. After the type has been set, you will kern the characters to optimize spacing. After converting the text to curves, you will stretch out the letters to form the arcing sign painter's style of the original design.

You will begin this exercise with two identically sized blocks of text. By the end of the exercise, though, they will be radically different in appearance. Through Convert To Curves, you will achieve dramatic results that would be difficult to produce with other drawing programs.

This design will fit on a landscape 8 1/2-by-11-inch page, so take care of the Page Setup dialogue box first. Make sure that the grid is turned on and set to six per inch. You will turn the grid off once the type has been converted to curves.

Using Nonprinting Guidelines to Lay Out Designs

CorelDRAW! version 3.0 introduced the Layers Roll-Up menu. This feature enables you to assign objects to specific drawing layers. In the following exercises, you will create a number of objects on the non-printing guide layer. You will lay out your design on a guide rectangle 9.17 inches wide by 7.17 inches deep. This will be your design boundary line. You can easily scale and align objects using this boundary line.

You can also use Draw's snap-to guidelines for many such situations. However, unlike most other programs, Draw supports more than just vertical or horizontal guidelines. For those times when you need an arc or diagonal guideline, Draw has you covered!

Anyone who has spent time at an old-fashioned drawing board is familiar with the idea of using guidelines. In Draw, non-printing rectangles, ellipses, and lines are invaluable drawing aids. Use them the same way you would draw blue lines on a board. While

PageMaker users will be quite familiar with the concept of snap-to's, these "do-it-yourself" guides are a bit different in theory and practice.

Set up your page and design boundaries, and then set the type. If there is something on the screen that should be saved, make sure that you save it now.

Setting Up the Page

Click **File**	The File menu appears.
Click **New**	A blank page appears.
Click **Page** Setup	The Page Setup dialogue box appears.
Click **Landscape**	
Click **Letter**	
Click OK	Page changes to landscape orientation.
Click **Display**	The Display menu appears.
Click **Grid** Setup	The Grid Setup dialogue box appears.
Change the grid frequency to six per inch	
Make sure that Snap-to-Grid is selected	
Click OK	
Click Arrange	The Arrange menu appears.
Click Layers Roll-Up	The Layers Roll-Up menu appears.
At Layers Roll-Up, *click* Guides	Guide-layer is selected.
Click right arrow	Layers fly-out menu appears.
Make sure that Multilayer *is selected.*	
Click the rectangle tool	

continues

Drag a rectangle	Make the rectangle 9.17" wide by 7.17" tall. Center it on the page.
Release the mouse button	A guideline rectangle is drawn.

Now the preparation is out of the way. A clean piece of paper is on the board, and the first guidelines are drawn. Now you can begin setting type for this design.

Setting Type

Corel includes over 150 typefaces on Draw version 3.0's distribution floppies, and more than 250 on the CD-ROM version. This collection is a nice variety of faces to select from, and, as you will see later on in the book, you can easily add more faces to your personal collection.

Each typeface has its own distinctive features, and each sets differently from other faces. In figure 5.2, you can see the differences in height and width between four of the sans serif typefaces supplied with Draw. The figure also gives a visual representation of some common typographical conventions.

Figure 5.2:

Typeface sizes and conventions.

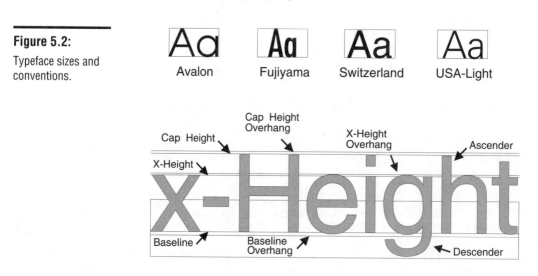

For the first block of text, you are going to use 144-point Brooklyn Normal, set centered. Brooklyn is Corel's version of Bookman, a fairly popular typeface included as one of the 35 standard PostScript fonts in many laser printers. Set the spacing at a moderately tight –0.05.

Setting THURSTONS

At Layers Roll-Up, *click* Layer 1	Layer 1 is selected.
Click the text tool	The cursor becomes a +.
Click the page	The Text I bar appears.
Type: **THURSTONS**	
Press Ctrl-T	The Artistic Text dialogue box appears.
Click **Center**	
Enter: **144** *in the point size window*	
Click Brooklyn	
Click **N**ormal	
Click **S**pacing	The Text Spacing dialogue box appears.
At Inter-Character, enter: **–5**	
At Inter-Word, enter: **65**	
Click OK	
Click OK *again*	The type is set according to your specifications.
Click the pick tool	
Drag THURSTONS *to the center* of the page	

Do not worry if the text runs over the edges of the page; you will condense it in a few moments. Next, you are going to repeat the last step to set the bottom line, BAIT & TACKLE. There will be a few differences. As mentioned previously, the type entry dialogue box "remembers" the last typeface and size specified; you do not need to re-enter the type specs. Just type in the text itself. Point size, typeface, and alignment are all retained; however, spacing information is not.

Setting BAIT & TACKLE

Click the text tool	The cursor becomes a +.
Click the page	The Text I bar appears.
Type: **BAIT & TACKLE**	The type is set according to the previous specifications.
Click the pick tool	
Drag BAIT & TACKLE *to the center of the page*	

Instead of opening up the Spacing dialogue box and re-entering information, use a shortcut to clone the type spacing information.

Borrowing Style

Copy Style From is a shortcut that can be used for a wide range of purposes on various objects, not just type. This command is a great time-saver because it makes it possible to copy object details from one item to the next.

In this case, you are going to copy type specifications from one block to the next. When you use this shortcut, you can avoid the Spacing dialogue box altogether and ensure that the typographical attributes will be consistent from line to line. While you could use Save As Default Setting in the Text Spacing dialogue box, many times this may be an afterthought.

Copying Style

With BAIT & TACKLE still selected, take the following steps:

Click **Edit**	The Edit menu appears.
Click Copy **S**tyle From	The Copy Style From menu appears.
Click **T**ext Attributes	
Click OK	The "from" arrow appears.

Click THURSTONS	The type specifications are copied.

The Text dialogue box remembers previous type specifications. Notice that you did not have to enter typeface, size, or alignment information. However, because spacing information is not re-tained—it returns to the default setting—you need Copy Style From.

There are many occasions where the Copy Style From command comes in handy. Later in this exercise, you will use the command to copy fill and outline information from one object to the next.

Condensing Type

The next step is to squeeze the two text blocks to fit into your design boundary. Looking at the screen (see fig. 5.3), you can see that while the height of the characters is correct, both lines of type are too large for the design. In order to make the two lines of type fit, you must stretch them to size horizontally.

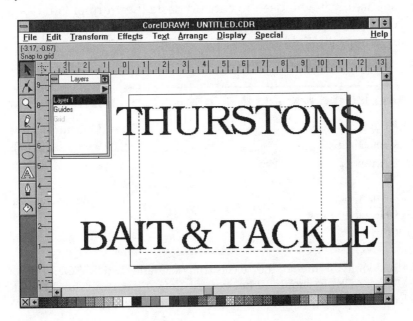

Figure 5.3:
The text is too wide.

Stretching was covered way back in Chapter 1, and you even condensed some type in Chapter 4, so these next few steps should be getting familiar by now. Begin by aligning the left side of the two text lines to your nonprinting design boundary by using align/horizontal/left. You will then vertically align the text to the boundary. Finish by horizontally scaling the text to fit and grouping all the objects.

Notice all the arranging, grouping, and ungrouping going on. To align multiple objects, you often need to work in this fashion. When aligning an assortment of objects with different orientations, grouping enables you to maintain the relationship between two objects while aligning them with other objects. As an example, two objects may be horizontally left-aligned with each other and grouped; then, the group may be horizontally right-aligned with a third object, and so on. For more information about grouping and aligning, refer to Chapter 3.

A note of caution: if you group objects with guide-layer objects, the guide-layer objects will be pulled forward from the guide layer, and will become "normal" objects on the active layer. In addition, they will then be assigned the default outline and fill. In these cases, you will need to cut and paste the "former" guide-layer object back onto the guide layer (after you are finished with your group-aligning)!

Aligning the Text and Design Boundary/Condensing Type

Click **Edit**	The Edit menu appears.
Click **Select All**	All objects are selected.
Click **Arrange**	The Arrange menu appears.
Click **Align**	The Align menu appears.
Click **Horizontal Left**	
Click **OK**	The objects are horizontally left-aligned.

At this point, all three of the objects (the rectangle, THURSTONS, and BAIT & TACKLE) should be horizontally left-aligned and should still be selected. By shift-clicking BAIT & TACKLE, it will be deselected.

Shift-click BAIT & TACKLE	The words are deselected.
Click **Arrange**	The Arrange menu appears.
Click **Align**	The Align menu appears.
Click Vertical **Top**	
Click OK	The two objects are almost vertically top-aligned.
Click **Arrange**	The Arrange menu appears.
Click **Group**	The objects are grouped.
Shift-click BAIT & TACKLE	The words are selected.
Click **Arrange**	The Arrange menu appears.
Click **Align**	The Align menu appears.
Click Vertical **Bottom**	
Click OK	The objects are almost vertically bottom-aligned.
Shift-click BAIT & TACKLE	The words are deselected.
Click **Arrange**	The Arrange menu appears.
Click **Ungroup**	The objects are ungrouped.
Shift-click the rectangle	The rectangle is deselected.
Drag THURSTONS *right-center handle to the left*	The handles are replaced by a blue dashed box.
Release the mouse button	When the status line reads: (approx.) 73 percent.
Click BAIT & TACKLE	The words are selected.
Drag the right-center handle to the left	The handles are replaced by a blue dashed box.
Release the mouse button	When the status line reads: (approx.) 61 percent.

continues

Notice that the type blocks do not vertically align with the rectangle. Use zoom to get a better view of the objects. You will need to turn the grid off to achieve proper alignment. Drag (or nudge) the text blocks into position. Turn the grid back on when you are done.

Click **Edit**	The Edit menu appears.
Click **Select All**	All objects are selected.
Click **Arrange**	The Arrange menu appears.
Click **Group**	The objects are grouped (see fig. 5.4).

If necessary, use Align to Center of Page (in the Align dialogue box).

Click **Arrange**	The Arrange menu appears.
Click **Ungroup**	The objects are ungrouped.
Click page *to deselect objects*	
Click **rectangle**	The rectangle is selected.
Press **Shift-Delete**	The rectangle is cut.
At **Layers Roll-Up,** *click* **Guides**	Guide-layer is selected.
Press **Shift-Insert**	The rectangle is pasted onto the guide-layer.

Figure 5.4:

Type in position.

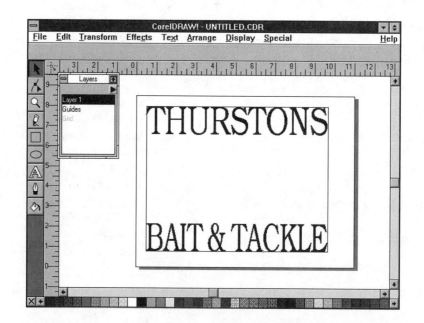

A wise typographer is careful as to what typefaces he or she scales anamorphically, and the percentages used. It is easy to create an unreadable mess by scaling the wrong face or by scaling too much. However, this project calls for a certain look, and Brooklyn seems to hold up fairly well. It will not win any awards, but it will do for this example.

Before you go any farther, take the time to save your file!

Saving Progressive Files

You will save your page under the file name TSHIRT. As a complex drawing progresses, it is wise to name the file in such a way that you can create multiple copies. Use a short prefix (up to five or six characters) followed by a numeric extension.

Each time a difficult maneuver is performed, use Save As to renumber the file. Make your first Save As TSHIRT01, and proceed on to TSHIRT02, TSHIRT03, TSHIRT04, and so on. With this routine, you have a file to fall back on if the current file gets ruined.

Saving the File

Click **File**	The File menu appears.
Click **S**ave	The Save File dialogue box appears.
At **File,** *type:* **TSHIRT**	
Click **S**ave	The file is saved as TSHIRT.CDR.

The next step is to add another nonprinting guideline. This will be the imaginary line that you will be stretching characters around.

Adding an Arc Guideline

You are going to add another object to the guide layer. This time, you will draw an ellipse, around which your type will arc. The ellipse will start out as 9.17 inches wide by 1.50 inches high, which is approximately the width and height of the word THURSTONS. You will then use a vertical stretch to scale the ellipse anamorphically to approximately 300 percent of its original height, and finish by centering the ellipse and ungrouping the other objects.

Drawing, Stretching, and Positioning the Ellipse

At Layers Roll-Up, *click* Guides	Guide-layer is selected.
Click the ellipse tool	The cursor becomes a + sign.
Align the cursor with top left corner of the rectangle	
Drag down and to the right	The cursor snaps to the grid as it is moved.
Release the mouse button	When the status line reads 9.17" by 1.50", an ellipse is drawn.
Click the pick tool	The ellipse is selected.
Position the cursor over the a ellipse's bottom-center handle	The cursor becomes a +.
Drag the bottom-center handle down	
Release the mouse button	When the status line reads y scale: 300% (vertical stretch).
Shift-click the rectangle	The group is selected.
Click Arrange	The Arrange menu appears.
Click Align	The Align menu appears.
Click Align to Center of Page	
Click OK	The ellipse is centered.
Press Ctrl-Y	Turns off the grid.

The top of the ellipse should approximately touch the baseline of the upper block of text, and the bottom of the ellipse should approximately reach the lower text block's cap height (see fig. 5.5).

You are done using the grid—you turned it off with Ctrl-Y at the

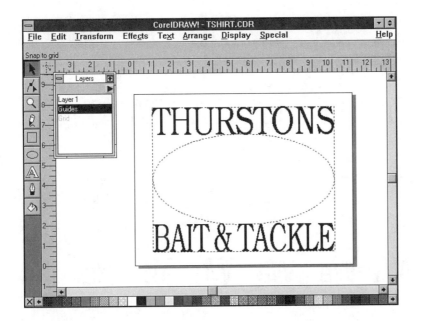

Figure 5.5:

Using an ellipse as guidelines.

end of the exercise. You will see why after you convert the text to curves and begin manipulating the individual outlines.

Kerning Text

Once the type is in position, you need to kern the text. Kerning is the art of reducing or increasing the space between character pairs to achieve an even visual appearance. Certain character combinations, such as LT, VA, To, and Wo are commonly tightened to give an aesthetic character fit. Figure 5.6 shows many of these commonly kerned combinations.

There are few skills in the graphic arts quite so esoteric as kerning. The amount of time spent kerning is entirely up to the kerner. Some people can spend hours on a single headline, while others have no qualms about setting unkerned type. If you fall in love with the craft of finely-kerned type, it's likely that your spouse (or significant other) will look at you with dismay when the conversation turns to kerning. Some—no, make that most—folks just do not understand, nor will they ever.

Figure 5.6:

The kern pair chart.

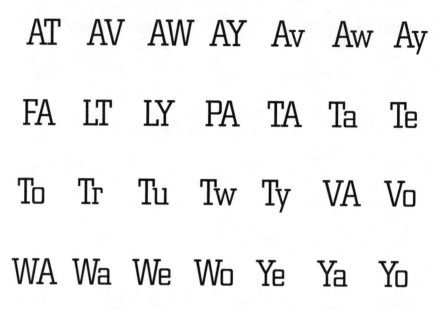

Typeface: Berthold City Light (Adobe)

Is kerning an acquired skill or an innate ability? Quite possibly, it is more than a little of both. Those who do not comprehend the concept of kerning are not alone. There are thousands of people out there who call themselves typesetters, or even typographers, who could not kern themselves out of a loose (as opposed to a tight) spot.

If you have the ability and the desire, you can learn to kern. But, you must *want* to learn. Developing an "eye" takes time and effort. It is all too possible to lose half a day kerning a headline. One of the keys is to make consistent changes and do so in small steps.

CorelDRAW! makes kerning easy for professional typographers. In addition to its excellent screen representations (from both TrueType and PostScript/ATM fonts), the program offers a number of kerning methods to select from. It offers the user a chance to make a precise numeric entry via the Character Attributes dialogue box, or use the visual click and drag approaches. Nudge is an additional way to finesse type in fine, measured increments. You can set up your Nudge preferences and massage letters into position. As you will see, each method has its advantage, and the different methods can be used in combination.

Drag-kerning text by eye is the fastest way to bridge a large space. Results are immediate—you can see exactly what is happening— and this will be the method you use most often. But not always. Nudge-kerning also is very visual and direct.

Kerning with Character Attributes

The Character Attributes dialogue box can move text in increments as fine as one percent of a character's point size. You will use this device when you need to squeeze just a hair between characters, or to move a measured amount in one shot. At larger point sizes, however, you may want to use nudge (with a fine setting) to finesse character fit. Character Attribute kerning is specified in a percentage relative to point size; Nudge kerning is denoted by absolute distances.

In the last chapter, you used the Character Attributes dialogue box to make the superior dollar sign for the Fast Freddie flyer. The dialogue box offers a variety of text manipulation tools in one easily accessible place.

In addition to typeface, point size, superior, and inferior typographic controls, the Character Attributes dialogue box offers control over other important character specifications. These include horizontal shift (kerning), vertical (or baseline) shift, and character angle (rotation). This section will cover the horizontal shift controls. The rest will come shortly.

By specifying -5 percent inter-character spacing, you asked for a relatively tight track. There should not be much individual letter pair kerning to do here, but once you learn how, you can take the practice as far as you want.

Begin by kerning the word THURSTONS. Remember to hold down Ctrl to constrain your movement to the baseline. Use the zoom tool to get a better look at what you are working with. You can move one or more characters at a time. Be sure to pay attention to the status line. If the Layers Roll-Up menu gets in your way, roll the menu up by clicking on the menu's up arrow button. You can roll it back down by clicking on the same button.

Kerning THURSTONS

At Layers Roll-Up *menu: click* Layer 1	Layer 1 is selected.
Click the Layers up arrow button	The Layers Roll-Up menu rolls up!
Click the zoom tool	
Click the +	
Marquee-select THURSTONS	
Release the mouse button	The screen zooms up on THURSTONS.
Click the shape tool	
Click THURSTONS	
Marquee-select the NS *nodes*	The nodes are selected.
Ctrl-Drag the NS *nodes to the left*	Move the nodes to (approximately) dx: -0.09.
Shift-click the N *node*	The N node is deselected.
Ctrl-Drag the S *node to the left*	Move the node to dx: -0.05.
Double-click on the S *node*	The Character Attributes dialogue box appears.
Type **-12**	At the horizontal shift.
Click OK	

Notice that when you used the Character Attributes dialogue box, the Horizontal Shift entry listed the approximate total distance from both moves (see fig. 5.7). This amount is the total cumulative distance from the original position. This can be a bit confusing since the Status Bar reports on absolute distances, while the dialogue box reports on a change in distance as a percentage of point size.

It is much easier and far more precise to handle the last tweaks with Nudge or the dialogue box, rather than by drag-kerning. Make your big moves with the mouse and fine-tune with Nudge and then the dialogue box (if necessary).

Shortcut

Double-click on a selected character node to get to the Character Attributes dialogue box.

The Character Attributes dialogue box can be accessed in one of two ways. The first (and more roundabout) way is to select a node and click Edit and Character Attributes. The second (and easiest) way is to simply double-click on a selected node.

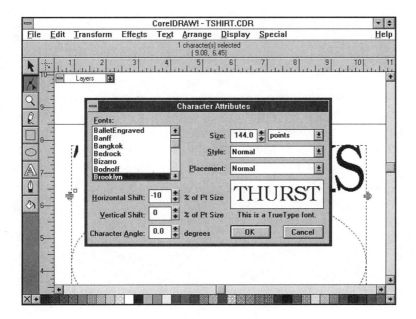

As you have seen, drag-kerning can be used on more than one character at a time. In the next exercise, you will move large blocks in one fell swoop.

Now that you have kerned the word THURSTONS, you will move on to the second block of text, BAIT AND TACKLE. Since this block of text was "squeezed" a bit tighter, it provides plenty of kerning opportunities.

Kerning goes both ways. Although most people think of kerning as something that is only done to tighten up text, this is hardly the case. Certain character combinations, in certain fonts, can cause a "too tight" situation to appear. Look at the AI, IT, and KL character combinations; they all should be "opened up."

Give It a Nudge!

Nudge was one of the most convenient features introduced in CorelDRAW Version 2.0. It enables you to move an object or objects (including type) by a pre-specified distance.

Using your keyboard's cursor keys, you can move objects up, down, to the left, or to the right in increments as fine as three tenths (0.3) of a point or as large as 12 picas. The amount of Nudge is specified in the Preferences dialogue box. You will find many opportunities to use this wonderful feature; kerning is but one of them.

To kern individual (or groups of) letters, click on the shape tool, select the nodes of the letters you want to move, and bang away at the appropriate cursor key. The characters will instantly pop into place. Another advantage of using nudge-kerning, as opposed to drag-kerning, is that baseline alignment is easily maintained.

Although the Preferences dialogue box will enable you to set the Nudge increment to as fine as one tenth (0.1), of a point, settings less then three tenths are disregarded. If you need to Nudge things in finer increments, there is a work-around. While three tenths of a point is the smallest effective Nudge setting, remember that you can initially set your type in a larger size and then scale it down after you are done tweaking. Using this method, you can kern effectively in minuscule increments. Just make sure that your type is not too tight once you reduce it!

Figure 5.8 shows what the word "BAIT" looks like on screen before you do anything to it. Figure 5.9 shows the results of the following exercise.

Figure 5.8:

Before kerning.

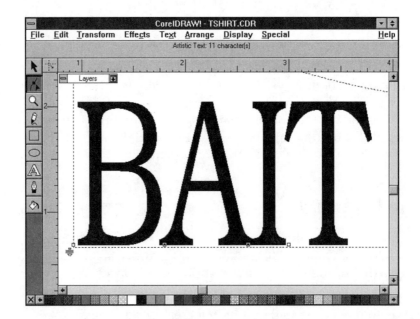

The BAIT & TACKLE Kernfest

Before you begin this exercise, call up the Preferences dialogue box and set Nudge to 0 picas, 1 point.

Click the shape tool	
Click BAIT & TACKLE	The words are selected.
Marquee-select the AIT & TACKLE *nodes*	The nodes are selected.
Ctrl-Drag the AIT & TACKLE *nodes to the left*	Move the nodes to dx: -0.07.
Release the mouse button	The text is kerned.
Shift-click the A *node*	The A node is deselected.
Drag the IT & TACKLE *nodes to right*	Move the nodes to dx: 0.06.
Release the mouse button	The text is kerned.
Shift-click the I *node*	The I node is deselected.
Ctrl-Drag the T & TACKLE *nodes to the right*	Move the nodes to dx: 0.02.
Release the mouse button	The text is kerned.
Shift-click the T & T *nodes*	The T & T nodes are deselected.
Ctrl-Drag the ACKLE *nodes to the left*	Move the nodes to dx: -0.05.
Release the mouse button	The text is kerned.
Shift-click the A *node*	The A node is deselected.
Ctrl-Drag the CKLE *nodes to the left*	Move the nodes to dx: -0.10.
Release the mouse button	The text is kerned.
Shift-click the C *node*	The C node is deselected.
Ctrl-Drag the KLE *nodes to the left*	Move the nodes to dx: -0.06.
Release the mouse button	The text is kerned.
Shift-click the K *node*	The K node is deselected.

Now, nudge-kern the last two nodes:

Press the right-arrow key seven times	The characters are kerned seven points to the right.
Shift-click the L *node*	The L node is deselected.
Press the right-arrow key twice	The character is kerned two points to the right.

NOTE

The type may need "more" or "less" kerning, depending on your personal preferences. Use either the drag- or nudge-kerning technique.

Figure 5.9:

After kerning.

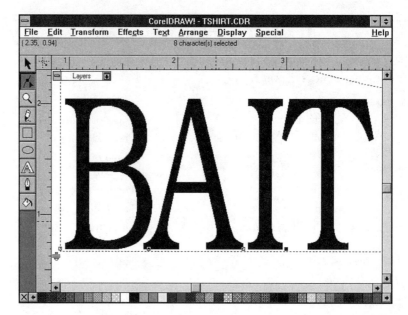

That seems like a lot of work for one line of text. Get ready, because it is going to get worse. Once you begin moving individual character nodes around, kerning will seem like a vacation at the beach!

Realigning Text to the Baseline

When you kern characters, it is very easy to pull them off their baseline. Perhaps you forgot to hold down Ctrl while you were drag-kerning. This problem is just as easily corrected with the Align To Baseline command.

Shortcut

Press Ctrl-Z to align text to baseline.

Align To Baseline can be used on a block of text while it is selected with either the pick or the shape tool. The command returns all text to its original horizontal baseline.

Using Align To Baseline

Click the pick tool
Click THURSTONS   The word is selected.

Click Text	The Text menu appears.
Click Align to Baseline	The text is aligned to the baseline.
Click BAIT & TACKLE	The words are selected.
Click Text	The Text menu appears.
Click Align to Baseline	The text is aligned to the baseline.

Now that you have finished kerning and aligning the second block of text to the baseline, it is a good idea to align the text horizontally. When you kerned the text, you changed the line lengths; consequently, the objects are no longer centered to the design boundary. You will use a variation of Align to Center of Page to restrain alignment to the horizontal plane.

Realigning the Text

Click THURSTONS	The word is selected.
Shift-Click BAIT & TACKLE	Both pieces of text are selected.
Click **A**rrange	The Arrange menu appears.
Click **A**lign	The Align menu appears.
Click Align to Center of **P**age	
Click Vertical **C**enter	Vertical Center is deselected.
Click OK	The objects are horizontally centered.
Click **F**ile	
Click Save **As**	Save the file as TSHIRT01.CDR.

Okay, all the easy work is out of the way. Now things start to get more complicated. It is almost time to convert your two lines of type to curves. Once you do that, there is no going back. You cannot unconvert to curves. Make sure that you have saved your file before continuing!

Editing and Manipulating Character Outlines

Converting text to curves enables you to modify individual character shapes. This can be extremely useful for custom logos and hand-lettering techniques. Figure 5.10 shows some samples of effects created with type that has been converted to curves. In the following exercise, you will be pulling text around the ellipse to give the look of a traditional freehand-rendered sign.

Figure 5.10:

Type that has been converted to curves.

After you convert a block of text to curves, you cannot edit the text with the Text dialogue box. It becomes just another curved object. That is why it is important to make sure that there are no typographical errors before converting text to curves!

Converting Text to Curves

Converting to curves is quite simple. It is the work you perform afterwards that is quite complex.

Converting **THURSTONS BAIT & TACKLE** to Curves

Click the pick tool	
Click THURSTONS	The word is selected.
Click **Arrange**	The Arrange menu appears.
Click Convert To Curves	Notice the nodes! The word THURSTONS is now curves.
Click BAIT & TACKLE	The words are selected.
Click **Arrange**	The Arrange menu appears.
Click Convert To Curves	BAIT & TACKLE is converted to curves.

Notice that individual nodes have appeared on the characters. As far as CorelDRAW! is concerned, the characters are now objects, not letters. You are about to see exactly what that means.

Remember fooling around with the clouds back in Chapter 3? You pushed and pulled on the clouds' nodes and control points to alter their sizes and shapes. You can now do the same thing to your letters.

You will begin the next exercise by zooming up on the first part of THURSTONS. Using the zoom tool, you will drag a marquee around the letters THUR. With the screen zoomed up, the individual character nodes will be apparent.

While you are dragging the characters out, watch the status line. To avoid an overabundance of node tweaking, try to maintain an x: 0.00 coordinate while dragging. Nonetheless, you will have to align the nodes anyway. Using the status line will help, but it will not circumvent all imperfections.

To keep from pulling the characters out of vertical sync, a keyboard drag modifier will help ease your pain. Hold down Ctrl while dragging a node (or group of nodes) to constrain movement to a horizontal or vertical plane.

Shortcut

Press Ctrl-V to convert to curves.

Shortcut

Use Ctrl-Drag to constrain node movement to horizontal and vertical.

Using Node Edit To Alter Character Shapes

Click the zoom tool	The Zoom fly-out menu appears.
Click the +	The cursor becomes a magnifying glass.
Marquee-select THUR	
Release the mouse button	The screen zooms up on THUR.
Click the shape tool	
Click THURSTONS	The word is selected. Nodes appear.
Marquee-select the nodes of the T's bottom serif	The letter's nodes are selected.
Hold down Ctrl and drag the nodes straight down to meet the ellipse	
Release the mouse button	The T is stretched.
Marquee-select the nodes of the H's left bottom serif	
Hold down Ctrl and drag the nodes straight down to meet the ellipse	
Release the mouse button	The H's left leg is stretched.
Marquee-select the nodes of the H's right bottom serif	
Hold down Ctrl and drag the nodes straight down to meet the ellipse	
Release the mouse button	The H's right leg is stretched.
Marquee-select the U's lower nodes	
Hold down Ctrl and drag the nodes straight down to meet the ellipse	
Release the mouse button	The U is stretched.

The R appears to be partially resting on the ellipse. Do not move the vertical foot that is touching the ellipse. The diagonal foot that extends below the ellipse can be altered later. Use the scroll bar to move over to fit STONS on the screen.

Shift-click the eleven lowest nodes on the S	
Hold down Ctrl and drag the nodes up about 0.05 inch	
Release the mouse button	The S is shortened.

You will notice that the S has lost a bit of its smoothness. It will be necessary to use the shape tool later to tweak the control points for the nodes involved. The next character, T, may already be resting on the ellipse. If it is, move on to the N.

Marquee-select the nodes of the T's bottom serif	
Hold down Ctrl and drag the nodes straight down to meet the ellipse	
Release the mouse button	The T is stretched.

Stretch the N before you do anything to the O. The N is a two-part stretch, like the H.

Marquee-select the N's six lower left nodes	
Hold down Ctrl and drag the nodes straight down to meet the ellipse	
Release the mouse button	The left side of the N is stretched.
Marquee-select the N's three lower right nodes	
Hold down Ctrl and drag the nodes straight down to meet the ellipse	
Release the mouse button	The right side of the N is stretched.

Figure 5.11 shows the results of this exercise.

You have reached an impasse. You were supposed to rotate the O. Unfortunately, it cannot be rotated with the node edit tool. If you had remembered to rotate the character before converting to curves—while the text was still text—it would have been no big deal. Now, the best way to accomplish the task is with Break Apart. While you are at it, you will use Break Apart on the final S too, so you can stretch it down without losing its overall proportions.

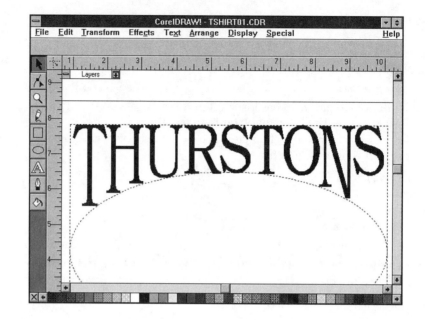

Break Apart

Break Apart is used for breaking up combined objects, such as text
that has been converted to curves, so that individual objects may
be altered without affecting the other objects.

You will duplicate the word THURSTONS and perform your
mutations upon the duplicated copy. After you have duplicated
the word, it is an excellent time to save your work using Save As.
Name the new file TSHIRT02.

There is one small stipulation when using Break Apart on text
objects. When you break apart a text object, characters such as the
upper case A, B, D, O, P, Q, and R lose their counters. The
counters (or holes) fill in with whatever color or tint the character
is filled with (see figs. 5.12 and 5.13). This can be quite disconcert-
ing at first, although you soon get accustomed to dealing with it.

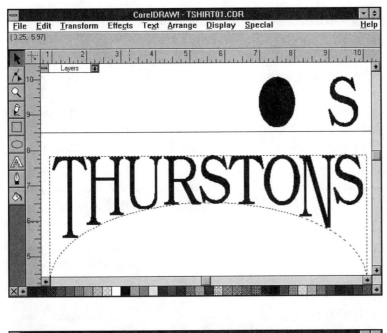

Figure 5.12:
Filled counters.

Figure 5.13:
Unfilled counters.

Using Combine To Reassemble Multiple Path Characters

Shortcut

Press Ctrl-C to combine objects.

There is a simple way to return a character with a filled-in counter to its proper state. In the next exercise, you will combine two paths into one object. The character will be returned to its proper appearance. This maneuver must be performed for every multiple-path character that is recombined. It is a necessary step.

Using Break Apart and Combine

Click the zoom tool	
Click the -	Reduces the artwork's size to show more surrounding space.
Click the pick tool	
Click THURSTONS	The word is selected.
Click **Edit**	The Edit menu appears.
Click **D**uplicate	The word THURSTONS is duplicated.
Drag the new THURSTONS *off the page*	
Click Arrange	The Arrange menu appears.
Click **Break** Apart	The word THURSTONS is broken apart.
Click the page	THURSTONS is deselected.
Shift-click the new THURST N *characters*	The characters are selected.
Press Del	The THURST N characters are deleted.
Marquee-select the O *and the* S	
Drag the O *and the* S	Position the letters above their counterparts.

Look at the O. It does not look good! The counter is filled with black because the O is two separate objects. The next step will solve the problem. Use Combine to fuse the two separate objects into one object.

Shift-click the S	The S is deselected.
Click **Arrange**	The Arrange menu appears.
Click **Combine**	The two parts of the O are combined.

You now have your transplant letters. It is time to dig out the original characters and replace them with the new models. You will be selecting the old characters by shift-clicking all of their nodes. A simple delete will remove the characters.

Removing the Originals and Transplanting the New Letters

Click the zoom tool	
Click the +	
Marquee-select THURSTONS O S	To zoom up.
Click the shape tool	
Click THURSTONS	
Shift-click all the "old" O and S nodes	All "old" O and S nodes are selected.
Press Del	The "old" O and S are deleted.
Click the pick tool	
Click the "new" O	The "new" O is selected.
Drag the "new" O into position	
Click the "new" S	The "new" S is selected.
Drag the "new" S into position	

Now that the transplanted characters are in position, it is time to do something special with them. You will rotate the O -28 degrees. Then you will use Clear Transformations to return the S to its original pristine state (as it was in its original converted to curves condition).

You will add a second nonprinting ellipse to your design. This ellipse will be based on the first ellipse, and scaled 105 percent proportionally. It will be needed when you arc out the bottom serifs of the word THURSTONS.

Begin this next exercise by creating the second nonprinting ellipse and a fourth nonprinting guideline—a skinny, horizontal rectangle.

Adding More Guidelines

At Layers Roll-Up, *click* Guides	Guide-layer is selected.
Click the pick tool	
Click the ellipse guideline	The ellipse is selected.
Click Transform	The Transform menu appears.
Click Stretch & Mirror	The Stretch & Mirror dialogue box appears.
At stretch horizontally, enter: **105**	
At stretch vertically, enter: **105**	
Click Leave Original	
Click OK	A new ellipse is drawn, 105 percent of original size.
Click the rectangle tool	
Drag a rectangle	Begin at the left side of the design boundary, at the same level as the top of the bottom serif in the first T in THURSTONS. Make it 9.17" wide by 0.57" high.
Release the mouse button	A rectangle is drawn.

With the new nonprinting guidelines in, you will rotate the O and stretch the S to fit. Once rotated, the O looks a bit small, so you will also stretch it a little. At this time, you will also pull out the diagonal leg of the R.

Rotating the O and Stretching the S

At Layers Roll-Up, *click* Layer 1	Layer 1 is selected.

Double-click the O	The O is selected in Rotate/Skew mode.
Drag the top right rotate arrow down and -28 degrees to the right	
Release the mouse button	The O is rotated -28 degrees.
Drag the O *into position*	
Click the O	The O is selected in Stretch/Scale mode.
Stretch the O *horizontally to fit*	You can do this by eyeballing the letter.
Release the mouse button	The O is horizontally stretched.
Click the S	The S is selected.
Drag the S's *lower center handle down*	Adjust the amount of stretch to figure 2.14's specification.
Release the mouse button	
Drag the S *into position*	

Pay careful attention to the status line in this next maneuver.

Zoom up on the R	
Click the shape tool	
Click **R**	THURST N is selected.
Shift-click the lower four nodes of the R's *right leg*	
Drag the nodes down and to the right	
Release the mouse button	After the status line reads: dx:0.09 dy:-0.07 distance: 0.11 angle: -37. The R's diagonal stem is stretched.

Oops! You forgot the apostrophe in the word "THURSTON'S." Was it a planned mistake, or was that a mistake in the plan? Whichever it was, you have to remedy the situation and add the missing apostrophe.

Since you have already converted the text to curves, you do not have the option of inserting the apostrophe into the text stream.

You will have to drag it into place. Even though the apostrophe is added at this stage, the people who look at the sign will not know the difference!

To add an apostrophe to the word THURSTONS, you will have to create a new piece of text. Use the text tool to set a 144-point Brooklyn Normal apostrophe, and horizontally scale it approximately 76 percent. Zoom up on the NS and drag the apostrophe into position. The tighter you zoom in, the more control you will have in placing the character. An exercise is not necessary for this little blunder. By now, you should be able to handle this task without assistance. After you have finished, your screen should look like figure 5.14.

Figure 5.14:

Work in progress!

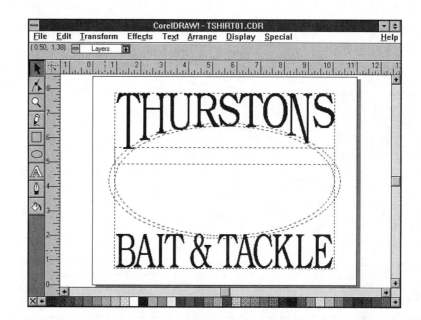

Use Snap to Objects for Precision!

What do you do if you want to move or stretch an object to a specific point? The solution is simple: use Draw's magnet-like Snap to Objects! Among the precision tools that were introduced in CorelDRAW! 3.0, Snap to Objects is your weapon-of-choice for accurate alignment. You can have any object snap to any other object at a predetermined point. This yields far more flexibility than using Snap to Guidelines, or Snap to Grid, alone.

Every object, from a block of paragraph text to an open line path, has a number of snap to points. Where do Snap Points occur? In general, you will find a Snap Point at every node along an object's path. Each object (except for an open line path) also has a Snap Point at its centerpoint.

If you want to snap to a point on an object, other than an existing point, use the shape tool to add a node at the exact point that you wish to snap to. To add a Snap Point to a rectangle or ellipse, you will first need to convert the rectangle or ellipse to curves, before adding the node.

For more accuracy, zoom in on the objects that you wish to snap. The magnetic effect is measured in absolute screen distances. Consequently, this means that the magnetism is relative to how far you are zoomed in or out. There is no preference setting to control snap distance.

Using Snap to Objects is easy. First, make sure that the function is toggled on via the Display menu. Then, with the pick tool, click (at the exact point you want to align) and drag the object you want to snap towards the (stationary) object you want to snap it to. When you get close enough, the magnetic effect will pull the object to the nearest Snap Point. You can maneuver the object from Snap Point to Snap Point.

Guide-layer objects have full Snap Point functionality, with an added bonus—they work even if the Snap to Objects function is toggled off (as long as Snap to Guidelines is toggled on)! In addition, when you use Snap to Objects with the function toggled off, you will not be hampered by the magnetic effect when selecting the Snap Point on the moving object. In other words, you are free to select any point along an object, rather than just its own snap to points.

Try using Snap Points when you complete the next phase of the exercise.

Arcing the Serifs

This design is developing a distinctive style, which is one of the basic reasons for converting text to curves. The availability of convert to curves is why CorelDRAW! is so much more than either a typesetting or drawing program. It is really a synthesis of both media.

To take this design to the next step, you are going to arc the serifs. Use the two ellipses as guidelines for the top and bottom of the serifs. This will give you the hand-lettered look of Thurston's original sign.

Arcing the serifs is a time-consuming task. The results, if properly rendered, make it time well spent. This feature will be one of the factors that sets this design apart.

Rather than go all the way through this next exercise one step at a time, you will learn the principles, modify a couple of serifs, and be invited to finish the exercise on your own. Because the work is getting rather complex, save your file frequently. By the end of the book, this will be drilled into your head. Save your files frequently!

The mechanics behind arcing serifs are rather straightforward. In practice, they can sometimes be difficult to attain. They consist of pulling the affected nodes down (or up) to meet the nonprinting guidelines. The smaller ellipse is the guide for the bottoms of the serifs. The larger ellipse is the guide for the tops of the serifs.

Begin by shift-clicking (or marquee-selecting) groups of involved nodes and dragging them down to meet the smaller ellipse. Proceed by dragging individual upper and lower nodes to intersect the outer and inner ellipses respectively. Remember that you can use Ctrl-Drag to keep your movements horizontal or vertical.

The curves that connect the serif to the character stems will become distorted. To clean them up, use the control points for the affected nodes. Use the ellipse as a guide to align the "knitting needles." Try to be as consistent as possible. The far ends of the ellipse will give you the most trouble. The best advice is to tweak and tweak some more.

Begin with the serif at the base of the first T in THURSTON'S. Create a new term for your purposes—call it *peer node*. A peer node is the node on the opposite side of a symmetrical character, relatively perpendicular to the node you are working with (see fig. 5.15). The peer node controls the parallel function of a selected node, but it does so on the opposite side of the character. The relationship between the two will control how "even" the serif curves appear.

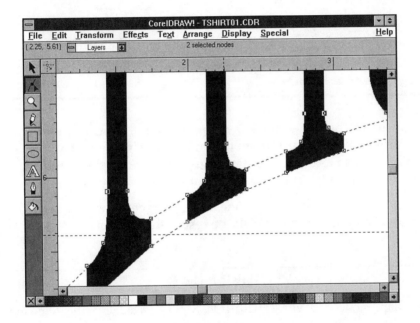

Figure 5.15:

Peer nodes on.

Arcing the First Serif

Click the shape tool	
Click THURSTON'S	The word is selected.
Marquee-select the four left nodes of the T's base serif	
Ctrl-drag the selected nodes down to the inner ellipse	
Release the mouse button	The nodes are moved.
Shift-click the lowest selected node	The node is deselected.

continues

Ctrl-drag the selected nodes up to the upper ellipse	The lowest node (of the three) should intersect the ellipse.
Release the mouse button	The nodes are moved.
Shift-click the lowest selected node	The node is deselected.
Ctrl-drag the selected node up	Align it on same horizontal plane as its peer node.
Release the mouse button	The node is moved.
Marquee-select the three upper right nodes of T's base serif	
Ctrl-drag the selected nodes up to meet the outer ellipse	The lowest node (of the three) should inter sect the ellipse.
Release the mouse button	The nodes are moved.

Notice that the curves have been pulled out of sync. Use the control points to return them to symmetry. This can get rather subjective, so use your artistic judgment. Click on the involved node, and pull the control points out to achieve the proper curve.

The next exercise will cover one more character, the H. You will then be on your own to finish the rest of the characters.

Arcing the H

In shape mode, and with THURSTON'S still selected, take the following steps:

Marquee-select the four left nodes of the H's left base serif	
Ctrl-drag the selected nodes down to the inner ellipse	
Release the mouse button	The nodes are moved.
Shift-click the lowest selected node	The node is deselected.
Ctrl-drag the selected nodes up to meet the upper ellipse	The lowest node (of the three) should intersect the ellipse.

Release the mouse button	The nodes are moved.
Shift-click the lowest selected node	The node is deselected.
Ctrl-drag the selected node up	Align it on same horizontal plane as its peer node.
Release the mouse button	The node is moved.
Marquee-select the two upper right nodes of the H's left base serif	
Ctrl-drag the selected nodes up to meet the outer ellipse	The lower node (of the two) should intersect the ellipse.
Release the mouse button	The nodes are moved.

That takes care of the left base serif. Now finish the character by doing the right base serif.

Marquee-select the three left nodes of the H's right base serif	
Ctrl-drag the selected nodes down to meet the inner ellipse	
Release the mouse button	The nodes are moved.
Shift-click the lowest selected node	The node is deselected.
Ctrl-drag the selected nodes up to meet the upper ellipse	The lower node (of the two) should intersect the ellipse.
Release the mouse button	The nodes are moved.
Shift-click the lowest selected node	The node is deselected.
Ctrl-drag the selected node up	Align it on same horizontal plane as its peer node.
Release the mouse button	The node is moved.
Marquee-select the two upper right nodes of the H's right base serif	
Ctrl-drag the selected nodes up to meet the outer ellipse	The lower node (of the two) should intersect the ellipse.
Release the mouse button	The nodes are moved (see figs. 5.16 and 5.17).

Figure 5.16:

The arced letters THUR.

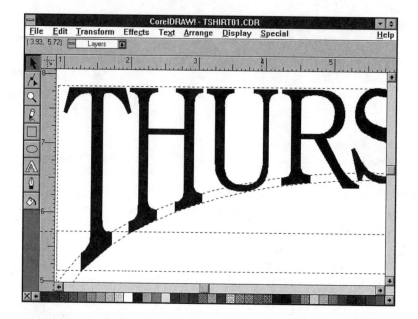

Figure 5.17:

Almost done.

No more examples are needed at this point. Use the techniques covered if you want to complete the design on your own.

Pushing the Envelope

Without a doubt, the Envelope effect is one of Draw's engaging features. This fabulous implement makes designing type that looks hand-lettered a simple task. You are about to see how the time and effort you spent on the last exercise can be substantially reduced. Though envelopes are less exact, you can use them to get similar results in a much shorter time frame.

Remember the Silly Putty you had as a kid? You could press it onto the Sunday comics for an image of your favorite cartoon character, then stretch and tug the likeness into bizarre shapes. A CorelDRAW! envelope works in a similar manner. After you apply an envelope to an object, you can control the overall shape of that object. Applying an envelope gives you eight handles around the selected object that you can drag until you are silly.

Enveloped text is still text. That is, you can still make changes to typeface, size, and spacing. This affords incredible flexibility. You can even access the text with Print Merge (which a later chapter will cover).

Envelope Basics

The four different styles of envelope are: Straight Line, Single Arc, Two Curves, and Not Constrained, as shown in figure 5.18. The icons that designate each style do a good job of explaining how each works, but the best way to gain an understanding is to try them out.

The Straight Line, Single Arc, and Two Curves choices enable you to apply those shapes *once* to each of the envelope's four sides (top, bottom, left, and right).

After you select Not Constrained, you are given control points at all eight handles. These work just like the control points on a curve. The side handles are smooth nodes and the corners are cusp nodes. Using this method, you can bend and twist objects (including type) into amazing shapes.

STRAIGHT LINE

SINGLE ARC

TWO CURVES

NOT CONSTRAINED

You can Copy An Envelope between two objects. This works just like Copy Style From, but you cannot copy multiple envelopes at once.

If you want to use one envelope around a number of objects, group or—if applicable—combine the objects. You cannot add a new envelope to a number of selected objects unless they are grouped (although you can copy an envelope to them). If, for example, you select three objects and copy an existing envelope to them, an envelope will be applied to each object rather than to the three objects as a whole. If you Copy An Envelope from an existing (enveloped) object onto those three (ungrouped) objects, you will get some wild effects.

An object can have multiple envelopes, although it may be easier to get the desired effect by using the Not Constrained mode. Look at figure 5.19. On the left, not constrained was used to get a straight line on the baseline, and a double curve on the cap line. On the right, a straight line envelope was used on the baseline. Then, Add New Envelope was used to add a second (two curves) envelope, and then the cap line was pulled out. Notice that the baseline is no longer straight.

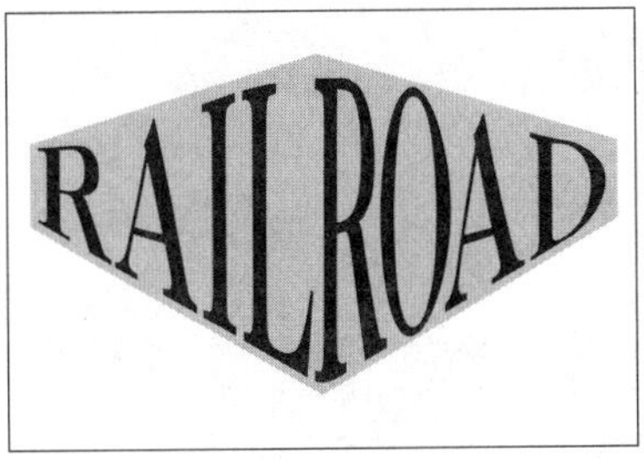

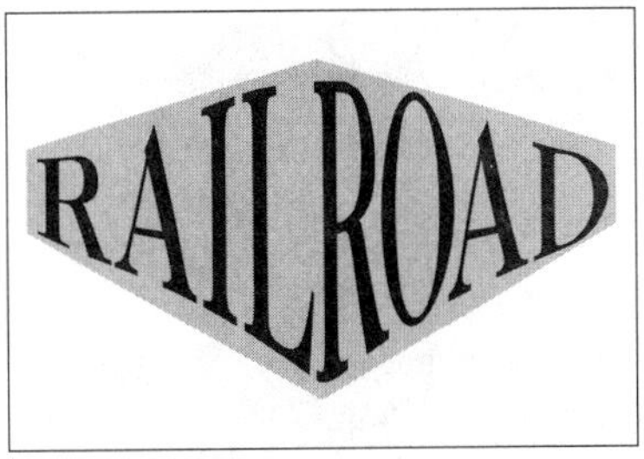

Figure 5.19:

Unconstrained and multiple envelopes.

When you are using envelopes, things can often get out of control. But there is an easy way to get your objects back to normal. You can remove an envelope (or multiple envelopes, one at a time) by using Clear Envelope. To remove all envelopes at once, use Clear Transformations.

The keyboard modifiers, Ctrl and Shift, have special functions when used with the envelope effect. If you hold down Ctrl and drag a handle, that handle and the handle opposite it will move in unison. If you hold down Shift and drag a handle, that handle and the handle opposite it will move in opposite directions. If you hold down Ctrl and Shift together and drag a handle, all four sides (or corners) will also move in opposite directions.

Before you get going on this next exercise, store your current file. You will need to bring back TSHIRT01.CDR, or the version of the THURSTON'S sign that you saved just before converting the text to curves.

Giving THURSTON'S an Envelope

Now you can try the envelope effect. Instead of doing something rigid at this point, just have some fun!

Click THURSTON'S	The word is selected.
Click Effects	The Effects menu appears.
Click E**d**it Envelope	The Edit Envelope selections appear (see fig. 5.20).
Click Single Arc	THURSTON'S is assigned a one-curve envelope.

continues

Click and drag the lower left handle down to meet ellipse	
Release the mouse button	THURSTON'S is re-drawn with a one-sided baseline arc.
Click and drag the lower right handle down to meet ellipse	
Release the mouse button	THURSTON'S is re-drawn with two-sided baseline arc.
Click and drag the lower center handle up to meet ellipse	
Release the mouse button	THURSTON'S is re-drawn with a big two-sided baseline arc.

Now that you have the idea, go ahead and try arcing BAIT & TACKLE downward (see fig 5.21). If your envelope goes wildly astray, clear it with the following procedure.

Click Effects	The Effects menu appears.
Click **C**lear Envelope	The envelope is cleared.

Next, try assigning the different envelope styles to the THURSTON'S design. You will find this tool easy to use, but it still takes some effort to master!

If you get your design almost to the point you want with the exception of few tweaks, you must use Convert To Curves to access the individual nodes and control points.

Take note that you can have only one style of envelope active at a time (even though you may have multiple envelopes). If you have more than one enveloped object on-screen, all envelopes will be assigned the same style. You may not like it, but that is the way it is! Use Convert To Curves on enveloped objects to get around this.

Did Envelope dazzle you? Just wait. The next effect you try—Extrude—is going to pull you overboard!

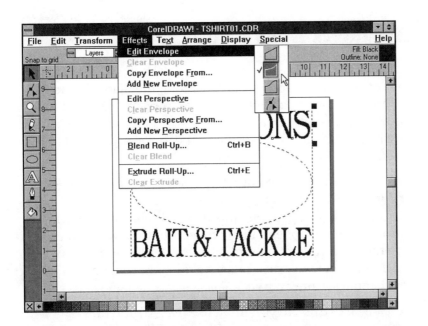

Figure 5.20:
The Effects menu.

Figure 5.21:
THURSTON'S envelope.

Extrude Is Heavy Stuff

The next time you look through your local newspaper, take a gander at the automobile section. Among the many screaming headlines, you are bound to find an example of extruded type. This effect gives new meaning to the word "weight" when used to describe a piece of type. Extruded type looks as if it has been carved from stone.

The Extrude effect was completely overhauled in CorelDRAW! Version 3.0. When it was first introduced in version 2.0, it offered revolutionary power, but was difficult to master. This latest incarnation has exponentially increased both power and ease-of-use. This is not to say that the Extrude effect is child's play (even though it is fun to use on a fast machine!). In fact, you can expect a considerable learning curve.

To create an extrusion, you must use the Extrude Roll Up menu, which is accessed by means of either the Effects menu, or the Ctrl-E keyboard shortcut. The illustration in figure 5.22, shows the Extrude Roll Up menu's five different modes which cover four different extrusion characteristics: Shape, Position (which has two menus), Lighting, and Color. Buttons for these four modes line the left side of the Roll Up. To switch to a different mode, click on the button corresponding to the mode you wish to switch to.

Shape

When you first access the Extrude Roll Up, it will be in the *Shape* mode. Here you assign *depth, perspective* and *direction,* enabling you to forge type (or any other object) to look as if it is zooming off into the distance towards an implied vanishing point. *Depth* controls how deep the extrusion is; setting it to a maximum value of 99 extends the extrusion all the way to the vanishing point. The extrusion appears flat (orthogonal) or with the illusion of distance if Perspective is clicked. Objects pop forward from the page, getting smaller as they get closer if Perspective and To Front are both selected.

Extrusions are assigned a *direction* corresponding to the menu's horizontal and vertical settings. By default, extrusions will zoom off to a vanishing point located at the ruler's zero/zero setting, which is (unless altered) found at the lower left hand corner of the page. You can reset the vanishing point in a number of ways. The first is to alter the ruler's zero/zero setting before applying any extrusions. The second is to numerically alter the horizontal and vertical settings. The third, and the most fun, is to interactively drag the vanishing point around the page. Once you have an extrusion vanishing point on a page, subsequent extrusions (on that page) will follow to the same vanishing point.

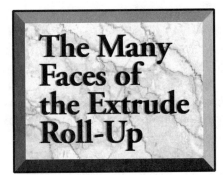
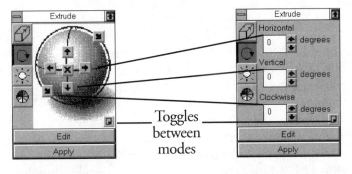

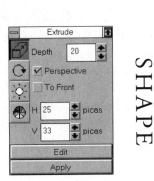

Toggles between modes

SHAPE

POSITION

COLOR

LIGHTING

Figure 5.22:
The Extrude Menus.

Position

Clicking on the *Position* button summons a globe-like object, surrounded by arrow buttons. The Position mode controls an object's rotation in three dimensions. Each click of an arrow button yields a five degree move in that direction of rotation. The arrow buttons on the perimeter of the circle control clockwise and counter-clockwise rotation. The horizontal arrow buttons control left and right rotation, while the vertical arrow buttons control over-the-top and under-the-bottom rotation. The best way to understand this one is try it out!

After you click on the page icon button in the lower right hand corner of the menu, the Extrude Position menu will change to a far more precise but far less graphical description of object rotation. Here, you can enter specific degrees of rotation. While each click of an up or down arrow will get you another five degrees, you can always type in a specific amount of rotation, in one degree increments.

Lighting

Clicking on the button that looks like a child's drawing of the sun brings you to the *Lighting* menu. Here you are given three choices. The first is an on/off toggle switch, which determines whether or not the Lighting effect is used. Flipping the light switch to the on position enables you to set the *lighting angle* and *intensity*. Once you turn the feature on, you will see a globe appear inside the wireframe box. The X on the wireframe box determines the location of an imaginary light source. As you move it around, you will see the globe's highlight change. The light source can only be set to one of the wireframe intersection points. The intensity setting controls the amount of light shining on the object.

Lighting affects all types of extrusion fills, adding shadows to the backsides of each object. Lighting is not a full-blown 3-D lighting implementation. There are no cast shadows. Each object is independent of the next.

Color

The last of the four Extrude buttons summons the Color menu. Here you are given three more choices, this time relating to the extrusion's color. *Use Object Fill* does exactly what you would expect. *Solid Color* enables you to assign a specific process color. *Shade* performs a fountain-fill-like gradation, which follows the contours of the extrusion.

Care must be taken when assigning shades, and/or lighting to an extrusion. This is one of the instances of what looks really cool on the screen may take ages to run on the printer, or worse, imagesetter. Shades and lighting are complex functions. Try not to over do them, or you will pay the price (literally, if you are sending work to a service bureau) for the time that it takes to image the file!

Extrude does have its limitations. You may extrude only one object at a time. You cannot extrude a group of objects, nor can you extrude a number of selected objects. You can extrude combined objects, however. Once you have executed an extrusion, the original object becomes tied to the extrusion. You can break them up by clicking *Separate* from the Arrange menu.

After Draw extrudes your object, the extrusion itself will be a group of objects, with the same outline and fill as the original object, by default. As you have seen, the Roll Up menus offer plenty of extrude fill options. You can also change the extrusion's outline and fill, either in its entirety or by separating, ungrouping, and making changes object by object. Remember to regroup and/or group with the original object so that the complete, extruded object can be scaled or moved without the risk of falling apart.

The math involved in the creation of the Extrude effect makes you glad that the Draw program handles the computations. You can worry about the structure of your design, not the equations necessary to complete it!

Shortcut

Press Ctrl-E to access the Extrude Roll-Up Window.

In the next short exercise, you will take the finished Thurston's sign and use Extrude to give it some depth. Save your current file, if need be, and call up your most recent (and complete) version of the Thurston's sign.

Extrusion, like Envelope, is a workout for your computer's processor. Depending on the speed of your computer, you may wait a while. But the end result is well worth it.

Extruding THURSTON'S

To make the screen less cluttered, go ahead and delete all those nonprinting guidelines. Ungroup the sign if necessary. Combine the word "THURSTON'S" into one object.

Click THURSTON'S	The word is selected.
Click Effects	The Effects menu appears.
Click Extrude Roll Up ...	The Extrude Roll Up menu appears.
Click Apply	THURSTON'S is extruded.

Now that you have extruded the word "THURSTON'S" downward, extrude "BAIT & TACKLE" upward. Notice that Draw remembers your last dialogue box entries.

Click Bait & Tackle	The words are selected.
At the Extrude Roll Up, *Click* Apply	BAIT & TACKLE is extruded (see fig. 5.23).

Now, go ahead and try different extrusion depths, positions, lighting, and fills! Drag the vanishing point icon around to see how different angles affect the extrusion. Notice how the pick tool changes to a + when you are interactively adjusting the vanishing point. Use Snap To Guidelines to position the vanishing point in a specific spot.

Extrusions look good when they have a hard edge. You can use a thin outline rule to make the surface pop out. Depending on the size of the extruded object, this can be anything from a hairline to a two-point rule, relative to the size of the objects you extrude.

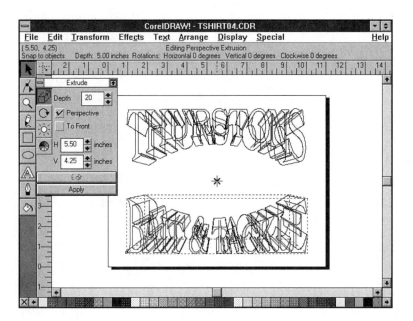

Figure 5.23:
Adjusting the
Vanishing Point.

Summary

This chapter introduced a fairly advanced project that will carry over into a later chapter (covering advanced fill and outline trapping techniques). You have tried out a variety of commands and techniques. Among them, Convert To Curves, Break Apart, and Combine played major roles. After fiddling with Draw's Envelope and Extrude effects, a new appreciation for Corel Systems' programmers is in order! You have seen that Draw is a program that builds upon its simplicity to provide design solutions.

As mentioned earlier, typography is perhaps CorelDRAW!'s strongest area. The program offers designers a world of fonts, with editable outlines. And remember, you are not limited to the range of fonts that came with CorelDRAW! There are literally thousands of PostScript fonts available today, from a host of foundries. On the other hand, as of this writing, there are relatively few TrueType fonts on the market. Chapter 11 will cover the subject of fonts and font conversion. And there is one text effect not covered as yet: Fit Text to Path. This powerful command will be examined in Chapter 8.

Outline, Fill, and Color

well-designed page can work either in black and white or in color. Structure is what makes the difference. Of course, a poor choice of colors can ruin a design from a chromatic standpoint, but the mere inclusion of color cannot make up for poor design. A flashy paint job on a leaky hull will not keep the boat from sinking.

Because color printing can be an expensive proposition, the place to experiment with color is certainly not on the printing press. Mistakes can be more than expensive; they can cost you your job or an account. It is important to take precautions at every step and to keep an eye on the meter. When you are working with color, the meter is always running. See Chapter 12 for more information on avoiding the pitfalls of color printing.

This is a rather ambitious chapter. It covers the color basics for both spot and process colors. In addition to color, the chapter also explains the many properties of the outline and fill tools, including full- and two-color patterns. To illustrate some practical applications of color, the chapter touches on the subject of charts and 35mm slides. CorelDRAW! version 3.0 introduced CorelCHART!, a powerful charting program, and an excellent complement to Draw. Slides, one of Draw's least-exploited output options, can be a relatively inexpensive way to experiment with color. Chapter 14 delves into CorelCHART! in-depth.

The only way to gain real experience with color is through trial and error. Like most subjects in the art world, learning through experience is mandatory. Understand the theory, and then practice, practice, practice!

Using CorelDRAW! and Color

Color is described in one of two ways, depending on the medium. Printed color involves layering partially transparent inks onto opaque paper. The subsequent printed piece is an example of *subtractive color*, which subtracts wavelengths (colored inks) from white light (paper). When you are working with video screens or producing 35mm slides, projected color entails *additive color*. Draw treats all color as subtractive, even when composing an image that will ultimately be used as a 35mm slide.

The CorelDRAW! program has two different methods for specifying color: *spot* and *process*. These refer to the two basic methods of reproducing color images on a printing press. Spot color is used when two or more specific colors are required for a print job. Process color is used to give the printed illusion of "full color."

For those who are just entering the world of printed color, the first place to start is with spot, rather than process, color. It is wiser to *wade* into uncharted waters, as opposed to diving in head first.

PANTONE Color

In most print shops, a scheme known as the PANTONE Matching System—commonly referred to as PANTONE color—ensures that the final printed color correctly corresponds to the color specified by the designer. Quite simply, PANTONE is a recipe book for mixing printing inks. The pressperson follows a predefined recipe to "cook up" the correct color, the same way a chef prepares clam chowder. A dash of this and a spot of that; three parts blue to two parts red.

When specifying a color using the PANTONE system, an exact color is requested. The printed color should match the one chosen from the PANTONE color swatch book. A few colors come "straight out of the can," but most colors must be mixed from combinations of other colors.

This process should eliminate inconsistencies, but the system relies on the press person to accurately mix the specified ink. If the ink is not meticulously mixed, the printed color will not match the requested color. If color printing is important to you, find a competent printer and stay with them.

Although CorelDRAW! does a laudable job with PANTONE color screen representations, do not, under any circumstances, trust the screen colors to be true. Buy a PANTONE book, and use it to accurately specify your colors. Most graphic arts supply houses carry them. They are not cheap, but they are worth the investment.

Process Color

As opposed to PANTONE color, process color mixes ink on the printed page, not before it is put on the press. Process color is commonly referred to as "four-color" printing, alluding to the four colors of ink used: cyan, yellow, magenta, and black (CMYK). Each color has a separate printing plate and, when printed, the four colors are combined in different ratios to give the illusion of a full-color photograph. When you specify a color using the process color model, you can enter specific percentages of each of the four process colors, blending them to create a full spectrum of color.

CorelDRAW! does an excellent job of creating either spot or process color separations. The power of the PostScript language enables you to send Draw files to a high-resolution imagesetter where negatives can be produced. These negatives are then used to burn the printing plates. By imaging directly onto negative film, you are assured of producing the highest quality image possible. Much of the manual (and costly) preparation that you may have formerly encountered with color printing is eliminated.

It is also possible to proof images on a color PostScript output device prior to sending the files out for separations. The best of these printers can print with either process or PANTONE color-simulating capabilities. Although they should not be used for final output, color printers can be helpful in the design process, allowing comps to be made in a short time frame.

Later in this chapter, you will specify both spot and process colors, and ultimately image them as 35mm slides. Preparing artwork for color printing—whether spot or process—is not something to be taken lightly. Fooling around with slides first gives you some slack. For more in-depth information on how to prepare your work for color printing, refer to Chapter 12.

For now, this chapter will move on to the extended functions of the outline pen tool, where it covers the fundamentals of specifying color.

Using the Outline Pen Tool

Draw's outline pen tool offers a wide range of outline pen colors, widths, and shapes. Until this point, you have worked with only the most immediate choices, those present on the Outline fly-out menu (see fig. 6.1; see also figure 2.18 in Chapter 2 for an annotated illustration). Although this menu offers enough options to render uncomplicated black-and-white drawings, you must delve further into the menu structure to make use of color outlines.

As your drawings become more and more complex and your familiarity with Draw increases, you will find that the possibilities are continually unfolding. The outline pen tool provides versatility without being cumbersome. Its options are there if needed, but their presence is not a hindrance if they are not needed for the task at hand.

The Outline dialogue boxes are accessed via the Outline fly-out menu. Notice the two icons at the far left of the menu in addition to the default line width and color choices. The upper icon—a pen nib—is a duplicate of the icon that opens the Outline fly-out menu; clicking on this icon accesses the Outline Pen dialogue box.

The lower icon—which represents a color wheel—gives you access to the Outline Color dialogue box. The icon next to the Outline Pen accesses the Outline Pen Roll-Up window.

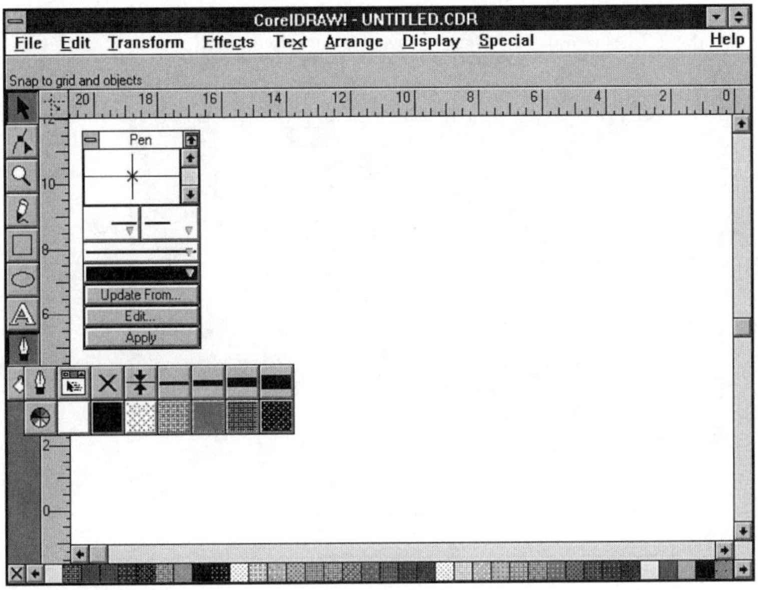

Figure 6.1:

The Outline fly-out and Roll-Up menus.

Customizing the Outline Pen

The outline tool is as versatile as a slew of "real" calligraphic pens. There is much to be explored here, so experiment with some different combinations.

Through the Outline Pen dialogue box, you can control pen type and shape, color, corners, line caps, dashing, and arrowheads (see fig. 6.2). Options are also provided for placing the outline behind the fill, and for scaling the outline with the image. Take a look at some of the choices.

Shortcut

Press F12 to get to the Outline Pen dialogue box.

Style: Draw offers great flexibility with regard to dashed and dotted line styles. Right out of the box, you get 15 predefined line styles (in addition to solid lines) with the option of adding up to 25 more. Dashed and dotted lines are accessed by clicking on the line under Style (which brings up the Dashed & Dotted Line Styles pop-up menu, shown in fig. 6.3). You use scroll bars to browse through the available line styles. To change a dashed line style into a dotted line style, select a short dash and click the round line caps selection.

Figure 6.2:

The Outline Pen
dialogue box.

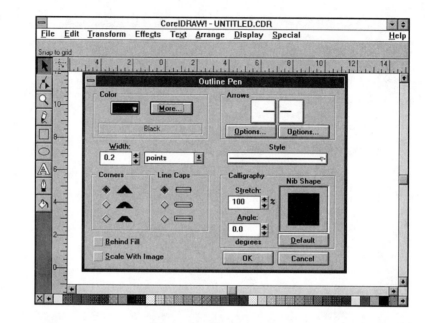

Figure 6.2:

The Outline Pen
dialogue box.

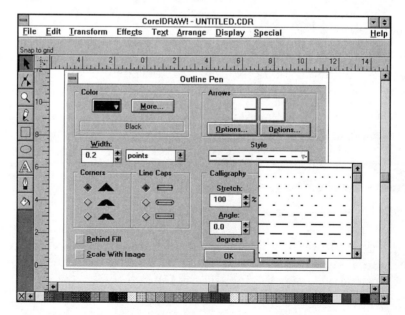

Figure 6.3:

The Dash and Dotted
Line Styles menu.

The dash sizes are scaled in direct proportion to the weight of the line specified. Hence, the thicker the line, the larger the dash pattern. The predefined line styles probably will not meet all of your needs. To add your own custom variations of dashed lines, you must edit CORELDRW.DOT, a text file that describes line styles (see fig. 6.4). You will find it in your CORELDRW directory.

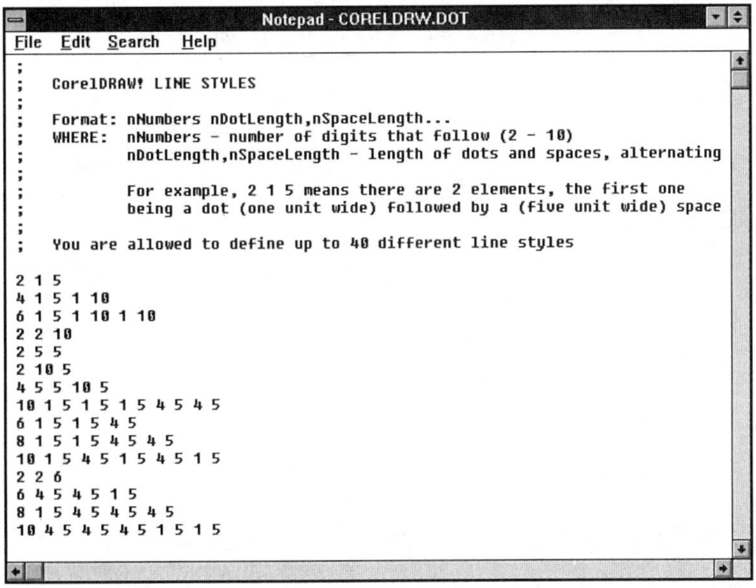

Figure 6.4:
CORELDRW.DOT.

```
Notepad - CORELDRW.DOT
File  Edit  Search  Help

;
;   CorelDRAW! LINE STYLES
;
;   Format: nNumbers nDotLength,nSpaceLength...
;   WHERE:  nNumbers - number of digits that follow (2 - 10)
;           nDotLength,nSpaceLength - length of dots and spaces, alternating
;
;           For example, 2 1 5 means there are 2 elements, the first one
;           being a dot (one unit wide) followed by a (five unit wide) space
;
;   You are allowed to define up to 40 different line styles

2 1 5
4 1 5 1 10
6 1 5 1 10 1 10
2 2 10
2 5 5
2 10 5
4 5 5 10 5
10 1 5 1 5 1 5 4 5 4 5
6 1 5 1 5 4 5
8 1 5 1 5 4 5 4 5
10 1 5 4 5 1 5 4 5 1 5
2 2 6
6 4 5 4 5 1 5
8 1 5 4 5 4 5 4 5
10 4 5 4 5 4 5 1 5 1 5
```

This procedure may sound difficult, but it is really quite easy. You will need to use an ASCII text editor, such as Notepad, to do the job. Just remember to make a duplicate copy of CORELDRW.DOT before you edit the original.

Take a look at figure 6.4. Each line style is defined by a row of text, which includes: the number of elements (maximum of ten), length of the dash, and the space between dashes. Dashed lines run in a continuous loop from left to right. One of the effects you can create with dashed lines is shown in figure 6.5.

To create a line style, type the specifications for the new line style on a new line (after the existing group of line styles is the best place to start). If you want, you can bring your favorite styles to the top of the chart with some cutting and pasting. After you have altered CORELDRW.DOT, you must save the file and restart CorelDRAW! for the changes to take effect.

TIP

You are limited to 40 line styles per the CORELDRW.DOT file, but you can have literally hundreds of available styles. How? Create multiple line style files, each with a different name (for example, DOT1, DOT2, DOT3, etc). When you want to use the line styles in a particular file, copy/rename the file you need to CORELDRW.DOT, and restart Draw each time you change.

Figure 6.5:

A dashed coupon border.

Behind Fill: The Behind Fill option is useful when working with text. If Behind Fill is enabled, the fill will print to the midpoint of the outline. If it is not enabled, the outline will encroach upon the fill. The thicker the outline, the more important it is to use Behind Fill. Failing to use this option may result in text that is unreadable or just plain ugly (see fig. 6.6).

Figure 6.6:

Use caution (and Behind Fill) when outlining text.

Another way to look at it is that with Behind Fill enabled, the outline will print at half its weight. This is because the outline's width is centered on an object's outline. You will find that the Behind Fill option will prove itself to be of definite interest when you attempt some rudimentary trapping in Chapter 12.

Scale With Image: The Scale With Image option is extremely important when creating artwork that is to be scaled or rotated. For instance, say that you create a logo at full-page size. Then you scale the logo for use on letterheads and business cards. If Scale With Image is not used, the outline weight will remain constant. This will result in the outline "filling-in" the logo. The logo that looked good at full-page size turns into mud when reduced (see fig. 6.7).

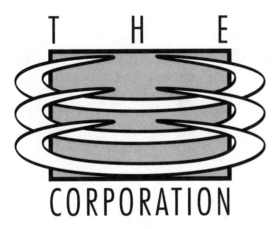

Scale With Image
NOT Selected

Scale With Image
Selected

Figure 6.7:

Scale with image logo.

In addition to affecting line weight, Scale With Image also plays an important role when scaling or rotating objects that have been drawn with a calligraphic pen shape. Enabling this option will ensure that the pen shape rotates along with the image. If Scale With Image is not clicked, the object will rotate, but the pen stroke will not.

Corners: There are three options for line corners: miter, round, and bevel. The options are rather self-explanatory (see fig. 6.8). Miter extends the outer edges of the two meeting lines. To avoid corners in small angles that "overshoot," the miter limit may need to be adjusted upward. The miter limit setting is accessed from the Preferences dialogue box.

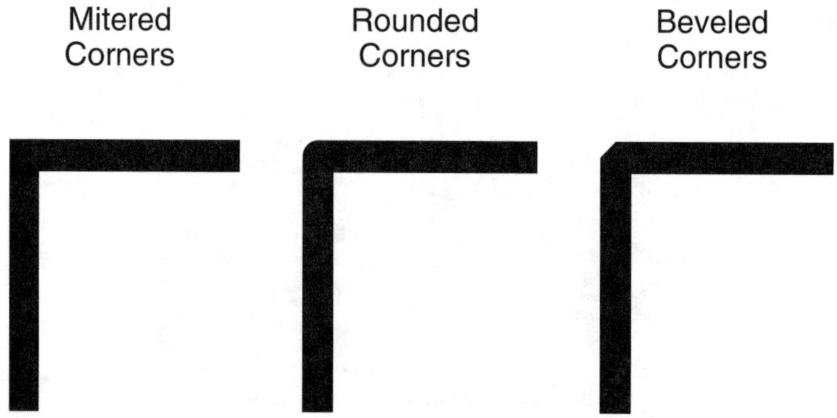

Figure 6.8:

Mitered, rounded, and beveled corners.

Mitered
Corners

Rounded
Corners

Beveled
Corners

For an example of what happens when the miter limit is improperly set, look at the word "SUMMER" in the "SEASIDE AQUARIUM" color plate. The *M*s show the spiky results.

Arrows: Draw comes with an array of arrowheads and other symbols necessary for technical illustrations. The program also enables you to create your own arrows and doodads. The Arrowhead pop-up menus are accessed by clicking on either the starting (left) or ending (right) Arrow buttons in the Outline Pen dialogue box (shown in fig. 6.9). Use the scroll bars to browse through the arrowhead styles.

When you find the arrowhead you want, assign it by clicking with the left mouse buttons. Choose an arrowhead from the left menu to place it at the start of the line; choose an arrowhead from the right menu to place it at the end of the line. To return a line to "non-arrowhead" form, click the flat line. To switch starting and ending arrowheads, click Options and Swap!

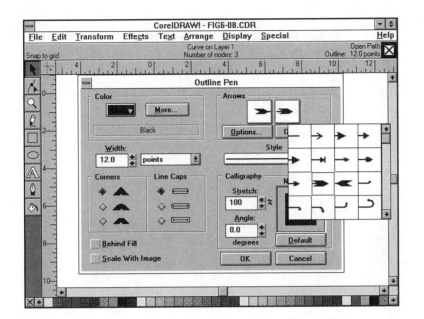

Getting a new arrowhead into the Arrowhead pop-up menu is
an easy task. You simply select any object (including combined
objects) and use the Create Arrow command (found on the Special
menu). Draw asks if you *really* want to create a new arrowhead
before it stores it. Note that the outline and fill attributes do not
carry over (for example, you cannot have a fountain-filled arrowhead); instead, these settings are governed by the outline color
and weight. If you want an arrowhead with no fill, you will either
need to draw a combined "doughnut" object or break a closed
path object, using Node Edit.

The Arrowhead pop-up menu also enables you to delete or edit
existing arrowheads. Deleting an arrowhead from the list is
simple: click the arrowhead you want to remove, and then click
Delete.

To edit an existing arrowhead, click Option, and then click Edit.
This summons the Arrow Head Editor (see fig. 6.10). The Arrow
Head Editor enables you to stretch/scale, re-orient, and position
the arrowhead in relation to the line. Stretching and scaling works
like stretching and scaling other objects in Draw, although the
keyboard modifiers (such as Ctrl and Shift) have no effect. Side
handles stretch; corner handles scale. Unfortunately, there is no
Undo within the editor (except for Cancel)!

Figure 6.10:

The arrowhead editor.

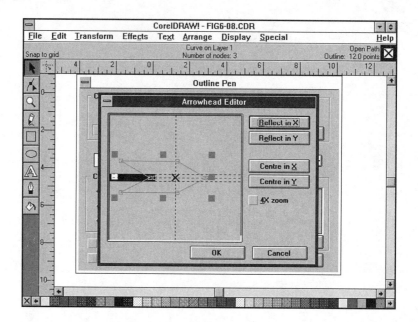

You cannot edit individual arrowhead nodes, but you can use them as snap-to points. By clicking and dragging on a node, that point becomes "magnetic" and will be attracted to the guidelines. Reflect in X and Reflect in Y flip the arrowhead on the vertical or (middle) horizontal guideline, respectively.

Center in X and Center in Y center the arrowhead to those same guidelines (also respectively). 4X Zoom zooms up by a factor of four.

Line Caps: In addition to arrowheads, there are three options for line caps. They are: butt, round, and square (see fig. 6.11). Line caps apply to both ends of a line. However, when using an arrowhead, the "non-arrowhead" end of a line can have a butt, round, or square line cap.

Pen Shape (Calligraphic Pens): The Pen Shape option gives flexibility to the pen width, shape, and angle. This feature is like being able to snap in a completely different pen nib with only a few clicks (see fig. 6.12). Show this feature to a calligrapher, and watch him salivate!

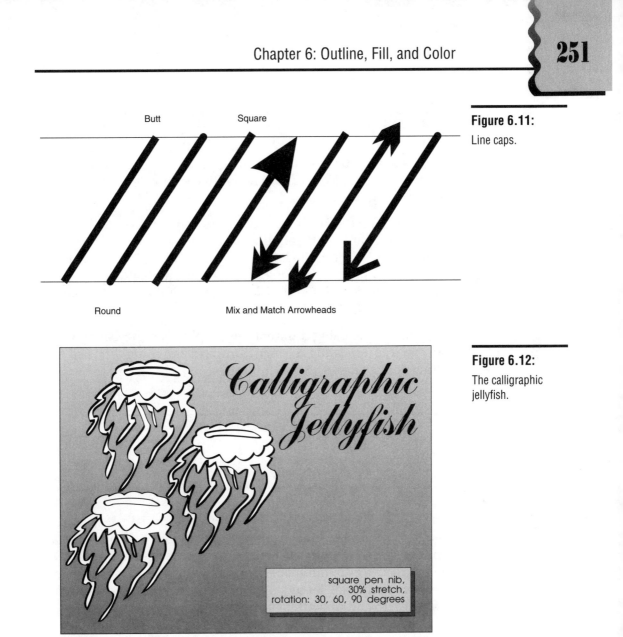

Figure 6.12:
The calligraphic
jellyfish.

Specifications are entered in typical Corellian fashion. Width
defines the size of the pen nib, and can be specified in inches,
centimeters, and fractional points, as well as points and picas.
Stretch alters the actual shape of the pen, while Angle rotates
the pen upon its axis.

A line width of 0.00 is *not* the same as a line width of NONE. Specifying a line width of 0.00 will yield a line at the output device's single-pixel width. A standard 300 dpi laser printer will output a line 1/300 in width; an imagesetter may be able to print lines that are 1/1270 or 1/2540 in width (possibly even thinner, depending on the model).

One of the nicest features introduced in CorelDRAW! 3.0 is the interactive capability to define a calligraphic pen shape. Try placing your cursor in the Nib Shape window, and click and drag around the window. The cursor will become a plus sign (+). You can freely adjust both the stretch and angle of the pen nib without ever touching the keyboard or size buttons!

To get the feel of using different calligraphic pens, try signing your name, duplicating the signature, and assigning different outline pen attributes to the duplicates.

Signing Your Name with Different Pens

Click pencil tool
Sign your name at the top of the page

Your signature probably looks pretty bad—especially if you used a mouse to do it. The creator of the illustration was lucky and had a cordless pen and graphics tablet. In any case, feel free to tweak your signature with the shape tool. Try to get the signature to look at least vaguely as it should. You are going to duplicate the signature twice, to end up with a total of three.

Duplicating the Signature

Click the shape tool
Tweak the nodes   Until you are content.
Shift-click all the paths in
the signature
Click **Arrange**   The Arrange menu
                                                 appears.

Click **Group**	The signature is grouped.
Click **Edit**	The Edit menu appears.
Click **Duplicate**	The signature is dupli-cated.
Drag the signature to the bottom of the page	
Click **Edit**	
Click **Duplicate**	The signature is dupli-cated again.
Drag the signature to the middle of the page	

There should be three signatures on the page. You will assign a different calligraphic pen type to each signature, so that you can see the differences between the various pen nib shapes. At this point, make sure that the preview window is turned on (press F9 to switch the window on or off).

Assigning a Pen Type

Click the pick tool	
Click the uppermost signature	The signature is selected.
Click the outline tool	The Outline fly-out menu appears.
Click the outline pen	The Outline Pen dialogue box appears.
Click the round corners	The corners are selected.
Change the pen width to **0.02** *inches*	
Change Angle to **0** *degrees*	
Change Stretch to **100** *percent*	
Click OK	
Click the middle signature	The signature is selected.
Click the outline tool	The Outline fly-out menu appears.
Click the outline pen	The Outline Pen dialogue box appears.
Click the square corners	The corners are selected.
Change the pen width to **0.03** *inches*	

continues

Change Angle to **40** *degrees*	
Change Stretch to **50** *percent*	
Click OK	
Click the lower signature	The signature is selected.
Click the outline tool	The Outline fly-out menu appears.
Click the outline pen	The Outline Pen dialogue box appears.
Click the round corners	The corners are selected.
Change the pen width to **0.04** *inches*	
Change Angle to **60** *degrees*	
Change Stretch to **20** *percent*	
Click OK	

If you have a printer available, try printing the file to see the distinction between pen shapes (see fig. 6.13). The differences in pen shape may be less than obvious. In general, the larger the pen nib and the more extreme the stretch, the more apparent the pen shape becomes. The rectangular pen nib will yield a harder, sharper edge, while the rounded pen nib will be softer and more flowing.

The Outline Pen Roll-Up Menu

Yet another of CorelDRAW! 3.0's time saving Roll-Up menus is the Outline Pen (see fig. 6.14). This Roll-Up offers point-and-shoot convenience for line characteristics, including line width, arrows, line style, and outline pen color. In addition, it enables you to Update From (which is the same as Copy Style From) any other line; and it also provides easy access to the Outline Pen dialogue box (via the Edit button). Like other roll-up menus, you must remember to click Apply to assign any changes!

Shortcut

Use the Search function to select PANTONE and TRUMATCH colors by number.

Understanding Draw's Color Selection Methods

Specifying color with CorelDRAW! may seem, at first, like a mystifying procedure. The color selection choices are vast and the methods may not be instantly comprehensible. The secret lies in using the proper palette (which depends on the printing method that you will be using). The first choice you will have to make is whether you will be specifying either spot or process color. If you specify spot, your choices are simple; you are allowed to choose PANTONE colors either visually, or by name.

Round Nib, 0.02 inches, 0% Angle, 100% Stretch

Square Nib, 0.03 inches, 40% Angle, 50% Stretch

Round Nib, 0.04 inches, 60% Angle, 20% Stretch

Figure 6.13:

The signature of John Q. Public.

If you are working with process color, your choices are far more varied. Draw enables you to specify process color from a number of color models. Choosing each method determines the layout of the Outline Color or Uniform Fill dialogue boxes. For the purposes of the exercises, you will be dealing with spot PANTONE and process CMYK color exclusively.

The Outline Color and Uniform Fill dialogue boxes have plenty of smarts. It is possible to specify a color with one color model (perhaps RGB), switch to another (say, CMYK), and retain a semblance of color integrity. However, only one type of process color model can be active at any time.

Figure 6.14:

The Annotated
Outline Pen roll-
up menu.

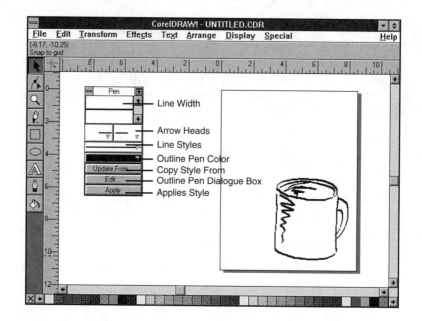

Figure 6.14:

The Annotated
Outline Pen roll-
up menu.

Each time you specify colors, CorelDRAW! remembers the mode
in which you left the color selector. For example, if you used
Process colors the last time you specified a color (either for an
outline or a fill) in CMYK, the dialogue box will pop back up in
the same mode the next time you access it. Like other portions of
the program, CorelDRAW! configures itself around the way you
work. The color specification methods may seem odd at first, but
you will soon become accustomed to them.

Outline Colors

Shortcut

Press Shift-F12 to
get to the Outline
Color dialogue box.

A full range of colors is available for outline use. These include
spot as well as process color choices. To access the Outline Color
Palette, click on the color palette icon on the Outline menu. When
you get into color fills later in this chapter, you will see that this
dialogue box is similar to the Uniform Fill dialogue box (see
fig. 6.15).

The first option in the Outline Color dialogue box is the choice of
color specification method: spot or process color. Choose a
graphic's color method according to the type of printing press that
it will ultimately be printed on.

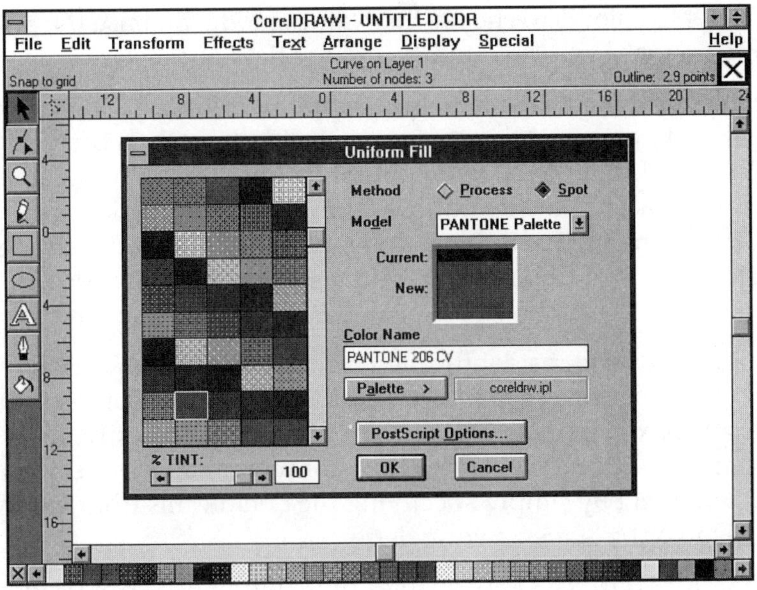

Figure 6.15:

The Uniform Fill Color dialogue box.

To select a color, click on it with the left mouse button. As you scroll through the different color choices, you will notice that Draw shows a color swatch and (possibly) a name for each selected color. Once again, use the on-screen color sample as a loose guide only. It is not accurate. To specify colors precisely, you *must* use an actual printed process or PANTONE color guide.

Spot Color Outlines: If the graphic is to be reproduced using PANTONE colors, click Spot. Draw enables you to choose PANTONE colors, either visually from the PANTONE palette or by name. To switch between the two, click on Model and choose your poison from the pop-up menu.

If you use the palette method, you will notice that, as you click on each color, its PANTONE number appears in the Color Name box. You cannot specify directly by number in this box, but all inks are in sequential order. Need a PANTONE 288 blue? Scroll to the blues, and start clicking while looking for 288 in the Color Name box. However, this is not the most direct method.

If you like to be dead sure about what you are selecting, you can specify by Name. Here, you can scroll through the ink colors numerically rather than visually. The fastest way to specify a

PANTONE color is to choose the Names model and use the Search String option. Type the number into the field and *Voila!*

With spot colors, it is easy to specify tint percentages. This can greatly extend the color range of a printed piece. Reds can yield pinks, dark blues can spawn lighter blues, and so on. When the file is output as color separations, each color's separation will include all the tints of a color, along with the color at full strength. To specify a Spot Color tint percentage, click on the up/down arrows at the % tint box, or type in the tint percentage directly.

Shortcut

A quick way to replace the number in any of the value boxes in CorelDRAW! is to position the cursor on the number you want to change and double-click. This highlights the entire number. You can then type in the new number without first deleting the old characters.

You can also render a depth-filled black-and-white graphic by using the full range of grays made available on the Outline Color dialogue box. Simply leave the color at Black and specify the percentage of tint. This can lead to a far more realistic effect than you would get by simply specifying the default fills from the fly-out menu or on-screen color palette.

PostScript Options: Draw enables those with PostScript printers to specify the PostScript screen type of any spot color outline. The subject of PostScript halftone screens will be covered in the Fill tool section. In addition, you can overprint spot or process colors using this dialogue box (more in Chapter 12).

Process-Color Outlines: If the graphic is to be printed on a four-color press, click Process. Outline colors will then be specified in percentages of cyan, yellow, magenta, and black (CMYK), or by one of the other process color models.

As you select different colors, you will notice that a descriptive name may pop up in the Color Name box. This is a nice touch that proves itself useful when you begin building your own colors. For instance, say that you are illustrating a woman's face. You can mix specific colors for each tone, calling them by descriptive names like ruby lips, earlobe, nostril, rosy blush, and so on.

How are process colors specified? While the Outline Color dialogue box is in Process color mode, click Model to summon a pop-up menu that enables you to specify process colors in a number of ways. Color can be chosen using one of a number of methods: CMYK (Cyan/Magenta/Yellow/Black), RGB (Red/Green/Blue), HSB (Hue/Saturation/Brightness), Named, or TRUMATCH. This diversity can be confusing; there are few reasons to use anything but CMYK (or TRUMATCH) for four-color print work. RGB and HSB are common in the computer video world but not for print graphics. If you specify colors using either RGB or HSB, the colors will be converted to CMYK values when the file is printed (although Corel states that the conversion will not be exact).

Once you have chosen a process color model (CMYK is recommended for print work), you can go about mixing colors via one of two methods. The first method is to specify the exact amount of cyan, yellow, magenta, and black ink via the slide bars or numeric entry. As you change the ink values, you will get an on-screen representation. The second method is to use the Visual Selector.

The Visual Selector

The Visual Selector is a snazzy way to choose colors. It consists of two separate but linked color boxes. The large box controls the amount of cyan and magenta while the skinny box controls the amount of yellow. As you click and drag the cursor around, the CMYK values are calculated; when you release the mouse button, they pop into place.

The Visual Selector uses a process known as "Gray Component Replacement" (GCR) to reduce the amount of ink used. The concept behind GCR is that you can remove equal amounts of cyan, magenta, and yellow, and replace them with black while rendering the same color. The black makes colors "snap" by adding contrast.

TRUMATCH Color

TRUMATCH color is one of the most significant additions to CorelDRAW! 3.0. It is a method for specifying process colors, by which hues are described in exact terms. For example, picking TRUMATCH 18-a from the color palette specifies a shade of green that is built from 100 percent yellow, 0 percent magenta, 85 percent cyan, and 0 percent black. By specifying exact colors, TRUMATCH provides a common ground for designers, service bureaus, color trade shops, and, most important, printers.

Shortcut

Spot color specified with PANTONE numbers can be converted to its process color equivalents (once again, this will not be exact). It is a neat little trick: specify a spot color, click Process, and boom—a process color! Unfortunately, this does not work in reverse.

To access TRUMATCH colors, you must first load the TRUMATCH palette. Clicking on the Palette button summons a menu that enables you to load palettes via the Open Palette dialogue box. As you may have guessed, clicking on TRUMATCH.PAL will load the TRUMATCH palette.

As with PANTONE colors, it is imperative to use a swatch book to choose accurate TRUMATCH colors. Once again, these swatch books require an additional investment that is well worth the few dollars you will spend. It is foolish to rely on your screen to pick colors that will be used on a printing press—even if you have a very expensive 24-bit display system! Of course, the better the display is, the closer the color will be.

Printing with process colors is a costly business that is best left to the professionals. One cannot expect that mere ownership of a program like Draw gives one the experience and wisdom to work with process color. This is not to say that it should not be attempted. But it should be approached with extreme caution (and deep pockets).

Using the Fill Tool

Tapping into the fill tool's capabilities is a little like sneaking into Grandma's jelly cupboard. There are so many delicious choices to pick from that it can be tough to decide on which one to use. Draw gives you enough choices so that you will not become bored with the same old flavors. Each one is a treat!

The Fill fly-out menu offers the default fills of black, white, 10, 30, 50, 70 and 90 percent tints, along with no fill. In addition, the menu gives you access to the Fill Roll Up menu, Uniform Fill, Full- and Two-Color Pattern Fill, Fountain Fill, and PostScript Texture Fill dialogue boxes. Figure 6.16 illustrates this menu, and figure 2.19 in Chapter 2 presents an annotated illustration of it.

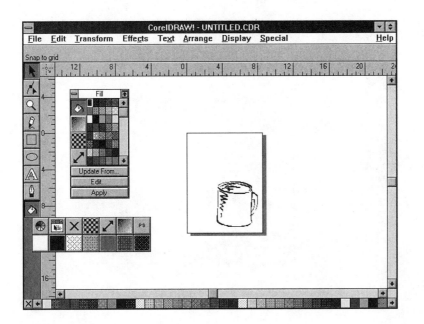

Figure 6.16:

The Fill fly-out and
Roll-Up menus.

Uniform Fills

At the far left of the Fill fly-out menu, you will find Uniform Fill.
It is accessed through a color wheel icon. A click on the color
wheel summons the Uniform Fill dialogue box.

This dialogue box looks and functions exactly like the Outline
Color dialogue box. You are once again offered the choice of spot
or process color, as well as access to the PostScript Halftone
Screen dialogue box.

Shortcut

Press Shift-F11 to
get to the Uniform
Fill dialogue box.

PostScript Screens

One of the more interesting features of the Uniform Fill and
Outline Color dialogue boxes is the opportunity to specify different PostScript halftones and to set screen frequencies and angles
(see fig. 6.17). This flexibility lets you design artwork that uses a
wide range of fill patterns.

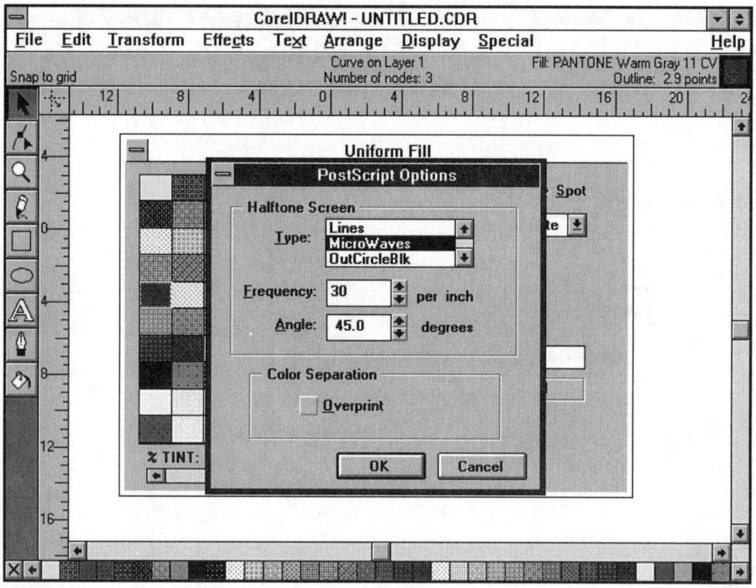

Figure 6.17:

PostScript Halftone
Screen dialogue box.

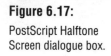

Screen Types: The PostScript halftone screens are most enticing when used with screen frequencies of 30 per inch or less. With low frequencies, the different screen types become prominent, and can be used to their best advantage. At higher screen frequencies, the eye loses focus on the patterns, resulting in the visual interpretation of gray rather than of black-and-white lines.

PostScript Halftone Screen types include: Default, Dot, Line, Diamond, Dot2, Grid, Lines, MicroWaves, OutCircleBlk, OutCircleWhi, and Star (see fig. 6.18). As with the Outline color choices, you cannot specify the PostScript Halftone Screen when using process color.

Screen Frequency and Angle: Every halftone screen has a frequency and angle. The common rule of thumb is that the higher the quality of printing, the higher you should go with screen frequency. The finer the screen, the less noticeable it will be to the naked eye. Newspapers customarily use halftone screens of 85 lines per inch while magazines use 110, 133, or even higher.

If you are outputting to a desktop laser printer, try not to specify more than 60 lines per inch. High resolution imagesetters can commonly handle screens of 150 lines per inch. Screen angle becomes readily apparent at low screen frequencies and is also a very important part of process color separations.

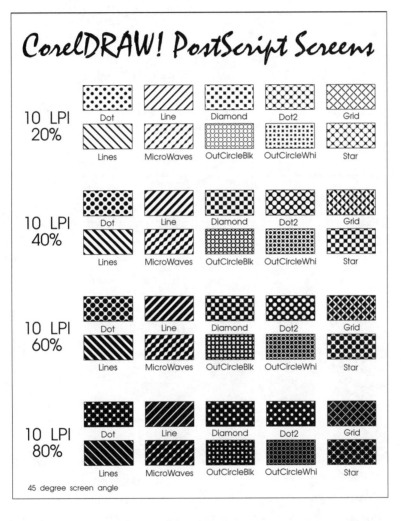

Figure 6.18:

Examples of PostScript halftone screens.

Overprint: If you are preparing spot colors for printing, there is a good chance that your printer (the person, not the machine) needs overprints or traps. Chapter 12 deals with this subject.

Fountain Fills

Fountain fill is one of Draw's most seductive features. Everyone has been (or will be) attracted to the smoothness that this tool provides in blending one color to the next. This appealing characteristic can be used with either spot or process color.

Draw provides two types of fountain fills: linear and radial, which you can specify by means of the Fountain Fill dialogue box (see fig. 6.19). Linear fountain fills start at one side of an object and migrate to the facing side (see fig. 6.20). Radial fountain fills start at the outside edges of an object and radiate inward to the object's center point.

Figure 6.19:

The Fountain Fill dialogue box.

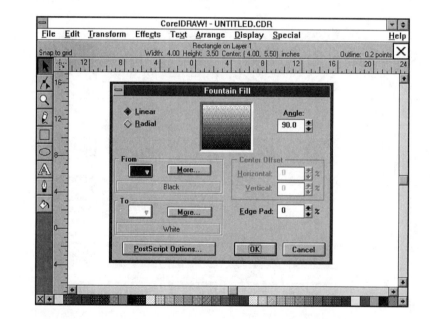

In the next exercise, you will set up a simple one-color linear fountain fill and try setting different fill angles. Full-color editing should be on for this exercise. If it is not, turn it on now by pressing Shift-F9.

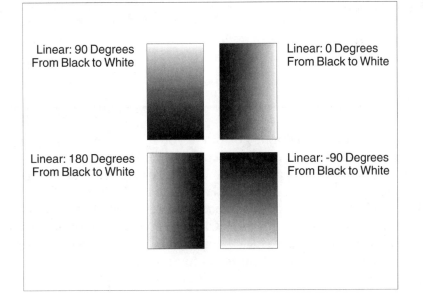

Figure 6.20:
Linear fountain fills.

Experimenting with Linear Fountain Fills

Click the rectangle tool

Hold down Ctrl and draw a
three-inch square

Click the fill tool   The Fill fly-out menu
                                               appears.

Click Fountain Fill   The Fountain Fill icon
                                               looks like a diagonal
                                               gradient.

The default fill should appear as follows: Linear; 90 degrees; Process;
From Black; To White. If these are not your settings, change them for the
purposes of this exercise.

Click OK   The square is fountain-
                                               filled.

At 90 degrees, the square is filled from the bottom up. Change the
direction of fill.

Click the fill tool   The Fill fly-out menu
                                               appears.

continues

Click Fountain Fill	The Fountain Fill dialogue box appears.
Change to **-90** *degrees*	
Click OK	The square is fountain-filled.

If you like, try setting the fill to 180 or 0 degrees.

Shortcut

Press F11 to get to the Fountain Fill dialogue box.

The Fountain Fill dialogue box offers you a choice of Draw's full complement of colors and PostScript Options. Colors may be freely specified using any color model. Clicking More brings up a dialogue box (that looks remarkably like the Uniform Fill or Outline Color dialogue boxes) that provides access to any possible color fountain fill (see fig. 6.21). Clicking PostScript Options while in Spot Color mode provides access to PostScript halftone screens, which can add dramatic effects to fountain fills.

Figure 6.21:

Centered and Offset Radial fountain fill.

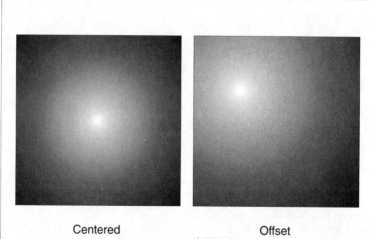

Centered

Offset
(-22% Horizontal, 18% Vertical)

Edge Pad enables you to increase the fountain fill starting and ending color bands by up to 45 percent. Since fountain fills follow an object's bounding box, irregularly shaped objects can be persnickety; Edge Pad assures that the starting/ending fountain fill colors hit the edges of the object, rather than fall outside.

CorelDRAW! version 3.0 introduced the capability to interactively alter linear fountain fill angles. Remember how you changed the Calligraphic pen shape earlier in the chapter? You can change angles just as easily! Just click and drag in the fountain fill display window. Your cursor will turn into a + sign, and a line will appear, drawing itself from the middle of the window through the cursor to the edge of the window. As you drag around the window, you will notice the angle percentage changing. When you release the mouse button, the display window will be redrawn with the angle you have specified. The easiest way to understand how this works is to simply click near the edge that you want the fountain fill to go *to*.

Radial Fountain Fills: Now that you have seen how a linear fountain fill works, try a radial fill. The Fountain Fill dialogue box enables radial fountain fills that flow to the center of an object. The From color spec refers to the outside of the object. The To color spec refers to the inside of the object. There are no angles. What if you want to have the radial fill flow to the top left corner? Don't worry; there is a very simple method to achieve the effect.

The easiest method of changing the "lighting angle" is to use the interactive click-and-drag technique. When you click in the radial fountain fill display window, crosshairs appear, enabling you to drag to any position you want. Alternatively, you can specify Center Offset in horizontal and vertical percentages. Positive values push the light source upward and to the right. Negative values push the light source downward and to the left. The Fountain Fill dialogue box also enables you to use Edge Pad.

Fill the square you just drew with a radial fountain fill and try different center offsets.

Using Center Offset To Alter the Lighting Angle of a Radial Fill

Click the square

Click the fill tool   The Fill fly-out menu appears.

Click Fountain Fill   The Fountain Fill dialogue box appears.

continues

Click **R**adial	
Set: From Black	
Set: To White	
Click OK	
Click **E**dit	The Edit menu appears.
Click **D**uplicate	The square is duplicated.
Drag the duplicate square below the original	

Now that you have set the fill and made a duplicate, use Center Offset to change the lighting angle.

Click the fill tool	The Fill fly-out menu appears.
Click Fountain Fill	The Fountain Fill dialogue box appears.
At Horizontal: type **-25**	
At Vertical: type **25**	
Click OK	The fountain fill is offset.

The center of the radial fill should now be in the upper left corner of the square. It is fairly easy to alter the lighting angle with this method, once you get the hang of it. Figure 6.22 shows samples of the effects you can achieve. Go ahead and alter the Center Offset by using the interactive method.

CorelDRAW! enables you to create fountain fills with either spot or process colors. You cannot have a fill that changes from a spot color to a process color. However, if you specify the first color as spot and the second as process, the first color will be automatically converted to process.

Fountain fills can give a dimensional look to an illustration. Care must be taken, however, to limit the use of the feature. Fountain fills are quite demanding on the printer, and the use of too many fountain fills, or fountain-filling objects with many nodes, will slow your printer down. Sometimes, using too many fountain fills or fountain-filling an object with many nodes will actually prevent a file from printing. The time it takes for your preview screen to redraw also increases dramatically. Fountain-filling a rectangle is safe; but doing the same to an object with dozens of curved nodes is just asking for a long run on your printer's RIP. Of course, you could go out to lunch while you are waiting!

Figure 6.22:

Texture fills.

If a fountain fill-laden file refuses to print, try replacing some of the fountain fills with solid color fills. Avoid rotating fountain-filled objects. Also try minimizing the number of nodes in any fountain-filled object. The trick is to construct the leanest file possible. The subject of building intricate illustrations is covered in Chapter 8.

PostScript Texture Fills

The PostScript Texture fills are located under the letters PS on the Fill fly-out menu. They are available only when printing on a PostScript output device. The 42 different characteristic fills can be individually altered to yield a seemingly limitless number of possibilities. Figure 6.22 shows some sample effects.

Draw's documentation contains a comprehensive section that displays the many texture fills, along with sample settings for each.

To specify a PostScript texture fill, click PS on the Fill fly-out menu. The PostScript Texture dialogue box (see fig. 6.23) enables you to specify the type of fill and its parameters, which may include: Frequency, Linewidth, ForegroundGray, and BackgroundGray. Parameters depend on the fill being used. These parameters differentiate the many possibilities within each fill type.

Figure 6.23:

The PostScript Texture dialogue box.

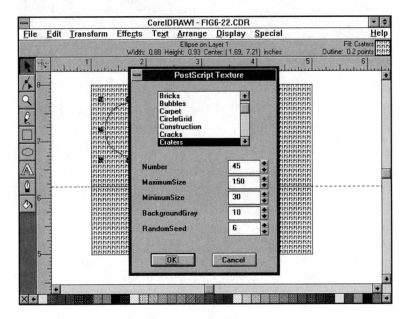

NOTE

Don't expect to see texture fills in the preview window. Rather than a screen representation of the fill, a PS motif will fill the object.

The warning given on fountain fills holds doubly true for PostScript texture fills. They may look real neat, but they can take a long time to print. These little critters (one is even called "Reptiles") are an extreme drain on output device resources. If plans include using texture fills, be sure to allow plenty of time for the printer to image the file.

Hopefully, advances in PostScript technology and increases in printer speed will make these warnings a thing of the past. Only PostScript printers can print PostScript fills—yet another reason to recommend using one!

Two-Color Pattern Fills

Although CorelDRAW! is basically a vector-based illustration package, the program ships with a number of two-color bit map patterns, and additional patterns are available from a variety of sources. Bit maps can be imported from scanned images or created in CorelPHOTO-PAINT!, Windows Paintbrush, or other paint programs. Draw's Two-Color Pattern editor can create new patterns or edit existing ones. There is even a Create Pattern option on the Special menu for creating bit map (as well as vector) pattern fills from existing CorelDRAW! objects.

The Two-Color Pattern Fill icon (located on the Fill fly-out menu) looks like a tiny checkerboard. Clicking on it summons up the Two-Color Pattern dialogue box (see fig. 6.24). Here, you can click on the preview pattern to access the pop-up menu, and use the scroll bars to select a bit map pattern visually. If you fail to find a pattern to your liking, you can import or create a new one.

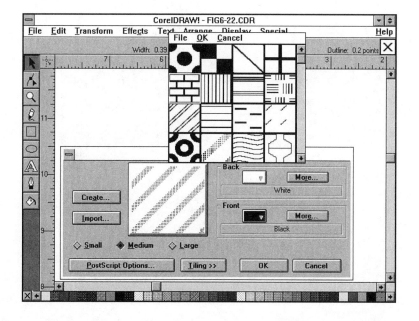

Figure 6.24:

The Two-Color Pattern Fill dialogue box, with pop-up menu.

As its name implies, each Two-Color Pattern fill can only have two colors: a foreground and a background. They are initially black and white (respectively), but they do not have to stay that way! You can use either spot or process methods to colorize patterns. However, it will not allow you to mix process and spot colors in a pattern. Plan your color scheme carefully; you can only use two process, or two spot colors. You can not use one spot and one process. The dialogue box includes a handy preview feature so that you can try applying different foreground and background colors without leaving the box. PostScript Options provide overprinting capabilities, and control over PostScript screens (in spot color mode only).

Pattern fills are based on the tile concept. The dialogue box provides three default tile sizes: small, medium, and large. Clicking on Tiling>>, expands the dialogue box, and your tiling options (see fig. 6.25). You are free to resize tile width and height to suit your needs. Although the maximum tile size is 3 × 3 inches, be careful not to stretch out or squish tiles too far. Remember, these are bit maps, and will become jagged or blurred once removed from their original size and scale.

Figure 6.25:

Two-Color Pattern Tiling Options.

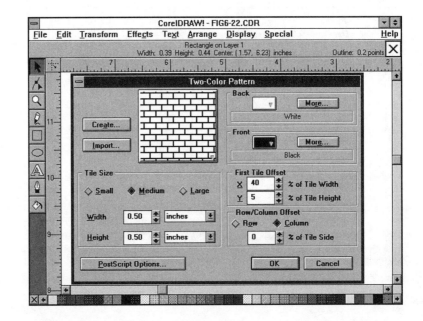

Patterns can be offset to compensate for discrepancies in object size the same way a tile man sets floor tile. If a pattern does not fit an object cleanly, you can use X and/or Y offsets to lay down the pattern precisely. You also have the option of using Inter Row/ Column Offset to stagger the pattern.

Working with matrix patterns takes some thought, but sometimes the best stuff happens by chance. Once again, the time spent here is worth the effort you put in. You will learn more about how patterns work by experimentation.

Two-Color Pattern Fills are print-time consumers. The more times a pattern is reproduced, the larger your print file will become and the longer it will take to print. For this reason, patterns should be used with caution. The caveats that apply to fountain fills also apply here.

The Two-Color Pattern Editor works in three bit map sizes and four pen sizes (see fig. 6.26). It is summoned by clicking on the Create button. The Editor may remind you of Windows Paint-brush in its Zoom Up mode. Click on a square with your left mouse button to turn it black, and click with your right mouse button to turn it white.

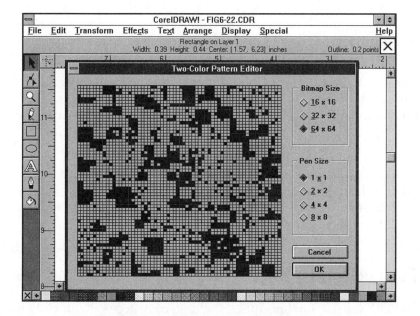

Figure 6.26:

The Two-Color pattern editor.

Full-Color Pattern Fills

Somewhere in between Two-Color Patterns and PostScript Textures lies Full-Color (or vector) patterns. Drawing from a little of both, Full-Color Pattern fills can offer more flexibility than either of the aforementioned fills. However, Full-Color Pattern fills fall to the same print-time malady as do all other "fancy" fills. If you want to use them, be prepared to wait for the printer.

Like Two-Color Patterns, Full-Color Pattern fills can be created from existing CorelDRAW! objects with the Create Pattern option on the Special menu. Unlike Two-Color Patterns, however, you can use more than two colors or tints.

Full-Color Patterns are stored as files. When you choose a Full-Color Pattern, you select a file from the Load Full-Color Pattern dialogue box. Thankfully, a preview window lets you check out the different patterns one by one.

Like Two-Color Patterns, you can control the tile size and offsets of Full-Color Patterns up to a maximum of three inches by three inches. However, you cannot alter the color of a Full-Color Pattern through the Full-Color Pattern dialogue box. To do so, you must edit the objects that the Full-Color Pattern was based upon, and recreate the pattern.

Editing an existing Full-Color Pattern fill is no more difficult than editing any other Draw file. To edit an existing Full-Color Pattern fill, you open it, edit it, and then use Create Pattern to save it (see figs. 6.27 and 6.28). The trick is to use the PAT file extension in the Open Drawing dialogue box in place of the CDR extension.

Unlike Two-Color Patterns, Full-Color Patterns can be resized without losing image quality. But once again, Full-Color Patterns are tough on the printer. The more patterns you use, the longer you can expect to wait!

The Fill Roll-Up Menu

The Fill Roll-Up enables quick-picking, easy access to almost all of Draw's fills: Uniform, Fountain, Two-, and Full-Color Patterns (see fig. 6.29). In addition, it enables you to Update From (which is the same as Copy Style From) any other fill, and can also whisk you to the supporting fill dialogue boxes (via the Edit button) to make more involved fill decisions. There is one slight omission: you cannot access PostScript Pattern Fills from the Roll-Up menu.

Figure 6.27:

Loading a Full-Color Pattern.

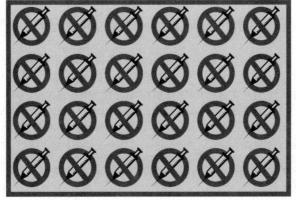

Figure 6.28:

The Full-Color Pattern printed.

You can save plenty of time with the Fill Roll-Up menu. Assigning existing Two- or Full-Color Pattern fills (from their respective pop-up menus) is a breeze, as is altering Fountain Fill characteristics.

Figure 6.29:

The Annotated Fill Roll-Up menu.

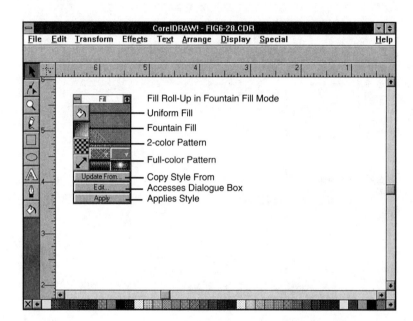

You have just covered a lot of ground, including learning how to specify color outlines, fills, and patterns. In the next section, you are going to put that theory to work as you build an opening slide.

Creating Charts and Slides

Producing charts and slides is important to many corporate electronic artists. Preparing business presentations makes up a large portion of many a corporate shop's workload. Many computer programs enable users to prepare colorful charts, graphs, and text for use in 35mm slide presentations. CorelDRAW! is but one of them.

Prior to version 3.0, CorelDRAW! had no built-in automatic charting capabilities. To produce charts with the program, you either had to import the chart or build it from scratch. Thankfully,

CorelCHART! was introduced with Draw version 3.0. This program fills a gap by providing advanced 3-D charting in the Corel environment. You can quickly and easily create stunning charts, and incorporate them with your other artwork. With spreadsheet import capabilities and other powerful features, Chart literally adds a new dimension to CorelDRAW!. Chapter 14 covers CorelCHART in-depth.

As you progress through the rest of the exercises, you will put Draw's fountain and color fill capabilities to use. Why cover color and slides in the same chapter? At the present time, color printers are too expensive to be commonplace. Proofing in color is important, but most people only have black-and-white printers—whether dot matrix, ink jet, or laser—hooked up to their computers.

When you proof an image that is intended to be black and white, you get black-and-white prints. That is no problem. But when you proof an image that is intended to be color, you still only get black-and-white prints. Currently, 35mm slides are among the least expensive ways to produce color output from Draw.

Producing Charts and Graphs

Before the advent of personal computers, charts and graphs were produced in one of two ways. The first method was the old-fashioned way, on a drawing board with skilled designers wielding technical pens, T-squares, and triangles. The second method was accomplished with programmers, mainframe computers, and plotters. If you worked either way in the past, you are sure to appreciate the changes that the past decade has brought.

Of these two methods, the drawing board was capable of yielding much more distinctive results. Artists are capable of making aesthetic decisions; computers are not.

Thankfully, today's dedicated PC graphing software programs offer far more flexibility than their mainframe ancestors did. With a trained operator, excellent results are possible in real time. With an untrained operator, however, you do not get what you do not pay for.

CorelDRAW! and CorelCHART! bring together the methods employed by designers and computer users. These two applications should form a cornerstone of your slide and chart-building repertoire. You should also have a spreadsheet program to round out the set.

Building Your Own Pie Charts

If necessary, you can build your own pie charts by using the shape tool to modify a circle into a pie slice (see fig. 6.30). This method is not automated, but it can be useful in a pinch. Simply click on an ellipse's node with the shape tool and drag it around. Dragging inside the ellipse will yield a pie slice. Dragging outside the ellipse will create an arc.

Figure 6.30:

A pie slice made with the shape tool.

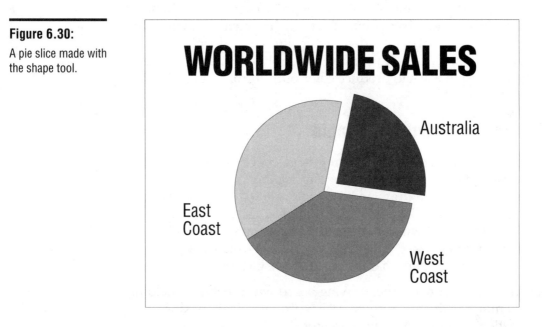

You need a separate circle for each slice. If you were planning six slices, for example, you would copy five more circles on top of the first circle.

The status line will show the angles of the pie slice/arc. Using Ctrl will constrain the pie slice to 15-degree (default setting) increments. To facilitate the alignment of pie wedges, the highlight box is the same size as the original ellipse. If you shift-click or marquee-select all the pie wedges and use horizontal/vertical center to align, things fall a bit short. Enabling Snap-to-Objects works well here.

Making Your Presentation Count

Presentations that consist of boring slide after slide will surely put the audience to sleep. On the other hand, arrays of flashy charts may leave the audience dazed and confused.

Cut presentations down to the minimum. Use only the charts that are absolutely necessary. This will help to prevent the audience from suffering from information overload. Remember, it is too easy for information to get lost in the delivery. The message is the important thing; do not let the medium get in the way.

It is a good idea to provide printed copies of the important information in your presentations. But do not take the visuals, print them out full size, and staple them together. That is just sloppy. Given the time, incorporate the visuals in a document that consists of a written recap of the presentation. Do not make it a rehash of the voice-over; include background information that would be too lengthy for the presentation itself. And do not just read from the slides. Instead, elaborate upon them.

The value of a presentation is not determined solely by its charts and graphs. The complete package is what sells. Make sure it is comprehensive. Artists should strive to eliminate cookie-cutter charts. Do not use a chart program's pre-set defaults for background and text colors if there is time to find something better. Above all, do not put style above substance; strive for style with substance. Use what works.

Right now, stop in at DeLook Design and see what kind of colorful work Joe is getting into.

DeLook Design Lands Rippin' Surfboards, Inc.

The crew at DeLook Design is elated. They have just hooked their first corporate client, Rippin' Surfboards, Inc.. It was not too hard since the president and founder of the company is Joe DeLook's old surfing buddy, Rip Raster.

Rip wants a presentation he can give to the local bank as part of his request for a loan. Rippin' Surfboards is thriving and has outgrown its present location (which is Rip's garage, of course). Rip has just found the perfect spot for his new production facility. The owner is eager to sell and Rip is ready to buy. Unfortunately, all of Rippin' Surfboards' capital is tied up in its inventory. Rip is counting on this presentation to save his business.

Joe DeLook has promised Rip that he can put a slide presentation together in just a couple of days. The presentation will consist of an introductory slide, a text slide, and a chart. In the following exercise, you will make an introductory slide for Rippin' Surfboards, Inc. (see fig. 6.31).

Figure 6.31:

The introductory slide.

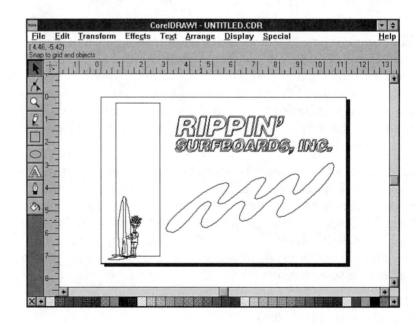

Building Slides

When building images that will ultimately become slides, the first thing you should do is change the page setup to match the aspect ratio of a 35mm slide. Since the size of a 35mm slide is approximately 24 by 36 millimeters, the aspect ratio is 2:3.

Do not worry about making any difficult calculations; once again, Draw makes things a snap. Just click on Slide in the Page Setup dialogue box, and your page size will be instantly configured for the correct aspect ratio. Because this translates to 7.33 inches by 11 inches, you can even proof your work on any Windows-supported printer.

If you do not use the proper page setup, the slide image will probably be clipped or incomplete. Right now, take the time to open a new page and properly set it up for 35mm slides. While you are in Page Setup, you can use Add Page Frame to place a rectangle which you will fill with the background color. When a page frame is initially placed, it will have the default object fill.

By using a page frame, you ensure that the background color will reach to the edge of the image area and no further. If the background color rectangle does not reach the page edge, your slide will be outlined in black or white (depending on how you export your slide).

Do not confuse Page Frame with Paper Color. A page frame is an object that can be filled with any color or pattern, while paper color is a device for on-screen print proofing. Paper Color assigns a "paper shade" of your choice to emulate printing on colored paper. The color exists only in the preview window; it does not appear on the copy that rolls out of your output device.

35mm Slide Page Setup

Click **File**	The File menu appears.
Click **Page Setup**	The Page Setup dialogue box appears.
Click **Slide**	

continues

Click Landscape	
Click Add Page Frame	A Page Frame is added.
Click OK	The page is set up in the proper aspect ratio.
Click **Display**	The Display menu appears.
Click **Grid Setup**	The Grid Setup dialogue box appears.
Change the grid frequency to **3** *per inch*	
Click **S**nap to Grid	
Click OK	

The slide presentation that you are about to construct consists of a group of repetitive elements. Chief among them is the slide structure itself, which is of a rather standard design, incorporating a solid color background with a fountain-filled bar running vertically along the left side.

Along with the overall design, there are three more repetitive elements: the logo and two motifs, a surfer and a wave. Remember, you are at the beach! You will build the slide structure first and then move on to setting the logotype. You will finish up by creating the wave pattern, and importing and coloring the surfer clip art.

Since you used a page frame, the background will reach the page edge. You will fill the Page Frame with a solid color from the Uniform Fill dialogue box.

As you have seen, the Uniform Fill dialogue box offers a choice between spot and process colors. You are going to address the spot colors first. Once you have clicked Spot Color, the dialogue box enables you to choose color as well as tint percentage.

Setting up the Background with a PANTONE Fill

Click Page Frame	
Click the fill tool	The Fill fly-out menu appears.

Click Uniform Fill	The Uniform Fill dialogue box appears.
Click **S**pot	The Dialogue box is configured for spot (PMS) color.

You need to scroll down a bit to get down to the color you want. Remember that when you select a color, the PANTONE number appears in the Ink Name box.

Scroll through the PMS colors
Select PANTONE 255

Click OK	The rectangle is filled with the selected color.

With the solid filled background in place, draw and fill a vertical rectangle along the left side of your slide layout.

Drawing and Fountain-Filling the Rectangle

Click **D**isplay
Click Show **R**ulers *(if they are not on)*
Click the rectangle tool
Position the cursor .67 inches from the left side and .33 inches from the top of the page
Draw a rectangle 2.00 inches wide by 6.67 inches tall, as shown in figure 6.32

Click the fill tool	The Fill fly-out menu appears.
Click Fountain Fill	The Fountain Fill dialogue box appears.
Click **L**inear	
At From, Click More	Fountain Fill color dialogue box appears.
Click **S**pot	

Select: PANTONE Process Blue
Click OK

continues

At To, Click More	Fountain Fill color dialogue box appears.
Select: PANTONE 255	
Click OK	
Click OK *again*	The rectangle is fountain-filled.

Figure 6.32:

Rectangle for fountain-filling.

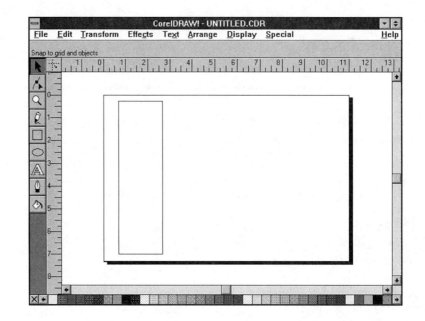

The rectangle should be 100 percent process blue at the bottom, fading to the background's PMS 255 at the top. An interesting twist to a standard layout.

Now, set the logotype. You are going to use another fountain fill on the word RIPPIN' and a solid color fill on SURFBOARDS, INC. Always be careful not to overdo it with fountain-filled text—large blocks of text or complex letter forms can lead to trouble.

Setting the RIPPIN' Logotype

Click the text tool
Click the center of the page

At the text I bar, enter: **RIPPIN'**
Press Ctrl-T

The Artistic Text dialogue box appears.

Scroll down to and click Switzerland-Black
At Style, click Italic
At Point Size, enter: **84**
Click **S**pacing

The Spacing dialogue box appears.

At Inter-Character, enter: **-1**
Click OK
Click OK *again*
Click the page below RIPPIN'
At the text I bar, type:

SURFBOARDS, INC.

Press Ctrl-T

The Artistic Text dialogue box appears.

At Point Size, enter: **48**
Click **S**pacing

The Spacing dialogue box appears.

At Inter-Character, enter: **-1**
At Inter-Word, enter: **50**
Click OK
Click OK *again*
Click the pick tool
Click RIPPIN'
Click the fill tool

The Fill fly-out menu appears.

Click Fountain Fill

The Fountain Fill dialogue box appears.

At From, Click More

Fountain Fill color dialogue box appears.

Click **S**pot
Select: PANTONE 354
Click OK
At To, Click More

The Fountain Fill color dialogue box appears.

Select: PANTONE YELLOW
Click OK

continues

Click OK *again*	The type is fountain-filled.
Click SURFBOARDS, INC.	
Click the fill tool	The Fill fly-out menu appears.
Click Uniform Fill	The Uniform Fill dialogue box appears.
Click **S**pot	
At Color, select: PANTONE 354	
Click OK	The type is uniformly filled.

Now, drag the type so that the words are in position with each other. Use the align horizontal left command if necessary.

Shift-click or marquee-select **RIPPIN'** *and* **SURF-BOARDS, INC.**	
Press Ctrl-G	The logotype is grouped (see fig. 6.33).

Now that the logotype is positioned and grouped, add a drop shadow behind the type to make the logo stand out. With the logotype still selected, take the following steps:

Press Ctrl-D	The logotype is duplicated.
Drag the duplicate logotype a few points below and to the left of the original	
Click the fill tool	The Fill fly-out menu appears.
Click Black	The drop shadow is filled with black.
Shift-click the original logotype	The shadow logotype should still be selected.
Click **A**rrange	
Click **R**everse Order	The drop shadow is behind the original logotype.
Press Ctrl-G	The logotype is grouped.

Figure 6.33:
The logotype
in place.

Now draw the squiggly wave symbol and fill it with a graduated
fill. Remember the warning about fountain fills? Keep the number
of nodes to a minimum to avoid trouble. You are going to be
assigning the exact same fill as the first RIPPIN'. If you would
like, you may use Update From (on the Fill Roll-Up menu) or
Copy Style From (on the Edit menu) instead of manually assigning the fountain fill. Of course, you will need to perform a couple
of ungroups first!

Drawing and Filling the Wave

Click the pencil tool	
Draw the wave symbol, as shown in figure 6.34	
Click the fill tool	The Fill fly-out menu appears.
Click Fountain Fill	The Fountain Fill dialogue box appears.
At From, Click More	The Fountain Fill color dialogue box appears.

continues

Click **S**pot
Select: PANTONE 354
Click OK
At To, Click More

The Fountain Fill color
dialogue box appears.

Select: PANTONE YELLOW
Click OK
Click OK *again*

The type is fountain-
filled.

Save the file with the name RIPPIN.

Figure 6.34:

The wave.

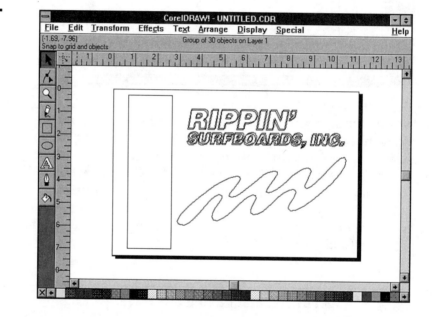

The last element is the surfer. Thankfully, you do not have to
draw him, just import him. You will find the surfer on the CD-
ROM that comes with CorelDRAW! version 3.0. He is located in
the Sport library.

Bringing in the Surfer from the Sports Library

Click File	The File menu appears.
Click Import	The Import dialogue box appears.
Maneuver to your CD-ROM drive	
Double-click clipart	
Scroll down, double-click sports	
At List Files of Type, select CorelDRAW!, *.CDR	
Roll down, double-click Surfer	The surfer appears (see fig. 6.35).
Click OK	

Figure 6.35:
The surfer.

On the slide, the surfer is a black-and-white dude in a multi-colored world. You do not want a boring-looking surfer, so pick him apart and fill him with whatever colors you like.

Because you want to produce a full-color slide, you need to ungroup the surfer and fill the individual objects with some surfer-like colors. To do this with the largest possible number of colors, use process fills to colorize the image.

Usually, mixing PANTONE and process colors together is an expensive situation. But since these compositions are to be imaged as 35mm slides, you can mix colors as you see fit. Just don't expect to do this with a normal print job—unless you have an unlimited budget and absolutely no conscience!

The process color uniform fill option works in a manner similar to the spot color option. The difference is that if you click Process instead of Spot, you can specify uniform fills by entering exact percentages of any combination of the four process colors in addition to selecting prespecified, named colors.

To reiterate: Don't get lulled into specifying color based on what you see on the screen. Use a PANTONE or TRUMATCH swatch book. If you are specifying color for a certain printing press, it is important to have an absolute reference. Your printer may be able to supply a comprehensive process color guide run from his own press.

Ungroup the surfer and individually color his parts. Color just his limbs, chest, head, and shorts. You can finish him up and regroup him later.

Coloring the Surfer

Click the zoom tool	The Zoom fly-out menu appears.
Click the +	
Marquee-select the surfer	The screen zooms up.
Click the pick tool	
Click the surfer	
Press Ctrl-U	The surfer is ungrouped.

Now that there are 34 separate objects , try to colorize them in a logical manner. Start by shift-clicking the surfer's legs, arms, and head.

You are going to create a named color that you will call *Surfer's Tan*. This will make it easy to identify in the Fill dialogue boxes and on the status line. You will notice that as you repeatedly go back into the Uniform Fill dialogue box, it remembers where you left it. The dialogue box will be in whichever mode you left it.

Creating a Named Color

Shift-click the surfer's legs, arms, and head

Click the fill tool — The Fill fly-out menu appears.

Click Uniform Fill — The Uniform Fill dialogue box appears.

Click Process — The dialogue box configures for process color.

At Model, click **CMYK**

At cyan, enter: **0**

At magenta, enter: **25**

At yellow, enter: **30**

At black, enter: **10**

At Color Name, type: **Surfer's Tan**

Click OK — The surfer gets a slight tan.

Marquee-select the nose and mouth

Click the fill tool — The Fill fly-out menu appears.

Click Uniform Fill — The Uniform Fill dialogue box appears.

At cyan, enter: **0**

At magenta, enter: **40**

At yellow, enter: **30**

At black, enter: **10**

At Color Name, type: **Surfer's Nose**	
Click OK	The surfer's nose gets a burn.
Click the surfer's shorts	
Click the fill tool	The Fill fly-out menu appears.
Click Uniform Fill	The Uniform Fill dialogue box appears.
At cyan, enter: **0**	
At magenta, enter: **77**	
At yellow, enter: **27**	
At black, enter: **23**	
At Color Name, type: **Surfer's Shorts**	
Click OK	The surfer puts on some bright shorts.
Click the surfer's hairdo	
Click the fill tool	The Fill fly-out menu appears.
Click Uniform Fill	The Uniform Fill dialogue box appears.
At cyan, enter: **0**	
At magenta, enter: **0**	
At yellow, enter: **100**	
At black, enter: **5**	
At Color Name, type: **Surfer's Do**	
Click OK	The surfer bleaches his hair.

That should give you the general idea of how the process (no pun intended) works. Remember, the only time you would be able to affordably mix this many PANTONE and process colors together would be when printing to a slidemaker or color proof printer.

Continue filling the Surfboard and puddle with whatever colors you like. Stick with a somewhat limited palette, that is, pick up the colors that have been used elsewhere. This will help to tie the slide together.

When you are done, scale the surfer down to 30 percent of original size, and drag him to just above the bottom of the vertical bar. You have created Rip's introductory slide!

Using Palettes to Your Advantage

Specifying colors in CorelDRAW! can be simplified through intelligent use of the on-screen color palette. You may have noticed it on the bottom of the Draw window, and wondered why you are not using that. Well, you *should* use the on-screen palette whenever possible, in the same manner a painter loads paint onto his palette. It is a great time-saver. But you must understand how to specify and mix the colors before you can start saving the time.

The on-screen color palette saves you time by allowing you to specify an object's fill or outline color with one mouse click. With an object selected, position your cursor over the chosen color, and click with the left mouse button to fill, click with the right mouse button to outline. Instant colors! See the "X" button at the far left of the palette? Selecting an object and clicking the X with your left mouse button will assign a fill of None. And clicking with your right mouse button will assign an outline of None.

The palette can be switched on—in either spot or process color modes—or off via the Display menu. To move through the on-screen color palette, there is a pair of scroll buttons. But, if you have to use them, you are overlooking the advantage of having the necessary colors loaded at the top of the palette.

When you start working on a piece of artwork, consider the color scheme. First, decide whether the image will be constructed with spot or process colors. As the artwork evolves into the production stage, you decide which colors you want to load onto your palette. Then you arrange them to fit your working style.

To make the most of the palette, you reorder the colors so that those you use most are at the top of the list. To shuffle the colors around, go to the Uniform Fill dialogue box palette. There, you can click and drag colors, positioning them to set up your palette in the order that best suits the artwork at hand. The order of the

Uniform Fill dialogue box palette matches the order of the on-screen color palette.

To create a new color and add it to the palette, switch Method to CMYK. You can then mix up a color to your liking and assign it a descriptive name of your choice. When you are done creating your custom color, click on the Palette button, and click Add Color To Palette. You then have the option of saving your custom palette. It is easy to both add and delete palette colors via the Palette button. Loading and saving palettes is also a breeze. In all, proper use of CorelDRAW!'s palettes will add to your enjoyment of the program and help you be more productive, to boot!

Summary

Draw provides a full range of outline and fill capabilities. This chapter has covered the advanced features of both, while using a "real world" example of 35mm slidemaking as a vehicle for displaying Draw's utility as a powerful communications tool. While Draw itself is not a charting or graphing program, CorelCHART! is a powerful addition to the Corel Graphics Toolkit.

Your role as an electronic artist is to help your clients get their messages across. Whether the medium is print, slides, or even (as you will see in Chapter 10) three-dimensional objects, Draw enables you to do it right. The program's control over color, in both PANTONE and process permutations, makes it an essential instrument in your quest for artistic success.

As you move through the rest of this book, Draw's potential should become increasingly obvious. It is up to you to harness that power, whether your field is commercial art or somewhere within the fine arts.

7

Bit Maps and Draw

raw is a vector-based drawing program rather than a bit-mapped paint program. Still, Draw does a nice job of importing bit-mapped images from other sources, and Draw can even be used to export bit maps of its own. This chapter discusses the different types of bit maps that can be used within the Draw environment. CorelDRAW! version 3.0 introduces CorelPHOTO-PAINT!, a powerful bit-mapped paint program. While Photo-Paint is touched upon here, you will find it covered in-depth in Chapter 13.

Unlike object-oriented images, a bit-mapped image is rasterized—that is, imaged dot by dot. Each pixel on the screen corresponds to a single dot on the output image. A bit-mapped image could be considered a grid of pixels or a matrix of dots. As you can see in figure 7.1, the individual dots in a bit-map matrix can be either on (in black, or in a variety of colors or grays) or off (white).

Figure 7.1:

The bit map
blown up.

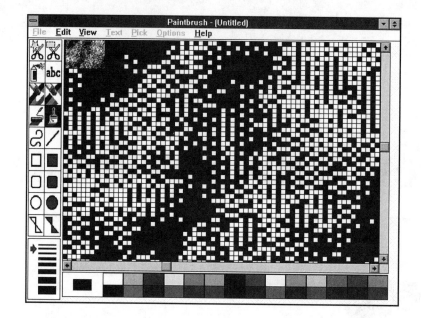

Finding Bit Maps

Bit-mapped images can come from a variety of sources. These
include scanned images, original paint-type graphics (such as
those you may create and export from Photo-Paint), and electronic
clip art. It is possible to import a limitless variety of images into
Draw, whether they begin as electronic files or printed originals.

It is even possible to incorporate "screen shots" or "screen
dumps" into Draw images. In fact, that is how many of the graphics in this book were reproduced. Screen shots are especially
useful for producing software documentation or promotional
materials. While New Riders Publishing uses a dedicated screen
capture program, for light duty you can use the Corel Screen
Capture utility, CCApture, supplied with CorelDRAW! version 3.0.

Scanners

A *scanner* makes it possible to bring a printed image or piece of artwork into a computer program. Scanners transform analog artwork into digital data through a process known as *digitizing*. Now these devices are commonplace, but just a few years ago they were playthings reserved for those with deep pockets, long vision, and a taste for the exotic.

Scanners are available in a variety of sizes and styles, from hand-held scanners at the low end to serious "heavy-metal" drum scanners at the high-end. While in the past very few shops combined six-figure scanners with CorelDRAW!, times are changing. Now that Photo-Paint is bundled in the Draw package, Corel users have the capability to alter 24-bit images. Chapter 13 includes an exercise in which you will manipulate a 24-bit file.

Today, many people buy scanners in the $200 to $2,000 range. These scanners may be limited in image quality, but they have come a long way in a short time. Line art and grayscale scanning is commonplace. As computers grow faster, more powerful, and less expensive, expect to see a corresponding increase in scanning accuracy and resolution.

One of the most interesting developments in scanner technology is the advent of drum scanners in the $30,000 to $40,000 range. Entries from Scanview and Howtek are changing the way people work with color. Instead of relying on outside suppliers, designers can create high-caliber scans at their desktops. Quality four-color work, however, has never been a poor (or an unskilled) person's game. It takes serious commitment, skill, and expertise to create realistic full-color scans. It may be subjective, but there is no replacement for having "an eye."

A Scanning Caveat

One must be careful, however, as to the images one scans. It is too easy to break the law by using images that belong to another person or organization. While the "copyright police" might not come knocking on the door, a little professional courtesy goes a long way.

If a client should ask to include an image of, say, a popular car-toon character, *do not* do this without obtaining the proper autho-rization from the copyright owner. In many cases, it is easy enough to contact the licensee, pay a fee, and avoid the legal ramifications.

Because Draw has no internal provisions for working with graph-ics on a bit-by-bit basis—other than bit-map fill patterns—a paint program, such as Photo-Paint, is necessary for dealing with bit-mapped graphics. Many other PC programs are available to accomplish this task, and one of them is included in the Windows program.

Windows Paintbrush

Anyone who has spent some time in the Windows environment knows that Microsoft was kind enough to include a program known as *Windows Paintbrush* along with the package. The latest version, included with Windows 3.1, is an improvement upon its predecessor, Windows Paint.

Windows Paintbrush's obvious advantage over any other paint package is that it is basically free, since it comes with the Win-dows package. Price aside, the powerful though diminutive program has enough horsepower to take care of many bit-mapped graphic needs.

The program can produce images that appear to have been ren-dered with charcoal or pen and ink, as shown in figure 7.2. When coupled with a graphics tablet, Windows Paintbrush is capable of surprising results.

Paintbrush's toolbox may seem abbreviated, but it contains enough versatility to get many a job done. And for the price, there should be no complaining. In a few moments, you will create some artwork with Paintbrush; and later in the chapter, you will import the file into Draw.

If Windows Paintbrush or CorelPHOTO-PAINT! does not have enough horsepower for you, there are a number of alternatives available. A capsule review of a few of the most popular bit-map paint programs available is included in Chapter 11.

Figure 7.2:
Paintbrush imagery.

Take a few moments to play around with Windows Paintbrush.
You will have to minimize Draw to an icon and bring up the
Windows Program Manager (see fig. 7.3) to launch Paintbrush
(see fig. 7.4). This chapter will not cover Paintbrush in depth, but
you will see that the program is easy to grasp.

Figure 7.3:

The Windows
program manager.

Figure 7.4:

The Windows
Paintbrush screen.

Launching Windows Paintbrush

Click the minimize arrow

In the upper right corner
of the screen. Draw
becomes an icon.

At the Windows Program Manager Accessories window:

Double-click the Paintbrush icon

Windows Paintbrush
launches.

Now that you have Paintbrush up and running on the screen, go
ahead and try out the various tools. Many are self-explanatory,
but here are the basics.

Along the left side of the Paintbrush window is the toolbox, with
its many easily identified painting implements. Beneath the
toolbox is the line size box, where line width is chosen. Along the
bottom of the window, the palette offers a choice of 28 colors
and/or shades.

You are going to create a drawing of a wave, like the one shown in figure 7.5. Later, you will import this file into Draw using black, white, and shades of gray. Once in Draw, you will colorize the bit map with the outline and fill tools.

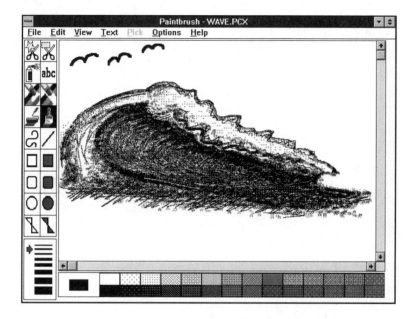

Figure 7.5:
The wave pattern.

At this point, you should get comfortable with Paintbrush's various painting tools. Pay particular attention to the airbrush tool (it looks like a spray can)—you are going to create a bit-mapped image using it. If additional material is required at this time, in-depth information on Windows Paintbrush can be found in the Microsoft Windows *User's Guide.*

DeLook Designs for Island Sports

The DeLook Design studio has become one hopping place! Word of the studio's new capabilities is spreading through Seaside like a red tide. Island Sports has just asked Joe and the gang to design the graphic elements and a logo for its next marketing campaign.

Ready to get to work? Okay, here is the first assignment. You need to draw a wave pattern for Island Sport's newspaper ad. It should be easy to crank out the image in a short time using the airbrush tool. If you use the smaller line widths, the airbrush will have less propensity to "spit." It's amazing how the software designers have also included this frustrating aberration. A little less realism would have sufficed!

Remember, Paintbrush maintains the standard Windows Undo function. If needed, it is readily available on the Edit menu. In addition to Undo, the eraser tool comes in handy for touching up mistakes.

Drawing a Wave Graphic with the Airbrush Tool

This should be a fun and easy exercise. Don't worry about getting everything exactly perfect. Just have a good time with it!

Click the airbrush tool   The cursor turns into a
                                             plus sign (+).

*Draw a wave graphic using only
black, white, and grays*

Click the paintbrush tool

*Draw a few sea gulls at the
top of the screen*

Before you leave the Paintbrush program, you will need to save your image (see fig. 7.6). Paintbrush offers five different formats for saving files, as shown in table 7.1. The program defaults to the Windows bit-map file (BMP). Draw is capable of importing any of these file formats—but make it easy on yourself and save the wave as a PCX file.

Table 7.1
Paintbrush File Formats

PCX
Monochrome bit map
16-Color bit map
256-Color bit map
24-Bit bit map

Figure 7.6:
Windows Paintbrush
Save screen.

Saving the Wave as a PCX File

Click **File**	The File menu appears.
Click **S**ave	The Save dialogue box appears.
At Save File as **T**ype:	
Click PCX files (*.PCX,	Saves the file as WAVE.PCX.
Type **WAVE** *in file name box*	
Click OK	
Click the minimize arrow	Paintbrush is minimized.
Bring Draw up	

Electronic Clip Art

You may have worked with object-oriented electronic clip art in CDR, EPS, and CGM formats, but these vector-based formats are certainly not the only formats in town. Many electronic clip-art libraries are also available in the ever popular PCX and grayscale information-laden TIFF formats. You need not limit yourself to object-oriented libraries alone. Using bit-mapped art expands the depth and breadth of your clip-art choices.

Working with bit-mapped clip art can be more difficult than working with vector-based art. It requires extra steps, which may (as you will see) include converting the raster image into vector format. This process is referred to as tracing, and can be handled in variety of ways.

There is a wide range of bit-mapped formats on the PC platform, and Draw supports most of the major players: BMP, GIF, PCX, TGA (Targa), and TIFF. Bit map file-format support was greatly enhanced in version 3.0, with the addition of color bit map export along with support for GIF and TGA. Draw's bit-map file export filters enable selectable image resolution and image sizing control. Bit map support does exclude two important formats. As of CorelDRAW! version 3.0b, neither CMYK TIFF 6.0 or DCS are supported. Hopefully, Corel's engineers will add these two formats—crucial to high-end graphic arts work—to Draw's burgeoning bit map list.

BMP

The summer of 1990 saw the introduction of the BMP Windows bit-map format. A few months later, with the release of version 2.0, CorelDRAW! had the capability to import these files. As you may recall from the Paintbrush File Save As dialogue box, Windows BMP files come in four flavors: monochrome, 16-color, 256-color, and 24-bit.

Take caution: as with other bit-map formats, the more colors in a BMP file, the larger the file. Hence, you should save BMP files using the file format with the smallest number of colors. There is no reason to save a 16-color image as a 24-bit file. BMP file compression is optional, although it is not available for 24-bit files.

GIF

In 1992, CorelDRAW! added support for the popular GIF (Graphic Interchange) file format, originally created for CompuServe. This format is supported by a number of programs, including Autodesk Animator. Draw can import and export black and white, grayscale, 16- and 256-color GIF files. File compression is standard.

PCX

As the most common denominator in PC bit-map formats, PCX was originally developed by the Z-Soft Corporation for PC Paintbrush (the forerunner of Windows paint programs). Because the PCX format is so popular, most paint packages should provide the option of saving files in PCX format.

Draw provides extensive support for the many flavors of PCX: black and white, 16-level grayscale, 256-level grayscale, 16-color, 256-color, and 16-million-color, with file compression standard. One of the distinct advantages of PCX images is that most PC printers can print them.

TGA

CorelDRAW! version 3.0 added support for the Truevision Targa (TGA) bit-map files. This format is immensely popular in the 3-D modeling, video, and animation worlds. While *Targa* (so named for the video board for which it was designed) files once lived only in those realms, they have now been brought to the PC graphics mainstream. You can save files in 16- or 256-level grayscales, and in 256 or 16-million colors as well. File compression is optional.

TIFF

TIFF is the acronym for *Tag Image File Format*. This type of image often contains more information than its PCX counterpart. Draw can import and export a range of TIFF images. You have your choice of black-and-white, 16-level grayscale, 256-level grayscale, 16-color, 256-color, and 16-million-color TIFF files. File compression is optional.

While Draw can import color and grayscale TIFF images, these images can only be correctly printed on a PostScript output device. Grayscale TIFFs are typically used to generate halftone reproductions of continuous tone originals. Draw supports the TIFF 5.0 file format standards. CMYK TIFF 6.0 is not supported.

Dealing with Bit Maps through Draw

Draw treats bit-mapped images in one of two ways, regardless of whether the file format is BMP, GIF, PCX, TGA, or TIFF. In the first method, Draw treats bit maps as bit maps. This is the method you would use to incorporate color and grayscale images, or line art that needs no tweaking. The second method involves tracing the outline of a bit-mapped file. Tracing converts bit-mapped artwork into object-oriented artwork. Tracing can be done automatically, using CorelTRACE! or autotrace, or it can be done manually. CorelTRACE! also has the capability to trace color or grayscale bit maps. Automatic tracing almost always requires some degree of manual clean-up.

To trace or not to trace is the question to ask yourself when importing a bit-map file. It is a far better thing to bring in a clean bit map than it is to spend hours cleaning up traced outlines in Draw.

Think of a pasteboard. When you bring in a bit map to be used "as is," it is as if you are pasting up a line art or halftone stat. Aside from cropping and scaling, you do not plan on messing with the image.

Now think of a light table. When you import a bit map for tracing, it is as if you are pasting the original to the light table and overlaying it with frosted acetate or tracing paper. If the original is choppy and uneven, you compensate for that as you trace, whether on the light table or on the computer monitor.

It is best to import bit-mapped images that are as clean as possible. Draw has absolutely no provision for cleaning up bit maps being used as originally drawn. If an image is to be traced, a messy original will yield an equally sloppy trace. Do not throw away your technical pens just yet!

Soon, you will import the wave graphic you drew in Windows Paintbrush and use it as a bit map (not for tracing). You will then use the bit-map image as a background for a text mask, an interesting effect that has many uses. After that, you will try tracing a bit map.

Using Bit Maps as Bit Maps

Most paint-type graphics are available as PCX files, whereas most high quality grayscale images are in the TIFF format. You saved the wave file as a PCX image. Whether a bit map begins life as a paint file or as a scanned image, the technique that you are going to use can be applied to either file type.

Incorporating Bit-Map Images

Next, you will import the WAVE.PCX file you painted in Windows Paintbrush. Importing a file into Draw should be a familiar procedure—strictly point-and-click!

Importing the Bit-Mapped Wave

This exercise assumes that the WAVE.PCX is stored in the C:\WINDOWS directory. If it isn't, substitute the appropriate drive and directory.

Click File	File menu appears.
Click Import	Import dialogue box appears.

continues

At List Files of **Type:**

Click down arrow button   Pull-down file type menu
                                                         appears.

Click CorelPHOTO-PAINT!,*.PCX, *.PCC

Maneuver to the directory in which the WAVE.PCX file is stored.

Double-click WINDOWS

Click WAVE.PCX

Click OK   The wave is imported.

Drag the wave to the center of the
page (click on the bounding box)

NOTE

If you are working in
wireframe mode and
the bit map does not
appear on the screen
(all you see is a
bounding box), the
bit-map display is
turned off. It can be
switched on and off
via the Display
menu.

The bit map appears to be quite small, but it will work for your purposes. Now that you have imported the wave, you are going to perform some interesting maneuvers with it. Bit-mapped images can be cropped, scaled, stretched, skewed, and rotated. You won't do all these operations on this particular bit map, but feel free to experiment on your own after you are done here.

Cropping Bit Maps

It is easy to remove unwanted image area by *cropping* the image with the shape tool. This procedure will be quite familiar to those who have done either conventional paste-up or desktop publishing. The advantage of cropping in Draw, as opposed to doing so on a "real" pasteboard, is that you can undo an errant crop. If your electronic razor blade wavers, you do not need to go back to the camera room for a redo!

Bit-map cropping is controlled by one of four cropping handles: left, right, bottom, and top. These handles are active only when the bit map is selected with the shape tool. Once the bit map is selected, the status line reflects the crop percentage for the four sides. When the cursor is properly positioned over a cropping handle, it will turn into a + sign.

Cropping the Wave Bit Map

The sea gulls may seem just a bit too trite for this graphic. Remove the birds by cropping them with the top cropping handle.

Click the shape tool	
Click the wave bit map	The bit map is selected. Cropping handles appear.
Position the cursor over the top cropping handle	The cursor becomes a +.
Pull the top cropping handle down	To remove the unwanted sea gulls.
Click the pick tool	To exit from cropping mode.

Draw enables you to crop bit maps, but it makes more sense to crop while in a paint program. Importing large bit maps and cropping them in Draw will lead to needlessly large file sizes. Smaller bit maps, obviously, make smaller files. These files can be loaded, displayed, and handled at much faster rates. In addition, the screen representations should be of a higher quality.

Scaling Bit Maps

Scaling bit maps within Draw can sometimes be disappointing. Anyone who has ever enlarged a minuscule piece of artwork—whether on an office copier or a litho camera—knows what happens when it is blown up too much. The artwork turns into mud. The same thing occurs on a computer when enlarging (scaling up) a bit-mapped graphic, only faster.

The results can best be appreciated by actually going through the motions. Try increasing the size of a bit-map graphic. Print it out and see what happens. It is possible that the resulting image may be useful for a special effect, but as a realistic rendering, forget it.

Always try to bring in a bit map that is the same size or larger than the final printed size will be. Bit maps reduce (scale down) more acceptably than they enlarge. Scaling up always results in a loss in image resolution.

Stretching, Skewing, and Rotating Bit Maps

Three bit-map manipulations that should be approached with caution are stretching, skewing, and rotating. This is not to say that these operations should not be performed, but they should be done with care. The same caveat that applies to scaling up bit maps applies here as well.

When a bit map is rotated or skewed, it will display as a rectangle in both wireframe and preview modes (see fig. 7.7). There will be a white triangle in the top left corner of the rectangle to denote the bit map's orientation. Rotated and skewed bit maps can only be printed on a PostScript output device.

Figure 7.7:

Rotated bit-map screen shot.

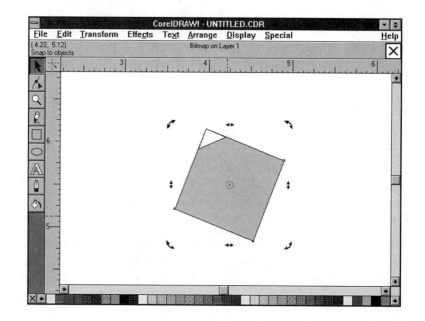

Scaling, stretching, skewing, or rotating bit maps in Draw does not always give pleasing results. If there is a real need to perform any of these functions to a bit map, do so in a paint-type program before you import the file into Draw.

In addition to eating up memory, imported bit maps can slow up printing times to an insufferable pace. This reason alone makes one seriously consider using a "real" stat rather than a scanned grayscale image.

Changing Bit Map Color and Fill

The bit maps imported into Draw may be either black and white or color. Once a black and white bit-mapped image has been imported, you can colorize it. Nevertheless, you are not allowed to change the hues of imported color bit maps from within Draw (these may be altered in Photo-Paint). The program's capability to deal with bit maps on a bi-color basis can lead to some interesting effects. For example, black-and-white bit maps can be changed to purple and pink, or to different shades of gray. Although changing the color of a bit map is a simple process, picking the right color can take time.

The black portion of the bit map is colorized by selecting the bit map and using the outline tool. Color choices can be spot or process. If a spot color is chosen, the tool also will enable you to render different halftone screen patterns on the bit map itself.

The white portion (or background rectangle) of the bit map can be colorized by using the fill tool. The same color/screen flexibility is provided as above.

In short, the outline tool affects the bit map, while the fill tool affects the background rectangle. In the following exercise, you will change the colors of the WAVE bit map that you previously imported.

Masking Bit Maps

While it is possible to alter the size of a bit-mapped image, color it, and even change the image's focal point with cropping, one of the most powerful modifications you can perform on a bit map is to mask it. A mask is similar to a stencil. Only the open areas show through. The term is adapted from its corresponding function in conventional printmaking and airbrush work.

In the next exercise, you will be using a mask as if you were sign painters employing a conventional airbrush. Remember using the airbrush tool in Windows Paintbrush? You are about to see why you did what you did.

You will perform the electronic equivalent of cutting a stencil. Once you build the stencil and position it over the bit-mapped image, only those areas that are open will show through. You will use this method to fill a word (WAVE) with a bit-mapped pattern consisting of two different tints of blue (see fig. 7.8).

Figure 7.8:

The mask equation.

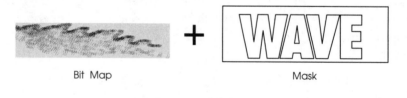

Bit Map   Mask

Masked Bit Map

Masking and Coloring the Wave

You will start out by drawing a rectangular mask outline larger than and centered around the bit map. Then you will add the word WAVE. The results are shown in figures 7.9 and 7.10.

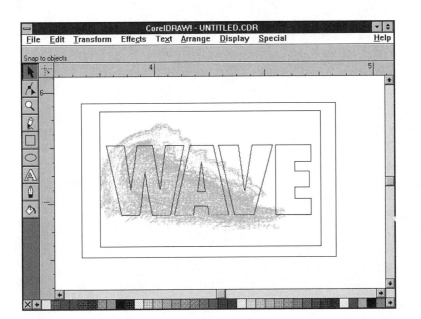

Figure 7.9:
WAVE in wireframe.

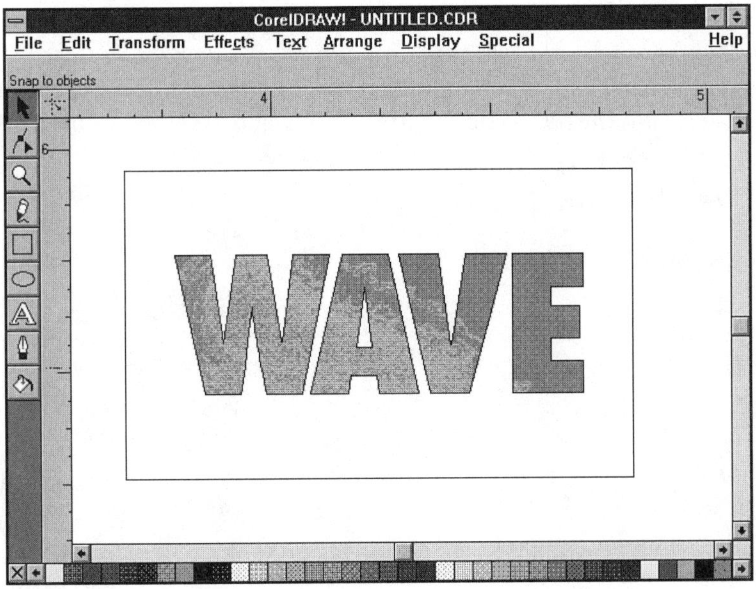

Figure 7.10:
WAVE in preview.

Click the rectangle tool

Draw a rectangle — Make it slightly larger than the WAVE bit map, and center it on the wave.

Click the text tool

Click the left side of the bit map

Type **WAVE**

Press Ctrl-T — The Artistic Text dialogue box appears.

Set type in Fujiyama Extra Bold, 30 point, centered

Click **S**pacing

At Inter-Character, *enter:* **-6**

Click OK

Click OK *again*

Now that you have set the type, use the shape tool to interactively kern the letters:

Click the shape tool

Tighten up the kerning between WAV

Now that WAVE looks pretty tight, center it horizontally and vertically, combine it with the rectangle to form a mask, and take care of the outline and fill:

Shift-click the rectangle — WAVE and the rectangle are selected.

Click **A**rrange

Click **A**lign — The Align dialogue box appears.

Click Horizontal/Vertical Center

Click OK — WAVE and the rectangle are aligned.

Click **A**rrange

Click **C**ombine — WAVE and the rectangle are combined.

Click the fill tool — The Fill fly-out menu appears.

Click white

Click the outline tool — The Outline fly-out menu appears.

Click hairline

You have just built a white mask with a hairline outline. Finish up by coloring the bit map:

Click the pick tool	
Click bit map	Bit map is selected.
Click the outline tool	The Outline fly-out menu appears.
Click Outline Color	The Outline Color dialogue box appears.
Click **Process**	The dialogue box configures for process color.
Click CMYK	
At cyan, *enter:* **60**	
At magenta, *enter:* **0**	
At yellow, *enter:* **20**	
At black, *enter:* **05**	
Click OK	The bit map is colored.
Click the fill tool	
Click Fill Color	The Fill color dialogue box appears.
At cyan, *enter:* **60**	
At magenta, *enter:* **0**	
At yellow, *enter:* **0**	
At black, *enter:* **25**	
Click OK	The bit map's background is colored.

If you want, try some other color combinations. Remember, you can use the on-screen color palette to save time. Clicking the left mouse button will change the bit map's background (fill), while clicking the right mouse button will change the bit map's foreground (outline).

This effect can be extremely useful for filling objects with halftones and intricate patterns that are not available from Draw's menus. These patterns can be built in Windows Paintbrush, CorelPHOTO-PAINT!, or another paint program. But be careful as

NOTE

You cannot change the color of an imported color bit map from within CorelDRAW! If you need to make changes, you will have to go back to a paint program (such as CorelPHOTO-PAINT!) that can work with the file.

to the number and size of the bit maps imported into a single file. System and printer speed are sure to suffer from an overabundance of bit maps.

If everything looks good with the WAVE image, take the time to save it now with the file name CATCHA. When you are done, open a new file; you are going to move on to composing your next graphic element.

Using Bit Maps for Tracing

In the first part of this chapter, you used bit maps as bit maps. Now, you are going to use bit maps as tracing patterns. Tracing a bit map gives you the capability to scale an image without fear of distortion, and the freedom to output that image to a variety of printers.

For example, what happens if you need to incorporate an existing logo or other artwork—which must maintain high resolution—into your design? Forget the idea of simply importing a scanned image unless you have access to a high-resolution scanner, a screamingly fast computer, and a huge disk drive. If scanned at the more pedestrian 300 dpi, art can be fuzzy, and more often than not, conspicuously jagged. Images scanned at high resolutions (1200 dpi) yield huge files. If at all possible, logos and other similar line art (which are to be used repeatedly) should be converted into vector format.

One way to digitize artwork is to trace the design with a digitizing tablet. The common mouse cannot compare to a high quality tablet; the rodent does not offer the same precision and intuitive drawing capabilities. Tablets are available from a variety of manufacturers, with a wide range of features and prices.

Digitizing tablets require that you trace artwork as if you were using tracing paper. Simply tape the original to the surface of the digitizing tablet and trace around the outlines with a specialized pen or puck. While this method is not perfect, it is vastly superior to attempting the same with a mouse. For more information on digitizing tablets, check out Appendix B.

The second choice for digitizing artwork is to scan an image and convert it to vector format with one of three on-screen tracing methods. The first of these three methods is like tracing with a tablet. Bring in the bit-mapped image and trace it on-screen with the pencil tool. This is rather time-consuming, but it definitely includes the human element, and requires a certain level of hand-eye coordination. The operator, not the computer, draws the outline.

Corel has also provided two automated methods of on-screen tracing. The first of these methods is known as autotrace. This feature is accessed from within the Draw environment by selecting a bit map and clicking on the pencil tool. This is a wonderful feature, but it has been overshadowed of late by CorelTRACE!, the flagship of Draw's tracing fleet.

CorelTRACE! is a stand-alone Windows program that is provided with every copy of Draw (version 1.2 and newer). CorelTRACE! is a highly automated method of tracing bit-mapped files, and can—if run on a 80386- or 80486- equipped computer—even be run in the background while you are using Draw or another program in the foreground (although this can tax your system). Pretty slick stuff.

Joe's next piece for the Island Sports account is built from a file (SIZZLE.PCX) you will find on the Inside CorelDRAW! disk. The file depicts a high-contrast image of a woman riding a personal watercraft (the Sizzler!). Joe scanned the image from a ratty piece of artwork that his client has supplied (see fig. 7.11).

Figure 7.11:
The Sizzler, before clean-up.

You will begin with the artwork as a big-map image. Thus so, you can alter it pixel by pixel. The file will be cleaned up with Paintbrush, saved under a new name, and imported into Draw. Finally, you will trace the artwork.

This method can be faster than attempting to do all the clean-up from within Draw. Take note of the horizontal lines that run behind the image. Joe wants to remove those lines. It is easier to do so prior to tracing in Paintbrush, or Photo-Paint, than it is to try to remove them after the file has been traced.

In this instance, you will use CorelPHOTO-PAINT! to clean up the image. While this may be the first time you have used Photo-Paint, it is fairly easy to use, and you can refer to the on-line help if you get stuck. Remember, Photo-Paint is covered in-depth in Chapter 13.

Cleaning Up a Bit Map

At the Windows Program Manager:

Double-click Photo-Paint	Photo-Paint is launched.
Click File	The File menu appears.
Click **O**pen	The Open File dialogue box appears.

Maneuver to the directory where you installed the *Inside CorelDRAW!* files.

Click SIZZLE.PCX	
Click OK	The file opens.

Now clean up the image with Photo-Paint. Remove the horizontal background lines, paying close attention to where they attach to the woman and her watercraft. Take out the logotype, and darken any lines which appear too thin for your liking. Use the eraser tool or the paintbrush (with white ink). To alter the size of the brush, you should have the Width and Shape workbox on the screen. For pixel-by-pixel editing, you will want to zoom in real tight.

Feel free to alter the image. Pay particular attention to the woman's sunglasses and lips—they both need to be touched up. Straighten out jagged lines as you see fit.

When you are done cleaning things up, and your image looks like figure 7.12, save the file as SIZZLER.PCX. You are going to import the cleaned-up file into CorelDRAW! and explore the tracing options.

Figure 7.12:
The cleaned-up hydrosport.

Importing a File for Tracing

There really is not too much to this one, folks. You will import the file the same way you import any other file. If you are not happy with the clean-up work you performed, you can cheat a little, and bring in SIZZLE2.PCX instead. That file has been cleaned up for you!

Importing Sizzler

Click **File**
Click **Import**

continues

At List Files of **Type:**

Click down arrow button	Pull-down file type menu appears.

Click CorelPHOTO-PAINT!,*.PCX, *.PCC

Maneuver to the directory that the SIZZLER.PCX file is stored in.

Double-click WINDOWS

Double-click SIZZLER.PCX

Click OK	The Sizzler is imported.

Now that you have the Sizzler on your system, do a little comparison between manual tracing and autotracing. As you have probably noticed, bit maps are selected by clicking on the *bounding box* or outline, rather than on the image itself.

Manual Tracing Versus Autotracing

Manual tracing is not a load of fun, but by going through the process you will gain an appreciation of autotracing, and ultimately, CorelTRACE!. Without the aid of a prompted exercise, try to trace the outline of the rower using the pencil tool. Make sure that the bit map is not selected before you click on the pencil tool. If you click on the pencil tool while the bit map *is* selected, you will get the autotrace tool, rather than the pencil tool.

It will help to zoom up on the bit map as much as possible. You may want to work in wireframe mode, rather than full-color preview. If you begin to get frustrated, don't fret. Manual tracing is not fun, nor is it an effective use of your time. After trying to trace the outlines by eye, you are going to really enjoy using autotrace. Instead of grinding teeth and splitting hairs, all you have to do is point and shoot!

Now, try tracing the Sizzler using the autotrace tool.

Giving Autotrace a Try

Click the pick tool

Click Bit map's bounding box	Bit map is selected.

Click the pencil tool

The cursor turns into the autotrace tool.

Position the right side of the autotrace tool on the edge of the Sizzler

Click mouse

The Sizzler is autotraced (see fig. 7.13).

This last step takes a few moments. When it is done, the cursor once again becomes the autotrace tool.

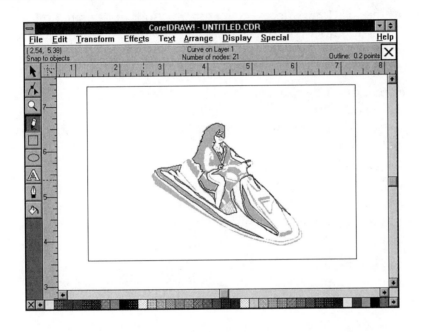

Figure 7.13:

The Autotrace tool in action.

That was far easier than manual tracing. Unfortunately, autotrace only traces exterior edges. The image you are working on consists of many individual objects. Each object within the image must be traced and assigned a fill, or combined with other objects. This, too, can be quite a time-consuming task. It helps to pre-set the autotrace preferences for the type of image being traced.

Autotrace Preferences

Properly setting up the autotrace preferences can alleviate many autotracing woes. There is no single correct setting for autotrace; the setting depends upon the image being traced. You are going to visit the Preferences dialogue box once again, this time to take a look at autotrace tracking, corner threshold, and straight line threshold, the three adjustments that affect autotracing. You will find these settings by clicking the Curves button.

Autotrace tracking affects the feature's affinity for detail. Low values will render complicated tracings that follow each and every variance in the bit map's outline. High values yield smooth, breezy outlines.

The second setting, Corner Threshold, determines the point at which a node is smooth or cusp. High settings will render smooth corners, while low settings deliver cusps. This setting also applies to freehand drawing.

Finally, straight line threshold makes the decision between using straight or curved line segments. A high setting will bias in favor of straight lines, while a low setting will give favor to curved lines. Use a high setting when dealing with very straight, angular originals.

Again, setting the preferences correctly is application-dependent. The settings hinge entirely upon the material being autotraced. Like corner threshold, this setting applies to freehand drawing as well.

Tracing the Better Way with CorelTRACE!

Now that you have done it the hard way, get ready to sit back and let the computer do all the work. CorelTRACE! is a blessing for those of you who do any amount of tracing.

Try tracing a file to see just how wonderful the CorelTRACE! program really is. In this next exercise, you will see how Trace converts bit-mapped files (either PCX or TIFF) into EPS—files which are then importable into CorelDRAW!.

While CorelTRACE! works, watch the lower left corner of the Trace window (see fig. 7.14). Trace Processing reports its progress as it works. After the trace is finished, a summary of trace file information will be displayed at the bottom of the window. This includes the number of objects and nodes in the EPS file, along with the elapsed time.

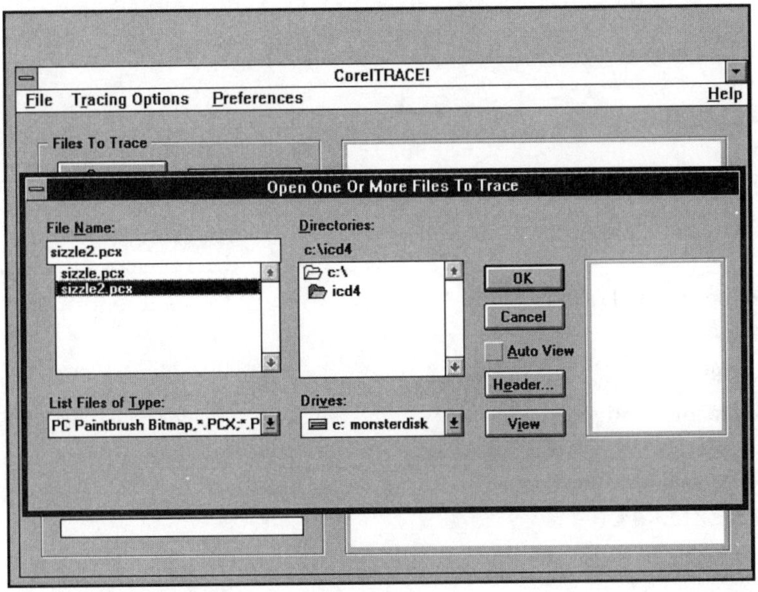

Figure 7.14:

The Trace open files dialogue box.

Using CorelTRACE!

You will use Trace to convert the same bit map that you previously imported into Draw. If there is something on the screen that needs to be saved, save it now, because you are going to exit the Draw environment for a little while.

Click File	The File menu appears.
Click Exit	If there is an unsaved file, a dialogue box asks if the file should be saved.

continues

At the Windows Program Manager:

Double-click the CorelTRACE! icon	Trace is launched. The program's main dialogue box appears.
Click **O**pen	The Open One Or More Files To Trace dialogue box appears.

At List Files of **T**ype:

Click down arrow button	Pull-down file type menu appears.

Click CorelPHOTO-PAINT!,*.PCX, *.PCC

Maneuver to the directory that the WAVE.PCX file is stored in.

Click C:

Double-click ICD4

Click SIZZLER.PCX	SIZZLER.PCX is selected.

Click OK

Click **F**ile

Click **O**utput Options	The Output Options dialogue box appears.

Make sure that Trace is set up to store the output files in the proper directory.

Click OK

Click Tracing Options	The Tracing Options menu appears.

Click Normal Outline

Click SIZZLER.PCX

Click **T**race All	Trace begins converting the Sizzler.

The Sizzler's image appears as Trace converts the file into EPS format. When Trace is finished, the hourglass once again becomes a cursor (see fig. 7.15).

Pretty neat trick! Just wait until you import the file into Draw—that is when it gets *really* impressive. While you can use Trace Partial Area (found on the Preferences menu) to crop images with the bounding box, many images include superfluous stuff that you will not be able to crop out. That is why it is important to first clean out the extra junk with a paint program.

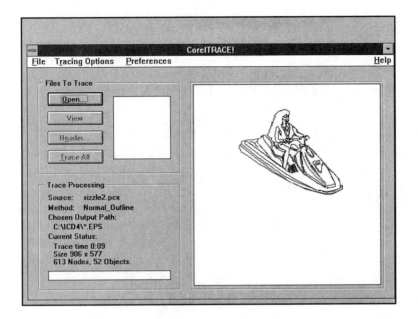

Figure 7.15:
Traced image in window.

Why should you exit Draw before running Trace? Well, running Trace and Draw at the same time can be a bit demanding for computers without enough system resources, so if you have such a system, it makes sense to shut one program down before opening up the other. If the system you are working on has a fast 80386 and plenty of RAM, you may be able to run the two programs concurrently. However, running Trace along with another program can slow tracing speed.

To speed things up, remember to load the bit-map file to your computer's hard disk before tracing. Floppy drives have a slow input/output (I/O) rate, and tracing a file stored on a floppy can take an interminably long time.

Trace can be set to batch trace a group of files. This is a very handy way to convert files while the computer is unattended. This works well for images that will not be cropped. Select the files you want to trace and let the computer do all the work. If you choose to do this, all images should be scanned at the same resolution. Make sure that Trace Partial Area is not selected; otherwise, someone will have to baby-sit your computer while it is tracing.

Setting Up CorelTRACE!

In the last exercise, you merely ran Trace with its factory defaults. Trace has two basic tracing methods. These are known as Outline and Centerline, and indicate the type of object that should be traced.

CorelTRACE! works amazingly well with either the Outline or Centerline default settings, but for those of you who are terminal tweakers, there are plenty of buttons to push. Tracing Options enables you to adjust the settings for Curve Length, Convert Long Lines, Sample Rate, Fit Curve, Outline Filtering, Remove Noise, and even enables you to Invert Bitmaps.

All of these settings can take some fiddling with, and sometimes it may be better to go with the defaults and clean up the resulting file. But, if you have time to fiddle, by all means do so. Trace enables you to save custom settings by typing a name in the Option Name box.

Follow Outline will trace the edges of a bit map and fill the resulting objects with black or white. If an area is black on the original, it will be black in the trace. The same goes for white. Outline works best on solid, heavy, filled originals. It is even possible to trace grayscale images using this method, resulting in a high contrast vector image. Figure 7.16 shows an example of a good outline trace.

Follow Centerline is best used for thinly drawn illustrations. This method assigns a thickness to the resulting lines, but it will not assign a fill unless a definitely filled object is found. Images traced with this method can only be black lines on a white background. Figure 7.17 shows an example of a good centerline trace.

Maximum Line Width can be adjusted when Centerline is chosen. The higher the setting, the more pixels Trace will remove; this results in smooth, consistent lines at the expense of image integrity. Lower settings will follow the original image more closely, resulting in a coarser line (although truer to the original).

Uniform Line enables you to stipulate an exact line weight.

Invert Bit map First will reverse the image (turn black to white, and vice versa) before tracing.

Figure 7.16:

An example of an outline trace.

Curve Length defines the span of individual curves. To be effective, this setting must be used in conjunction with Fit Curve and Sample Rate. Shorter curve lengths result in larger numbers of nodes and bigger files; hence, it should only be used when maximum detail is needed.

Convert Long Lines governs Trace's conversion of long lines into either curved or straight lines. Usually, a medium setting works fine. However, if a drawing consists solely of lines, select Lines. If the image is all curves, click Curves.

Sample Rate and **Fit Curve** regulate the extent to which the trace is true to the original. With a Sample Rate of Fine and Fit Curve set to Very Tight, Trace will yield the highest image integrity at the expense of file size. Setting Sample Rate and Fit Curve to the other extremes will smooth out a rough bit map.

Figure 7.17:

An example of a centerline trace.

Edge Filtering controls an outlined object's smoothness. The Mild or Smooth setting is useful for smoothing jagged originals or low dpi scans. A setting of None will hold the maximum detail.

Remove Noise is handy for deleting "scan dirt" (superfluous objects smaller than the indicated number of pixels). Higher numbers remove larger objects and result in leaner files. Lower numbers leave more dirt. The factory setting is 8 pixels.

Outline Filtering is handy when tracing low res (150 dpi or less) scans, like the Sizzler. It enables you to govern the smoothness of an outline. Using a Mild or Smooth Points setting can polish a jagged bitmap.

If you are working with grayscale or color images, you can convert them to black-and-white (1 bit) monochrome files, or lower the number of grays or colors, via the Color Reduction dialogue box (which you access through the Preferences menu). Grayscale bit maps can be traced as 4-, 8-, 16-, 64-, or 256-level images. Color bit maps can be traced as 8-, 16-, 64-, or 256-color images.

Needless to say, there is plenty of experimenting to be done here. To become a Trace-master, expect to spend plenty of time and be sure to set aside loads of disk space!

No Matter How You Trace...

Regardless of the method used to trace an object, there is always a certain amount of tweaking that must be done to clean things up. The computer has a propensity for node-overkill. As mentioned before, pare down objects to a minimum of nodes. Reducing the number of nodes in a trace can be done while tracing and once the tracing has been brought into Draw. This strategy saves in a multitude of ways. File size can be lowered, screen redraw time can be lessened, and printing time slashed, all by eliminating needless nodes. If a node is not needed, remove it; the lines will be smoother, and you will reap all the aforementioned benefits.

The Island Sports Logo

Joe plans to use the Sizzler in the Island Sports logo. You will finish your tracing and tweaking phase now, then use Fit Text to Path to finish the logo in Chapter 8. While you have Draw up and running, import the cleaned-up and traced SIZZLER file.

Importing the Trace

Click File	The File menu appears.
Click Import	The Import dialogue box appears.
At List Files of **Type:**	
Click down arrow button	Pull-down file type menu appears.
Click CorelTRACE!,*.EPS	

continues

Maneuver to the directory that the sizzler.eps file is stored in.

Click C:

Double-click ICD4

Click SIZZLER.EPS   SIZZLER.EPS is selected.

Click OK   The cleaned-up Sizzler appears.

The power of CorelTRACE! will become apparent just as soon as you click preview (if full-color editing is not already on). The program does an amazing job of converting bit-map files to object-oriented drawings.

You should take the time to clean up some of those excess nodes. This can get a little hairy, but you have a little trick that will make tweaking tracings just a bit easier.

A Tracing Tweaking Tip

Whenever you trace something, be it electronically or convention-ally, it helps to have some guidelines to follow. This next exercise will demonstrate an easy way to align your lines as you remove needless nodes and fine-tune your drawing.

You are going to duplicate the tracing. Then you will center the two tracings horizontally and vertically. You will ungroup the top tracing and click the shape tool. When you do that, the bottom grouped tracing will not be modifiable by the shape tool. You can use these lines to guide you as you remove the excess nodes. Remember, the fewer the nodes, the smoother the drawing, and the faster it loads, redraws, previews, and prints.

As you work through the drawing, removing excess nodes, you will find that the Snap-to-Nodes feature can be a mixed blessing. You will end up toggling the feature on and off, as needed. In addition, you may need to frequently redraw the screen. This can be accomplished in a number of ways: you may click on the scroll bar thumbs, choose Refresh Window (from the Display menu), or press Ctrl-W.

Following Outlines While Tweaking

With the Sizzler selected, take the following steps:

Click Edit	The Edit menu appears.
Click Duplicate	The Sizzler is duplicated.
Marquee-select both watercraft	
Click Arrange	The Arrange menu appears.
Click Align	The Align dialogue box appears.
Click Horizontal/vertical center	
Click OK	The Sizzlers are horizontally and vertically centered on each other.
Click Page	Deselects the Sizzlers.
Click the top Sizzler	Selects the top Sizzler.
Click Arrange	The Arrange menu appears.
Click Ungroup	The top Sizzler is ungrouped.
Click the shape tool	The bottom group is not editable.

Now comes the challenge of removing the excess nodes while retaining the integrity of the drawing. Start by removing one node at a time, and move on to marquee-or shift-deleting groups of nodes once you feel comfortable with the process. Figures 7.18 and 7.19 show before-and-after views. Remember, you can always use Undo if you remove the wrong node. Before you get too far along, remember to save the file as SIZZLER2. Now go for it!

After you have removed the excess nodes, remove the background Sizzler. Otherwise, all of your node-tweaking will have been in vain.

To select the background group, repeatedly press Tab. When the status line reports that it is a group of objects, you have found the background group. Delete it with Del. Group the remaining Sizzler-parts.

Finish things by triplicating the Sizzler.

Figure 7.18:

Before tweaking.

Figure 7.19:

After tweaking.

Duplicating with Move

Rather than drag-duplicating, you will use the convenient Move dialogue box to create your duplicate Sizzler. This handy command enables you to drop the dupes with precision. You can access the Move dialogue box from the Transform Menu or with a keyboard shortcut, Ctrl-L.

The Move command can be especially useful for executing precise step-and-repeat procedures. As you will see in this next exercise, once you perform the first step-and-repeat, subsequent moves can be performed with the Repeat command (Ctrl-R).

You will perform two step-and-repeats. The first will use the Move command while the second will make use of the Repeat command. Finally, you will assign different tints to the watercraft. The results should look like figure 7.20.

Shortcut

Press Ctrl-L to access the Move dialogue box.

Shortcut

Press Ctrl-R to repeat the last function performed.

Shortcut

Press Ctrl-Q to access the Stretch and Mirror dialogue box.

Step-and-Repeating, and Tinting the Cyclists

With the Sizzler selected, take the following steps:

Click **Transform**	The Transform menu appears.
Click **Move**	The Move dialogue box appears.
At Horizontal *type:* **.25**	
At Vertical *type:* **.25**	
Click **Leave Original**	
Click OK	The Sizzler is step-and-repeated.
Click **Edit**	The Edit menu appears.
Click **Repeat**	The Sizzler is step-and-repeated again.
Click the left Sizzler	The left Sizzler is selected.
Click the fill tool	The Fill fly-out menu appears.
Click 10 percent black fill	The left Sizzler is assigned a 10 percent black fill.

continues

Click the center Sizzler	The center Sizzler is selected.
Click the fill tool	The Fill fly-out menu appears.
Click 50% black fill	The center Sizzler is assigned a 50 percent black fill.

Figure 7.20:

The Sizzler gets triplicated.

One slight problem has cropped up. Because the Sizzler is not a solid object, it is transparent! You will have to create a white object with no outline, and place it underneath the top Sizzler to knock out the other images. Go ahead and whip one out with the pencil tool. Try to keep the number of nodes to a minimum. Use the move command to move the different elements precisely.

You are done for now. And guess what? You do not have to clean up your drawing pens, pencils, or charcoal! Just make sure that you save this file under the name SIZZLERS.CDR, before you forget. You will be needing the file to complete the logo at the end of the next chapter.

Summary

While Draw is strictly a vector-based drawing program, its bit maps are treated with care. You cannot do any bit-map editing, but you are free to crop, scale, rotate, and stretch bit maps beyond the realm of good taste. As shown in the first series of exercises, Draw lets you use bit maps as a background to a mask, whether text or otherwise.

Draw offers a wide range of choices for converting bit-mapped originals into vector-based artwork. Through its various methods—manual tracing, autotracing, and the formidable CorelTRACE! utility—Draw gives the user great power to quickly and confidently transform bit maps into objects.

The wise bit-map tracer knows that what the computer gives is not what should be ultimately used. There is always more tweaking to be done, and fine-tuning tracings is a tweak's redemption. CorelPHOTO-PAINT! (covered in Chapter 13) provides a power tool for pre-scan bit-map editing.

If you find that you need a bit-map paint program with more power than CorelPHOTO-PAINT! or Windows Paintbrush, check out the reviews of Image-In-Color, Aldus PhotoStyler, and Fractal Design Painter in Chapter 11.

8

Assembling Complex Images

So far, this book has covered most of the fundamentals of creating electronic artwork with CorelDRAW!. Along the way, it has tried to stress the proper way to assemble modular images so that they can be easily altered and printed with confidence.

Those who come into the world of Draw with an art background may have a distinct advantage, although such experience does not ensure success. An artist may make wondrous achievements with oil colors but fail to grasp Draw's theory. The vector-based, object-oriented environment can be daunting to those without the vision to use it to their benefit.

An artist whose training includes print-making, whether artistic or commercial, also has an advantage. Many of Draw's core principles are also found in the arts of serigraphy (screen printing) and lithography. An artist who is comfortable with the gist of print-making will be comfortable with Draw.

It is vital to understand that success with Draw entails more than just drawing a pretty picture. The intent is to build working drawings—illustrations that have the flexibility to change at a moment's notice. To accomplish this goal, a drawing must not only be designed and rendered, it must be engineered.

Building Images That Work

No matter what the application, solid design is the key to success. A well-engineered building stands the test of time. A precisely crafted automobile handles impeccably. A well-thought-out computer program runs flawlessly. This last example is the key here—because when you create an image with Draw, you are writing a computer program.

DRAW (CDR) files are source code. Windows' print drivers could be considered compilers. The files that Draw sends to the printer are object code. If a Draw file is not properly drawn, the resulting program will not run.

There is a right way and a wrong way to solve a problem, write a computer program, or execute a drawing. If a computer program functions, but is slow and difficult to use, it is a flop. If a Draw file fails to print or takes half a day to do so, it too is a failure.

What good is a drawing that you cannot print? A pretty picture on the screen does nothing for you at deadline time. Who do you blame for nonprinting images—the manufacturers of the program, the operating system, the description language, or the artist/ operator responsible for using them?

No one should take the blame, but the artist should take the ultimate responsibility. Through in-depth working knowledge, the experienced Draw artist knows the program's limitations. He or she knows what the program can and cannot do. Pushing the design envelope should not be done at deadline time, or at least should be done only with extreme prudence.

There are a variety of concepts that can help you build working images. The following pages cover many of the basic points necessary to achieve success with Draw.

Getting the Most from Combine and Group

The Combine and Group commands are significant players at Draw's cutting edge. While the inexperienced Draw user may see little use for these two commands, it is crucial to understand the difference between them. Combine is a function of systematic design, while Group is a function of composition convenience. Combine makes a huge difference in screen redraw and printing. Group is of great assistance in image construction. These two commands are similar, but far from the same.

Combine is one of the most important, yet least used, of Draw's command set. It enables you to fuse objects together, so they act as one. Although they are not physically connected, combined objects share the same outline and fill characteristics. Thoughtful use of Draw's Combine command can make it possible to print drawings that would regularly choke a printer. To effectively challenge Draw's frontiers, you must first become practiced in the proper use of Combine.

Here are some general guidelines for using the Combine command effectively:

- **Combine like objects.** For maximum efficiency, try not to combine more than 20 to 25 objects at a clip. Larger combinations can cause problems at print time. Also, avoid combining complex, multi-node objects.

- **Use Combine to reduce file size.** Combined files are well-designed files. They take up less space, since file size is kept to a minimum. This is an important consideration for disk space, whether it is fixed or removable.

- **Use Combine to reduce screen redraw time dramatically.** Upon preview redraw, it is easy to tell whether a group of objects has been combined. Uncombined objects pop in, one by one. Combined objects pour down the screen—from top to bottom—in a fraction of the time.

Unlike Combine, Group does not affect screen redraws, file size, or print times. Group simply collects objects, acting mainly as an item of convenience. In the playing card exercise from Chapter 3, you grouped clusters to make assembly easier.

In the exercises in this chapter, you will see how Group and Combine can simplify image manipulation, speed up screen preview, reduce file size, and enable complex images to print with ease.

Keeping Things in Control with Layers

When your drawings start to get complex, CorelDRAW!'s Layer controls are essential to maintain order—not to mention your sanity. The Layers Roll-Up menu (which is accessed via the Arrange menu or by the keyboard shortcut, Ctrl-1) is a powerful device. It will help you create artwork that would otherwise be impossibly complicated, if not beyond the realm of sense entirely.

Layers are easy to work with, once you understand the basics. You can have an endless number of layers, each with a distinctive name (of up to 32 alphanumeric characters). Individual layers can be made invisible, as well as nonprinting, for the sake of clarity while working, previewing, or manipulating your drawing. Draw also gives you the option of assigning a color override that designates a specific color outline to all objects on a layer (in addition to making them transparent). Color override affects only the on-screen appearance; it has no effect on output. Layers can be locked, to avoid disturbance while working on other layers.

Artists who render technical drawings will find Layers invaluable. In most basic drawings, artwork can be on one layer while annotation is on another. It may have taken Corel a number of releases finally to include layer control, but now that it is here, it's up to you to make use of it!

Using Fountain Fills Properly

Using too many fountain fills is a sure way to choke an output device. If you are imaging a file with fountain fills and the file refuses to print, you have one realistic option. Get rid of some or all of those fountain fills. Of course, you can always increase curve flatness when printing, but that is another story (covered in Chapter 11).

Complexity for complexity's sake is pointless. Slapping layer upon layer of over-noded fountain-filled objects is an exercise in futility. If you really want to waste your (or your employer's) time, you can slap on as many as you want. But the ultimate result will seldom be printable. If you have the latent desire to work your imagery to death, you should buy a canvas, a few brushes, and some oil paints.

This is not to discourage the use of fountain fills. But one must realize that they can exceed the capabilities of the output device. Use them with great discretion. Additionally, try to avoid fountain-filling objects with a large number of nodes, such as strings of intricate type. This can be an extremely processor-intensive task; and, at the very least, the output device might take hours to print the file.

Eliminating Excess Nodes

Like too many fountain fills, excessive nodes can choke a printer fast. When executing a freehand drawing or tracing a bit-mapped file, Draw will invariably lay down far too many nodes. It is the artist's responsibility to go back in and strip out the unnecessary nodes.

It is possible that tracing an image can yield a hundred nodes where two might suffice. This depends on the quality of the original and the user settings. Once again, it is the artist's duty to rectify the situation.

The fewer the nodes in a file, the smaller that file will be and the faster it will image, both on the screen and at the output device. In short, file sizes, screen redraw, and print times will improve if you eliminate excess nodes.

Some file types (such as CGM and WPG) are vector formats, even though they contain line segments instead of Bezier curves. Any time a file is imported in either of these formats, it will contain far more line segments than are necessary in CDR format. In addition, the object will not scale with the smoothness that one would expect from a Bezier curve-based object. When using imported CGM images, select and delete excess nodes before sending the images to a high-resolution output device.

Joe DeLook Takes an Early Lunch

A hungry Joe DeLook has cut out for an early lunch and some fishing. With his lunch bag and fishing gear in hand, he is ready for a few hours of relaxation. He reaches his favorite spot, throws in a line, and opens up his lunch pail.

While nothing seems to be biting today (save the mosquitoes), Joe welcomes the time out of the office. The quiet bay-front setting is a calming relief from the pandemonium back in the studio. Joe's eyes briefly focus on a Monarch butterfly, flitting from flower to flower, before he slips into a peaceful snooze.

Building a Working Drawing

You are going to use an exercise that greatly relies upon your creativity as well as your discipline. This next segment will demonstrate the advantages of using Combine and Group in building a working drawing. You will be drawing a butterfly to illustrate some of the principles of complex work.

Since a butterfly can be a rather subjective thing, feel free to take off in a different direction from the Monarch that is assembled here. If, after completing this exercise, you want to try another critter, do so by all means.

A butterfly is used for this exercise because there is no hard and fast right or wrong. Who is going to know if the butterfly is not exact? Above all, it is important to have fun with this exercise.

The butterfly exercise is broken down into eight separate steps. For clarity's sake, you will be working in wireframe mode. You will proceed in a methodical fashion, grouping each set of objects as you go along. Grouping makes it easy to move sections around the drawing, while Combine makes a big difference in preview speed. You will get one wing finished before you start combining objects. Draw will not enable you to combine grouped objects. Hence, you will select each group, ungroup, and combine.

Before you actually draw your first object, you will set up the Outline Pen New Object default for a one-point outline. This will be a great time-saver, and beats going back to the outline menu every time you need the same weight rule.

The first step consists of drawing the silhouette of the butterfly's left inner and outer wings. Here it is shown using only four nodes; you may need a few more. The wings are filled with black and outlined with a one-point black rule (see fig. 8.1).

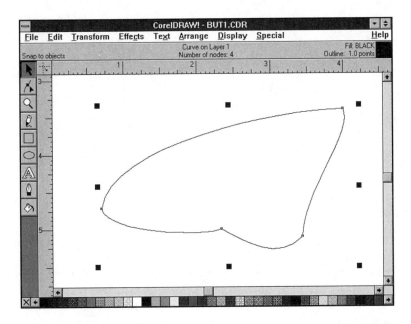

Figure 8.1:

The wing's silhouette.

If you have problems creating closed path curves, check the AutoJoin setting in the Preferences dialogue box. Setting Autojoin to 10 will zap curves closed. You may want to experiment with different settings. Remember: 1 is the least likely to close, while 10 is most likely.

Drawing the Silhouette

Set up the page for letter size, portrait orientation:

Click the pick tool

continues

Click the outline tool	The Outline fly-out menu appears.
Click the outline pen	The Outline Pen for New Object dialogue box appears.
Click Other Objects	
Click OK	A different Outline Pen for New Other Object dialogue box appears.
Set width to 1.0 points	
Click Scale With Image	
Click OK	The outline pen new other object's default is set.
Click the pencil tool	
Draw the wing	
Click the fill tool	The Fill fly-out menu appears.
Click black	The silhouette is filled with black.
Click the shape tool	
Click and delete the extra nodes	
Tweak the control points to achieve the proper shape.	
Save the file as BUT1	

Beginning with the next section, you will be laying colors on top of the silhouette. At this point, the file is about as compact as files get. This one measures in at 9256 bytes (but your file sizes may differ slightly).

The second step entails drawing nine large orange segments on the wing. All segments are filled with a uniform fill of 40 percent magenta and 100 percent yellow, and outlined with a one-point rule of 60 percent magenta, 100 percent yellow. The segments are then grouped (see fig. 8.2).

Once you open the Uniform Fill and Outline Color dialogue boxes and configure them for Process Color CMYK mode, they will stay that way. Each time you call one of these dialogue boxes, it will appear in the same mode as you last left it.

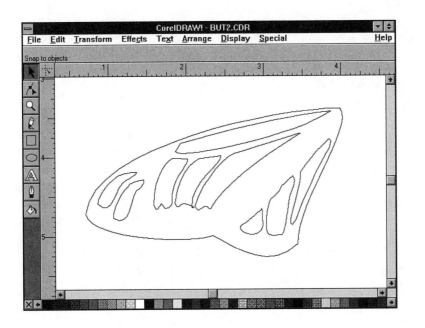

Figure 8.2:
The wing begins to develop.

Adding the Nine Orange Segments

Take a look at the preceding illustration for an example of how the nine orange segments should look.

Click the pencil tool

Draw nine segments

Click the shape tool

Click and delete the extra nodes

Tweak the control points to achieve the desired shapes:

Shift-click or marquee-select all nine segments

Click **Arrange**	The Arrange menu appears.
Click **Group**	The segments are grouped.
Click the fill tool	The Fill fly-out menu appears.
Click Uniform Fill	The Uniform Fill dialogue box appears.
Click **Process**	The dialogue box configures for process color.

continues

If the dialogue box is in CMYK mode, leave it that way. If it is not, change it.

At magenta, enter: **40**

At yellow, enter: **100**

Click OK   The nine segments are
                                          filled.

Click the outline tool   The Outline fly-out menu
                                          appears.

Click Outline Color   The Outline Color
                                          dialogue box appears.

Click Process   The dialogue box
                                          configures for process
                                          color.

If the dialogue box is in CMYK mode, leave it that way. If it is not, change it.

At magenta, enter: **60**

At yellow, enter: **100**

Click OK   The nine segments are
                                          outlined in orange-red.

Save the file as BUT2

The wing is starting to develop, and the file size is growing: 11654 bytes.

Step three places 11 oval shapes near the left-most section of the wing (see fig. 8.3). The ovals are grouped and then filled with 10 percent magenta and 100 percent yellow. They are outlined with a one-point rule of 40 percent yellow.

Placing the Oval Shapes

Click the pencil tool

Draw 11 oval shapes

Click the shape tool

Click and delete the extra nodes

Tweak the control points to achieve the proper shape:

*Shift-click or marquee-select
all 11 ovals*

Click **Arrange**	The Arrange menu appears.
Click **Group**	The ovals are grouped.
Click the fill tool	The Fill fly-out menu appears.
Click Uniform Fill	The Uniform Fill dialogue box appears.
At magenta, enter: **10**	
At yellow, enter: **100**	
Click OK	The 11 ovals are filled.
Click the outline tool	The Outline fly-out menu appears.
At yellow, enter: **40**	
Click OK	The 11 ovals are outlined in light yellow.
Save the file as BUT3	

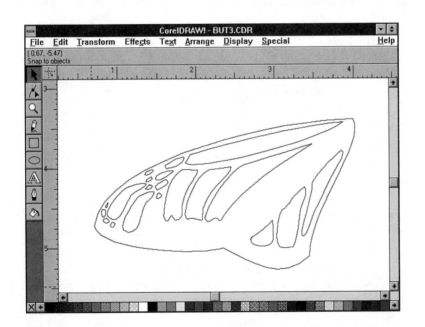

Figure 8.3:

The wing gets some spots.

Figure 8.3 shows how the 11 oval shapes should look.

As the file grows in complexity, so do screen redraw times and file size. At this point, the file weighs in at 14342 bytes. (Again, your file size may differ slightly.)

Step four adds 66 spots to the bottom of the wing (see fig. 8.4). These spots are filled with 20 percent yellow, and outlined with a one-point rule of 40 percent yellow. The spots are broken into three groups of 20, 23, and 23 items. The slickest way to accomplish this is to build one group and duplicate it. Then add or delete spots as needed.

Get Your Kicks with Sixty-Six (Spots)

Click ellipse tool

Draw approximately 6 ellipses

Instead of drawing a zillion spots, you will use these six as a base. Using Rotate or Mirror with Leave Original will make each spot seem almost unique.

Click the pick tool	
Double-click a spot	To display rotate/skew handles.
Use a corner handle to rotate the spot	
Press and release the + on the numeric keypad	This leaves the original in place.
Release the mouse button	
Click another spot	
Drag a side handle to the opposite side to mirror the spot	
Press and release the + on the numeric keypad	To leave the original in place.
Release the mouse button	

You should now have eight spots. Repeat the two techniques you just used to create 15 more. When you're done, you will then group, fill, and outline the spots.

Shift-click or marquee-select all 23 spots	
*Click **Arrange***	The Arrange menu appears.

Click **Group**	The spots are grouped.
Click the fill tool	The Fill fly-out menu appears.
Click Uniform Fill	The Uniform Fill dialogue box appears.
At yellow, enter: **20**	
Click OK	The 23 spots are filled.
Click the outline tool	The Outline fly-out menu appears.
Click Outline Color	The Outline color dialogue box appears.
At yellow, enter: **40**	
Click OK	The 23 spots are outlined in light yellow.

Now, you need to duplicate the group of spots two times, and drag the groups into position:

Press Ctrl-D	The group of spots is duplicated.
Drag the new group into position	
Press Ctrl-D	The duplicate group of spots is duplicated.

Drag the second new group into position

You may or may not need to ungroup one of the groups, depending on whether you can fit 69 spots, rather than the 66 you originally specified.

Save the file as BUT4

Figure 8.4 shows the 66 spots.

The file is getting larger, and screen redraw should be getting longer and longer. At this point, the file size is 29796 bytes.

In the fifth step, you combine your first objects—a large number of orange-red one-point rules. Outline them with 80 percent magenta and 100 percent yellow. These are open path objects and can have no fill. After you're done, check your screen redraw time.

Figure 8.4:

The wing gets some
more spots.

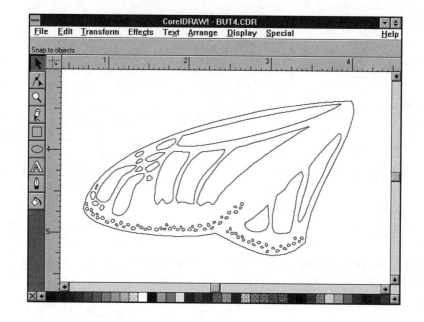

Adding and Combining Lines

Now you can combine the lines in two clusters:

Click the pencil tool

*Draw three or four straight lines
in each of the orange segments*

*Draw a freehand line at the bottom
of both the inner and outer wings*

Click the shape tool

*Click and delete the extra nodes
on the freehand lines*

Shift-click half of the lines

Click **Arrange**   The Arrange menu
                                                  appears.

Click **Combine**   The lines are combined.

Click the page   Deselects the lines.

Shift-click the remaining lines

Click **Arrange**   The Arrange menu
                                                  appears.

Click **Combine**	The lines are combined.
Click the first set of lines	
Click the outline tool	The Outline fly-out menu appears.
Click Outline Color	The Outline color dialogue box appears.
At magenta, enter: **100**	
At yellow, enter: **40**	
Click OK	The lines are drawn in deep orange-red.
Click the second set of lines	
Click Edit	The Edit menu appears.
Click Copy Style From ...	The Copy Style From dialogue box appears.
Click Outline **Color**	
Click OK	From? arrow appears
Click first set of lines	Outline color is copied.

If you want, go in and change the straight line segments to curves. Tweak the control points to have the lines follow the dimensions of the orange segments.

Save the file as BUT5

Figure 8.5 shows the results of this exercise.

In the sixth step, you combine everything of like fill and outline into assemblies of no more than 25 objects. This procedure considerably speeds up screen redraw time.

Combining the Wing

The time has come to combine each cluster of objects. This will be made easier because you have grouped them along the way. The procedure in this case goes like this: select, ungroup, and combine—simple, clean, and effective.

Click the pick tool	
Click an orange segment	
Click **Arrange**	The Arrange menu appears.

continues

Click **U**ngroup	The segments are ungrouped.
Click **A**rrange	The Arrange menu appears.
Click **C**ombine	The segments are combined. Notice that their fill color now displays on the status line.
Click a yellow oval	
Click **A**rrange	The Arrange menu appears.
Click **U**ngroup	The ovals are ungrouped.
Click **A**rrange	The Arrange menu appears.
Click **C**ombine	The ovals are combined.
Click a group of spots	
Click **A**rrange	The Arrange menu appears.
Click **U**ngroup	The spots are ungrouped.
Click **A**rrange	The Arrange menu appears.
Click **C**ombine	The spots are combined.

Repeat the procedure for the last two groups of spots.

Save the file as BUT6

Now you are seeing the fruits of your labor. Notice the speed at which the wing displays in full-color editing mode or in full-screen preview. The wireframe may look identical, but the redraw time tells the story. If you take a look at the file size, you will see that it has dropped dramatically: fallen from 29796 to 14652 bytes since last checked.

The seventh step merely involves grouping and mirror/duplicating the first wing, then dragging it into position and rotating it, if necessary. Then group the two wings together to allow the pair to be moved as one unit.

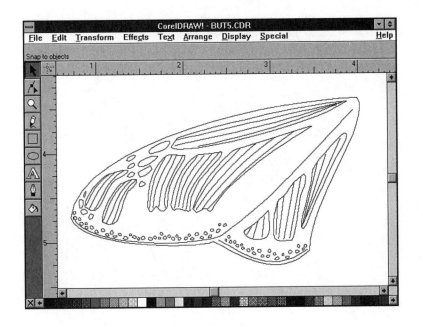

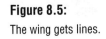

Figure 8.5:
The wing gets lines.

Duplicating and Positioning the Second Wing

Marquee-select the wing

Click **Arrange**	The Arrange menu appears.
Click **Group**	The wing is grouped.
Click **Transform**	The Transform menu appears.
Click **Stretch & Mirror**	The Stretch & Mirror dialogue box appears.
Click **Horiz Mirror, Leave** Original	
Click OK	The wing is mirror/duplicated.

Drag the new wing into position and rotate if necessary (see fig. 8.6).

Figure 8.6:

The wing gets mirrored and rotated.

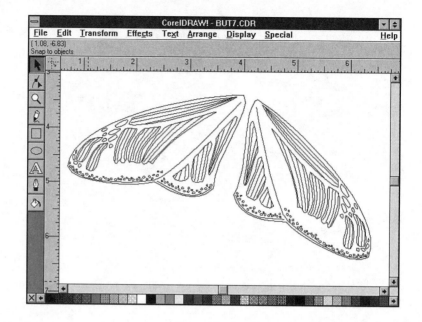

Finally, you will build the butterfly's body. You will draw a silhouette body (in black), and squeeze it anamorphically a couple of times, using Repeat. Then you will use the Blend effect to fill the area between the objects with a variety of tones. Blending the original outline into a skinny highlight will give the body a more three-dimensional look. The different tones will provide the illusion of lighting.

Now you will construct the head, eyes, and antenna. Use the pencil and ellipse tools to build these, and remember to combine like objects. The black outline around the body came from the very first "unsqueezed" silhouette. You did not start changing the tints until *after* you squeezed your first duplicate.

Blend and Repeat

The Blend effect, introduced with CorelDRAW! version 2.0, is a powerful drawing tool. With Blend, you can interpolate between two different objects. The outline color and width, fill, and object shape are melded together. Blend had a wide variety of uses. For instance, you can turn apples into oranges, dogs into cats, and purples into reds. In the last case, you will notice that there is functional overlap between the Blend effect and fountain fills.

CorelDRAW! version 3.0 features great improvements to the Blend effect. Most importantly, blends are now dynamic. This means that once you have created a blend, you can make changes to the starting or ending objects, and the blend will re-create itself.

Blend is accessed via Roll-Up menu, which offers incredible control over a number of blend characteristics. In the following exercise, you will use only a fraction of Blend's capabilities. The engineers put their efforts to good use on this one! Blend is now one of Draw's nicest features.

Repeat may not be as flashy as Blend, but it is certainly as utilitarian and you will use it quite frequently. You can automate repetitive tasks in CorelDRAW! with the Repeat command. Repeat reiterates the last maneuver performed. You will use this technique to add a number of "belts" to finish off the butterfly's body.

As you use Blend and Repeat to finish off the butterfly's body, it will help to draw the butterfly's body vertically, without any diagonal angle, so that the initial horizontal stretch does not distort the body. You can rotate the completed body later.

Shortcut

Press Ctrl-R to repeat the last function.

TIP

Perhaps you want to shrink (or enlarge) an object, but are not sure what the object's final size should be. Scale the object down (or up) by a small percentage; say, 2 percent. Then, use the Ctrl-R shortcut to repeatedly scale the object down (or up) to the exact size. This technique can also be used for rotating objects.

Using Blend To Build the Butterfly's Body

Click the pencil tool

Draw the silhouette of the body

Click the fill tool — The Fill fly-out menu appears.

Click black — The silhouette is filled with black.

Draw a body section

Click the shape tool

Reduce the number of nodes in the body section to about 11

Tweak the nodes as needed

Click the fill tool — The Fill fly-out menu appears.

continues

Click Uniform Fill	Uniform Fill dialogue box appears.

At cyan, enter: **100**

At magenta, enter: **50**

At yellow, enter: **10**

At black, enter: **60**

Click OK

Now that you have the first body section down, you will squeeze it to create the highlight. You will use two keyboard modifiers, Shift +, to stretch from the middle of the object and leave the original.

Click the body section	The body section is selected.

Click and drag the side handle,
scaling down 29 percent at the same time

Press + while pressing and holding
down Shift

Release the mouse button	The body is stretched, leaving an original.

Now, fill this body segment. With the squeezed segment selected, take the following steps:

Click the fill tool	The Fill fly-out menu appears.
Click Uniform Fill	The Uniform Fill dialogue box appears.

At cyan, enter: **100**

At magenta, enter: **80**

At yellow, enter: **40**

At black, enter: **40**

Click OK

Shift-click or marquee-select both body segments

Click the outline tool	The Outline fly-out menu appears.
Click none	

You are almost there! Now it is time to use Blend. You are going to add two steps between the inner and outer body objects. The interpolated objects will blend in shape as well as color.

With both body segments selected, take the following steps:

Click Effects	The Effects menu appears.

Click **B**lend Roll-Up ...	The Blend Roll-Up menu appears (see fig. 8.7).
At Steps, type **2**	
Click Apply	The body segments are blended (see fig. 8.8).

Notice that the blended segments are grouped together. This makes them easy to delete if they do not come out looking quite right. Of course, you can ungroup the blend and work with the individual objects, tweaking nodes and colors as you see fit.

Blend works on object shapes, fills, and outlines, but there are some restrictions. You can only blend between two entities at a time, but these can be groups of objects or multiple path objects (see figure 8.9). Blending between objects of different fills or outline colors has certain constraints, as outlined in Table 8.1.

Shortcut

Press Ctrl-B to access the Blend Roll-Up menu.

Table 8.1
Blend Characteristics

Starting/Ending Object Fill	*Blend Objects Fill*
No Fill/Any Fill	No Fill
Uniform/Linear Fountain	Uniform to Linear Fountain
Uniform/Radial Fountain	Radial Fountain
Radial Fountain/Linear Fountain	Radial Fountain
Two Fountains of Same Type	Similar Fountain
Uniform/Pattern	Uniform
Pattern/Any Fill	Other Fill
Two Patterns	Top Object's Pattern
Spot Color/Process Color	Process Color
Two Different Spot Colors	Process Color
Two Tints of the Same Spot Color	Spot Color Tints

Figure 8.7:

The Blend Roll-Up menu.

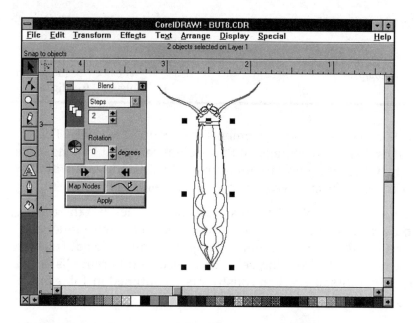

Figure 8.8:

The body after blending.

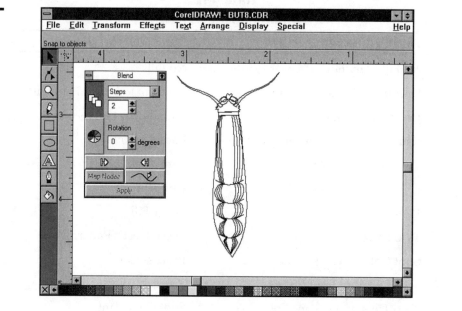

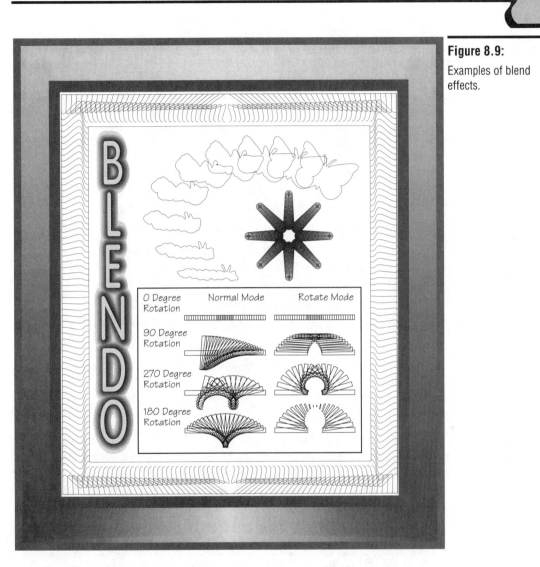

Figure 8.9:
Examples of blend
effects.

In addition to the blend fills mentioned earlier, you can set specific
blend color attributes. By clicking on the Blend Roll-Up's color
wheel, you are able to access an HSB color wheel. Clicking on
Rainbow enables you to apply a rainbow effect—in either a clockwise or counter-clockwise direction—to your blend.

The Blend dialogue box offers a variety of different effects. The first value you may enter is the number of blend steps. This value (from 1 to 999) governs the number of interpolating objects created between the starting and ending objects. Remember that the more objects you use, the smoother the blend; but file size (and print time) will grow proportionately.

You can use rotation for some interesting arcing effects. Figure 8.9 displays settings for 270-, 180-, 90-, and 0-degree (clockwise) rotation. Using negative values will rotate the objects in the opposite direction. In addition, you can pull out an object's center of rotation before blending to give the blend a twisting path.

Editing intermediate blend objects can yield some interesting results. Ctrl-double-click on any intermediate blend object, and you can alter that object's position, outline, fill, size, and shape. You can even get into some heavy node editing!

The position and number of nodes in each object affect the blend. By default, blends act upon the starting nodes of both objects. You can alter this by selecting Map Matching Nodes. This option enables you to choose the nodes—in effect, temporarily reassigning the starting nodes—to achieve different blends.

Blending along a path became a reality in CorelDRAW! 3.0. You can now have a blend follow a specific, editable trail. When blending along a path, you have the option to use either predefined spacing, or a number of steps. A blend can follow the full path, or just a portion of it, with magnetic accuracy. You also can rotate the blend objects to follow the curve of a path.

Now that blending is interactive, you can move or otherwise alter a starting or ending blend object, and watch the blend redraw. You even have the capability to reshape the blend path interactively. The blend objects will instantly and precisely align themselves to the path.

There are many uses for Blend. The more you work with the effect, the more you will find. In figure 8.9, a caterpillar was turned into a butterfly with seven intermediate steps. The butterfly came from Draw's animal symbols. It was duplicated and rearranged into a caterpillar shape with the node edit tool. By blending two objects with the same number of nodes, some of the bizarre effects that happen when blending two wildly different objects were avoided. You will notice that the blend steps are always equally spaced; however, you can separate and ungroup the blend after its completion and space the interpolated objects as you see fit.

The neon effect on the word "Blendo" was easy to create. First, the word was set with a fat 10 percent outline. Then, the word was duplicated and centered on the original. The duplicate was given a 100 percent hairline outline. Eight blend steps were used between the two. Presto! Instant neon. For a step-by-step exercise in creating neon type, check out Chapter 9.

Now that you have covered the blend basics, it's time to get back to finishing off Joe DeLook's butterfly.

Finishing Off the Body with Repeat

The butterfly's body should be starting to look pretty good. You have a few more additions to make, and you will be home free. The next brief exercise uses the Repeat command to duplicate and move an object.

Shortcut

Press Ctrl-R to repeat the last maneuver performed.

Look at the lower section of the butterfly's body. You are going to "tie a belt" around each of the four "waists," to give some shadow. Start by drawing the first "belt" around the uppermost "waist."

Finishing the Body with Repeat

Click the pencil tool

Draw a single line segment

Click the shape tool

Change the nodes to curves, to fit the belt

Tweak the control points

Click the pick tool

Press and drag the belt down to the second waist

continues

Release the mouse button   A duplicate belt is
                                             drawn.

Now, as you are about to see, Draw can remember and repeat that last
maneuver:

Click **Edit**   The Edit menu appears.

Click **R**epeat   Another belt is drawn,
                                             spaced exactly the same
                                             distance.

Try that one more time to get the last belt. When you are done, take the
following steps:

Shift-click all 4 belts

Click the outline tool   The Outline fly-out menu
                                             appears.

Click the one-point rule

Click **A**rrange   The Arrange menu
                                             appears.

Click **C**ombine   The belts are combined
                                             (see fig. 8.10).

Figure 8.10:

The butterfly's body
in position.

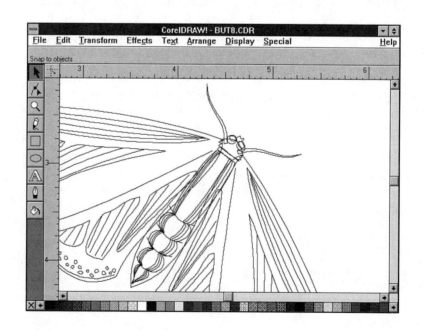

When everything is done, group (do not combine) all the body parts and drag the body into a more natural position (see fig. 8.11). If you combined all the body parts now, it would be a waste of effort; combining objects gives them identical outline and fill characteristics. To finish off the butterfly, remember to group the wings with the body—you would not want his wings to fall off!

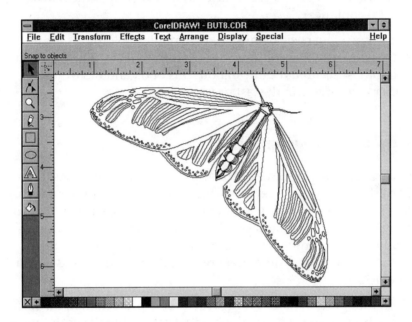

Figure 8.11:

The finished butterfly.

After completing this last exercise, the advantages of using Combine, Group, Blend, and Repeat should be quite apparent. The author's final file size came in at 23884 bytes, almost 6K less than the original uncombined wing alone!

Before moving on to the next subject, take the time to print your butterfly. If you encounter any problems with printing, check out Chapter 12. While the butterfly is not a hopelessly complex piece of art, it may tie up your printer for ten minutes or more.

Preventing Problems

It would be tough to find an electronic artist, or any computer user, who has never lost a file—or at least a few hours of work—because of lackadaisical file management. Most people learn the hard way. That is why it is crucial to follow proper file management techniques.

There are a few basic details to keep in mind. Nothing earth-shattering here, just common-sense stuff. In fact, you have been using these techniques throughout this book and have done so rather extensively in the last group of exercises.

Save Files Frequently!

Once again, use the Save command to write working files to the hard disk at regular intervals. This procedure will prevent file loss in the event of a power outage (barring a disk crash). It also provides a "super undo," for those occasions when the file gets really trashed through a series of unfortunate choices. With a saved file on hand, you merely reopen the file, relax, and get back to work.

Even though CorelDRAW! provides some protection in the form of the backup file, get into the habit of saving the file each time an intricate maneuver is performed. This will help to thwart the gremlins.

In addition to simply saving files, you also can make multiple copies of intricate files (as you did with the butterfly). This provides extra insurance in case a version gets trashed along the way. Number these files sequentially to make it easy to go back in and rework the file at any stage of completion.

CorelDRAW! version 2.0 introduced Timed AutoBackup. This is yet another mechanism for safeguarding work. You will learn how to alter the backup timing in Appendix A.

Use Undo Immediately!

This next point may also seem obvious, but run through it one more time. It is imperative to use Undo immediately after fouling up. Do not try to "fix" what has gone wrong. Do not touch anything else, be it an object or a tool.

The second that you say "Oops," stop everything. Then, without delay, click Edit/Undo, or use the keyboard shortcut Alt-Backspace. This will ensure that Undo will perform its function. Failure to use Undo immediately may jeopardize the drawing.

Always Back Up Important Files!

The final preventive measure to mention is file backup. So many of you have so much information stored away on your hard disks without realizing the potential for disaster. Hard disks are like bank vaults. They are great places for storing things, but if the disk should crash, it would be akin to throwing away the key to the vault. Salvaging data from a trashed hard disk can be tougher than breaking into a bank.

Fortunately (or is that luckily?), the author followed strict backup procedures while working on a previous edition of this book. Deep into the production process, one of the computers had a hard disk failure. While it was a setback, it was not monumental. All important files had been backed up to floppies. A spare hard disk was slapped into the computer and all the software and data files were reloaded. In half a day, everything was once again running at full speed.

Which files should be backed up? All important CDR files, for starters. Imagine putting days, weeks, or even months into building a library of images, only to have them lost to a disk crash. There are disk utilities on the market that may enable the user to salvage files that would otherwise be lost. One of the most popular is the Norton Utilities.

Backing up important CDR files to floppy disks is an inexpensive way to safeguard against loss. Use the Windows File Manager on a regular basis to copy all pertinent files from the hard disk to floppies.

Preview Strategies

A good deal of the material discussed in this chapter concerns operating efficiency. The time it takes to get things done is vital. Most people have grown up in a world that refuses to wait for anything, including the time it takes for computers to process information.

Shortcut

Press Shift-F9 to switch between wireframe and full-color editing.

When building complex drawings, the screen redraw times can get to be quite substantial. Here are a few strategies that can help to cut down the waiting time. Of course, you could go out and get the fastest computer available, and outfit it with a speedy hard disk and powerful graphics card, but no matter what, you will eventually find yourself (broke and) seeking something a little faster. The concepts you are about to learn will work with any PC running CorelDRAW!

The simplest advice is to work in wireframe mode most of the time. This obviously cuts down on screen redraw time. You must determine what works best for you. When speed is the prime consideration, work with wireframes. When it is imperative to do full-color editing, press Shift-F9 and go for it!

Shortcut

Press F9 to invoke full-screen preview.

If you like the biggest preview screen possible, then you will want to use true full-screen preview. By pressing F9, you instantly summon up a nice big preview, unencumbered by windows, toolboxes, and the like. The disadvantage is that you must return to editing mode to make any changes to the image.

Interruptible Display

When you are working on a large file, screen redraws can get to be quite time-consuming. One way to speed things up is to use Interruptible Display. This feature enables you to perform a function before the screen has been completely redrawn. This time-saving feature can be switched on and off at the Preferences dialogue box.

Auto-Panning

Auto-panning was introduced in CorelDRAW! version 3.0, but PageMaker users will be quite familiar with the concept. With this feature enabled, the screen will scroll automatically when you drag an object past the Draw window's border. You can switch Auto-panning on or off via the Preferences dialogue box.

Getting the Most from Layers

Among the Layer Options, you may decide to make a layer invisible, or apply a color override. By hiding a complex layer, your screen will redraw faster and your drawing will be easier to work with. Assigning a color override can yield much the same result, without "losing sight" of those layers.

Preview Selected Only

The last time-saving strategy involves using the Preview Selected Only option, also found on the Display menu. This method is useful when composing very complex drawings with a multitude of objects. Using this function speeds up redraw times enormously, because the program only displays selected objects, rather than the entire drawing.

It is also useful for isolating objects. If an image contains a heap of objects, each indiscernible from the next, Preview Selected Only can be instrumental in sorting things out. With this option on, merely click on, or Tab through the objects until the correct one is located, and press F9 to preview.

TIP

Click the right mouse button while dragging to leave an original. This has no effect on any of the programmable mouse functions.

Save Time by Programming Your Mouse

One last way to speed things up is to set up your mouse button to perform a frequent task. The Preferences dialogue box provides the means to instantly pop into four different modes. You can set your right mouse button to summon: 2× Zoom, Edit Text, Full

Screen Preview, or Node Edit. This can save a great amount of time, and it is possible that future versions of CorelDRAW! may provide additional choices.

It is obvious that Corel Systems truly listens to its user base. Many of the features that were incorporated into the latest incarnations of Draw were requested by users. If you have a feature request, be sure to let Corel know about it.

Joe Wakes Up

When you last left Joe DeLook, he was asleep at his favorite fishing spot. A sharp tug on the line has brought Joe back into the waking world, but, alas, the fish took the bait and swam off. Belatedly, Joe remembers the Island Watersports project that he was working on.

With only a few hours to deadline, Joe hustles back to the studio. The work is not too far from being finished, but there is one important thing yet to be done—fitting the company name around the logo.

Fitting Text to Path

One of CorelDRAW!'s most engaging features, Fit Text to Path, enables you to take a string of text and set it around a circle, an oval, a square, or another object (see fig. 8.12). This feature is a valuable asset to the artist who is thrown a curve, and then asked to set type to it.

To fit text to a path, you need two obvious things: the text and the path. The mere implementation of the command is easy; select both the text and the path, summon the Fit Text to Path Roll-Up menu from the Arrange menu, make your choices, and click Apply. Achieving perfection can be time-consuming, however; it is not just a point, shoot, and print procedure. There is always plenty of room for tweaking.

Once type is aligned to a path, it is still moveable. You can reposition individual characters with the shape tool, and adjust inter-character and inter-word spacing. The shape tool will also enable you to access the Character Attributes dialogue box to change the size, typeface, and rotation of individual characters. This last capability is quite important, because characters tend to require a touch of rotation to achieve a smooth look.

Unfortunately, text is not directly editable while on a path. You must use the Edit Text command to make changes (like correcting typos). Furthermore, it is uncommon for type to be perfectly set to a path at first shot. It usually takes at least a few tries to achieve the proper combination of text alignment, character spacing, and rotation. Don't feel too bad if it takes a while to get the hang of it. Once you understand the principles, things will begin to make sense; and soon you'll be able to fit text to a path like a pro.

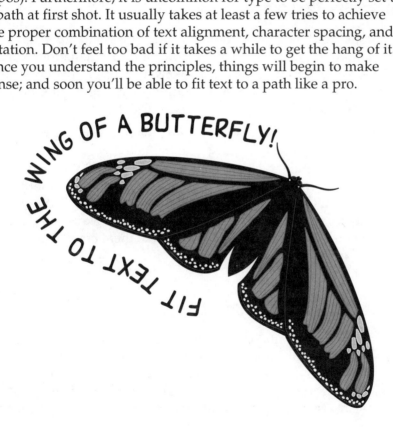

Figure 8.12:

Text made to fit almost anything.

Fit Text to Path Roll-Up Menu

Corel's engineers totally overhauled the Fit Text to Path effect in CorelDRAW! version 3.0, and with great success. By using a Roll-Up menu, they were able to create a full-featured implementation of what was once just a frustrating and underpowered tool. The Fit Text to Path Roll-Up menu gives you total control of the command.

Character Orientation

The "look" and "set" of fit-to-path text is governed by the text orientation setting. You can choose one of four orientations: Rotate Letters, Vertical Skew, Horizontal Skew, or Upright Letters. The accompanying figure (8.13/8.14), Path-O-Logic, illustrates how each setting affects text.

It is safe to say that for most designers, the traditional Rotate Letters setting will get the most use. In the following exercise, you will use that setting to complete the logo for Island Watersports (that you began in Chapter 7). You will likely save the other three settings for special effects, or for more abstract work. Setting the wrong piece of type with Vertical or Horizontal Skew could send your clients into convulsions. It may make them crazy, but, by all means, experiment (as in fig. 8.15)!

Character/Path Alignment

Draw gives you plenty of flexibility with respect to character/path alignment. You can choose between five alignment settings: baseline, variable, top-of-caps, descenders, and centerline. All except for the top-of-caps alignment are variations of the same theme—in essence, variations upon character baseline alignment.

As shown by the ever-handy Path-O-Matic, your character/path alignment choices are controlled by the Character Orientation setting. While you are limited to baseline or variable alignments when using either of the skewed settings, both the Rotate and Upright Letters settings allow access to the full range of character/path alignment.

Figure 8.13/8.14:
The Path-O-Logic Chart.

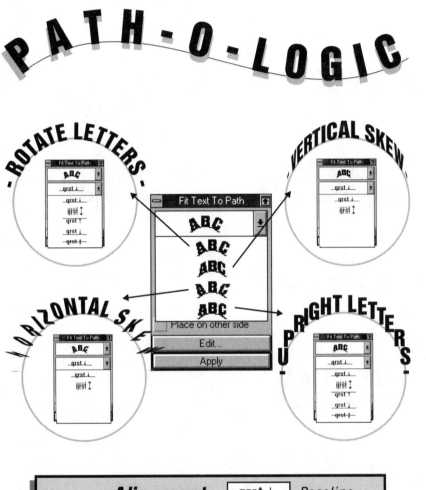

Figure 8.13/8.14: Continued

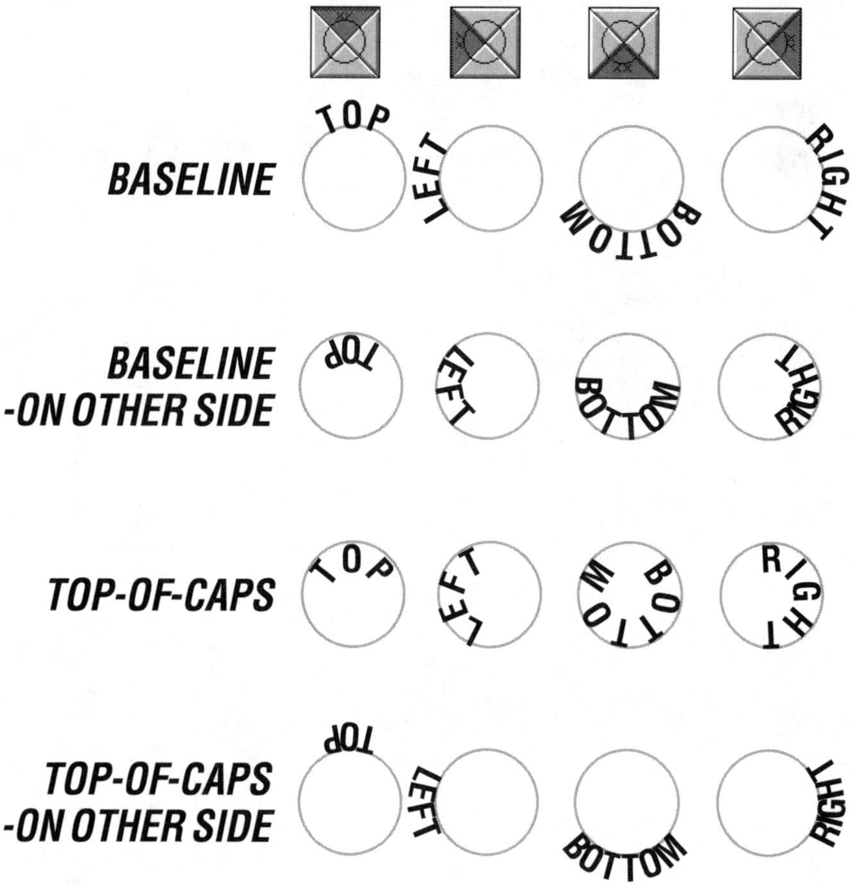
BASELINE
TOP
LEFT
BOTTOM
RIGHT
BASELINE -ON OTHER SIDE
TOP-OF-CAPS
TOP-OF-CAPS -ON OTHER SIDE

TIP

Finding it tough to select the text to make edits? Here are two hints. You can use the tab key to cycle between objects. Or, click on the text with the shape tool, select the pick tool, and *voila!* You can now press Ctrl-T to access the Artistic Text dialogue box.

If you decide that you want to change the text's distance from the path (regardless of the original alignment setting), simply click on the text, and drag it inward or outward. The Vertical Offset marker will appear, and the status line will report on the text's distance from the path. When you release the mouse button, you will notice that the alignment setting will have changed to variable. You may also make similar changes (or fine-tuning tweaks) by clicking on the Fit Text to Path Roll-Up menu's Edit... button. This summons the Fit Text To Path Offsets dialogue box, where you can alter the Distance From Path and Horizontal Offset settings.

Influence of Fit To Path Text Justification

The Fit Text To Path Roll-Up menu configures its text justification settings differently for rectangles and ellipses than it does for other objects. This provides a satisfactory interface for both situations.

Rectangles and Ellipses

When you work with a rectangle or ellipse as your path, the Fit Text To Path Roll-Up menu provides an instant visual clue as to how your text will set on the path. A four-cornered button controls how you center your text: on the top side, left side, bottom side, or right side of the path. Simply choose the side you want to center your text on and click the corresponding side of the button.

If you want your text to run on the other side of the path, click Place On Other Side. This will flip the text over to the inside or outside of the path, depending on whether you are aligning via character baselines or top-of-caps, respectively. Take another look at the Path-O-Matic chart (figure 8.13/8.14).

Figure 8.15:
Skew yourself silly!

Other Objects

Text is always fit to a path based on the path's starting and/or ending nodes. Open path objects (or lines) have obvious starting and ending points. Closed path objects start and end at the same point. If you are drawing an object which you will ultimately use as a path to which text will be fit, you must take this into consideration.

All text justification is governed by the Fit Text To Path Roll-Up menu, as any other alignment settings are overruled. Left Alignment will force the text string to be set from the path's starting node. Center Aligned will force the text string to be centered between the starting and ending nodes. Right Aligned will force the text string to end at the path's ending node.

How can you tell where a closed path starts? No problem. When an object is selected with the shape tool, the start/end node will appear larger than the other nodes. If you select an object with the pick tool, look closely and you will see the starting node (this works best when you are zoomed out). Want to move a starting node? It's a hassle, so you should try not to! Objects can always be mirrored or rotated, but the best strategy is always to try and draw the object with text-alignment in mind. Start the drawing in the place that you plan to align from. Luckily, there is one possible "cheap out." If you click Place On Other Side, the text will start from the ending node and on the opposite side of the path (180 degrees).

Separate/Align to Baseline/Straighten Text/Undo

As you are going through the process of fitting text to a path, you will invariably need to return the text to its original state as you alter character spacing information, or correct a typo. In short, the best way to accomplish this is immediately to Undo the fit. If you have made a move (and made Undo unavailable), you still have a couple of options.

In these cases, you must first break the text from the path, by clicking Separate (from the Arrange menu). Then, you must deselect the text by clicking the page. Once you have reselected the text, both Align to Baseline and Straighten Text will reset text strings to a straight baseline. Straighten Text, however, will also remove any Character Attributes, such as typeface and size. It will also reset vertical shift, horizontal shift, and character angle values to zero. This is not a good thing to do after you have just spent half an hour adjusting these settings.

Unlike Straighten Text, Align to Baseline will not erase the horizontal shift or character angle values. However, Straighten Text, will hold all kerning and rotation information. Unfortunately, the text will land in a nasty-looking lump if it has been rotated.

How do you get around this dilemma? Usually, the best choice is simply to undo the maneuver. If you make Character Attribute changes, make a duplicate of the block of type for safekeeping.

Right now, you are going to use Fit Text to Path to finish off the Island Watersports logo. Start by opening up the file SIZZLER.CDR that you saved at the end of the last chapter. You will add four ovals (see fig. 8.16). Later, you will use two of them as nonprinting guidelines to fit the text to. The other two ovals will be part of the design and will outline the logo.

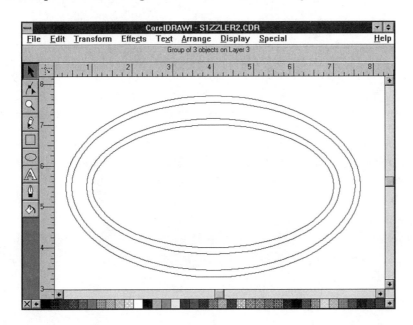

Figure 8.16:

Beginning the Island Watersports logo.

Creating a Text Path for the Island Watersports Logo

Click File	The File menu appears.
Click **O**pen	
Double-click SIZZLER	The SIZZLER file opens.

You are going to need four ovals. The first oval is for the inner outline and the second is for the inner text path. The third is for the outer text path, while the final oval is for the perimeter outline. It may sound like overkill, but you will use them all. To begin, set the grid to 1 per inch. You will turn it off again almost immediately.

Drawing the Inner Oval

Click **D**isplay	The Display menu appears. Note whether Snap To Grid is on.
Click **G**rid Setup	The Grid Setup dialogue box appears.
Set Frequency to: 1 per inch	
Click Snap To Grid	If the grid is not already on.
Click the ellipse tool	
Draw an oval	Make it 6.00" wide by 3.00" tall. This is the inner oval.
Press Ctrl-Y	Turns off grid.

You have created the inner oval. Scale up three more ovals, each from the preceding duplicate. You will notice that you are using percentages that are proportional to the horizontal and vertical dimensions of the oval.

Drawing the Rest of the Ovals

Click the inner oval	The inner oval is selected.
Click **Transform**	The Transform menu appears.
Click **Stretch & Mirror**	The Stretch & Mirror dialogue box appears.
At Horizontal, enter: **105**	
At Vertical, enter: **110**	
Click **Leave Original**	
Click OK	The oval is scaled up to create the inner text path.
Click the inner text path oval	Selects the inner text path oval.
Click **Transform**	The Transform menu appears.
Click **Stretch & Mirror**	The Stretch & Mirror dialogue box appears.
At Horizontal, enter: **112**	
At Vertical, enter: **124**	
Click **Leave Original**	
Click OK	The oval is scaled up to create the outer text path.
Click the outer text path oval	Selects the outer text path oval.
Click **Transform**	The Transform menu appears.
Click **Stretch & Mirror**	The Stretch & Mirror dialogue box appears.
At Horizontal, enter: **104**	
At Vertical, enter: **108**	
Click **Leave Original**	
Click OK	The oval is scaled up to create the outer perimeter.

Next, set the text. You will be using the default settings, baseline, and top of object, when you fit the first piece of text to the path. Consequently, all you will need to do at the Roll-Up menu is click the apply button.

Setting Text to a Path

Click the text tool	The cursor becomes a +.
Click the page	The text I bar appears.
Type: **ISLAND WATERSPORTS**	
Press Ctrl-T	The Artistic Text dialogue box appears.
At Point Size, enter: **40**	
At Type, choose: **USA-Black**	
Click **S**pacing	
At Inter-Character, enter **-10**	
At Inter-Word, enter: **120**	
Click OK	
Click OK *again*	
You have the text and the path, so go for it!	
Click the pick tool	
Shift-click ISLAND WATERSPORTS *and the inner text path*	
Click Text	The Text menu appears.
Click Fit **T**ext To Path	The Fit Text To Path Roll-Up menu appears.
At Fit Text To Path Roll-Up menu:	
Click Apply	ISLAND WATERSPORTS is set to the inner path.

So how does the text look? It probably needs some tweaking and kerning. Take note of the places that need to be tightened or loosened and then click Undo to break the text off the path. Now is the time to make those initial kerning adjustments. When you are done, refit the text to the path. Continue to use interactive kerning and the character attributes to rotate individual characters.

If you happen to do something to make Undo unavailable, you can use Straighten Text to do the job, although you will lose any kerning information. You will find Straighten Text on the Arrange menu. Using Align to Baseline will not work well; the characters will remain rotated, and you will wind up with a lumpy mess. Once again, the best strategy is to make a duplicate of any seriously tweaked chunk of text.

Now, set the text for the bottom of the logo.

Setting the Bottom Text

Click the text tool	The cursor becomes a +.
Click the page	The text I bar appears.
Type: **ESTABLISHED 1966**	
Press Ctrl-T	The Artistic Text dialogue box appears.
At Point Size, enter: **40**	
At Type, choose: **USA-Light**	
Click **S**pacing	
At Inter-Character, enter **-10**	
At Inter-Word, enter: **120**	
Click OK	
Click OK *again*	
Click the pick tool	
Shift-click inner text path	
At Fit Text To Path Roll-Up menu:	
Click Alignment down arrow button	Alignment menu appears.
Click Top-Of Caps	
Click Bottom button	
Click Place on other side	
Click Apply	ESTABLISHED 1966 is set (top-of-caps, on other side, and bottom aligned) to the inner path (see figs. 8.17 and 8.18).

Figure 8.17:

Setting top-of-caps, on other side, and bottom alignments.

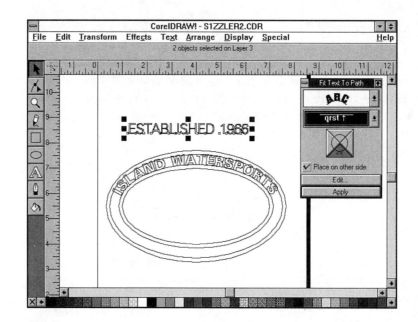

Figure 8.18:

The logo with type fit to path.

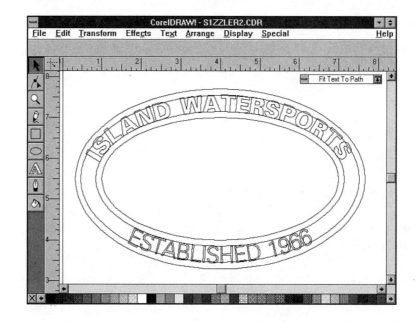

This type may not need nearly as much refining as the type at the top of the logo. Feel free to do any kerning or rotating you think appropriate.

You are almost done, but you have a few things to tidy up. The two text paths should be nonprinting, and hence must be assigned an outline and fill of NONE. Alternatively, the text path outlines can be deleted without disturbing the text. However, if you want to go back in and tweak some more, you will have nothing to align to. The inner and outer outlines (which you do want to print) should be combined, given a fill of white, and a two-point outline. The results should look like figure 8.19.

Bring the Sizzler art into position, rotate and scale to fit, and save the file. The logo is done!

As you have seen, fitting text to path is a powerful feature which enables the user to make the final aesthetic adjustments. This exercise gives you just a taste of what the procedure is all about. Do not feel that you are done as soon as Draw has fit the text to your path. More often than not, you will need to go in and adjust kern pairs, as well as character rotation. Avoid setting text to tight curves, if at all possible. If it is a must, try setting the type in a smaller point size.

Figure 8.19:
The finished logo.

Here is one general rule of advice with regard to inter-character spacing. Text fit to the outside of a path should initially be set with a tight track. Text fit to the inside of a path should initially be set with a loose track. This is because outside text opens up, and inside text closes up, once they have been fit to their respective paths.

Now that you have the logo finished, move on to perspective, the final subject in this chapter.

Perspective

The Perspective effect was introduced in CorelDRAW! version 2.0, to great acclaim. It is a means to apply one- and two-point perspective to any object (see figs. 8.20 and 8.21). If you are not familiar with perspective, briefly go over the theory basics presented here. If you are interested in learning more background information, consider taking a course in two-dimensional design.

There are many familiar examples to refer to when speaking about perspective. The most common may be the ubiquitous railroad tracks and telephone poles. Think how these objects fade off into the distance, shrinking to tiny spots on the horizon.

When working with perspective, there are always two constants. You must have a horizon line and at least one vanishing point. The horizon line, as its name implies, is a horizontal "edge of the earth," while the vanishing point is the point of convergence on the horizon line. As objects get farther away, they grow vertically closer to the horizon line.

Remember that the horizon line is at eye level. If eye level is five feet and seven inches, so too is the horizon line. Consequently, any object that is at eye level—regardless of its location on the plane—will hit the horizon line.

The best way to lay down a horizon line with CorelDRAW! is to drag in a horizontal guideline. Then, you can drag in a vertical guideline (or two) to set up your vanishing point(s). This method is especially handy when aligning the vanishing points of a number of objects.

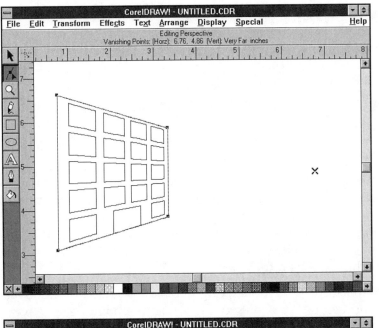

Figure 8.20:

One-point perspective.

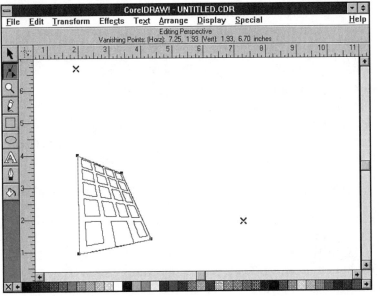

Figure 8.21:

Two-point perspective.

Using the Perspective Effect

When you select an object and click Edit Perspective (on the Effect menu), CorelDRAW! applies a bounding box to the object while the cursor turns into the shape tool. To alter one-point perspective, click and drag on a corner handle. If you want to constrain the movement horizontally or vertically, hold down Ctrl. To effect perspective on two opposite handles simultaneously, hold down both Ctrl and Shift; the handles will move in opposite directions.

To alter two-point perspective, click and drag a corner handle toward (or away from) the object's center. Watch for a pair of X markers on the screen; these markers are the object's vanishing points. Once they are on-screen, you may find it easier to change an object's perspective by clicking and dragging on the object's vanishing points rather than on the object's handles.

Not too surprisingly, one-point perspective enables for one (usually horizontal) vanishing point, while two-point perspective affords two (vertical and horizontal) vanishing points. You can use the click-and-drag positioning technique on either variety.

The Perspective effect can be used on a single object, a group of objects, or a number of (ungrouped) objects. But if you want to apply perspective to an illustration of a building with doors and windows, for example, you should group the objects on each "face." Otherwise, the perspective will be applied to each object rather than to the objects as a whole, and you would have to adjust the perspective for each object (see fig. 8.22).

Remember Copy Style From? It is possible to Copy Perspective From too! Select the object that you want to copy the perspective to, click Copy Perspective From (on the Effects menu), and the From? arrow will appear. Then click the object you want to copy the perspective from. Instant perspective! Note that if you copy to a number of ungrouped objects, a separate perspective will be applied to each object.

Right now, give the perspective effect a try. You will take the finished Island Watersports Logo and see how it looks on a shopping bag (see fig. 8.23). This exercise should ease you into perspective. You will be drawing a couple of rectangles, a couple of handles, and setting some type before you get around to applying perspective.

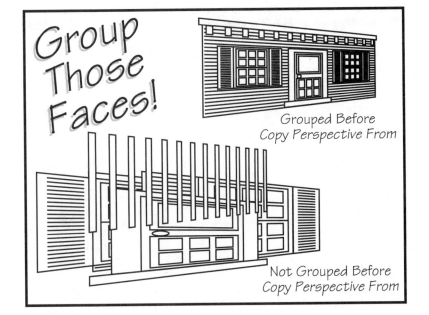

Figure 8.22:
Remember to group before copying perspective!

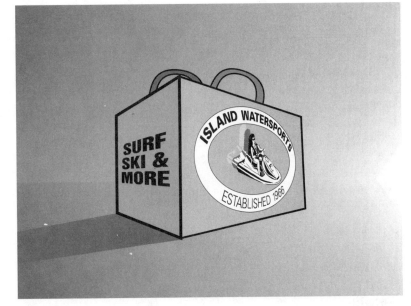

Figure 8.23:
The Island Watersports shopping bag.

Using Perspective To Put the Logo on a Shopping Bag

Set the grid to an easy 2 per inch, and turn it on. This exercise may remind you of the box kite you built way back in Chapter 2!

Click the rectangle tool	
Draw a rectangle	Make it 2" wide by 2.5" high.
Click 20% tint	
Click the outline tool	The Outline fly-out menu appears.
Click the two-point rule	
Draw a second rectangle	Make this rectangle 1" wide by 2.5" high. Place it to left of, and vertically aligned with, the first rectangle.
Click 30% tint	
Click the outline tool	The Outline fly-out menu appears.
Click the two-point rule	
Drag the horizontal guideline down 1.5 inches below the top of the rectangles	This is your horizon line
Drag the vertical guideline over 1.5 inches from the left of the rectangles	This is your vanishing point.
Drag the vertical guideline over 2.5 inches from the right of the rectangles	This is your right vanishing point
Press Ctrl-Y	Turns off grid.

Now, you will set some text for the left side of the bag and draw a couple of handles:

Click the text tool	The cursor turns into a +.
Click the inside of the left rectangle	The text I bar appears.
Type **SURF** *and press Enter*	
Type **SKI &** *and press Enter*	
Type **MORE!**	
Press Ctrl-T	The Artistic Text dialogue box appears.

At Size: enter **24**

Click **Center**

Specify SwitzerlandInsert

Click OK

Click the pick tool

Click the skinny side of the bag

> The text and the side of the bag are selected.

Press Ctrl-A

> The Align dialogue box appears.

Click horizontal center

Click vertical center

Click OK

> The type is centered on the side of the bag.

Press Ctrl-G

> The type is grouped with the side of the bag.

Click the pencil tool

Draw a pair of handles

> Now it should look like figure 8.24.

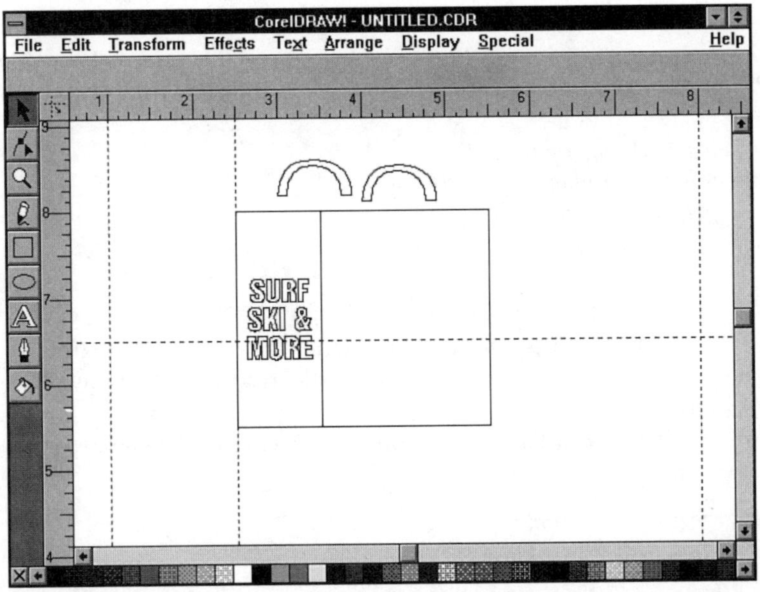

Figure 8.24:
Building the bag.

Okay, give this bag some perspective. You will be dragging corner handles until the vanishing points appear. Then you will drag the vanishing points onto the snap-to guideline intersections.

Finishing the Shopping Bag

Click the pick tool	
Click the skinny side of the bag	The text and the side of the bag are selected.
Click Effects	The Effects menu appears.
Click Edit Perspective	A bounding box appears around the side of the bag.
Click and drag the top left handle down until the vanishing point appears	
Click and drag the vanishing point onto the left guideline intersection	The bag's left side now has perspective!
Click the bag's front side	Selects the bag's front.
Click Effects	The Effects menu appears.
Click Edit Perspective	A bounding box appears around the front of the bag.
Click and drag the top right handle down until the vanishing point appears	
Click and drag the vanishing point onto the right guideline intersection	The bag's right side has perspective, too! Figure 8.25 shows the results.

Drag the handles into position and give them the appropriate tints of 40 and 50 percent for the front and back handle, respectively. Now all you have to do is add the logo to the front of the bag, copy perspective to it, and give it a tweak or two. Make sure that the logo has been grouped *before* you copy perspective!

Drag the logo onto the front of the bag	
Scale the logo to fit	
Click Effects	The Effects menu appears.

Click Copy Perspective from	The From? arrow appears.
Click the front of the bag	The perspective is copied.

The logo may need to be resized once perspective has been added. Go ahead and resize as necessary. When you have it right, click on the shape tool and reposition the vanishing point. Finish up by reshuffling the objects, and group when you are done.

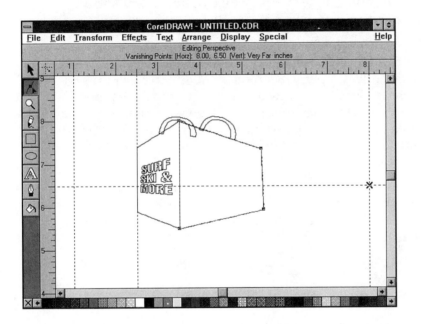

Figure 8.25:

The bag gets some perspective.

If an object's perspective gets out of hand, it can be easily removed with the Clear Perspective command. On objects with multiple perspectives, the command clears each perspective, one at a time. Clicking Clear Transformations removes all perspectives (as well as envelopes) at once.

Like the Envelope effect, text that has been given a perspective remains in an editable state. This makes it easy to change the wording on a packaging mock-up (like your shopping bag) or on a billboard rendering.

Phew! That winds up this chapter. It covered a lot of ground, so take a break while Joe makes his big presentation to the marketing executives at Island Watersports (see fig. 8.26).

Summary

CorelDRAW! is a relatively simple program that is capable of some very complex work. It takes a little talent and a general understanding of the concepts behind the program to be successful in its use.

In this chapter, you have focused on ways you can work more efficiently. Properly combining and grouping your work will ensure that files redraw and print in a timely manner. Using the preview window to your advantage is another way to save valuable time. You also learned about Draw's Fit Text to Path command, and how it can help you manipulate type in minutes instead of hours.

While artistic skill is one thing and electronic design know-how is another, the two are not mutually exclusive. Through a synthesis of both, Draw can help you achieve your goals in both art and business.

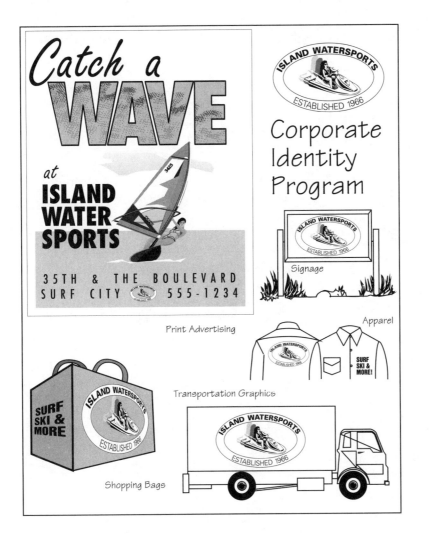

Figure 8.26:

Island Watersports marketing campaign.

9

Special Type Effects

emember Felix the Cat? The cartoon feline with his bag of tricks? This chapter is your equivalent to Felix's magic bag. When you run short of ideas, turn to this chapter for an instant concept, a creative jump-start, or a new way to solve a design dilemma.

The majority of this chapter is devoted to type effects. Some techniques may be familiar, but others may not be quite as obvious. Each effect is illustrated along with a quick how-to exercise, providing a fun and easy way to perfect your technique.

The chapter closes with an exploration of backgrounds. Textures can come from a variety of sources. With a scanner and a bit-map paint program, you can misappropriate any pattern from marble tile to spattered paint to achieve a unique look. And in the vector world, you learn how to create a Zooming Grid with the Perspective effect.

Using Typographical Pyrotechniques

As you have seen in previous chapters, CorelDRAW! enables users to produce a slew of impressive tricks with type. Serious design power comes into play when you use those effects to create multi-faceted pieces of artwork. Images that are exhaustively time-consuming, incredibly expensive, or almost technically impossible to create conventionally can be produced on time and under budget. But this does not mean that projects require little time or effort!

This section investigates a number of effects that are not "one-click" endeavors but require a bit of savvy and technical skill. As you work through the type effects, you soon realize that many of these tricks can apply to objects other than text. Most of the examples in this section strive to conjure up illusions of depth, texture, or motion.

With a depth effect, you can add a three-dimensional look to two-dimensional artwork. Draw enables you to quickly add pop to your work with effects like extrude. To effectively add depth, you need to take the extrusion apart and apply different tints to each side of an object to add the illusion of lighting angles. The concept of lighting angle figures strongly in creating bevel type, embossed type, and tube type. The artist must fool the beholder's eye into accepting different tints as different faces of a multi-dimensional object.

Drop Shadows: Variations on a Theme

A drop shadow is a duplicate of an object, filled with a different tint and placed behind the original object (see fig. 9.1). The fill can be lighter, darker, or a completely different color. The drop shadow is usually the first type embellishment discovered by neophyte desktop publishers, who sometimes overuse it brutally. In the right hands, however, a drop shadow is perfect for popping text off the page. When the drop shadow effect is correctly rendered, it makes type look as if it were magically suspended, floating above the page. Although drop shadows are commonly created with shades of gray, color adds far more subtleties than shades of gray alone can portray. In color advertising or packaging, the drop shadow is almost a necessity.

Figure 9.1:

A standard drop shadow effect.

Even though a plain vanilla drop shadow is hardly worth writing (or reading) about, a few variations of the theme are definitely worth discussing. This section presents perspective shadows, knockout drops, and embossed type. A number of methods are available to create the drop shadow. CorelDRAW! enables you to: use the Duplicate command (Ctrl-D); the Move command (with leave original); and Drag-duplicate. And starting with Version 2.01, the numeric "+" leaves a duplicate exactly on top of the original.

The Move command and the Duplicate command offer the most accuracy. The Move command enables you to change the distance moved each time you use the command; you can set the Duplicate command in the Preferences dialogue box. When you work with a number of objects that all must have the same exact drop shadow, the Duplicate command is your most convenient choice.

If you are only shadowing one object, drag-duplicating (pressing the numeric "+" while dragging) is an excellent option. After the duplicate object is on the page, the nudge function (when set at 0.01 inch) is the slickest way to reposition objects in fine increments.

Perspective Shadows

Figure 9.2 shows an example of a perspective shadow. The words are sitting on the horizon line, backlit by an offset radial fill. The foreground is a linear fountain fill, with the fill angle set to flow from the focal point of the background. The perspective shadow completes the illusion by following the same imaginary light source.

Figure 9.2:

The perspective shadows effect.

The procedure to set a perspective shadow either behind or in front of a piece of type is simple. Contrary to popular opinion, you can create a perspective shadow without using the perspective effect—by using the Skew function.

You begin this exercise by drawing a pair of rectangles to form the background and foreground of your graphic. Draw the first rectangle with the rectangle tool, and duplicate the second from it, using Ctrl-drag. Then add the type, with its baseline resting on an imaginary horizon line. Pull a perspective shadow forward, and manipulate it with skew. Finish up by setting the fill of each object.

Creating Long Shadows

Click the rectangle tool   The cursor changes into a +.

Draw a rectangle, 5" wide by 1" high
Click the pick tool

Click and drag the rectangle's top center handle down; hold down Ctrl and press +	
Release the mouse button when the y scale is (-100%)	A duplicate rectangle is created.

The two rectangles should butt against each other. This line will form the horizon.

Click the text tool	The cursor becomes a + .
Click the center of the top rectangle	The Text I bar appears.
Type **LONG SHADOWS**	
Press Ctrl-T	The Artistic Text dialogue box appears.
Change to 48 point, Jupiter Normal	Changes the point size and face.
Click OK	A 48-point LONG SHADOWS appears.
Click the pick tool	
Click and drag LONG SHADOW's *top center handle down; hold down Ctrl and press +*	
Release the mouse button when the scale is (-100%)	A duplicate, mirrored LONG SHADOWS is created.
Click the mirrored LONG SHADOWS	The Skew/rotate handles appear.
Position the cursor on the bottom center two-headed arrow	The cursor becomes a+.
Drag the cursor to the right	The cursor goes into skew mode.
Position the cursor for approximately 50 degrees of skew	
Release the mouse button	LONG SHADOWS has some pseudo-perspective.
Click LONG SHADOWS *base text*	
Press Shift-PgUp	To bring the base type to the front.
Click **Edit**	The Edit menu appears.
Click Select **A**ll	The status line reads: 4 objects selected.
At the On-Screen Palette, right-click No Outline	

Drag the shadow into position, butting baseline to baseline, at the horizon line (see fig. 9.3). When everything is in place, assign object fills. Give the perspective shadow a 60% black fill, and the base type a black fill. The background (top rectangle) should get a radial fountain fill, from 40% black to white. Use the options box to offset the center, -50% in both x and y. The foreground (bottom rectangle) uses a linear fountain fill, running from 60% black to 10% black, at a 110-degree angle.

Figure 9.3:

The Long Shadows wireframe.

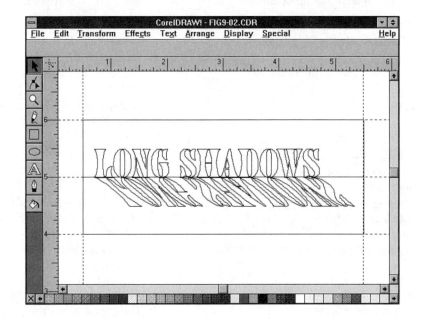

Shortcut

Click the right mouse button to leave an original when dragging.

Notice that the shadow's fill is set to be as dark as the darkest point of the foreground, to ensure that it is, in fact, a shadow. Try setting the shadow to an intermediate tint (say, 40% black) for an interesting effect.

Knockout Drops

No, knockout drops are not leftover barbiturates from a 1940s spy movie. *Knockout* refers to the fact that the white outline of the text knocks (or drops) out of the drop shadow (see fig. 9.4). You can use this effect when printing a multiple color job, where the drop shadow is a different color from the type itself, and the printer's specifications call for loose register. This is one way to avoid problems with trapping (see Chapter 12).

Figure 9.4:
The knockout drops effect.

This exercise is simple. Enlarge the size of the first letter in each word to give a "small caps" effect, and reposition a number of characters to make the type follow a jumpy baseline. Notice that when you create knockout drops, Behind Fill is selected in the Outline Pen dialogue box. This extra step prevents the outline from choking the fill, avoiding an undesirable result. The results of this exercise are shown in figure 9.5.

Creating Knockout Drops

Click the text tool	The cursor becomes a +.
Click page	The Text I bar appears.
Type **KNOCKOUT** *, press Enter, type* **DROPS**	
Press Ctrl-T	The Artistic Text dialogue box appears.
Change to 72 point, Dawn Castle bold	To change point size and face.
Click OK	A 72-point KNOCKOUT DROPS appears.
Left-click 100% black	To fill text.

continues

Right-click White	To outline text.
Click outline	Outline Pen fly-out menu appears.
Click Outline Pen Options	Outline Pen dialogue box appears.
*Click **B**ehind Fill, and Scale With Image*	
Click Rounded Corners, and Line Caps	
*At Width, enter **0.06***	
Click OK	
Click the shape tool	
Drag a marquee around K and D	
Double-click on the K's node	The Character Attributes dialogue box appears.
*At Point Size, enter **100***	
*At Vertical Shift, enter **-10***	
Click OK	Initial Caps are enlarged.

Use the shape tool to select and position individual characters to achieve a jumpy baseline:

Click the pick tool	
Click and drag KNOCKOUT DROPS down and to the left, and press +	
Release the mouse button when x and y are both approximately -0.07	A duplicate KNOCK OUT DROPS is created.

Assign a 20% black fill to the duplicate, and preview. The drop shadow will be in front of the base text. Use Shift Page Down to send the drop shadow to the back.

Embossed Text

Unlike standard drop shadows, which make type look as if it were floating above a page, embossed text makes type look as if it were pressed into the page (see fig. 9.6). This effect is useful when rendering type that should look as if it were "set in stone." CorelPHOTO-PAINT! and other bit-map paint programs can apply an embossed look to text or artwork with a built-in command, but vector-based CorelDRAW! does not offer a one-click solution.

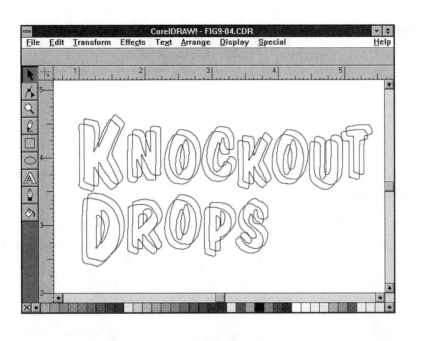

Figure 9.6:
The embossed text
effect.

CorelDRAW! does, however, enable you to quickly emulate
embossed text by setting two drop shadows—one above and one
below the base text. This provides the illusion of highlight and
shadow. Although this solution is not the most elegant, it is
effective and easy to accomplish. You can create interesting effects
by setting the base type with the same tint or color as the background, or by carefully highlighting sections of the embossed text
with slivers of tint, color, or fountain fill. If you work from a
textured background, you can achieve a granite look, especially if
you bring in a granite scan!

Creating Embossed Text

Click the rectangle tool	The cursor changes into a +.
Draw a rectangle 5.25" wide by 1.5" high	
Left click 30% black fill	
Click the text tool	The cursor becomes a +.
Click the center of the rectangle	The Text I bar appears.
Type **Emboss**	
Press Ctrl-T	The Artistic Text dialogue box appears.
Change to 96 point, Arabia	To change point size and face.
Click OK	A 96-point Emboss appears.
Click the pick tool	
Left-click 30% black	Fills base Emboss with 30% black.
Click and drag Emboss, *then press +*	
Release the mouse button when x and y are both approximately 0.02	A duplicate Emboss is created.
Press Ctrl-R	To create a third Emboss.
Press PgDn	Sends the third Emboss back one layer.
Left-click White	Fills highlight Emboss with white.
Click the leftmost Emboss	
Left-click 50% black	Fills the shadow emboss with 50% black.
Drag a marquee around all three Embosses	
Press Ctrl-G	Groups Emboss.
At On-Screen Palette, right-click No Outline	The Embosses have no outline.
Shift-click the rectangle	The Emboss and the rectangle are selected.
Click **Arrange**	The Arrange menu appears.
Click **Align**	The Align dialogue box appears.

Click Horizontal **C**enter
Click Vertical **C**enter
Click OK

The Emboss is centered in the rectangle (see fig. 9.7).

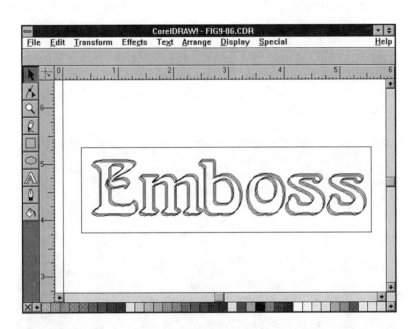

Figure 9.7:
Emboss wireframe.

In the previous example, the lighting angle is set to come from the upper right hand corner of the page. To change the way the embossing is "lit" (altering the angle by 180 degrees), give the leftmost Emboss a 10% black tint, and the rightmost Emboss a 40% black tint.

Neon Type

Neon signs are back in vogue. This part of American culture has made the jump from the real thing in Las Vegas and Times Square to hand-lettered signs, pickup trucks, and print advertising. CorelDRAW! makes it easy to create lettering with a neon look (see fig. 9.8). Such typography can work beautifully in black and white, spot, or process color. Certain typefaces work exceptionally well as neon type. One of the best faces to use is Vogue; its rounded ends give the perfect tubular feel. For script faces, try Freeport or Koala. In general, use a face that is of equal weight throughout the letterform.

To build neon type with CorelDRAW! is not incredibly difficult, but it does take time, patience, and experimentation to get things perfect. The Outline Pen dialogue box is essential when you create Neon Type. Be sure that you select Scale With Image, Rounded Corners, and Line Caps. This ensures that you can scale your neon type reliably and that it does not present any spiky outline surprises. Use the Blend effect, at its default setting of 20 steps, to create the illusion of neon.

Figure 9.8:

Examples of neon and tube type.

Back in the summertime paradise of Seaside, your hero, Joe DeLook, has just landed a design contract with his favorite waterfront bistro, The Neon Newt. The first project they want Joe to create is a full-color menu cover (see fig. 9.9). The cover depicts who else but Ned, namesake of The Neon Newt, and is lettered in their corporate typeface, VAG Rounded (which is known as Vogue in CorelDRAW!).

Joe has decided upon a simple design for the menu cover, which is to measure 6 inches by 8 inches. To begin the exercise, create a custom page with Page Frame.

Figure 9.9:
The Neon Newt
menu cover.

Creating Neon Type

Click **File**	The File menu appears.
Click **New**	A new page appears.
Click **File**	The File menu appears again.
Click **P**age Setup	The Page Setup dialogue box appears.

continues

Click **Custom**	
At Horizontal, enter **6.0** *inches*	
At Vertical, enter **8.0** *inches*	
Click Add Page Frame	
Click OK	A 6" × 8" page is created with a page frame.
Click Page Frame	
Click FILL	The Fill fly-out menu appears.
Click Uniform Fill	The Uniform Fill dialogue box appears.
Click *Process*	The dialogue box configures itself for Process Color.
Click *Names*	The dialogue box configures itself for Named Color.
Scroll down and select Deep Navy Blue	
Click OK	Page Frame is filled with Deep Navy Blue.

Click and drag on vertical ruler to create a guideline 0.5 inches from the left margin.

Click and drag on vertical ruler to create a guideline 0.5 inches from the right margin.

Click the text tool	The cursor becomes a +.
Click the page's top left corner	The Text I bar appears.
Type **NEON**	
Press Ctrl-T	The Artistic Text dialogue box appears.
Change to 96 point, Vogue	To change point size and face.
Click **Bold**	
Click OK	A 96-point Vogue bold NEON appears.
Click the pick tool	
At the On-Screen Palette, left-click No Fill	
Click outline	The Outline Pen fly-out menu appears.

Click Outline Color	The Outline Color dialogue box appears.
Click *Process*	The dialogue box configures itself for Process Color.
Click Names	The dialogue box configures itself for Named Color.
Scroll down, select Deep Navy Blue	
Click OK	NEON is outlined with Deep Navy Blue.
Click outline	The Outline Pen fly-out menu appears.
Click Outline Pen Options	The Outline Pen dialogue box appears.
Click **S**cale With Image	
Click Rounded Corners and Line Caps	
At Width, enter **0.222**	
Click OK	Base NEON has a fat outline, the same color as the background.
Click and drag NEON *to butt against the left guideline*	
Click the shape tool	
Click NEON	NEON is selected.
Click and drag the letterspace arrow to the right guideline	NEON is letterspaced.
Click the pick tool	
Click and drag NEON *to the bottom of the page*	
Hold down Ctrl and press +	
Release the mouse button	A duplicate NEON is created.
Press Ctrl-T	The Artistic Text dialogue box appears.
Backspace over NEON *and type* **NEWT**	
Click OK	NEWT is set in 96-point Vogue bold.

Now that you have set the type, get Ned the Newt! Use Draw's Symbol Library to summon the slimy creature:

continues

Click the text tool	The cursor becomes a +.
Hold down Shift and click the center of the page	The Symbols dialogue box appears.
Click Animals	
At Symbol #:, type **32**	To select Ned the Newt.
At Size:, type **5** *inches*	To change size of Ned the Newt.
Click OK	A five-inch Newt appears.
Click the pick tool	
At the On-Screen Palette, left-click No Fill	
Click outline	The Outline Pen fly-out menu appears.
Click Outline Color	The Outline Color dialogue box appears.
Scroll down, select Grass Green	
Click OK	Ned is outlined with Deep Navy Blue.
Click outline	The Outline Pen fly-out menu appears.
Click Outline Pen Options	The Outline Pen dialogue box appears.
Click **S**cale With Image	
Click Rounded Corners and Line Caps	
At Width, enter **0.167**	
Click OK	

At this point, all the base elements are on the page. You need to create the highlight elements to blend the base elements into. CorelDRAW! has a handy one-button shortcut to place duplicates directly on top of their originals. You may remember pressing + while dragging an object to create a duplicate. You also can select any object and press + without moving the object to create a duplicate.

Click NEON	
Press +	NEON is duplicated.
Click outline tool	The Outline Pen fly-out menu appears.
Click Hairline	
Click outline	The Outline Pen fly-out menu appears.

Click Outline Color	The Outline Color dialogue box appears.
Scroll down, select Magenta	
Click OK	Highlight NEON is outlined with Magenta.
Drag a marquee around both NEONs	Both NEONs are selected.
Click Effects	The Effects menu appears.
Click **B**lend	The Blend Roll-Up menu appears.
Use the default settings of 20 Blend Steps and 0 degrees Rotation.	
Click Apply	NEON is blended (see fig. 9.10).

Now press F9 to look at what you have done so far. Notice that the outline seems to fade into the background. If you recall, this effect was created by using the same color for both the background and the type's base outline. Repeat the last steps (duplicate outline, change outline width and color, then blend) to "neonize" the word NEWT. Then finish off Ned himself. Use a Turquoise Hairline for Ned's highlight. Notice how different Ned looks, as opposed to the type (see fig. 9.9). Ned appears to be popping off instead of fading into the background because of his base outline color.

Sharp eyes will notice that their newt is different from the newt shown in the figure. This is because the newt shown in the figure is from CorelDRAW! 2.0's Animal Symbol font. If you happen to fancy the old newt over the new, you can convert the 2.0 WFN font file (assuming that you still have it) to PostScript or TrueType format with Ares FontMonger.

Tube Type

Tube type is similar in concept, execution, and appearance to neon type. Once again, the Blend effect is used to create an illusion. But instead of a blend radiating outward, tube type grows inward, to create a three-dimensional effect (see fig. 9.11). Think of gel tooth-paste, silicon caulk, or the lettering on a birthday cake, to get the gist of what tube type is all about.

Figure 9.10:

Creating the Neon Newt menu cover.

Figure 9.11:

Tube type.

Neon type gets its magic from blending two similar pieces of type with different outline widths and tints. Tube type, on the other hand, does not necessarily use an outline at all. It works its wonders with an object's shape and fill.

To create tube type, start with a flowing script like Freeport. Take care of any character pair kerning, duplicate the text string, and drag the duplicate off to the side (you will use this for a drop shadow). Give the original text string a black fill/no outline, convert it to curves, and break it apart. Recombine any multiple path characters (such as A, B, D, and so on). Then, working letter by letter, create a duplicate of each letter. Make sure that the duplicate is on the top, and use the shape tool to create a character just a little bit shorter and narrower, but more important, thinner than the original.

Do not break the duplicate character apart to manipulate the individual paths! If you do, the blend will not work properly, and you will go crazy trying to fix it. Fill the skinny character with a 10% gray highlight fill. Marquee-select the skinny character together with the original character, and use Blend to impart the illusion of depth.

Creating Tube Type

Instead of rendering an entire word of tube type, create only one letter: a 500-point Q. Working in large scale gives you greater precision in line placement, which is crucial in developing different lighting angles.

Click the text tool	The cursor becomes a +.
Click the center of the page	The Text I bar appears.
Type **Q**	
Ctrl-T	The Artistic Text dialogue box appears.
Change to 500 point, Freeport	To change point size and face.
Click OK	A 500-point Freeport Q appears.
Click the pick tool	
Click fill	The Fill fly-out menu appears.
Click 100% black	The Q is filled with 100% black.
At the On-Screen Palette, right-click No Outline	

continues

Click **S**pecial	The Special menu appears.
Press + on numeric keypad	The Q is duplicated.
Click fill	The Fill fly-out menu appears.
Click 10% black	The Q is filled with 10% black.
Click **A**rrange	The Arrange menu appears.
Click Convert to Curves	The Q is converted to curves.
Click the shape tool	

Move individual nodes inward and adjust control points to form a skinny Q inside the original. Take your time and adjust the control points as needed, pushing the highlight to the top right of the letter (see fig. 9.12). Remember not to break the duplicate character apart into its individual paths! Next, create the blend by using Draw's default (20 step) setting (see fig. 9.13).

Creating the Blend

Click the pick tool	The skinny Q is selected.
Shift-click the original Q	Both Qs are selected.
Click **E**ffects	The Effects menu appears.
Click **B**lend	The Blend Roll-Up menu appears.
Use the default settings of 20 Blend Steps and 0 degrees Rotation.	
Click Apply	A 20-step blend appears.

Shortcut

Click the numeric keypad's plus symbol (+) to duplicate any selected object.

Go ahead and preview the tube type Q. If you are not happy with the way the lighting angle looks, delete the blend, tweak the skinny Q, and blend again.

To finish off a piece of tube type, use the duplicate you made to set a drop shadow behind it; it will provide the extra oomph to pop the image off the printed page.

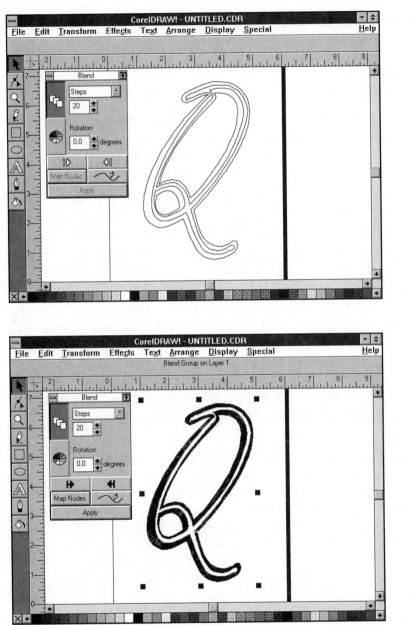

Figure 9.12:
Before the blend.

Figure 9.13:
After the blend.

Tube type may seem like a long way to get the same effect as neon type, but it actually offers more. Although it takes more time and patience, tube type provides far more control over each individual character. It may take all afternoon to create a one-liner, but the results can be well worth the effort.

Punk Text

On occasion, you may need to use an informal typeface that looks as if it were hand-lettered. In these cases, you will find that the standard-issue CorelDRAW! fonts do not fit the bill—until you pull a cheap trick out of the bag: punk text.

The name may conjure up visions of black leather and adolescent angst, but punk text is one of the best-kept secrets to create fast, easy, and distinctive display heads. Where would you use such unique typography? Just think rock and roll. T-shirts, concert flyers, compact disk and cassette-tape packaging, and band logos are all fair game.

You can create punk text quickly. By using the text tool, plug in the type in your choice of "base" typeface—sans-serif faces like Bahamas Heavy, Penguin Bold, and Ottawa Bold are good choices. Next select the text and convert to curves. Switch to the shape tool and drag a marquee around the entire text block. Double-click any selected node to bring up the Node Edit dialogue box, and change all the line segments to straight lines. There you go: punk text (see fig. 9.14).

You may need to tweak the type a bit—and this may take some time—but this is one of the slickest ways to create random lettering. Some characters fare better than others in the conversion process, as do certain typefaces. Angular characters, like A, E, and F, may not change at all, and require artistic persuasion. Use the shape tool to finesse the letterforms. Certain effects require you to break apart and possibly recombine characters; for example, when using different colors/tints for each letter, or when rotating individual letters.

As a general rule, the more complex a face, the poorer a choice it may be for creating punk text, because the results are often unreadable. On the other extreme, a face that already consists of purely straight lines—such as Motor—is not a candidate for conversion.

If you create a punk face that you really like, you can always save it as a PostScript or TrueType typeface by using the Symbol/Typeface Export Filter. By doing this, you will save even more time when you set type for the same account. After you do this, you can export the font for use with other applications (that can't use PS or TT), by converting the font with Ares FontMonger.

After you have created your punk text, you can apply any CorelDRAW! treatment. Just remember that when you convert text to curves, you will not be able to edit it, so be sure to check for typos before converting to curves. To finish things up, try using punk text with drop shadows or knockout drops.

Tweaked Vogue Bold

Figure 9.14:

Punk type.

Hand-Altered: R

Hand-Altered: B, C, E, G, O, R

Punk Text Revisited

Another quick way to create punk text is to duplicate a text string, drag the duplicate down the page, and change it to a completely different typeface. Then, use blend to mutate between the two different typefaces. Zingo...Instant punk text! The more blend steps, the more gradual the change is. Separate the blend elements, ungroup the blend, and delete the iterations you don't need.

This technique surely leads you into uncharted typographical territory. Font creation has never been as immediate, not to mention random. Certainly, much of what you get with this technique is unreadable, but you are bound to create at least one style that is usable!

Bevel Text

Have you ever wanted your type to appear as if it had beveled edges? By following this straightforward but exacting process, you can create multidimensional type like a pro. To bevel a piece of type, you must add facets to each side (see fig. 9.16). You can accomplish this through diligent use of the pencil tool, snap-to guidelines, and the pick tool.

The trick to maintaining your sanity when creating beveled type is to start with a typeface with a minimum of curves. Motor is a good choice, because it does not contain any curves at all. You also can try beveling punk text for an ultra-custom look. If the face contains curves, expect to spend extra time to get the curves to work out properly.

When you bevel text, the idea is to once again create the illusion of depth. To do this, use different tints of gray or base color on each side of a character. With process colors, you easily can add different percentages of black to the base CMYK mix. Spot colors (or good old black) can be altered with different screen densities. If you want to get real tricky (and spend an additional amount of time), you can use fountain fills on each facet, altering colors, angles, and edge padding appropriately.

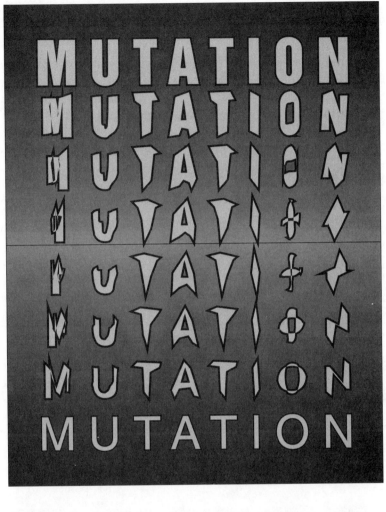

Figure 9.15:
More mutant punk type, courtesy of the blend effect.

Figure 9.16:
The bevel text effect.

In the following exercise, you bevel just one character, an E, set in 600-point Motor. Like the previous tube type exercise, this illustrates technique, without becoming too cumbersome. Create the E with a full beveled surface, as opposed to a flat surface with beveled edges. You can try to create the latter on your own. Use the approach illustrated here, along with a variation of the tube type technique, to apply a flat surface bevel (see fig. 9.17).

Figure 9.17:

A slightly different bevel effect.

Creating Bevel Text

Click the text tool	The cursor becomes a +.
Click the center of the page	The Text I bar appears.
Type **E**	
Press Ctrl-T	The Artistic Text dialogue box appears.
Change to 600 point, Motor	To change point size and face.
Click OK	A 600-point Motor E appears.
Click **Display**	The Display menu appears.

Make sure that Snap-to Grid is off, and that Snap-to Guidelines and Show Rulers are on.

Click the zoom tool	The Zoom fly-out menu appears.
Click +	
Marquee-select E	To zoom up on E.
Click the pick tool	

Position the cursor over the vertical ruler

Click and drag the guideline to the left edge of the E, and repeat for each vertical edge

Position the cursor over the horizontal ruler

Click and drag the guideline to the top edge of the E, and repeat for each horizontal edge

Now that the edge guidelines are in, draw the center guidelines by using a sneaky little trick. You may recall back in Chapter 5, you used nonprinting, guideline-layer ellipses to help balance your composition. This time, cut a few rectangles in half to determine the centerlines of the E. After the center guidelines are drawn, the rectangles will be deleted (see fig. 9.18).

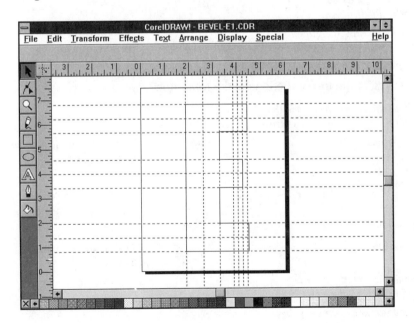

Figure 9.18:

Beveling the E on the screen.

Drawing the Centerlines

Click the rectangle tool

Starting at the left side of the E, take the following steps:

Click and drag a rectangle the width of the E's downstroke	
Click the pick tool	The rectangle is selected.
*Click **T**ransform*	The Transform menu appears.
*Click **S**tretch & Mirror*	The Stretch & Mirror dialogue box appears.
*At Horizontal: type **50***	
Click OK	The rectangle is half as wide.
Snap the rectangle to the leftmost guideline	
Position the cursor over the vertical ruler	
Click and drag the guideline to the rectangle's right edge	A centerline is drawn.
Click the rectangle tool	

Starting at the top of the E, take the following steps:

Click and drag a rectangle the depth of the E's top cross-stroke	
Click the pick tool	The rectangle is selected.
*Click **T**ransform*	The Transform menu appears.
*Click **S**tretch & Mirror*	The Stretch & Mirror dialogue box appears.
*At Vertical: type **50***	
Click OK	The rectangle is half as tall.
Snap the rectangle to the uppermost guideline	
Position the cursor over the horizontal ruler	
Click and drag the guideline to the rectangle's bottom edge	A centerline is drawn.

Use this procedure to draw centerlines throughout the E's cross-strokes. Drag two more vertical guidelines to denote the right side cross-stroke facets. Then delete the four boxes.

Click the pencil tool

Draw a series of three- and four-sided polygons to form the facets of the E (see fig. 9.19).

Finish up by assigning a fill to each of the facets. Use an 80% black fill for all the southsides, a 20% fill for all the northsides, a 60% fill for all the eastsides, and a 40% fill for the westside (see fig. 9.20). Experiment with and without object outlines.

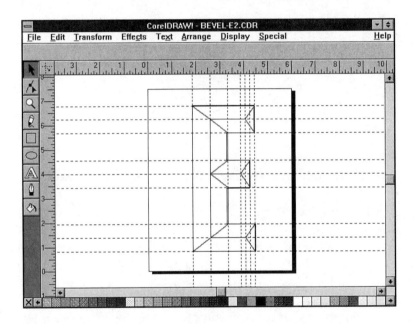

Figure 9.19:

Beveled E wireframe.

Chrome Type

The chrome look is almost as overdone as the common drop shadow, but many desktop designers are asked to set type in this style. To render chrome type correctly takes time and effort; it is not a point-and-click affair. Well-executed chrome type looks as shiny as the emblems on a custom show car. But poorly constructed chrome type can be complex and time-consuming to print. You must take two considerations into account: visual appeal and image engineering. If it looks great but does not print, you have not done your job. The same is most certainly true for the reverse scenario.

Figure 9.20:

Beveled E in full-color mode.

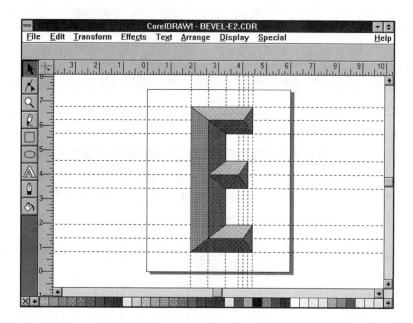

Hopefully, after working (and reading) through the rest of this book, you will understand how to work with fountain fills to reap the rewards yet not choke your printer, or worse, your service bureau's imagesetter where you may be required to pay overtime charges for intensive pages. The trick to creating chrome type that looks great and prints reliably is to construct the fountain fills as very simple objects layered on top of the original type. Mindlessly fountain-filling large strings of type—as type—can needlessly tie up a printer's RIP. Your responsibility is to put your files together properly.

Traditionally, chrome type is rendered with an airbrush. But because CorelDRAW! does not have an airbrush tool, you must make do with a combination of methods. High-end chrome type is constructed by using both fountain fills and blends to achieve a metallic luster. Starbursts—glints of light—also can be built by using either a radial fountain fill or a blend between a fat and a skinny object, using a tube type-like methodology. When used sparingly, these sparkles add the finishing touch.

The method you are going to use makes heavy use of the shape tool to break character outlines into smaller chunks. The chunks are then assigned different fountain fills, depending upon their geographical location upon the face of the character. At the very least, you may find that breaking a character into two chunks, upon a base character, provides a good foundation to build on. The bottom edge of the fountain fill of the top chunk can fade into the base character, while the top edge of the bottom chunk can contrast sharply with the base.

Once again, you create just one character—C—due to the complexity of the process. Good-looking chrome type takes a bit of effort and experimentation. When you are done with the letter C, try setting the rest of the word, CHROME (see fig. 9.21).

Figure 9.21:
Chrome type.

Creating Chrome Type

Click the text tool	The cursor becomes a +.
Click the center of the page	The Text I bar appears.
Type **C**	
Press Ctrl-T	The Artistic Text dialogue box appears.
Change to 500 point, Aardvark	To change point size and face.
Click OK	A 500-point Aardvark C appears.

continues

Click **Display**	The Display menu appears.

Make sure that Snap-to Grid is off, and that Snap-to Guidelines and Show Rulers are on.

Click the zoom tool	The Zoom fly-out menu appears.
Click +	
Marquee-select C	To zoom up on C.
Click the pick tool	
Position the cursor over the vertical ruler	
Click and drag the guideline to the left edge of the C's downstroke; repeat for the right edge of the C's downstroke	
Position the cursor over the horizontal ruler	
Click and drag the guideline to the bottom edge of the C's top serif; repeat for the top edge of the C's bottom serif	See figure 9.21.
Press + on the numeric keypad	The C is duplicated.
Press Ctrl-V	The duplicate C is converted to curves.
Click the shape tool	

At each of the four guideline intersection points, take the following steps:

Double-click	The Node Edit dialogue box appears.
Click **Add**	A node is added.

After the four extra nodes have been added, take the following steps:

Marquee all four new nodes	
Double-click on one of the selected nodes	The Node Edit dialogue box appears.
Click **Break**	The object is now two paths.
Double-click the line segment on the left side, between the broken nodes	The Node Edit dialogue box appears.
Click **Delete**	The line segment is deleted.

Double-click the line segment on the right side, between the broken nodes	The Node Edit dialogue box appears.
Click **Delete**	The line segment is deleted.
Click the pick tool	
Click **Arrange**	The Arrange menu appears.
Click **Break** Apart	The C is now two separate (open path) objects.
Click page	Deselects the two objects.
Click the top half of the C	The top half of the C is selected.
Click the pencil tool	The cursor becomes a +.
Draw a line between the top half's two lower nodes	Closes the path.
Click the bottom half of the C	Selects the C's bottom half.
Click the pencil tool	The cursor becomes a +.
Draw a line between the bottom half's two upper nodes	Closes the path (see fig. 9.23).
Click **Edit**	The Edit menu appears.
Click Select **All**	All the objects are selected.

At the On-Screen Palette, right-click No Outline

You now have three separate objects: the original C, along with the top and bottom halves of the duplicate C. Give the original C a 10% black fill. Experiment with different linear fountain fills for the top and bottom halves of the duplicate C. Start with a 10% to 60% 90-degree fill for the top, and a 30% to 70% 90-degree fill for the bottom. Try adding a duplicate C, with an outline but no fill, and bring it to front. Then, add a neon effect for a glowing result, as shown in figure 9.24.

Combining effects and techniques is one way to render distinctive, eyecatching artwork. Use the chrome, bevel, and neon effects together to yield impressive results. When used in combination with CorelDRAW!'s Extrude effect, the resulting type has an almost photographic quality.

Figure 9.22:

The C with guide-
lines drawn.

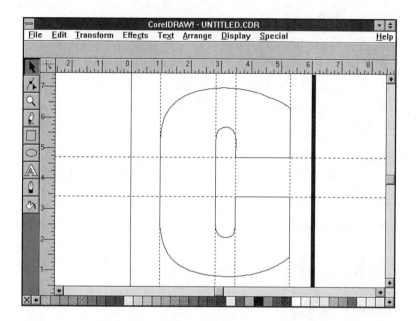

Figure 9.23:

The finished C
wireframe.

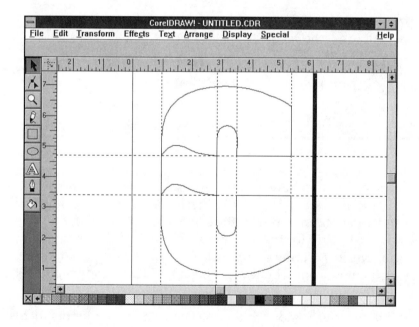

Spin Type

Spin type is often seen in program manuals and advertisements, but gets little work in the real world. This effect can be used to add the illusion of motion or depth to an object (see fig. 9.25). Spin type is fast and easy to do. You can use one of two techniques: the Multiple Repeat-Rotate-Leave Original technique or the Blend effect. Each technique has advantages. If you are not sure how

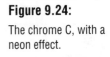

Figure 9.24:

The chrome C, with a neon effect.

much rotation you want, try the Multiple Repeat-Rotate-Leave Original technique. If you want to change tint as the type rotates, use the Blend effect.

Remember back in Chapter 1, when you rotated the 300zx? Now you are going to move the object's rotation point, and use the rotate tool to rotate the piece of type one degree, while leaving an original. Then, you will repeatedly use the keyboard shortcut, Ctrl-R, to repeat the step. You may be amazed at how fast you can grow a piece of spin type!

Figure 9.25:

Spin type created with Multiple Repeat-Rotate-Leave Original.

Using the Multiple Repeat-Rotate-Leave Original

Click the text tool	The cursor becomes a +.
Click the center of the page	The Text I bar appears.
Type **SPIN TYPE**	
Press Ctrl-T	The Artistic Text dialogue box appears.
Change to 48 point, Centurion Old Italic	To change point size and face.
Click OK	A 48-point Centurion Old Italic SPIN TYPE appears.
Click the pick tool	
At the On-Screen Palette, left-click No Fill	

SUSAN KRUPP/90

RIPPIN'
SURFBOARDS, INC.

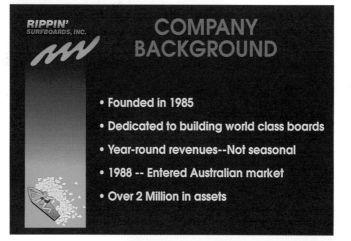

COMPANY BACKGROUND

- Founded in 1985
- Dedicated to building world class boards
- Year-round revenues--Not seasonal
- 1988 -- Entered Australian market
- Over 2 Million in assets

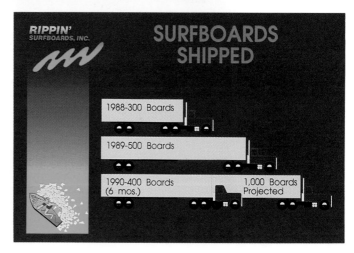

SURFBOARDS SHIPPED

1988-300 Boards

1989-500 Boards

1990-400 Boards (6 mos.)   1,000 Boards Projected

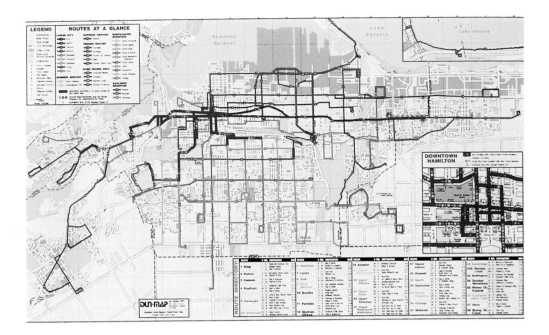

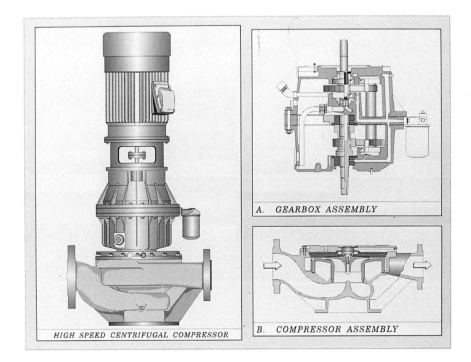

HIGH SPEED CENTRIFUGAL COMPRESSOR

A. GEARBOX ASSEMBLY

B. COMPRESSOR ASSEMBLY

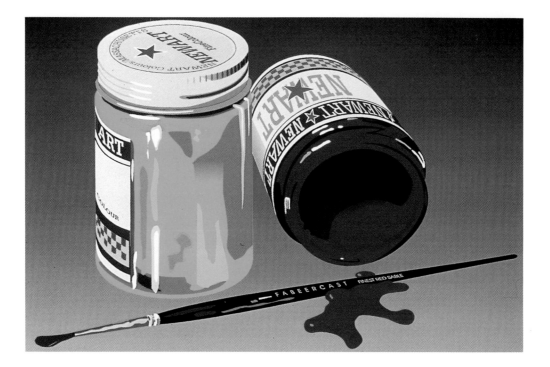

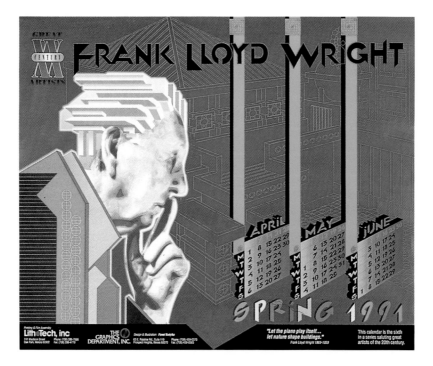

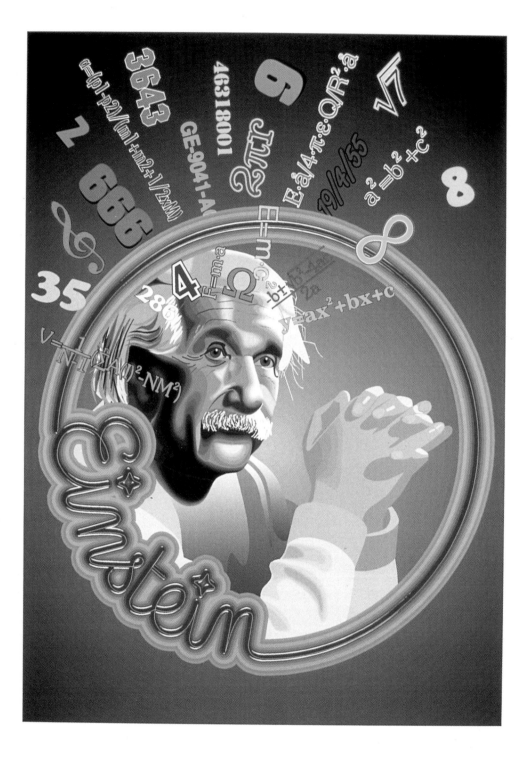

Click the outline tool	The Outline Pen fly-out menu appears.
Click Hairline	
Click the outline tool	The Outline Pen fly-out menu appears.
Click 30% black	
Click SPIN TYPE	The Rotate arrows appear.
Position the cursor over the center of rotation	
Drag center of rotation below and to the left of SPIN TYPE	
Position the cursor over the top right handle	The cursor's pointer becomes a +.
Drag the top right handle up and left	A blue dashed box replaces the arrow handles. The status line shows amount of rotation in degrees.
Press +	The status line reads: Leave Original.
When Angle is 1.0 degree, release the mouse button	A duplicate SPIN TEXT is created, rotated 1.0 degree from the original.
Press Ctrl-R	Repeats the procedure.

Use Ctrl-R another 28 times, and give the last object no outline and a 100% black fill.

The Multiple Repeat-Rotate-Leave Original technique used to create spin type is also valuable to create objects that radiate from a central point, such as petals on a flower or spokes on a wheel.

Next, try the same thing a little differently. This time, make use of the Blend effect to create your SPIN TYPE (see fig. 9.26). This next exercise uses the very first and last SPIN TYPEs you just created, so save the file if you want to hold onto it.

To begin, select and delete all but the very first and last SPIN TYPEs. When you have done that, proceed with the following steps:

Figure 9.26:

Spin type created
with the Blend effect.

Using the Blend Effect

Click the bottom SPIN TYPE	
Click fill	The Fill fly-out menu appears.
Click 10% black	
At the On-Screen Palette, right-click No Outline	
Click the top SPIN TYPE	
Click fill	The Fill fly-out menu appears.
Click 50% black	
At the On-Screen Palette, right-click No Outline	
Shift-click the bottom SPIN TYPE	Both SPIN TYPEs are selected.
Click **Effects**	The Effects menu appears.
Click **B**lend Roll-Up ...	The Blend Roll-Up menu appears.
Click Apply	A 20-step blend appears.
Click Arrange	The Arrange menu appears.
Click Separate	The Blend is separated.
Click page	To deselect the blend.
Click the top SPIN TYPE	
Click fill	The Fill fly-out menu appears.
Click 100% black	

Notice how the Blend effect SPIN TYPE differs from the first technique. Of course, the outline and fill characteristics were set up differently, but it is more than that. See how the Blend effect text moves in a straight line? Now take a look at the Multiple Repeat-Rotate-Leave Original Type; it moves in a gentle arc. Try each technique with different fills, outlines, and rotation percentages. To have the spin layer in the opposite direction when using the Blend effect, select both originals and click Reverse Order (on the Arrange menu) before blending.

Two-Tone Type

Have you ever had the need for a piece of type that is half positive (black letters on a white background) and the other half reversed (white letters on a black background)? CorelDRAW! provides a straightforward way to accomplish this effect (see fig. 9.27). By combining the text with an object, you can create two-tone type in a matter of mouse clicks.

This one is so easy that it may bring tears to the eyes of any graphic designer who ever had to do this conventionally, with reversal stats and a technical pen.

Remember that once you combine text with any other object, it is not editable; always make a duplicate of the type and objects you are about to combine, for safekeeping. Drag the duplicates off to the side, just in case you need to make an edit or adjust character kerning.

You also can easily add a spot color to the design by dragging a duplicate of the original shape behind the combined object. Change the tint/color of the duplicate object, and send it behind the original.

Creating Two-Tone Type

Click the text tool	The cursor becomes a +.
Click the center of the page	The Text I bar appears.
Type **TWO-TONE TYPE**	
Press Ctrl-T	The Artistic Text dialogue box appears.

continues

Figure 9.27:

Two-tone type.

Change to 72 point, Penguin, and then click **Center**	To change the point size, face, and alignment.
Click OK	A 72-point Penguin TWO-TONE TYPE appears.
Click the pencil tool	The cursor becomes a +.
Draw a triangle taller than, but not as wide as, TWO-TONE TYPE	
Click the pick tool	
Shift-click TWO-TONE TYPE	Both objects are selected.
Press Ctrl-A	The Align dialogue box appears.
Click Horizontal and Vertical **Center**	
Click OK	The objects are horizontally and vertically aligned.
Press Ctrl-C	The Objects are combined.
Click fill	The Fill fly-out menu appears.
Click 100% black	
At the On-Screen Palette, right-click No Outline	

Preview your work. If it does not look quite the way you want it, immediately undo the combine. Then, adjust the elements and recombine.

Letterspaced Type

Letterspaced (or blown-out) type, also known as force-justified type, is a simple task with Draw's snap-to guidelines and interactive letterspacing. By dragging out a pair of vertical guidelines, you can adjust type to fit any width (see fig. 9.28). Set your type with the left side hitting the left guideline, and switch to the shape tool. Draw displays the type's interactive spacing controls. Drag on the horizontal (intercharacter) marker to pull the type out to the desired width. To set interword space, hold down Ctrl while you drag.

DeLOOK DESIGN

SEASIDE, U.S.A. 800/555-1234

Figure 9.28:
Blown-out text.

Creating Blown-Out Text

Position the cursor over the vertical ruler	
Click and drag the guideline to the left side of the page	
Position the cursor over the vertical ruler	
Click and drag the guideline four inches from the first guideline	
Click the text tool	The cursor becomes a +.
Click the left guideline	The Text I bar appears.
Type **DeLOOK** (use 3 spaces) **DESIGN**	
Press Ctrl-T	The Artistic Text dialogue box appears.
Change to 24 point, Erie Light	To change point size and face.
Click **None**	To change justification.
Click OK	A 24-point, Erie Light DeLOOK DESIGN appears.

continues

Click the shape tool	
Drag DeLOOK DESIGN*'s intercharacter marker to the right guideline and release the mouse button*	DeLOOK DESIGN is letterspaced.
Click the text tool	The cursor becomes a +.
Click the left guideline	The Text I bar appears.
Type **SEASIDE, U.S.A.** (use 3 spaces) **800/555-1234**	
Press Ctrl-T	The Artistic Text dialogue box appears.
Change to 12 point, Erie Light	To change point size and face.
Click OK	A 12 point, Erie Light SEASIDE,U.S.A. 800/555-1234 appears.
Click the shape tool	
Drag SEASIDE, U.S.A. 800/555-1234*'s intercharacter marker to the right guideline and release the mouse button*	SEASIDE, U.S.A 800/555-1234 is letterspaced (see fig. 9.29).

Figure 9.29:

Force-justified letterhead.

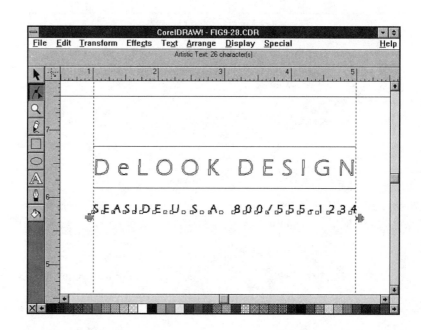

Texture Type

You fooled around with texture text in Chapter 7. Remember creating the Wave masked bit map? You can use the same technique, along with a scanner to create some interesting texture type (see fig. 9.30). Of course, you can use bit maps with type, without masking. When combined with beveled, embossed, or a carefully extruded technique, texture type can be even more striking (see fig. 9.31).

Figure 9.30:

Texture type.

Figure 9.31:

Texture type combined with other techniques.

Exploring Backgrounds and Design Elements

As mentioned in the last section, bit-mapped textures add visual impact to the artwork you create with CorelDRAW! Many sources are available for bit-map images. You can use scanners to create images, or you can use paint programs like Paintbrush or

CorelPHOTO-PAINT! and high-end image retouching programs such as Image-In-Color. You will find a number of Photo-Paint textures on the 3.0 CD-ROM disk. You can also find bit-map images in the public domain and from a variety of clip-art companies.

Using TIFF/PCX/BMP/GIF/TGA Textures

Some of the more popular textures are "organics," such as marble, granite, or wood. A local tile or flooring store is an excellent source of marble patterns. Ask if you can borrow a few tiles to scan. When you return the tiles, bring your finished artwork with you. Although the store owners may be skeptical at first, you may end up with a new account once they see what you can do!

"Non-organic" textures, like drybrush (see fig. 9.32) or splattered paint (see fig. 9.33), are also quite popular. The drybrush and splattered paint techniques that have been all the rage in recent years have their popular base in custom car paint jobs, and their inspiration in the work of Jackson Pollock. Although CorelDRAW! does not enable you to create drybrush or splattered effects from directly within the program, you can easily import TIFF or PCX scans of conventional artwork. Once the TIFF or PCX image has been imported into Draw, you have the full range of color and tints. In the process of colorizing black-and-white (1 bit) line art, the fill color affects the (white) background, while the outline color affects the (black) foreground.

Figure 9.32:

A drybrush accent.

Figure 9.33:

A splattered
background with
punk type.

Crumpled paper is an interesting background that can be quickly
created with a grayscale scanner. Once brought into CorelDRAW!
as a TIF, PCX, or BMP grayscale bit map, crumpled paper can be
assigned a fill of any color or tint you want, becoming an intriguing design element (see fig. 9.34). An even slicker trick is to set a
piece of type, print it on laser paper, crumple the print, and scan.

Figure 9.34:

The crumpled paper
effect.

The grid is one of the most overused graphic gimmicks in design.
Nonetheless, you can easily create perspective grids with
CorelDRAW!'s Perspective effect (see fig. 9.35). And when properly used with a tasteful fountain fill, the results can be so handsome as to make one forget that it has been done before (a zillion
times).

Figure 9.35:
The grid effect.

True innovation is hard to come by. In many cases, tried and true not only gets the job done, but leaves the client feeling comfortable with what you have designed. Like all the other design effects reviewed in this chapter, the grid is an iteration of what other artists have repeatedly created before.

Don't be afraid to innovate. But do not kill yourself for a client who does not appreciate, expect, or truly want innovative work. It can be too frustrating to attempt to convince someone who has no artistic appreciation. Do not waste their time or yours; if they expect formula, give it to them.

Summary

In this chapter, you have learned the basics behind a gamut of special effects, from the ubiquitous drop shadow through neon and punk type. Through it all you should come away with the realization that beauty takes time (and work).

CorelDRAW! has many built-in effects, such as Extrude and Blend. These magical implements can work wonders when used properly. But when an effect is used as an effect, without thought and overall design concept, you run the risk of losing focus. You easily can be caught up in the mechanics and technique (and fun) of creating a piece of electronic artwork and forget the real purpose of what you are doing.

Design should come first, not the computer. If you lose sight of your overall design concept, your finished product suffers. Use Draw's design power to your advantage. Do not let the constraints of the computer control your design.

You have a new set of brushes in your hands and a fresh canvas. Each time you approach a blank screen, you are faced with the same question that has faced artists since the beginning of time: how do I convey the message?

10

The Galleries

ow that you have learned the basics of creating beautiful illustrations and fine typography, this chapter presents a little show-and-tell. This edition of *Inside CorelDRAW!* features two full-color galleries. New Riders is proud to feature the work of some of the leading members of the CorelDRAW! community.

The following sections describe the artwork that appears in one of the galleries. The first gallery begins with some full-color work by the author.

Daniel Gray

Daniel Gray and Gary Cartwright of ArtRight Software are the first to admit to taking shortcuts in assembling two of the drawings for their part of the color section. The first of the two is the sexy advertisement for "The Navel Base," an imaginary bikini store in downtown Seaside. The second is the poster for the Seaside Aquarium.

How did they cheat in building these beautiful graphics? It was easy; they simply opened up some electronic images (this stuff is too impressive to be simply called "clip art") from the ArtRight Image Portfolios, and went to work.

The Navel Base

The Navel Base advertisement consists of a young woman in a very short T-shirt, along with some simple yet effective type, set tight (see fig. 10.1). These elements were dropped on a linear fountain-filled background.

The linear fountain fill has an angle of 133 degrees. The color ranges from 100-percent cyan, 20-percent magenta, and 5-percent yellow to 3-percent cyan, 10-percent magenta, and 100-percent yellow. The intent is to render a bright day at the beach, although it is a bit on the green side. Maybe the tide has brought in a load of algae and seaweed!

Figure 10.1:

Tight type.

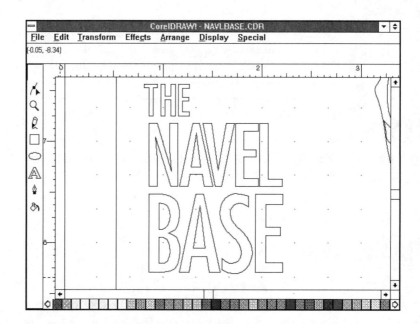

The conservative typography was set in various weights of Fujiyama (Futura) for a clean look. The type was heavily kerned, and scaled to fit. Draw's interactive kerning and scaling were instrumental in achieving this look.

The image of the sun-worshipping woman was left almost exactly as it was opened, with no changes made other than scaling. Dan and Gary decided to leave the skin tones alone (although they had given thought to perhaps a deeper tan). The image as you see it is contained in ArtRight's People Image Portfolio.

A zoom up on the girl's face (see fig. 10.2) reveals ArtRight's trademark accuracy without redundancy. The skin tones and shadows are painstakingly assembled, taking full advantage of CorelDRAW!'s Bezier curves. These guys do not waste a node!

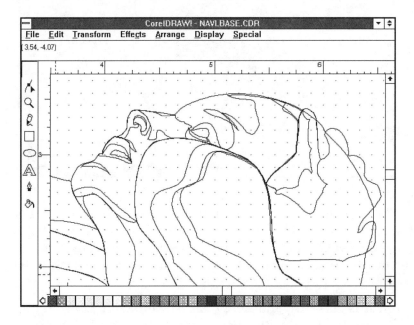

Figure 10.2:

Detail of the face.

Seaside Aquarium

The second of Dan and Gary's instant-art twosome is even more of a stunner. The Seaside Aquarium poster is almost slick enough to be sold as an art print. On this piece, they again used images from ArtRight. This time, they did just a bit of tweaking (on one of the fish; see fig. 10.3).

For this work, Dan and Gary turned to ArtRight's Animal Portfolio. As you can see, they brought in two gorgeous fish and one very pink squid. They placed these aquatic beauties on (another) linear fountain-filled background and finished up with some simple, yet elegant, typography.

Figure 10.3:

An intricate fish.

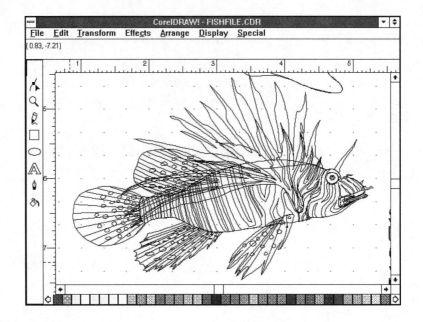

The background is a linear fountain fill with a -90-degree angle. The color spreads from 100-percent cyan, 3-percent magenta, and 20-percent yellow at the top of the page to 100-percent cyan, 60-percent magenta, 60-percent yellow, and 30-percent black at the bottom of the page.

The words SEASIDE and AQUARIUM were set in USA-Light (Univers), and filled with 20-percent magenta and 100-percent yellow. Character spacing was blown out using the interactive mode (with the shape tool).

The summer hours were also set in USA-Light, although in a different color, with an added drop shadow to pop the text off the background just a bit. The text was filled with 100-percent cyan and 20-percent yellow, echoing the color at the top of the page.

If you look at the MM in SUMMER in figure 10.4, you notice some nasty things happening with the miters on the drop shadows. These spikes were not noticeable on the preview screen, and did not rear their ugly heads until the file was color-separated. Dan and Gary decided to leave the aberration in to show that what you see is only an approximation of what you get. Outlining type is a tricky proposition that should be approached with caution (and the proper miter limit).

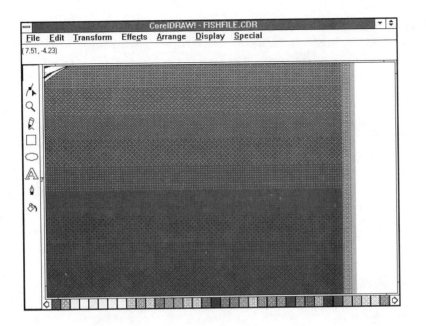

Figure 10.4:
Beware the miter.

While the outline type was set with a miter limit of 10 degrees, a setting of 25 degrees would have alleviated the problem. This is the perfect example of why color proofs are necessary before going to press. Things that are not apparent on-screen or on a 300-dpi laser print can become glaring defects when imaged at high resolution. It is always a wise idea to proof your work before signing off on it.

Color printing can be full of pitfalls. But the quality inherent in ArtRight's work lends some deserved confidence to the Draw user who needs immediate color images he can depend on. Every file the artists opened simply popped to the screen and printed flawlessly, and in outrageous color to boot!

The Monarch Butterfly

What more can be said about the Monarch butterfly? Since you spent much of Chapter 8 building the colorful little insect, see the exercises in Chapter 8 for the exact coloring schemes. The artists added a very simple background of various shades of green.

The large stalks of foliage were constructed with the same technique as the butterfly's body. An outline was drawn and stretched (with Leave Original), and the process color percentages altered. A few nodes were tweaked, and the process was repeated.

The leafy plant at the bottom of the illustration was built by using two original leaves. Duplicate leaves were stretched, scaled, rotated, and tweaked to alter the characteristics of each leaf. This method can save time, but it can be rather blatant if you are not careful. When you are using this technique, it is also important to construct clean and lean objects without a lot of nodes or fountain fills. The more times you paste, the more complex the file will grow.

Susan Krupp

Susan Krupp, a resident of Toronto, Ontario, has been a Draw user since the beginning. Her wildly imaginative designs have won her much attention, as well as first and second place awards in the in-house division of the inaugural Corel Systems International Design Competition. As you can see, her highly colored, surreal images carry quite a charge.

Fashion Block

An intriguing work, Fashion Block immediately challenges the viewer. Is the woman in the fish tank, or is she outside, and what is she doing there in the first place? The bold graphic style of this illustration operates on many levels with interesting perspective. The aquatic cast splashes onto the woman's blue lips, perhaps signifying the passage of life, or possibly just a new trend in lipstick.

This is a relatively complex file, with a correspondingly large file size. The CDR file weighs in at a healthy 85K, and the PostScript print-file balloons to over 800K. As you saw in Chapter 8, file size could drop dramatically with a judicious use of Combine.

Susan does a beautiful job of rendering the spotted and striped fish in bright magenta-pinks and muted blues. Fish images form a significant portion of Susan's work (see fig. 10.5). You see just a hint of a fountain fill in the fish's port-side fin, in addition to sweeping background fill.

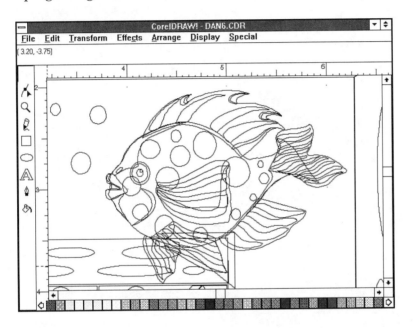

Figure 10.5:

Susan's fish in detail.

The curvaceous woman's torso (another one of Susan's repetitive images; see fig. 10.6) was grouped and rotated to achieve the kaleidoscopic effect used here to great advantage.

Dudes

This piece is a whimsical farce of an advertisement for a television situation comedy of polywogonian proportions. The TV show's namesakes, Stan and Suzanne, resemble nothing less than former New York City Mayor Ed Koch and Jessica Rabbit with gills (see fig. 10.7).

The advertisement's headline typography is deftly executed with Renfrew (Review) fit to a slightly arcing path. This typeface is best used in special headline treatments such as this, and should never be used for body text. You notice a fountain fill in the headline, as well as a pronounced drop shadow.

Figure 10.6:

The torso.

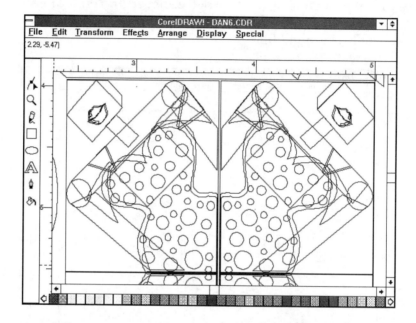

Figure 10.7:

What a pair!

At the lower right corner of the illustration, Susan set the tagline A TRUE AMPHIBIAN ROMANCE in Stamp (Stencil) on a diagonal plane (see fig. 10.8). Stamp is another one of those tricky display faces that should be used sparingly, as it is here. The yellow outline is a bit heavy, although it does help to pop the type off the background.

Figure 10.8:

Stamp text.

On the subject of the background, experienced Draw users may have taken note of the two fountain fills that merge behind the headline type. You may be interested to know that there are approximately eight in this illustration. Susan reports that this file printed in less than five minutes on a QMS color PostScript printer, although the color separations took considerably longer to image.

Susan's work shows a bold use of color, eclectic style, and riveting imagery. Her polymorphic shapes pull the audience in and leave them thinking.

Steve Lyons

Steve Lyons is a San Francisco Bay Area electronic artist. His distinctive works have appeared in many national publications, including *Rolling Stone, PC World, Personal Publishing, Publish,* and the *Washington Post Magazine.* Steve's style is quirky yet familiar; echoes of traditional print-making meet Gumby and the Block-heads.

While Steve is most at home using Adobe Illustrator '88 on his Macintosh, the jigsaw-puzzle desk shown in the color pages is a stunning sample of his work on the PC platform using CorelDRAW!.

Steve's skill and expertise translate across platforms. An in-depth knowledge of Illustrator helped Steve master the intricacies of Draw. Proficiency with one object-oriented drawing package can greatly shorten the learning curve of the second.

Michael Ward

Michael Ward is a veteran designer who has successfully incorpo-rated CorelDRAW! into the tools of his trade. He uses the pro-gram daily to produce a wide variety of printed material. Michael's regular undertakings include marketing materials, print advertisements, corporate presentations, and other similar projects.

Michael was asked for what he considered to be the most unique projects that he has done with CorelDRAW! New Riders is proud to present an awesome twosome: an acrylic clock and a cloisonne pin, both designed with Draw.

These two pieces are excellent examples of what can be done with Draw, aside from producing artwork for the printed page. The clock and cloisonne pin demonstrate that while Draw works only in two dimensions, it can be used to design objects that will ultimately be produced in three dimensions.

The Clock

A fabulous example of how far a simple design can be taken, the Pacific Financial Clock is a well-executed piece. As evidenced by the accompanying photograph, the clock's two-dimensional graphic elements translate perfectly into three dimensions.

Of particular note is the swallow that rotates around the clock face on a clear acrylic disk, giving the illusion of flight. The bird is really the second hand, and floats completely around the clock face once every minute (see fig. 10.9).

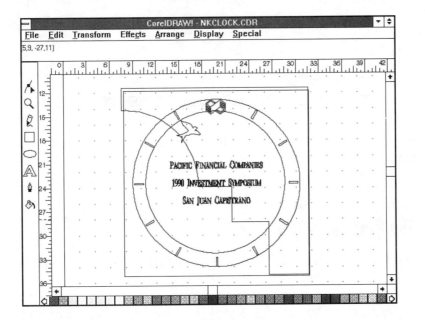

Figure 10.9:

The clock.

You will also notice the precise rendering of the Pacific Financial logo, reproduced here in a very zoomed-up screen shot (see fig. 10.10). The logo's stark geometric design is perfectly suited to vector-graphic reproduction.

The Draw file was printed in an oversized format and subsequently reduced by the company that manufactured the clock. Colors were not specified in Draw. Instead, a conventional tissue overlay was prepared, denoting color breaks.

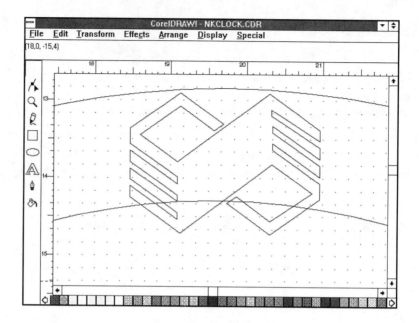

As you can see, promotional pieces like the Pacific Financial clock can be marvelous opportunities to explore Draw's design capabilities without breaking your budget.

The Cloisonne Pin

The Victorian house in Michael's cloisonne pin looks as if it has been plucked right off the streets of Cape May or San Francisco. Although the image may—at first glance—seem basic, it is actually quite complex (see fig. 10.11). The precision and attention to detail are awesome.

The house is expertly assembled, with a maximization of CorelDRAW!'s Combine feature. As you will notice in the close-up of the roof, all the shingles have been precisely drawn, duplicated, placed, and combined. The lines and nodes that extend into the area of the window frame are not seen on the preview screen or output device because the window frame has been sent to Front (see fig. 10.12). This is a perfect example of how these functions can be used to the artist's full advantage. It is impossible to imagine drawing or placing that many elements without Draw's precise duplication settings.

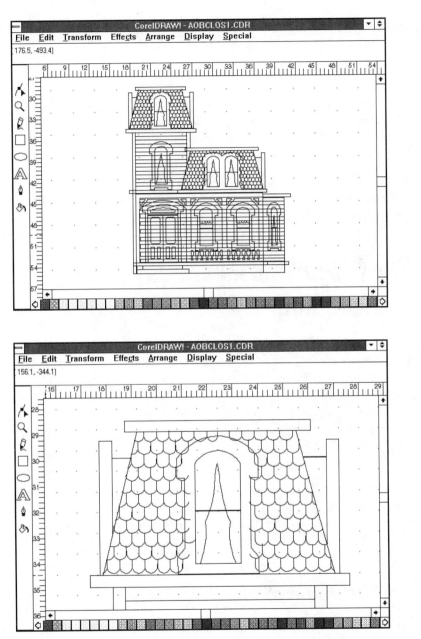

Figure 10.11:

The Victorian house.

Figure 10.12:

Shingled with precision.

Precise line placement is key to the design's success. Michael set his grid to Draw's finest setting: an accurate one per point (72 points equals one inch). This ensures the highest level of accuracy.

He also implements the concept of creating images in proportionately larger size and shrinking the final output. While the design is in the neighborhood of four inches tall, the finished pin is approximately one-fourth that size.

The cloisonne pin was printed in oversize format and was reduced to its final size by the pin's overseas manufacturer. Once again, a traditional tissue overlay was prepared, specifying the PANTONE color breaks.

Michael's work shows him to be a Draw craftsman of the highest caliber. Everyone can take a lesson in precision from the two pieces that he has contributed.

The Rippin' Surfboards, Inc., Presentation

You may remember the Rippin' Surfboards, Inc., 35mm slide that you constructed at the end of Chapter 6. That project has been resurrected here (using the clip-art surfer from CorelDRAW! version 1.2), to show you how the final presentation slides turned out for Joe DeLook's client, Rip Raster. Considering that this was Joe's first foray into the world of 35mm slides, he did a laudable job.

These three pieces have little artistic merit, but at least they are not offensive. The colors used in the series are bright, but not overdone. There is a consistency running from slide to slide, making good use of iteration without being too repetitive. For business slides, these three do just fine.

The Introductory Slide

This slide introduces the repetitive design elements for the subsequent presentation. The background, fade bar, logo type, wave design, and surfer motif are all present, although the wave and logo are in a larger size than the slides that follow. The background for all the slides was specified for PANTONE 255. The fade bar is a -90-degree linear fountain fill from PANTONE 255 to PANTONE Process Blue.

Elements of the surfer were specified in process colors. If these slides had been intended as images for print media, mixing process and spot colors would have been expensive. However, since these were imaged as slides, no one had to worry about paying for the press. Both the process and spot colors go through a conversion process when imaging on a film recorder (slidemaker).

The 35mm slides were then used to make conventional color separations. It is perfectly acceptable to do this for images that are not going to be reproduced at a far larger size than the original. If you need full-page color artwork, you are better off doing the separation on a Lino. But remember that you cannot play the same spot-to-process tricks that you can with a film recorder.

The Company Background Slide

This text slide follows the conventions set up by the intro slide. The headline, COMPANY BACKGROUND, was set in Avalon Bold, and filled with PANTONE 354. The bulleted text was also set in Avalon Bold and filled with a 20-percent cyan tint.

Basic typographical conventions were followed. Except for the headline, all text was set in upper- and lowercase, ensuring readability. The bulleted items were kept to a minimum, reducing clutter. The end result is an easily digestible bite of information. It is good practice to limit the amount of text on a slide. Too much text can make the image uninviting, and the slide may leave the projection screen without being read.

The Surfboards Shipped Slide

Chapter 6 mentioned the virtues of pictographs (graphs built using icons or symbols, rather than mundane bars). SURFBOARDS SHIPPED is a simple example of the genre.

The tractor trailers began as CGM files imported from the New Vision Technologies Presentation Task Force clip-art collection. To begin, the truck was duplicated three times, and then the individual trucks were positioned and ungrouped. The trailer portions were stretched, and the wheel/tire assemblies were repositioned.

The slide's typography follows the conventions set by the other slides. The headline is set in the same position, font, style, size, and color as the headline in the Company Background slide. The text within the trailer/bars was also set in Avalon, although in a smaller size and regular, rather than bold.

While pictographs can take far more creative effort than conventional charts, the results can be well worth the extra time spent. A little thought can go a long way.

The Artists of the First Gallery

In many cases, it may be more advantageous to commission an artist to produce a specific work, rather than hacking it out yourself. To this end, the names and addresses of the contributors are included:

Artwright Software
Corel Systems Corporation
1600 Carling Ave.
Ottawa, Ontario, Canada K1Z 8R7
613/728-8200

Susan Krupp
Suite 3105
65 Harbour Square
Toronto, Ontario, Canada M5J 2L4
416/868-0418

Steve Lyons
320 Cypress Drive
Fairfax, CA 94930
415/459-7560

Michael Ward
3033 Warren Lane
Costa Mesa, CA 92626
714/966-3008

The Second Gallery

This edition of *Inside CorelDRAW!* also features a second gallery of full-color illustrations—a collection of award-winning artwork created in CorelDRAW! by artists from around the world. These color illustrations were contributed to New Riders Publishing by Corel Systems Corporation.

The second color gallery includes the following illustrations:

"Temple"
Bernaert Mario
Benelux

"Go-Fish"
Susan Krupp
Canada

"Draw 1"
Michael Heffner
USA

"Satchmo"
Serge Duguay
Canada

"Butterfly"
Chris Purcell
USA

"Rainbow"
Paulette Hubach
USA

"Dun Map"
Ian Dunlop
Canada

"Farboetp"
Joachim Flugel
Germany

"Calendar"
Paul Bodytko
USA

"Cloudface"
Lloyd R. Hill
USA

"Einstein"
Xavier Broke
Spain

Summary

As you have seen, CorelDRAW! is capable of producing a variety of work, ranging from simple elegance through mind-boggling complexity. The wild card in the hand is the artist in (or slightly out of) control. It is up to the artist to conceive and execute the design; Draw merely follows the orders.

The work shown here is just a start. CorelDRAW! is a relatively new product; its user base is only beginning to mature. You can expect to see amazing things produced by the Draw community over the next few years.

Part Three

Past Your Own PC

The Windows DTP Arsenal
Printing Considerations

The Windows DTP Arsenal

The competition for graphic design work has never been tougher. More and more designers are going electronic—most of them arming themselves with the obligatory Macintosh. You have seen the TV commercials. You have read the magazine advertisements. You have heard the hype: "You want to go DTP, you have to go Mac." Well, it just is not true. Not any more.

The information in the following pages should help to round out your perception of Draw's place in the DTP arsenal. This chapter touches on the subject of Windows (with more coverage in Appendix A). It also reviews the various export file formats, delves into fonts, and covers Ares' FontMonger font conversion utility. The chapter also includes a list of publications to help you obtain further information about the publishing field. Mosaic, Corel's visual file manager, is covered at the end of the chapter.

This chapter is dedicated to those professionals who have decided on the PC platform for their desktop publishing work. It presents resources that can be instrumental in helping you achieve success. Professionals must keep abreast of the ever-changing industry. Graphic arts veterans can attest to the fact that systems go in and out with the seasons. The current crop of DTPers who feel a blind allegiance to any platform had better open their eyes.

When the next (not necessarily intended as a pun) greatest system rolls along, well-heeled and far-sighted designers will jump from both ships. The rest will soon follow. While the Macintosh camp is presently entrenched, and the PC troops are strengthening their position, you should watch for stray bullets.

Traditionally, the Macintosh has ruled the DTP market. In fact, it made the market. But it now runs the risk of losing the market. Prior versions of Windows have held back the PC, and with Windows 3.0, Microsoft had almost made amends. The latest incarnation of Windows, Version 3.1, is faster, more stable, and has incorporated TrueType. Although the Mac still has the edge in many designers' eyes, the gap is narrower than it was.

PC-based DTPers have a few distinct advantages over their Macintosh-based brethren. Their hardware choices are greater. They are not tied to the Apple mother ship for systems. They can buy PCs from countless manufacturers, thus lowering overhead. A comparatively equipped PC costs far less than a Macintosh.

PC-based DTPers are compatible with more computers. Far more PCs are installed than are Macs. This makes it easier to share files, not tears. However, since the introduction of Apple's Super Drive, Macs have become far more compatible. They can now read from and write to PC disks. Score one for Apple.

But finally, do not forget. You have CorelDRAW!

Taking Charge

As the year 2000 approaches, graphic communications are playing an increasingly important role in society. Once upon a time people outside the publishing field knew little about type and design, but the savvy business person of today looks at the subject with a discerning eye.

Concurrently, society has begun to demand instant gratification. Witness the success of fax machines and overnight delivery services. These are not new developments, both having been used by the publication industry for years; but today's business world accepts these privileges as undeniable realities.

In addition to bringing design to the forefront and paving the field for faxes and overnight mail, newspapers and magazines were some of the first heavy-duty computer terminal users. For the industry, timeliness is everything. Business has borrowed heavily from the experiences of professional publishers.

In today's world, demanding business people have begun to expect overnight design magic as well. You can probably blame this partially on those infamous computer commercials stating, "My department can do it." Although the computer has brought wonderful innovation to people's lives, it has also wrought havoc. People expect more from the designer, and they expect it faster. The aim of electronic artists is to stay competitive.

You are going into battle. Arm yourself. You need to become as cunning and shrewd as your competitors. You have to know what is out there and what works. You must form a strategy, yet be able to roll with the tide. Plenty of resources are available—it is up to you to use them.

Working with Windows

Because CorelDRAW! is a Windows-based program, it makes sense to outfit your software library with other Windows-based programs. In other words, to achieve the full potential of the environment, equip your computer with the proper software.

Just what does that mean? Primarily, if you need a certain program to perform a particular function, you should choose a Windows-based program over a DOS or other operating system-based alternative.

Rebooting your computer to change from program to program is not fun, and it is an incredible strain on productivity. Although Windows 3.1 is far more forgiving and offers more alternatives than its earlier versions, it asks more from the machine it runs on. Previous generations of PC programs have been coded to run on the (now) lowly 8088 processor. Windows programs are drawing the line between the power machine haves and have-nots.

Buying the Right Hardware

Windows eats up memory, both on the hard disk and in RAM. The first edition of this book was written and illustrated on an 80286 computer equipped with only a 20M hard disk and 2M of RAM. But Windows is (and you will be) far happier with a more powerful computer, a larger/faster hard disk, and loads of RAM. Subsequent editions of the book were produced on a 33 Mhz 386 with (4M and later) 16M of RAM and a 124M IDE drive—a mid-level machine, by today's standards.

Historically, computers keep getting faster and cheaper. Prices drop as power rises. This is one of the lucky truths (at least for now) of the computer industry. Although prices for such commodities as memory chips tend to rise and fall due to market volatility, the general trend is toward more power for less money. The author's new machine cost no more (adjusting for inflation) than his old machine did just three years previously.

The best advice here is to buy the fastest, most powerful computer that you can afford. Do not take out a second mortgage to buy it, but do not scrimp on a few hundred bucks, either. The time you save will be your own.

Buying the Right Software

The Windows user is naturally prejudiced towards Windows software. Programs that share a common graphical user interface (GUI)—in this case, Windows—operate more intuitively and integrate with other programs that have been designed with the same interface. For example, why buy a word processing program that does not run in the Windows environment if you are already running Draw and, perhaps, PageMaker?

Although this is not the place to get into the Aldus PageMaker versus Ventura Publisher argument, the marketplace tends to favor PageMaker. When Windows Quark Xpress finally arrives (hopefully by the time you read this), it will be a completely new game!

This is typical of the tumultuous industry, and an example of why it is important to keep track of an ever-changing game. The ante is constantly being upped. More programs are being released in Windows-compatible format. As computers progress along the PC-GUI path, it is safe to say that Windows will become the norm, if only as a precursor to OS/2.

Using Paint and Image Manipulation Programs

If you are reading this book, you probably already own the best object-oriented drawing package available for the PC. You probably even use a page layout package or two. And even though Draw now comes bundled with CorelPHOTO-PAINT!, you may want more firepower in the critical bit-mapped paint arena.

Aldus PhotoStyler

If you have ever had the chance to use Adobe PhotoShop on a Macintosh, you will find yourself right at home with Aldus PhotoStyler. Formerly marketed by U-Lead, PhotoStyler is one of the first high-end bit-map image-manipulation packages available for Windows. In the summer of 1991, Aldus acquired the rights to market PhotoStyler, and by fall, had subsequently rebadged and repackaged the product.

PhotoStyler provides all the serious tools that you need to retouch, enhance, and compose full-color images on your PC. The program can read and write files in a number of formats, including BMP, GIF, PCX, TGA, and TIF. In addition, it can write files in EPS format. Scanners from Epson, Nikon, and Microtek are supported, along with most popular printers.

A number of built-in filters provide an array of smoothing, sharpening, and spatial effects. In addition, the program allows user-definable filters for ultra-custom work. The ubiquitous illustration tools—airbrush, paintbrush, pencil, and eraser—are included as well; however, this program is designed for prepress work, rather than image creation. PhotoStyler provides support for GCR (gray component replacement) and UCR (under color removal)—essential tools for CMYK printing.

Aldus Corporation
411 First Avenue South
Seattle, WA 98104-2871
206/628-2320

Fractal Design Painter

Many PC-based artists have been frustrated by the lack of serious paint software for the Windows environment. This dearth of applications has been breached by an entry from a new software publishing firm formed by three veteran desktop software developers. Fractal Design Painter, from the Fractal Design Corporation, breaks new ground for Windows bit-map image creation. Its creators, Mark Zimmer, Tom Hedges, and Lee Lorenzen, are responsible for a few of the most powerful DTP programs available today. Zimmer and Hedges developed ImageStudio and ColorStudio; Lorenzen was a co-creator of Ventura Publisher.

Unlike Image-In-Color and Aldus PhotoStyler, Fractal Design Painter was developed to be a tool for the fine artist rather than the prepress photo retoucher. Although the program can import images in a variety of file formats, you do not want to use it merely to remove dust and touch up scratches. Painter for Windows supports BMP, PCX, RIF, TGA, and TIF formats, and is compatible with the Wacom tablet's pressure-sensitive pen.

When coupled with a Wacom tablet, Painter provides an environment so realistic that your nose may begin to twitch from the pastel dust, and your eyes may water from the turpentine. Painter's toolbox includes: chalk, charcoal, crayons, felt-tip markers, and other amazingly true-to-life implements. The program even has settings to enable artists to paint in the brush strokes of Van Gogh and Seurat! The paper you create on is changeable, giving artists the freedom to alter the tooth of the work surface.

It is hard to find a forgotten tool. Image cloning is supported with a twist; cloned images can be rendered in a variety of media, turning a photographic image into something far more organic. Painter includes electronic tracing paper and friskets, to protect the original copy.

Painter—like other high-end programs—is demanding of the PC it runs on. It requires a 386 or 486 computer, equipped with 6M of RAM, a suitably large hard disk, a high-resolution monitor, and video card. Fractal calls for Super VGA/256 colors as a minimum. You will be happier with 32,768 colors or 24-bit color. This is one powerful program—you will want to load it on the most powerful machine you can muster.

> Fractal Design Corporation
> 101 Madeline Drive, Suite 204
> Aptos, CA 95003
> 408/688-8800

Image-In-Color Professional

Minnesota-based Image-In Incorporated has one of the hottest little programs on the PC publishing scene today. Positioned to go head-to-head with Aldus PhotoStyler, Image-In-Color Professional is fighting a "David-against-Goliath" battle for the PC-image retouching crown. Image-In-Color was the first Windows program to support the Wacom pressure-sensitive tablet.

With color separation controls developed in cooperation with AGFA Compugraphic, such as: GCR, UCR, press gain compensation, and three color-absorption settings, Image-In is going after the serious prepress crowd. Color trade shops that have grudgingly accepted that the Mac is here to stay are in for a surprise. PC workstations are a whole lot more affordable!

Targeted at the high-end professional market, the program supports BMP, EPS, IMG, PICT, PCX, TGA, and TIF (including 6.0) formats, along with the direct loading of Kodak Photo CD images. Color correction controls enable savvy users to create customized printer tone curves. A full range of more than twenty photographic filters is standard issue, as is the capability to create user-definable custom filters. The Wacom tablet's pressure-sensitive input is well implemented in the program's painting tools, metering the flow of paint or density of a brushstroke.

Color scanners supported include: Epson, Marstek, Microtek, Nikon, Nisca, Ricoh, Sharp, Howtek, and Umax. Options include an OCR package, Image-In Read, along with an autotracing package, Image-In Vect.

Image-In Incorporated
406 East 79th Street
Minneapolis, MN 55420
612/888-3633
800/345-3540

Using Other Drawing Programs

You may have asked yourself: "Is there any reason to use a drawing program other than CorelDRAW!?" There may be. For the most part, Draw does a fine job, but it does fall short in a number of places. The program's three chief competitors are: Adobe Illustrator 4.0, Aldus FreeHand 3.1, and Micrografx Designer 3.1. Rather than a feature-by-feature comparison, what follows are the strong points of those programs.

Adobe Illustrator 4.0

The latest incarnation of Illustrator more than makes up for the dismal debut of the first version of the program. A number of features are worth mentioning. The most convenient of these features is that you can open multiple files (or versions of a file) at one time. Just as important, masking is fully supported, and the charting tool is built into the program—it is not called as a separate module.

As you might expect, Illustrator possesses the highest level of typographical refinement (to a thousandth of an em) of all the

Windows drawing programs. The program allows an infinite number of characters in a text block. You can automatically wrap text around objects and link text blocks. Unlike Draw, AI 4.0 lets you define leading in true points, and allows for hanging punctuation. Text can be entered and edited directly on a path.

Adobe Illustrator allows for more color selection choices. In addition to PANTONE spot, PANTONE process, and TRUMATCH, you can also specify color with either the FOCALTONE or TOYO color models. Adobe Separator offers a wealth of choices when it comes time to actually generate color separations, and the program also supports monitor color calibration.

> Adobe Systems Inc.
> 1585 Charleston Road
> P.O. Box 7900
> Mountain View, CA 94039-7900
> 415/961-4400

Aldus FreeHand 3.1

Developed by Altsys—the folks who brought you Fontographer—Aldus Freehand 3.1 provides a number of amenities. As with WinIllustrator, FreeHand offers support for color calibration, and enables you to paste objects inside other objects. Unlike Illustrator, however, FreeHand enables you to assign a default spread size. This feature can be thought of as an auto-trapping mechanism, although it is not the ultimate solution.

One of FreeHand's most notable features is the program's support for pressure-sensitive drawing tablets. This is the first vector-based Windows drawing program to use pressure-sensitivity, and the implementation is quite impressive. When you use the pressure tool, the harder you press, the fatter your drawn object becomes.

> Aldus Corporation
> 411 First Avenue South
> Seattle, WA 98104-2871
> 206/628-2320

Micrografx Designer 3.1

Prior to the arrival of CorelDRAW!, Micrografx Designer was the PC drawing program champ. Recent years have not been kind to the program's market share, but there are still a number of areas where Designer has enviable features. Color is but one of them. Like Illustrator and FreeHand, Micrografx Designer supports color calibration. The program also has an auto-spread feature, similar to FreeHand's; unfortunately, it does not support object-by-object overprinting.

Micrografx is legendary for Windows printer drivers. This latest version of Designer continues that fine tradition. The program supports a huge 128" by 128" image area, and the company offers 24-hour support.

> Micrografx, Inc.
> 1303 Arapaho
> Richardson, TX
> 800/733-3729

Importing and Exporting Vector Files

As you have seen in past chapters, Draw imports and exports a wide variety of graphic file formats, be they vector or bit map. Of the two, vector is usually preferable, if only for the fact that the subsequent images will scale smoothly. You will find bit-map formats covered in Chapter 7.

You have already learned how to import and export files in earlier chapters. Now turn your attention to some of the more interesting things that happen when you export vector files to other programs.

Draw is capable of exporting files in a plethora of file formats that will meet almost every need. Regardless of the final destination for the graphic involved, you need not go without for want of the proper format.

AI/EPS

The most desirable export file formats are Encapsulated PostScript® (EPS) and Adobe Illustrator (AI). These two provide the most information possible about an image.

Interestingly, Draw cannot reliably import the files it exports as EPS files. This makes it crucial to save all files in CDR format before exporting. In this way, you will be able to reuse your files with future versions of CorelDRAW!.

Draw cannot import files that it has exported as EPS because its EPS import filter only recognizes the Adobe Illustrator standard formats. Draw's EPS export filter includes more file information than the AI standards. Hence, the file contains too much information for the import filter to read. Part (or even all) of a file may appear, but the EPS import filter will not reliably import any but the Adobe Illustrator 1.1, 88, or 3.0 standards.

Of course, you can always export the file in AI format. CorelDRAW! enables you to export AI files in your choice of AI 1.1, 88, or Version 3.0 file formats. A file exported from Draw in AI format can be reimported. In the next exercise, you can do just that.

You will take the Monarch butterfly you created in Chapter 8 and export it as both an AI and an EPS file. Then, you will try to import both (only the AI file will import), and save the imported version as a new CDR file.

What will all of this teach you? For starters, you will see that the CDR format is far more compact than either the AI or EPS formats. You will also see that an imported AI file, originally created from a CDR file, will yield a far larger file the second time it is saved.

Exporting and Importing AI/EPS Files

The last version you saved was BUT8.CDR. If your most recent version is named differently, substitute your file name.

Click **File**   The File menu appears.

continues

Click **O**pen	The Open Drawing dialogue box appears.
Click BUT8.CDR	
Click **O**pen	BUT8 opens.

Now, you are going to export the file, first in EPS format and then in AI format. As you export, Draw will assign the appropriate file extension. It may look as if you are exporting to the same file, but you are not. The program takes care of that for you.

Exporting the File

First export the file in EPS format:

Click **F**ile	The File menu appears.
Click **E**xport	The Export dialogue box appears.
Click Encapsulated PostScript, *.EPS	
Click OK	The Export EPS dialogue box appears.
Click OK	The Export PostScript (EPS) dialogue box appears.
Click OK	The file is exported as EPS.

Now export the file in AI 3.0 format:

Click **F**ile	The File menu appears.
Click **E**xport	The Export Drawing dialogue box appears.
Click Illustrator 88, 3.0, *.AI, *.EPS	
Click OK	The Export AI dialogue box appears.
Click Adobe Illustrator V**3**.0	
Click OK	The file is exported as AI.

Image Headers

The Image Header option from the Export dialogue box gives you a TIFF file embedded in the EPS file. The TIFF file provides a screen preview for the image when it is imported into a document prepared with another program, such as PageMaker or Ventura. In the exercise, you selected low, which is the most compact of the three preview choices. It also provides the crudest screen representation of the three. The other choices, medium and high, provide higher resolution screen images, with the downside being considerably larger EPS file sizes.

More important, medium- and high-resolution image headers can choke the program into which you are importing the EPS file. Your system may lock up, and you may need to reboot. For this reason, it is a good idea to stick with low-resolution headers. You also can export without an image header. The EPS file will be smaller, with the imported file displaying as a bounding box.

Text as Text or Text as Curves?

You may have noticed that the AI export filter asked how to export text into the AI file. Although you did not have any text in the file, you still need to answer the question. Use Text as Text only if the fonts used in the file will be resident at the printer; otherwise the printer will substitute the Courier font. The AI filter does something interesting to text with special character attributes—it breaks those characters into separate text objects. The same is true for text on a path. Exporting text as curves can get around this by converting the text outlines to objects. However, the resulting object-text can be unacceptable; aberrations may crop up that, at best, affect the subtleties of type. If you can, try to export logotype files as EPS to avoid these shortcomings.

Now that you have exported to both EPS and AI formats, you will see that it is currently impossible to import an EPS file that was exported from Draw. Clear up the screen by opening a new file.

Trying To Reimport a File

Click File	The File menu appears.
Click New	A new file opens.
Click File	The File menu appears.
Click Import	The Import Drawing dialogue box appears.

Click Illustrator 88, 3.0, *.AI, *.EPS

Click BUT8.EPS

Click OK

Draw attempts to open the file, but it will probably not be successful. A "Corrupt or Invalid AI File" dialogue box may appear.

Click OK

Now that you have seen Draw's incapability to reimport files that it has exported as EPS, try to bring in an AI file. You should meet with success this time.

Importing an AI File

Click File	The File menu appears.
Click New	A new file opens.
Click File	The File menu appears.
Click Import	The Import Drawing dialogue box appears.

Click Illustrator 88, 3.0, *.AI, *.EPS

Click BUT8.AI

Click OK

Notice how long it takes to import the file. Watch how the individual objects pop in one at a time, as opposed to the turbo-charged CDR file, which literally pours in. The AI format throws away all that valuable combining information.

Now that the file has been reimported into Draw, resave it as a CDR file. Be careful not to overwrite the original file. You will name this file BUT8ASAI, to denote the Adobe Illustrator format.

Resaving the File as a CDR File

Click **File**	The File menu appears.
Click Save **As**	The Save Drawing dialogue box appears.
At File, type: **BUT8ASAI**	
Click OK	The file is saved.

Now, go out to the File Manager and take a look at the various sizes of the files you just created. You will be in for a surprise! As you can see, the original CDR file is quite compact at about 24K. The first EPS file doubled in size to over 52K. We shaved a hair more than 3K by exporting another EPS file without a header. When exported through the CorelDRAW! 3.0 Adobe Illustrator export filter, the AI file grew to 176K, seven times the size of the original.

The real revelation here is the size of the AI file that was imported and saved in CDR format. That file zoomed all the way up to 192K—that hurts! After this exercise, the advantages of storing files in the CDR format should be quite apparent. Unfortunately, none of the page layout programs support the CDR format.

AI/EPS Export Caveats

A few more things need to be mentioned (or reiterated) on the subject of AI/EPS file export before moving on to the other file formats. The first of these has to do with the computer bombing during file export. Over time, you may find that your computer will go out to lunch in the middle of file export. If so, the file you are exporting may be too complex. Always save the CDR file before exporting. You may need to go back into the CDR file to simplify things. If possible, pare down objects that contain a lot of nodes, and avoid combining large numbers of objects, especially if they are complex.

If you are having trouble accurately placing your EPS files into other programs (such as PageMaker), here's a little trick. Before you export your artwork, draw a rectangle (in the exact dimensions of the space you are importing the file into) around it, give the rectangle an outline and fill of none, and export the file. When you go to place the file, the bounding box should make placement an exact science. Just be sure to correctly position the artwork within the box *before* you export it. Doing so makes it easy to use the lowest resolution screen preview.

Export text as text when possible. This will ensure compact file sizes, and hopefully reduce the amount of time you spend waiting for (and possibly rebooting) your computer.

Computer Graphics Metafile (CGM)

The CGM format has a compact, object-oriented structure. Unfortunately, the format uses no Bezier curves—only straight lines—to form images. This drawback can cause "jaggies" to occur when scaling up an image, or when printing on a high-resolution output device. For some software packages, CGM may be the only choice. If so, you will have to use it.

One such example is earlier versions of Harvard Graphics. Although the program is extremely popular, it was notoriously hostile when it comes to importing art. Harvard had the capability to convert only CGM files to its own format. To make matters worse, the conversion program does not like complex CGM files!

However, a shareware program, written by Bob Cranford and known as LCD, promises to simplify and "fix" CGM files so the Harvard conversion program can understand them. You can find it in CompuServe's IBMAPP forum, Library 10, under LCD.ZIP.

Newer versions of Harvard (3.0 and WinHarvard) have improved import filters, so you may want to use a more appropriate export filter. If you must use CGM, you should be aware that it does not support bit maps or PostScript texture fills. And if your file contains fountain fills, you can play with the banding by changing the Preview Fountain Stripes setting.

AutoCAD (DXF)

Engineers, draftsmen, and architects will be glad to know that Draw is capable of exporting to the DXF format. Although the export filter does pose severe limits, the results can be worth the effort.

The DXF export filter supports object outlines only. All fills, whether solid, texture, or fountain, are discarded, as are bit maps. In default mode, all Draw-exported text is converted to curves, which means it cannot be edited as text in the DXF file. You can export text as text by changing the ExportTextAsCurves setting to "0" (in the CORELDRW.INI file). Dashed lines and calligraphic pens are converted to 0,003" solid lines. Curves become polyline segments. Finally, you have your choice of converting your colors to either AutoCAD's standard 7 or full 255 color set.

Scan Conversion Object Description Language (SCODL)

SCODL is widely used in 35mm slide making. Chapter 12 touches on a bit of slide making. You may want to flip ahead a few pages for more information.

GEM

The compact, vector-based GEM format is an excellent choice for exporting to Ventura documents. However, certain limitations must be taken into consideration. The first of these is a 128 nodes-per-object limit. Objects with more than 128 nodes will be broken into strips and grouped. For this reason, remember to limit the number of nodes per object.

Another limitation of the GEM format has to do with color support. GEM is limited to only 16 colors; Draw has over 16 million. This presents more than a slight problem, especially with fountain fills. Draw attempts to get around this by dithering the color. If you are planning on exporting color files in GEM format, be prepared to go back to the original Draw file once or twice to get the colors in synch.

The GEM format does not support bit maps—no matter whether they are scans or pattern fills. If your Draw file contains bit maps, you will need to trace them or rethink the artwork. Dashed lines are nixed, as are PostScript texture fills (which become rather boring gray fills).

IBM PIF (GDF)

If you need to upload graphics into an IBM mainframe computer, you will probably require the PIF/GDF export filter. This filter supports many of CorelDRAW!'s features, but there are notable exceptions.

Because PIF is limited to a 16-color palette, stick to this restricted palette when designing your artwork. PostScript textures, pattern fills, and bit maps are not supported. Fountain fills now work, but results can be disappointing.

Windows Metafile (WMF)

Windows Metafile files can be thorny critters for the page layout programs to import. These files impose a number of restrictions, such as no PostScript textures or halftones, no bit maps, and no patterns. Avoid these files if you can.

But even if Windows Metafiles still sound like a good idea, there is one more (big) caveat. If you import WMF files into PageMaker, and subsequently attempt to image those PM files on a Lino by using a Mac, you will be disappointed. The WMFs won't make the translation from the PC to the Mac. You'll be left with a bunch of bounding boxes and a bill from your service bureau.

WordPerfect Graphic (WPG)

WordPerfect, one of the most popular word processing programs available today, boasts its own graphic format, WPG. This format can be used when exporting files to WordPerfect (5.0 and later) documents that will not be printed on a PostScript output device. However, use the EPS export if the document will be printed on a PostScript printer.

The WPG format has its limitations. For starters, fountain fills are extremely crude, and PostScript textures and halftone screens are no go (for obvious reasons). In addition, bit maps are not supported, and Corel recommends that you convert all text to curves.

Draw's WPG export filter enables you to export either 16 or 256 colors. Although 256 colors may sound great, the results are subject to WordPerfect's screen and printer drivers. Stick to 16 colors for more reliable results.

Finally, image rotation should be done in Draw prior to exporting the file. Images rotated in WordPerfect may not print properly. Make sure the drawing looks right before exporting.

Searching for DTP Information

To get what you need to stay abreast of the DTP field, you must know where to look. The fact that you are reading this book shows that you have a thirst for knowledge and an appetite for information. The stronger that craving is, the more successful you will be.

The design revolution that has taken place since the advent of the Apple Macintosh, Adobe PostScript, and Aldus PageMaker is staggering. The immediacy of desktop publishing is now available to far more designers at increasingly affordable prices. Programs and computers have become more powerful than previously thought possible. And the trend shows no sign of subsiding.

The huge retail industry that has sprung up around the personal computer market is, to a large extent, mail order-based and service-oriented. You do not need to drive out to the store and lose a few hours of valuable time. Just pick up the phone, dial a toll-free number, place an order for whatever you could possibly need, and receive it the next day in the overnight mail.

Your job is to find resources and make contacts. Discover which programs and outlets are reliable, and support them. To that end, this chapter presents a selection of interesting products and firms that can make a difference in your day-to-day operations.

Adonis Corporation: Clip Art by Modem

For those of you who do not have the resources—whether talent or time—to create art in a pinch, Windows Shopper™ from the Adonis Corporation offers an exciting and innovative new service: on-line clip art. Just boot up Windows Shopper and search for a graphic by category or by publisher. Once the correct image is located, use the built-in communications capabilities to access Adonis' on-line electronic clip-art database and download the art you need. The service runs 24 hours a day.

Windows Shopper lets users preview the clip-art files by providing "thumbnail" images. The thumbnails are small monochrome bit maps, for preview purposes only. Adonis states that there are over 20,000 thumbnails in its library. The thumbnails are distributed in a compressed format that yields approximately 1800 images on each high-density floppy disk. By keeping thumbnails on the user's local PC, communications charges are kept to a minimum. You do not need to buy complete clip-art collections just to get a single piece of art, but per-piece rates can run on the high side. Adonis states that the price usually ranges from about $4 to $20, although you can save money by not paying for any extra images that you will not use.

Although most subscribers to the service download and purchase individual files, you can also purchase complete collections. Although the complete collections are not downloadable—telephone costs and time factors make it prohibitive—Adonis promises 48-hour shipping and competitive pricing.

Vendors include: T/Maker, 3G Graphics, Studio Advertising
Art, Metro Creative Graphics, ArtRight, Micrografx, ArtBeats,
DreamMaker, MicroMaps, and others. Payment is billed through
most popular credit cards.

> Adonis Corporation
> 12310 NE 8th Street #150
> Bellevue, WA 98005-9832
> 800/234-9497

Using Shareware

The personal computer software community is an oddity in
today's society. Where else can you find people willing to give
you their products without making you pay for them up-front?
Shareware is software that is distributed free of charge, with a
proviso: You try it. You like it. You buy it. If you do not like (and
use) the program, you need not pay for it.

The entire premise is based on trust. The shareware developers
trust that if you like the program, you will buy it. They have no
marketing, distribution, or production costs to speak of, other
than the cost of living. The registration fees they ask are paltry in
comparison to the utility of their programs.

This type of personal computer program can be a boon to the
electronic artist on a budget. There are literally thousands of
programs out there for the asking. They can be found on computer bulletin boards around the world.

Calendar Publisher for CorelDRAW!

Calendar Publisher is a Draw file that contains a template to create
customized calendars. This formerly time-consuming task has
been greatly simplified by this marvelous template.

The idea in Calendar Publisher is that each day of the month is
shown as a tile. You can select a tile or tiles because the numbers
of the month are grouped together with the box in which the
month is contained. You can then slide those tiles to a new

location to create a new month. If Grid is ON and set to 1", all the movable tiles snap into place.

Calendar Publisher's creator is Keoni Ahlo, of Honolulu, Hawaii. You may recognize the name; Keoni created the file SCREENS.CDR, a screen density guide that began as shareware, and now comes with CorelDRAW! Version 3.0. If you installed the sample files that came with Draw, you will find SCREENS.CDR in your SAMPLES directory.

Calendar Publisher for CorelDRAW! is shareware, and carries a measly $15 registration fee. It is worth every penny. You can find a PKZIPPED copy of the file in CompuServe's DTPFORUM Library 6 under the file title DTPCAL2.ZIP.

CALENDAR PUBLISHER
Keoni Ahlo
781 Ahukini St.
Honolulu, HI 96825
CompuServe ID: 76226,3303

PKZIP

One of the most wonderful shareware utilities available, PKZIP will compress file size for cost-effective telecomputing. For transmitting your files by modem, PKZIP can save big bucks in telephone costs and on-line charges. PKZIP is available on many bulletin boards, including its own. It is commonly distributed in a compressed, self-extracting EXE format. The program contains utilities for compressing, uncompressing, password encryption, and more.

The author received a copy of the program along with his Image Center introductory kit—a pleasant surprise (see Chapter 12). He used the program a few times and gladly sent in his ($25) registration fee.

Table 11.1 shows the results of running tests on some typical files. The files that were compressed included a database file, a word processing file, a file in native CorelDRAW! format, and various exported (EPS, SDL, CGM) versions of the Draw file.

Table 11.1
Compressed File Sizes

Type of File	Original Size	PKZIPPED Size
CDR	2584	1273
EPS	18606	6098
CGM	48088	23816
SCD	48916	24684
Database	85504	32918
Word Processing	54423	17759

Depending on your modem speed, you can save the cost of registration in no time at all. PKZIP is a utility that no telecomputing electronic artist should be without!

PKZIP
PKWARE, Inc.
7545 N. Port Washington Rd.
Glendale, WI 53217-3422
414/352-3670
414/352-7176 BBS
414/352-3815 FAX

CODE TO CODE

Bruce Robey, a type shop owner, programming professional, and university instructor based in Washington D.C., offers two excellent shareware resources for typesetters and desktop publishers. The first of these two, CODE TO CODE, is a typesetter/DTP utility collection.

With CODE TO CODE, you can update typesetter/DTP files without the hassle of reading through strings of obscure codes. A coded file, while fine for a typesetter experienced in editing around lengthy, intricate codes, can cause headaches for an editor who only wants to make text changes.

Although the program is not intended to be used with Draw, it certainly has a place in the DTP arsenal. Hard-core Ventura users, as well as high-end typographers, will find CODE TO CODE to be of great use for removing delimited codes. Removed codes can be stored in a separate file at the user's option.

CODE TO CODE is shareware and is available for an economical $29.00 registration fee. The latest version and printed documentation are available through registration directly from the author. CODE TO CODE is also available on a free trial basis by downloading it as CTOC21.EXE from the CompuServe IBMAPP forum LIB 12. The program is also available through BIX, GENIE, and MAGNALINE, and through disk distributors across the country.

ALPHAQUOTE

Bruce Robey's other offering, ALPHAQUOTE, is a typesetting and DTP estimating and copyfitting program. The program was originally sold as commercial software and has been used by thousands of typesetters world-wide. ALPHAQUOTE has been completely rewritten and re-released as shareware.

If you bill for your work, you will find ALPHAQUOTE indispensable for estimating and copyfitting books, magazines, and newsletters. The menu-driven format is practical and easy to use.

ALPHAQUOTE Version 3.0 is available for $29.00. Interested parties may call for a registered version or download the shareware version from COMPUSERVE, IBMAPP LIB 12 as AQ30.EXE.

> CODE TO CODE 3.0
> ALPHAQUOTE 3.0
> Bruce Robey
> AlphaBytes, Inc.
> 111 Eighth St. S.E.
> Washington, D.C. 20003
> 202/546-4119
> CompuServe ID: 71131,2734

The Association of Shareware Professionals

Just because a program is shareware does not necessarily mean that it comes "as is" and without software support. The Association of Shareware Professionals (ASP) was formed in 1987 to bolster the image and ensure the future of shareware as an ongoing alternative to conventional/commercial software.

ASP software developers must subscribe to a code of ethics and commit themselves to the concept of shareware. The association publishes a regularly updated catalog of programs, which includes file descriptions, locations, and registration fees. The ASP catalog is available in Library 8 of the CIS IBMJR forum, and must be extracted from ARC format using the shareware program ARC-E.COM.

Although the ASP does not review members' software for functionality or usefulness—its philosophy is to let the buyer try before he buys—the association does provide an ombudsman to deal with any post-registration disputes. However, the ombudsman cannot provide technical support for members' products.

Organizations such as the ASP have all of your best interests in mind. The concept of shareware is simple, elegant, and fragile. Electronic artists must support it if it is to survive.

> The Association of Shareware Professionals
> P.O. Box 5786
> Bellevue, WA 98006

Publications for Publishers

Information-hungry electronic artists have many avenues to pursue in your quest for knowledge. To stay on top of developments, it is important to have a variety of information resources. Many publications are available on the subject of graphic design, typography, and DTP.

Aldus Magazine

Okay, okay, so this is a house organ. But it is still worth mentioning. This slick four-color publication—sent free-of-charge to registered Aldus users—is a testament to what can be done at the high-end of desktop design. Although the first issues were a bit unpolished, Aldus Magazine has evolved into a fine publication.

The ambitious premise behind the bi-monthly Aldus Magazine is a complete redesign with each issue. These redesigns are potential nightmares for its designers, but tasty pickings for those of you who may be short on ideas. Subscriptions are available for those folks who are not registered Aldus users.

Aldus Magazine
Aldus Corporation
411 First Avenue South
Seattle, WA 98104-2871
206/628-2321

Corellation

Corellation, "The Official Magazine of the Association of Corel Artists and Designers" (ACAD), is an independent publication produced by Draw-loving publishing professionals. Each issue is full of information that suits Draw artists of all levels. There are articles and how-tos for everyone from beginners through advanced users. The monthly magazine includes listings for training centers and service bureaus, along with product reviews and interviews.

Randy Tobin, Corellation's Editor/Designer, does a fine job. The magazine is light and airy, making good use of editorial white space. Both design and content are of high caliber. It is exceedingly well printed for a magazine of its type, making good use of spot varnishes and soy inks. Yearly subscriptions are bundled with a yearly membership in ACAD (a non-profit group).

Association of Corel Artists & Designers
1309 Riverside Drive
Burbank, CA 91506

Corel Magazine

Corel Magazine is published by Texas-based, Adams Publications, Inc. The slick, four-color magazine provides a monthly look into what's happening in the ever-expanding Draw world. You will find plenty of tips, tricks, and tutorials within its pages. The Marketwatch and Hot Tech sections keep readers up-to-date with the latest developments in hardware, software, and related areas.

Articles by veteran Draw users offer valuable insights and new perspectives. The Letters section is refreshingly candid, and the product reviews are timely and relevant.

> Corel Magazine
> 719 Park Boulevard
> Austin, TX 78751

Desktop Publisher

The Desktop Publisher is a monthly tabloid devoted to serving the Mid-Atlantic publishing community. This publication is a fabulous place to find a new service bureau, read about the latest DTP hardware and software, and find out what is going on in the industry at a local level.

> Desktop Publisher
> P.O. Box 3200
> 1841 Norristown Rd.
> Maple Glen, PA 19002

TypeWorld

TypeWorld, founded in 1977 and edited by the venerable (and opinionated) Frank Romano, now runs under the tagline, "The first and only newspaper for electronic publishing." Recently purchased by the PennWell Publishing Company, TypeWorld is published twice a month. Though not for the low-end DTPer, Typeworld provides pages upon pages of product information for service bureaus and electronic publishers. Chances are, a product hits the pages of Typeworld before it hits the streets.

The newspaper also includes a good-sized classified section which lists equipment for sale, from low-end desktop stuff through six-figure high-dollar systems.

TypeWorld Editorial Offices
One Stiles Road
P.O. Box 170
Salem, NH 03079
603/898-2822

U&lc

A true treasure, U&lc, or "Upper and lower case," bills itself as the international journal of type and graphic design. U&lc is a quarterly celebration of the typographer's craft. Within its large format, you are treated to design at its best, whether black and white, spot color, or process color. Each issue brings incredible spreads that beg the mind for thorough consideration. Typographic history is taught here, and it is taught quite well.

Published by the International Typeface Corporation and available for a nominal fee, U&lc is a resource that you should not be without.

U&lc
International Typeface Corporation
2 Hammarskjold Plaza
New York, NY 10017
212/371-0699

Using CompuServe Information Service (CIS)

Have a question that needs to be answered, and cannot afford to spend the time or money to call Ottawa? Try CompuServe.

CompuServe is one of the most amazing resources in the computer world. It is a support network, offering you thousands of people who are ready to offer advice on whatever your computer problems might be.

Type up a note covering the problem in your favorite word processor. Then save it as an ASCII file and upload it to either the Corel or DTP Forums. Within a day, sometimes even hours, you will get the answer you need without waiting on hold or spending big bucks on telephone calls.

The DTPFORUM

The desktop publishing forum (DTPFORUM) is the place where savvy desktoppers hang out to trade advice, talk shop, and shmooze. There is the message board, with its winding threads of questions, answers, and conversations on topics ranging from DTP issues to what is the best Canadian beer. In the libraries, you will find demo programs, fonts, clip-art samples, and more. Every Tuesday night at 9 p.m. Eastern time, the DTPFORUM sponsors an on-line conference where DTPers can visit and trade information.

The ZENITH FORUM

The Zenith Forum (ZENITH FORUM) was originally created to support owners of Zenith Data Systems computers, most notably the Zenith portables. It has since grown to support portables in general, as well as Windows products. ZENITH FORUM is an excellent place to scour for shareware programs—from graphics converters to Windows utilities.

For the convenience of forum members, an up-to-date catalog of library files is posted on the first of every month. It is always LIBSUM.EXE in the New Files Library (Library 1). This forum is especially sensitive to the needs of new CompuServe users and holds beginners' conferences every Sunday night to give them live help. To get to the ZENITH FORUM, just type GO ZENITH.

The COREL FORUM

In late spring, 1992, Corel opened their own CompuServe forum. Just type GO COREL, and you'll be whisked to one of the most interesting forums on CIS! Here, you can ask specific Draw-related questions, and expect a prompt response from a number of folks well-versed in the program's intricacies. You can even upload problem files, connect-time-free, for Corel's on-line sleuths. In addition to the message board, there are libraries which contain bug-fixes, various CDR sample files, and a number of utilities.

> CompuServe Incorporated
> 5000 Arlington Centre Blvd.
> Columbus, OH 43220

Fooling with Fonts

In the not-too-distant past, the idea of purchasing a typeface from one manufacturer, loading that typeface onto a machine from another manufacturer, manipulating the typeface with a program from a third manufacturer, and printing it on a printer from yet a fourth was a wildly speculative concept. Today, it is a hard and fast reality. The key component in this tricky equation is what is known as the page description language (PDL). As you might have already deduced, the PDL that has made it all possible is Adobe Systems' PostScript language.

The arrival of the PostScript language has opened doors that were once locked with proprietary keys. In days gone by, if one wanted a new typeface for his or her particular printer, there was only one source: the printer's manufacturer. Typefaces from company A did not run on typesetters from company B, and vice versa.

Today, thanks to PostScript, you can buy fonts everywhere—even, as you will see, from a mail-order firm dedicated to selling just fonts. In addition, you have the flexibility to create your own fonts on the PC platform using Altsys' Fontographer or a combination of CorelDRAW! and Ares FontMonger.

Where Are All of CorelDRAW!'s Fonts?

CorelDRAW! Version 3.0 changed the way that Draw accesses fonts. Previous versions of the program relied upon the proprietary WFN font format, and included a utility program, WFNBOSS, to convert fonts between formats. Draw 3.0 can now use either TrueType, PostScript, or WFN fonts.

Accessing all of Draw's fonts can be a problem if you do not have a CD-ROM drive on your computer. Over 150 fonts are supplied in TrueType format from the installation disks. In addition, there are 100 or so TrueType fonts on the CD-ROM disk distributed with every copy of Draw 3.0. And all of the PostScript fonts are supplied on the CD-ROM. The symbol fonts are installed from floppies, and are in WFN format.

Although Windows has a limit of 1000 TrueType fonts, Draw has an internal limit of 900 fonts (which may be a combination of TrueType, PostScript, and WFN formats). If you have more than 900 fonts, you will want to use the newly announced Ares FontMinder to manage your fonts.

Ares FontMinder

Need a way to control a burgeoning array of fonts? Ares FontMinder tames the font-beast by organizing your fonts into easily installable (and de-installable) font packs. These font packs can contain any array of Type 1 and/or TrueType fonts. You can arrange your fonts according to clients, recurring jobs, or operators. With an easy way to swap between font load, your system will operate faster, and with less overhead. The idea is to load only the fonts you need, rather than the whole collection.

FontMinder evolved from the successful shareware program, FontManager. Developer Dennis Harrington's pet project became so popular that it attracted the attention of Ares, and has now grown into a full-fledged commercial application worthy of any serious DTPer.

Ares FontMonger

Ares FontMonger is one of the most useful pieces of software that a power-Draw user can own. The program is designed to convert, enhance, modify, and even create typefaces, and is a perfect complement to Draw's ability to export TrueType or PostScript Type 1 typefaces. However, FontMonger's font conversions are far more advanced, and include font hinting, which improves the appearance of laser-printed text.

FontMonger can convert fonts from a slew of PC font formats: Win 3.1 TrueType, PostScript Type 1 and 3, Intellifonts, Nimbus Q, Corel WFN, LaserMaster LXO; not to mention NeXT PostScript Type 1, as well as Mac TrueType, PostScript Type 1 and 3. These typefaces can be converted into: Win 3.1 TrueType, PC PostScript Type 1 and 3, Nimbus Q, NeXT PostScript Type 1, along with Mac TrueType, PostScript Type 1 and 3. That covers just about all the bases!

Converting fonts between formats is a sticky legal issue. The Ares documentation states that the creation of beautiful and practical typefaces is an art rather than a science, sometimes requiring years of work for the creation of a single typeface. Ares Software supports existing copyrights and the efforts of those who designed them and supports the work of the companies who publish fonts. You should check the license agreement for your fonts before using FontMonger to convert or alter them. For more information, please contact the supplier of your fonts directly.

As important as format conversions, the program enables you to do some serious modifications to existing fonts. You can build special fractions, symbols, or custom small caps. You also can import CorelDRAW! artwork into a font, so that you can create a logofont for distribution throughout your company. The power inherent in FontMonger is disproportionate to its price. Take a look through your CorelDRAW! 3.0 package for a special deal on FontMonger!

Ares Software Corporation
P.O. Box 4667
Foster City, CA 94404-4667
415/578-9090

FontHaus

FontHaus was born in Norwalk, Connecticut, in 1990, out of a desire to fill the growing needs of graphic designers. The firm is dedicated to providing timely, exceptional service and advice to the designer in need of a specific typeface. The only things they sell are fonts and font-related software. With over 6000 fonts in stock and ready to ship, FontHaus is a boon to the artist with heavy deadlines to meet.

In addition to being service-oriented from a delivery point of view, FontHaus offers unequalled depth and typographic expertise. While larger computer mail-order firms may offer just the Adobe library of fonts, FontHaus is a one-stop source for fonts from all the major foundries, as well as many small foundries. They offer typefaces from: Adobe, Agfa, ATF, Autologic, Berthold, Bitstream, Elsner+Flake, The Font Bureau, ITC, Lanston, Letraset, Linotype-Hell, Monotype, Panache, and Treacyfaces (just to name a few). To complement the depth of their wares, the people answering the phones know type—they are not just order-takers.

Dedicated to pushing the design envelope, FontHaus also actively seeks new and leading-edge type designs from today's most prominent designers, which they issue under the FontHaus label. These fonts are not available anywhere else, and include exciting new designs, as well as revivals of classic typefaces. Each and every font sold by FontHaus (regardless of foundry) is fully licensed, thus protecting the rights of the original designer and foundry. All told, FontHaus is a class act, and a resource that no typographer worth his (or her) pica gauge should be without.

> FontHaus Inc.
> 15 Perry Avenue
> Norwalk, CT 06850
> 800/942-9110
> 203/846-3087
> 203/849-8527 (FAX)

Adobe Type Manager

One of the biggest things to hit the PC DTP market in 1990 (right after the arrival of Windows 3.0 and CorelDRAW! Versions 1.2 and 2.0, that is) had to be the introduction of the Windows PC version of Adobe Type Manager (ATM).

The program uses vector printer fonts to produce screen fonts, eliminating the jagged or stick-like characters everyone had resigned themselves to for years. ATM makes on-screen type look the way it should. And, as a boon to folks who do not have access to PostScript printers, it enables you to print PostScript fonts, as well!

The publishing world speaks PostScript. CorelDRAW! Version 3.0's CD-ROM provides an instant library of over 250 PostScript Type 1 format fonts that can be used with any other Windows programs, such as PageMaker or Word for Windows. If you use Windows, and you do not have ATM, what are you waiting for?

Using Mosaic: Corel's Visual File Manager

CorelDRAW! enables the electronic artist to amass volumes of work in a short period of time. This productivity is a mixed blessing. Although it is easy to create stunning artwork, the sheer number of files can soon pile into an unmanageable tangle of obscure files. CorelMOSAIC! (first introduced in Version 2.0) helps you to cut through the confusion in a number of ways, and adds even more versatility to CorelDRAW!.

The first means of file management is the Visual File Selector. This icon-based feature provides an instantly recognizable vignette (a compact bit-map screen representation) of the artwork contained in a file. Whether stored in a library or as a stand-alone file, each image can be summoned through strictly visual association. The need for the user to remember specific file names is greatly diminished. Scroll through a directory with Mosaic, find the image you want, double-click—and CorelDRAW! opens with that file.

Mosaic is greatly enhanced in CorelDRAW Version 3.0. It can now display images in a wide variety of formats, in addition to CDR. You can view thumbnails of AI, BMP, CCH, DIB, EPS, GIF, PCC, PCX, SHW, TIF, and TGA format files. So it's easy to sort through your files, regardless of the format, before you import them into Draw. Displaying all those files, however, can take some time. Thankfully, Mosaic allows you to turn off the bit-map preview in its Preferences dialogue box.

Mosaic also enables you to compress and organize your files. Compressing files and storing them in libraries saves on disk space. The libraries can be organized to suit your working style through the Get Info dialogue box.

Using Mosaic Libraries

Mosaic libraries store CorelDRAW! artwork files in a compact, orderly manner. The library function uses a compression routine when compressing files and when expanding them back to usable form.

Working with existing library files is a straightforward affair. To open a file contained in a library, double-click on the file name, select a directory to place the expanded file into, and click OK. Alternatively, you can select the file and choose Open from the File menu. If you want to expand a number of files at once (to CDR format) without actually opening them in Draw, shift-click the files and then select Expand Image(s) to CDR from the Library menu.

Creating Mosaic libraries and adding to existing libraries is an easy task. To create a library, select a number of CDR files, click Library, and click Add Image(s) to Library. Mosaic will ask you which library you want to add the files to, and will ask you to verify the inclusion of each file. If you are creating a new library, Mosaic will ask you to verify that as well.

NOTE

When you add a file to a library, the original CDR file remains untouched. You must decide if you want to remove the file or leave it on your system.

Organizing and Annotating Your Files

The Get Info (File Information) dialogue box that is accessed through Mosaic's Edit menu enables you to add information to file listings in two powerful ways. The first involves *keywords*, which can be used to perform word or subject searches. By entering a number of descriptive words (separated by commas or plus signs) in the Keyword field of the Get Info dialogue box, you can build a database of artwork that you can easily search by categories.

The second field in the Get Info dialogue box is Notes. It can include a variety of information relevant to a file, such as a color summary or other description, client information, and so on. Because Keywords and Notes are Windows text fields, you can cut and paste information into them from other Windows applications.

Gang Printing with Mosaic

Do you need laser copies of a number of Draw files? In Mosaic, Shift- (or Ctrl-) click the required files, click Print Selected Files.... This saves you the time and hassle of opening files one at a time and sending each to the printer. You set up the printer dialogue box for the first image, and the rest of the pages print unattended.

Mosaic even enables you to extract and merge text from a number of selected files. For many people, this function can seem a bit obscure. But this can be a powerful tool for database-publishing everything from certificates to business forms.

Mosaic Thumbnails

One of the handiest things that you can do with CorelMOSAIC! is to print thumbnail representations of your files. This can be a great timesaver, and a boon to the production-minded. Mosaic's Page Setup dialogue box enables you to title pages and images in your choice of typeface and justification. You can vary the size of your thumbnails—both on screen and on the printed page—by changing the thumbnail width using the Mosaic Preferences dialogue box. These features came in handy during the production of this book!

Summary

CorelDRAW! is but one of many weapons you will use in your electronic graphic arts arsenal. Thankfully, it does a tremendous job of integrating with many different packages. The trick is to know which packages to use, and what to buy. The only way to do so is to stay current with the steady stream of information in this industry. This is not done by keeping your ear to the ground; it is done by keeping your nose in the trades.

The resources presented in this chapter are a starting point. To be successful, you must be informed. The ultimate business weapon is knowledge. It is up to you to go out and get it.

Printing Considerations

aving a pretty picture on the screen is one thing, but getting it printed is quite another. This book has stressed the concept of working drawings. The ultimate goal is to assemble an image that can be reproduced in a timely fashion. To that end, this chapter covers the issues of working with Draw in a production environment.

In the Monarch butterfly exercise in Chapter 8, you constructed a process color image that is a compact, streamlined file. Well-constructed images are the key to cost-effective printing. Not only do they image faster on the computer, they should also image faster on the output device, saving on "per-minute" charges.

Spot color images should also be carefully constructed. *Trapping*—the almost imperceptible overlap of different colors—is extremely important for many printing techniques, from screen printing T-shirts through fine art lithography. As you will see later in this chapter, you can set up traps with Draw, but only if the image has been put together with this in mind. While some artists may consider the extra work involved hardly worth the effort, others will welcome the ability to provide chokes and spreads.

This chapter focuses on getting your Draw files to the printer—not just the printer on the desk next to you, but also to the guy down the street who will ultimately print umpteen copies. Start out by taking a look at how Draw enables you to access its print options.

Using Draw's Print Options

CorelDRAW!'s print savvy is controlled by the Print Options dialogue box. Please note that this means the print options as they relate to a PostScript® output device. Although Windows can drive plenty of non-PostScript devices, it is hardly worth using CorelDRAW! with anything but a true Adobe PostScript-licensed printer.

The one exception is a relatively inexpensive color ink-jet printer, which can be a real convenience when used as a design tool. However, do not use an ink-jet printer as a prepress proofing device for images that will ultimately be output on a PostScript printer. The continuity just is not there.

Take a look at the various options that Draw gives you when printing files (see fig. 12.1). To access the Print options dialogue box, click File and then Print, or press Ctrl-P.

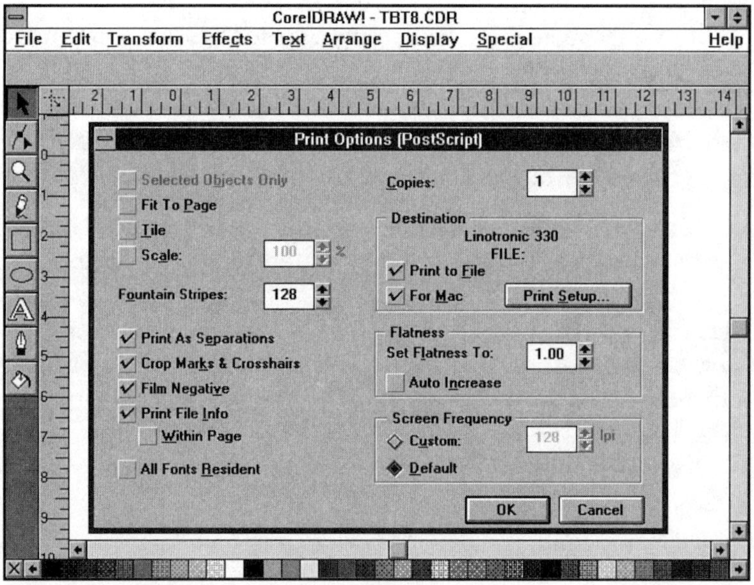

Figure 12.1:

The Print Options dialogue box.

Selected Objects Only. This is a time-saving option that is valuable when working with images that consist of many objects. It works in a similar manner to Preview Only Selected. In this mode, the printer outputs only those objects that are selected at the time the Print Options dialogue box displays. If you want to print just one or a few objects without waiting for the printer to image all the objects, use Selected Objects Only.

Fit to Page. This option is a subset of Scale. With one click, the oversized image will be scaled down to fit on the selected output page.

Tile. The Tile option prints an image that is larger than the output device's largest paper size. For example, when proofing a tabloid-sized image on a printer whose paper size is limited to 8 1/2 inches by 11 inches, click Tile. The printer will break the image up into pieces (or tiles), which can then be taped together for proofing.

Scale. Scale, like Tile, is a convenient way to print oversized images. Unlike Tile, however, Scale can fit the image on one piece of paper, although at a reduced size. The reduction percentages are variable.

Fountain Stripes. The Fountain Stripes option governs the number of stripes in a printed fountain fill. Low values will print faster (with visible banding), while high values will look smoother (and take longer to print). For high-resolution imagesetters, Corel recommends 128 for 1270 dpi, and 200 for 2540 dpi.

Print As Separations. This option is used for color printing. Each color used is broken into its own plate. If you are using process color, this means there will be separate plates for cyan, magenta, yellow, and black. With spot color, each spot color used will have its own plate. This option will also work with a combination of spot and process colors, just in case you want to pay for that seven-color press!

When Print As Separations is selected, Draw will automatically select Crop Marks & Crosshairs, Film Negative, and Include File Info. You can turn these options off as required.

Crop Marks & Crosshairs. As discussed briefly in Chapter 1, the Crop Marks & Crosshairs option adds registration marks to the output image. These are imperative for aligning the printed image on the press, and are absolutely necessary for color printing.

Film Negative. Film Negative sets the PostScript output device to invert the file image, turning black to white and white to black. This is necessary when imaging negatives that will be directly burned to the printing plates. Film negatives give the highest possible quality, short of burning plates right on the Lino.

Print File Info. This option prints all pertinent file information along with the image. This includes the name of the file, the plate color, the screen frequency and angle, and the time and date that the file was printed. This data will be printed outside the image area unless you click Within Page.

All Fonts Resident. This option is another time-saving feature, and one that is important for the serious typographer who regularly uses a service bureau. This option sets up the output file so that it calls the fonts directly from the output device. If this option is not checked, the file contains all the font information.

Output files that contain a number of fonts can grow quite large. If you click All Fonts Resident, you (or your service bureau) must have the corresponding fonts at the printer (otherwise, the printer will substitute fonts and the file will not print correctly). When All Fonts Resident is on, Draw does not send the extra font information. The result is a smaller print file and faster printing times.

In addition to speeding up print time, selecting All Fonts Resident will yield the actual PostScript font, rather than Draw's interpretation of it. This may not be important to many folks, but discerning typographers can tell the difference, subtle though it may seem.

The important thing to remember when using All Fonts Resident is that the required fonts must already be loaded on the printer. When you are using the standard 35 PostScript fonts, this is no problem for most printers. In fact, if your file contains only fonts from among the 35 standards, there is no reason to click the option; Draw will automatically use the printer's resident fonts. But using, for instance, Ottawa without having Optima loaded on the printer will result in font substitution. Make sure that your service bureau can provide a list of its available fonts. And don't forget to include a list of the fonts used with each file you submit to your service bureau.

Flatness. Flatness governs the smoothness of curves in PostScript output files. The lower the setting, the smoother the curves (and the more difficult a file is to print). Complex objects can sometimes choke a printer. Raising the Flatness setting enables Draw to simplify the curves, making the file more palatable to PostScript printers. While high-resolution imagesetters are more finicky than desktop lasers, a larger Flatness setting will be more apparent at high resolution. For this reason, you should always try to break large curves into smaller segments.

Auto Increase Flatness. This option was introduced in CorelDRAW! 3.0. As you may have gathered, Draw makes it too easy to create overly complex images that can be trouble at print time. When you click this option, Corel takes control of printing by setting up the PostScript file to automatically increment the flatness setting (up to a maximum of 10) each time the printer bombs out on a print job. If the object is still too complex to print, the printer will go on to the next object.

Screen Frequency. This option sets up the output device's halftone size. Although many folks may overlook this setting, it is of extreme importance when attempting serious color work. Failing to set a proper screen frequency will yield a rough-looking image. Do not waste your client's money by printing process color at 60 lpi.

To ascertain the correct screen frequency to use, check with the printer (the person, not the machine) who will ultimately print the job. He should be able to give you complete specifications.

The Screen Frequency setting is overridden by any individual changes in the Outline or Fill PostScript screen options dialogue boxes, for those objects only. This makes it possible to use, for instance, a 110 screen for an entire image with the exception of the logo, which may require a special screen effect. Corel advises using a 90-lpi screen frequency to avoid fountain fill banding on high-resolution output devices. On desktop laser printers, use 40 to 60 lpi.

NOTE

The color plates in this book were imaged to negatives at 133 lines per inch, and 1270 dots per inch.

Print to File is most commonly used when outputting an image to a printer that is not directly connected to the computer it was composed on. This is often the case for files being sent to high-resolution imagesetters, such as the ubiquitous Lino. The dialogue box gives you the option of specifying For Mac if you are sending the print file to a Mac-only service bureau. The For Mac option (added in version 2.0) strips the first and last characters from the print file, saving a step.

When you select Print to File, Draw asks for a file name. The program automatically assigns the PRN file extension to identify the file as a print file. After you click Print, Draw displays the PostScript Printer dialogue box (see fig. 12.2).

Figure 12.2:

The Print Options (PostScript) dialogue box.

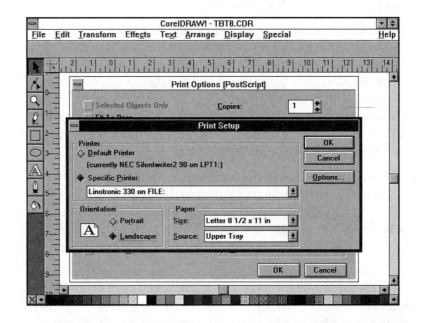

Here, you may select from among many of the popular PostScript output devices. If the printer you are using is not shown on the list, check with your printer manufacturer for a Windows 3.1 driver. In addition to printer type, the paper source and paper size are also selectable. The paper size is important when running a file with crop marks and crosshairs to the Lino. When imaging such a file, always use a paper size larger than the file you are printing. For example, when printing a letter-sized page with crop marks and crosshairs, use Letter Extra (if available).

In the Print Options dialogue box, you are also given another option to scale the output file, as well as to set the number of copies to be printed. Windows can be slow to print multiple copies of a file conventionally. It can be faster to print multiple copies to a file, and download (copy) the subsequent file to the printer.

You will also notice that there is a box marked Use Color. This option is dimmed unless a color printer is selected.

One final note on the Print Options dialogue box. If you have problems with your output device "timing-out" (failing to print), check to see that Device Not Selected is set at its default setting of 15 seconds, and Transmission Retry is set to 600 seconds or higher.

Windows 3.1 Print Driver Woes

Early versions of Microsoft's Windows 3.1 PostScript printer drivers have been problem-ridden. The 3.53 driver was released in late July, 1992, just months after the new release of Windows 3.1. This version added support for the Linotype L/300—arguably the world's most common PostScript imagesetter. Why Microsoft failed to include it in the initial release is unfathomable. In any case, you should be running with the latest release of the driver. You can download the latest PostScript drivers from Microsoft's BBS at 206/936-6735. You will find them in the file LINO.EXE (which is a self-extracting archive file).

The 3.52 driver does have one obvious shortcoming. When you specify a specific dpi setting (in the Print Options dialogue box), the imagesetter's control panel must be dialed into the identical setting. The imagesetter always overrules the driver's resolution. Be sure to let your service bureau know what resolution you need for each file.

Printing in Color

Unless you are lucky enough to have a color printer, the only way to check your images is to send out for a color proof. You have three options. The first is to send out for a color print from a service bureau that offers color PostScript output from a color PostScript printer such as the QMS ColorScript. These devices offer 300-dpi proof, which is suitable for comp work (but not prepress proofing) and can emulate either process or PANTONE colors. But rather than use these devices for *final* proofing, consider them marvelous, though costly, design tools.

The second, and preferred, color proofing option is to have your service bureau burn negatives on its Lino. Then, if you are using process colors, have the negatives made into a DuPont Chromalin™ color proof (commonly referred to as a "chrome"). For PANTONE colors, there are similar proofing systems.

The final option for color proofing is to have your printer show the color breaks with transparencies—such as 3M Color Keys—prior to running the job. Regardless of method, you should always have proofs made before going to press.

Negatives are a necessary step for high-quality printing. If your printer will not work with negatives, he is probably using direct-to-plate technology. He might think that this is high-tech, but it is not usually suitable for high-quality color printing. Look for another printer.

Process color is an intricate, expensive affair. If you intend to use CorelDRAW! to produce process color separations, make sure that you have plenty of time and money before proceeding. Each set of separations and chrome can easily cost more than $100. Do not expect to save by scrimping on the proof print. The dollars you save might cost you fifty times that if a press job must be rerun.

Trapping

Trapping, or *spreads and chokes*, as the procedure is commonly called, is the way printers compensate for variations in press registration when running multiple color jobs. Quite simply, one color is spread out, or the other color is choked in. This creates a slight overprint and counteracts any fluctuations in registration while a print job is running.

Figure 12.3 shows a simple trap. The darker outline color over-prints the lighter fill color resulting in a trap.

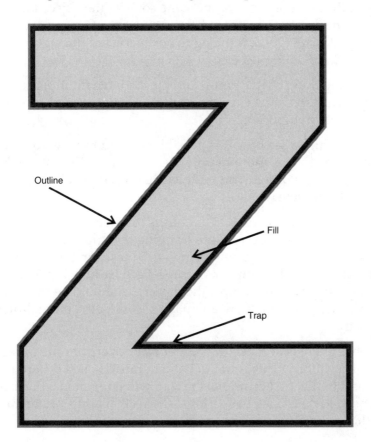

Figure 12.3:
An example of a trap.

There is good news when it comes to traps. With version 2.0, CorelDRAW! introduced a semi-automated capability for trap-ping artwork. However, it is a tricky business—a manual, trap-by-trap procedure—that should be approached with caution. The secret is in the way you construct your images.

Each press and pressman has different trapping requirements. Some need no traps at all and are perfectly content with butt registration. Others require varying spreads and chokes. Ink and paper types also have a lot to do with the trap amplitude.

If a color image can be separated into layers by colors, it may be possible to set traps. In a multiple color image, each color becomes a layer. By using outlines of the same color as the object's fill, a trap can be drawn. The secret here is to use the Overprint option in the PostScript Options dialogue box (accessed through the Outline Color dialogue box).

As with anything of this nature, it helps to have multiple copies of your file, just in case. Leave the original file untouched and play around with a duplicate.

You are going to see how it is possible to build traps with Draw— not necessarily easy, but possible. Remember the Thurston's Bait & Tackle T-shirt design you built in Chapter 5? Trot that file out now and complete it.

Screen printing in general, and T-shirts (or other textiles) in particular, tend to require more trapping than precise offset presses. To this end, you will begin with the Thurston's design as a way to explain the simplest of traps. Because all you will be dealing with is outlined type, the principles should be rather obvious. The more intricate an image becomes, the more difficult it is to trap.

The object here is to make the lighter color overprint the darker color just slightly. This is not done with mirrors, just different outlines! In this first example, the trap will happen in a flash. All you need to do is click overprint and select an appropriate line width.

Trapping the Thurston's Design

After you have gone through the following exercise, you will get the idea behind the trap solution. You will use a pair of suitable aquatic colors to bring the design to life.

As you will see, trapping with Draw can be a tricky maneuver. Sometimes it is simple and obvious; other times complex, puzzling, and ultimately impossible.

Setting a Simple Trap

You will start out by opening up the last version of the Thurston's file. This one happens to be TBT8. Substitute the name of your completed file, if it is different.

Click **File**	The File menu appears.
Click **O**pen	
Double-click on filename	The file assembles itself on-screen.

You need to group the words "Thurston's Bait & Tackle" so that they can be modified easily.

Shift-click all elements in Thurston's Bait & Tackle	
Press Ctrl-G	The words are grouped.

Next, you need to give the type a spot color fill and an overprinting outline.

Click the fill tool	The Fill fly-out menu appears.
Click Uniform Fill	The Uniform Fill dialogue box appears.
Click **S**pot	
At Model, click Names	Dialogue box configures for names.
Click PANTONE Process Blue CV	To fill with PANTONE Process Blue CV.
At Tint, enter: **100**	
Click **O**K	
Click the outline tool	The Outline fly-out menu appears.
Click the outline pen icon	The Outline Pen dialogue box appears.
Click the round corner	
Click the round line cap	

continues

At Width, enter **0.04**	Use inches.
Click OK	
At Color, click **More** ...	The Outline Color dialogue box appears.
Click **S**pot	
Roll down and click **PANTONE 316**	
At Tint, enter: **100**	
Click PostScript **O**ptions ...	The PostScript Options dialogue box appears.
Click **O**verprint	
Click OK	
Click OK again	
Click OK one last time	

You have created an outline that will overprint the fill by .02 of an inch. Now, you are going to print that outline to a file. You will be testing this setup on your desktop laser printer.

Click **F**ile	The File menu appears.
Click **P**rint	The Print dialogue box appears.
Click Print As **Se**parations	
Deselect Film **N**egative	You are printing POSITIVES.
Click Print To **Fi**le	
Click For **M**ac	
Click OK	

The Color Separations dialogue box appears (see fig. 12.4). The only colors that should be present are PANTONE Process Blue CV and PANTONE 316 CV.

Click **A**ll Colors	
Click OK	The Print to File dialogue box appears (see fig. 12.5).
Click OK	The Printer on FILE-NAME dialogue box appears.

The print file will automatically be assigned the same prefix as your current file, but with a PRN file extension.

Click OK	The Thurston's sign is printed to a file.

The PostScript Printer on FILENAME dialogue box enables you to set up your file for a specific media size. In order to choose an imagesetter, such as the Linotronic 300, you must have the imagesetter's drivers loaded on your system, through the Windows Control Panel.

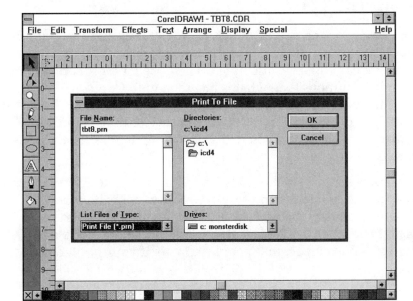

Figure 12.4:

The Color Separations dialogue box.

Figure 12.5:

The Print to File dialogue box.

Congratulations, you just created a simple trap with CorelDRAW! In this exercise, you printed your image to a file rather than to a laser printer. These files would be taken to a service bureau for film positive output. The film positives would then be used to produce the photo stencils required for screen printing. By contrast, lithographic printing usually requires film negatives.

Since you were preparing the file for screen printing, the trap you set was very large and very obvious. If you have a laser printer, send the separations to it, so you can see the trap. Remember to reset your printer options!

NOTE

Do not click Behind Fill in the Outline Pen dialogue box, or you will be left with no trap at all.

Although the preceding example is admittedly the most rudimentary of chokes and spreads, it illustrates the concept. Every day, artists all over the world are trapping with Draw. Here is a salute to all those groundbreakers willing to take the arrows in the forehead!

More complicated traps require that you duplicate objects, giving the duplicate (trap) no fill and an overprinting outline in either the fill or background color. Things can get quite complicated. One of the best ways to keep your head is to set up your images in overlays.

Avoiding Traps

No one is twisting your arm into trapping. In fact, many printers would rather handle the traps themselves, rather than try to correct what you have attempted. There are far more sophisticated trapping solutions than what is included with CorelDRAW! 3.0. If you are not comfortable with trapping your work, don't. Talk with your printer, color trade shop, or service bureau; they may be able to offer a solution that will save everyone time, headaches, and cash.

Designers and artists should not have to worry about how the ink hits the paper, just the end result. Unfortunately, the current situation requires that you *must* worry about it, although you don't have to worry about it alone. If you do not possess print production expertise, find people who do. If your printer does not have the electronic smarts to help you, check around. If you have a good relationship with your printer, let him know what you need. He can be an excellent resource, even if he can't handle everything in-house.

High-end systems, such as Scitex, set up traps once the image has already been ripped into a huge bit map. This can be the most expeditious method for trapping an intricate four- (or more) color design. It takes serious computer power and prepress expertise to do it right! The high end may not be for you, however. If you use a lot of hairlines in your work, you may not be pleased with the results. Once again, the best plan is to consult with folks who know the game. Let them guide you through the process, but expect to pay for their expertise. The costs will be trivial when compared to what it will cost you for a print job gone bad.

Playing with the Bands

If you have been working with CorelDRAW! for any significant amount of time, you are bound to have been disappointed at times by fountain fill banding. This unwanted phenomenon creates visible stripes in what should be smooth transitions of gray (or color) in images printed on a PostScript printer. Banding is due to the restrictions of the PostScript language and the resolution of your output device.

Avoiding Banding in PostScript Fountain Fills

In many cases, banding can be eliminated by following a few basic rules. These caveats have to do with the imaging capabilities of your (or your service bureau's) printer, along with the optical capabilities of the human eye.

Unfortunately, the secret to avoiding banding requires that you perform a mathematical equation or two. You can use the Windows Calculator to handle all the hard work. All you have to do is apply the rules.

The fundamental rule regulates the number of fountain fill stripes that are available to the printer. This figure depends upon the printer's resolution (dpi), the screen line frequency (lpi), and the percent of gray change. The gray change is the difference between the starting and ending percentages:

The Number of Stripes = (dpi/lpi)2 × (% Gray Change)

For example, typical desktop laser printers image at 300 dpi/60 lpi. A fountain fill that went from black to white—100 percent black to 0 percent black—would be a 100 percent gray change.

25 Stripes = (300/60)2 × (100-0)/100

If you were to print the same image on a Lino at 1270 dpi/110 lpi, you would have a greater number of stripes, due to the increase in resolution.

133 Stripes = (1270/110)2 × (100-0)/100

As shown in table 12.1, the number of stripes goes down as Line Frequency (lpi) at any given resolution goes up. While it may be advantageous to avoid banding by lowering the screen frequency, remember that the screen dots will be larger and more noticeable. Instead, it may be worth your while to run the file at high resolution. For example: if you are having trouble with banding in a fountain fill at 1270 dpi/120 lpi, running the same file at 2540 dpi/120 lpi may alleviate the problem by providing a significantly larger number of stripes. However, the file will take longer to print; consequently, your service bureau will probably charge a higher rate for high resolution.

Table 12.1
Number of Stripes at Various Resolutions

% Gray Change	dpi lpi	300 60	1270 90	2540 120	133	120	133	150
10		2	19	11	9	44	36	28
20		5	39	22	18	89	72	57
30		7	59	33	27	134	109	86
40		10	79	44	36	179	145	114

% Gray Change	dpi lpi	300 60	1270 90	2540 120	133	120	133	150
50		12	99	56	45	224	182	143
60		15	119	67	54	256	218	172
70		17	139	78	63	256	255	200
80		20	159	89	72	256	256	229
90		22	179	100	82	256	256	256
100		25	199	112	91	256	256	256

There is a boundary, however. Notice that at higher resolutions, the PostScript interpreter sets a maximum limit of 256 stripes. This is apparent in longer fountain fills, and those with smaller amounts of gray change, which leads to the next important item.

The human eye disregards bands that are 1/32" (0.03") or less. So what does that mean in the real world? Simple. You will get visible banding when individual bands are wider than 0.03". Hence, banding is usually noticeable in longer fountain fills. Why? Multiply 0.03" by the maximum allowable number of bands (0.03" × 256 = 7.68"). That is why you are always going to get a degree of visible banding in a large fill—even at high resolution (2540 dpi). Since lower resolution printers have far fewer stripes, banding is far more prevalent.

Before you print a fountain-filled object on a Lino, try running the numbers through the "Number of Stripes" equation. Then, multiply the number of stripes by 0.03". If the resulting number is larger than the length of the fountain filled object, it is a good candidate for banding. You may want to rethink the fill, and use a lower screen frequency, larger gray change, or run the file at a higher resolution.

Since the maximum number of stripes is limited by resolution, laser printers are far more prone to banding than are high-resolution imagesetters. Even so, a quick check with the calculator can save you money at Lino time. Now that you have the basics of black-and-white fountain fill banding characteristics, take a look at how it works with color fountain fills.

What about Color Fills?

In the last section, you learned the basics of avoiding banding in black-and-white fountain fills. With color fountain fills, you follow the basics and add one last equation. Before you can determine the gray change percentage for a color fountain fill, you need to come up with gray values for the starting and ending colors. The good news here is that CorelDRAW!'s color palette makes it easy to perform the equation.

Although you may be working with CMYK or Pantone colors, the PostScript language deals with your colors in their Red/Green/Blue (RGB) equivalents. Draw's color palette enables you to instantly change a color from its CMYK or Pantone values into RGB values. With your starting fill color selected in the dialogue box, change the fill type from its original setting to RGB. Presto! The color's RGB values appear. Write the values down, cancel out of the dialogue box, and repeat the procedure for the ending fill color. Then, plug the numbers into the following equation for each of the colors. (This equation is reprinted from the *PostScript Language Reference Manual*, Second Edition. Published by Addison-Wesley Publishing Company, Inc. Copyright © 1985-1988, 1990 Adobe Systems Incorporated. All rights reserved.)

%Gray = 30%(Red Value) + 59%(Green Value) + 11%(Blue Value)

With the gray value of the starting and ending fill colors calculated, proceed with the first equation you learned: The number of stripes = (dpi/lpi)2 × (% Gray Change). Then, multiply the number of stripes by 0.03" to determine whether or not you are going to get any banding.

In Short...

Your budget and time frame dictate how you handle fountain fills. Laser printers will produce bands on everything but the shortest fills. Printing files on a higher resolution output device will result in an increase in quality—up to a point. By following the rules set forth in this section, you can alleviate many unhappy surprises when you get your printed output back from the service bureau.

Printing Other Items with CorelDRAW!

One of the beauties of CorelDRAW! is that the images you create can be taken to many platforms and output on many devices. But the attraction is not solely in the range of printers that Draw can drive. The depth lies in the imaging possibilities, or more appropriately, the potential of what can be done with the output images.

By now, you have probably used Draw to prepare a variety of printed material, and you may even have a few different digitized logos on hand. You probably have a knowledge of laser printers and high-resolution imagesetters like the Linotype L-300, as well.

As you have seen in the last exercise, images can be easily made into Lino film positives and screen printed.

Print Merge

At some time, you may be asked to produce boilerplate prints merged with variable data, such as diplomas or awards (see fig. 12.6). You are in luck. CorelDRAW! version 2.0 introduced Print Merge, a marvelous feature that allows a data file containing a number of records to be combined with a static layout (including art and typographic effects) on the fly.

Print Merge applies most, but not all, of Draw's effects to variable data. Specifically, merged text cannot be fitted to a path, blended, or extruded. Most other attributes apply. This is an incredibly powerful feature, although it may yield questionable results when used with some of the more intricate effects, such as envelope.

The merge file must be saved in plain-vanilla ASCII format, with a TXT file extension. You can use Notepad, Write, or any other word processor that is capable of producing a clean ASCII file.

All merge files must follow the same general format. The first line lets Draw know how many data fields are to be replaced. The lines that follow are the fields (separated by beginning and ending backslashes) with the exact words to be replaced in the boilerplate file. After a blank line, the variable records start. Each individual field is separated by backslashes. A blank line separates each record.

Figure 12.6:

The BITE diploma.

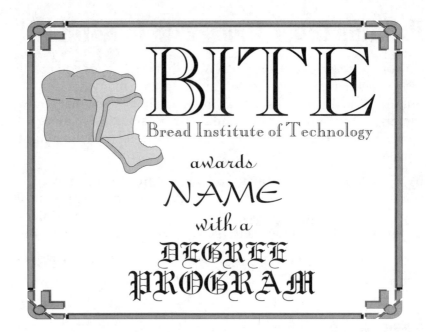

The following example is a file prepared for the Bread Institute of Technology:

```
3
\NAME\
\DEGREE\
\PROGRAM\

\Harry Pumpernickel\
\Doctor of\
\Yeastology\

\Rhonda Rye\
\Master of\
\Grainology\

\Sonny Sourdough\
\Bachelor of\
\Crustectomy\
```

35mm Slides

Back in Chapter 6, you put an image together for a 35mm slide presentation. You learned the basics of slide setup; you may remember that Joe DeLook sent the files off to a slide service bureau.

A staple of the typical board meeting, 35mm slides are a costly proposition for most businesses. Many companies send their sketches out to slide houses and pay hefty bills for the service they receive. Some large companies have expensive, dedicated, in-house departments and systems to churn out the celluloid.

Many firms are finding that they can control their own destinies by producing quality slide images with a desktop system and a qualified operator. Images built with CorelDRAW! can be sent to a 35mm slide service bureau in much the same way one would send files to a Lino service bureau. There is no need to switch to another software package. You can continue to use Draw to integrate and enhance elements originally generated in other programs.

Companies that produce slides in volume may consider purchasing their own desktop slidemaker. These handy devices will enable you to output directly to 35mm film, which you then take to a local photo lab for processing. If you are interested, there is a wide range of cameras available. Prices start in the low four-figure range, while a high-end camera can easily cost more than $20,000.

If you intend to produce slides, as in Chapter 6, there are a few things to be aware of. For starters, it is a wise idea to use a slide service bureau that is familiar with CorelDRAW! Secondly, allow plenty of time; you do not want to be experimenting at deadline time. Finally, it helps to know the lingo, so here is a bit of the buzz.

Imaging Formats

When your slide service bureau images your files, they will probably ask for the file in one of three formats. These are, beginning with the least desirable: CGM, SCODL, and EPS. There are caveats with all three of the popular slide formats.

The CGM (Computer Graphics Metafile) format does not support bit maps, nor does it support PostScript textures. In addition, fountain fills are not fully implemented. Linear fountain fills are no problem, as long as they are applied to non-rotated rectangular objects. But if you have to export CGM, and your files contain other types of fountain fills, you will get your best results by using a masked fill rather than a filled object. Use the CGM format only if you absolutely must.

For slide work, the SCODL (Scan Conversion Object Description Language) is far preferable to the CGM format. If Include All Artistic Attributes is selected, SCODL will support any type of object corners, pen shapes, calligraphic pen effects, and fountain fills with the same limitations as CGM. Bit maps are not supported, nor are PostScript Fills. Only rounded or butted line caps are supported. SCODL does not recognize dotted or dashed lines.

SCODL supports certain fountain fills, but only linear on rectangles and radial on circles. The best way to use a fountain fill with SCODL files is to build a clipping mask. Be wary of radial fills because they will overprint the circle by approximately ten percent—which leads to the next SCODL caveat.

When exporting SCODL files, do not leave any objects outside the page. If you do, your slides will not image properly. If you have objects lying outside the page area when you try to export in SCODL, CorelDRAW! will issue an error message. Take heed and correct the problem.

The best way to image slides is in PostScript EPS format. PostScript slides support all of CorelDRAW!'s features. Check with your slide service bureau to see if it can work with EPS before sending your files in one of the lesser formats. EPS slides are more expensive than SCODL or CGM slides, but the results are well worth the extra expense.

CorelDRAW!'s *Technical Reference Manual* covers each of the export file formats in depth. You will find the information you need in the "Exporting Graphics Files to Other Software Packages" section.

The Image Center

One of a rare breed, the Roanoke, Virginia-based Image Center is an authorized CorelDRAW! imaging center. This status is not bestowed on just any slide bureau.

While most slide bureaus will accept Draw-generated SCODL files, few can offer Image Center's flexibility and amenities. Unlike most bureaus, Image Center will work with native Draw files. Just send them a CDR file, and they will image it at 8,000 lines resolution. Eight thousand lines is twice the resolution of most bureaus, at a very competitive price.

Image Center can also provide PostScript slides in addition to the more pedestrian formats. This ensures that your slides are imaged with all the good stuff intact. Anything that can be output as EPS will image: fountain fills, dashed lines, and so on. Image Center does not ask for the EPS file, only the CDR, saving on communication time and, ultimately, cost.

In addition to the convenience of transmitting either SCODL or CDR files, Image Center accepts other formats like CGM, PCX, PIC, GIF, and the ever-popular TGA (Targa) files.

Image Center uses Matrix MVP raster image processors and MGI Solitaire digital film recorders to image your CorelDRAW! slides, assuring you of the highest possible quality. If you require Ektachrome color overheads, they can be shot at 4,000 lines resolution on Kodak Ektachrome 8-inch × 10-inch film.

With Image Center, you have the accessibility of on-line file transfer. You can transmit your files one day, and have slides the next. They promise delivery within 24 to 48 hours. You do not even need to buy any communications software—Image Center provides a copy of its own communications program free of charge!

The program is called IC-COM, and it accompanies your free user kit. Along with the program, you will find easy-to-follow instructions that will have you uploading your Draw files in minutes. Simply dial and telecommunicate your images. Very few slide bureaus offer this much utility and value.

Image Center, Inc.
P.O. Box 2570
Roanoke, VA 24010
1011 Second Street, S.W.
Roanoke, VA 24016
800/433-8829
703/343-8243
703/343-0691 (FAX)
703/344-3549 (MODEM)

Vinyl Lettering

One of the lesser known uses for CorelDRAW! is that of producing vinyl lettering for signmaking. Currently, Draw cannot directly drive vinyl cutting plotters. However, a software program known as CADlinkPlus from ThermaZone Engineering, Inc., makes vinyl cutting from Draw files a reality.

CADlinkPlus can import files and enable the user to scale drawings by percentages or by forcing the size to a specific dimension. This alleviates Draw's page size limitation. The drawings can then be sent to plotters from over ten different manufacturers. But CADlinkPlus (and vinyl cutters in general) supports object outlines only; none of Draw's fills are usable.

ThermaZone also offers an Outline/Inline/Distortion module program, which can apply some pretty tricky effects to the imported images. The text/graphics distortion software is capable of impressive three-dimensional perspective distortions, convex or concave arch distortions, fit to globe, and many other valuable effects. The software module enables the user to combine up to ten different distortions. And, as an added bonus, CADlinkPlus images can be converted into DXF or EPS files and reimported into Draw. This last factor alone would make the package a valuable addition to anyone's graphic software library.

Vinyl cutting from Draw images is expensive; you will obviously need a vinyl cutting plotter as well as CADlinkPlus to do the task. Unfortunately for most users, vinyl cutting plotters can be prohibitively costly. It could easily cost more than five thousand dollars to buy the additional hardware and software required to cut vinyl.

ThermaZone Engineering, Inc.
2285 St. Laurent Blvd. Unit D-8
Ottawa, Ontario, Canada K1G 4Z7
613/523-2715
613/523-0932 (FAX)

Colossal Graphics: Large Format Output

Have you ever needed a huge print of a CorelDRAW! or other PostScript/EPS file? If so, you probably had a hard time finding a way to image those big files, especially when considering Draw's maximum image area. Luckily, a company has broken the barrier to large format output. Colossal Graphics, Incorporated of Palo Alto, California, has pioneered the service by selling the PowerScript workstation, which enables printing Colossal Color Prints—full color images up to 40 inches × 12 feet in one piece! Even larger images (billboards, anyone?) can be created by tiling a single EPS page into multiple panels with precision accuracy using PosterWorks, a program from S. H. Pierce & Co.

Although a color PowerScript system can be quite expensive (in the same ballpark as an imagesetter), you do not have to own one to take advantage of its virtues. A local PowerScript bureau can output your file on premium bond paper or 4 mil clear film, at a maximum resolution of 400 dpi. The prints can then be dry mounted or laminated for durability.

PowerScript output should not be thought of as prepress proofing. Instead, it is a way to economically print a short run of posters, meeting/trade show signage, flip charts, in-store displays, architectural renderings, or site plans. The possibilities are inexhaustible. Output costs start at roughly $7 per square foot for black and white output, and around $10 per square foot for color. Considering the cost of conventional alternatives, imaging files at a PowerScript bureau can save thousands of dollars and plenty of time.

Colossal provides a thorough CorelDRAW! step-by-step user's guide for creating large format artwork. Basically, you need to provide a scaling percentage to "blow up" your images, along with font usage information. Although Colossal provides a scaling formula, a graphic arts proportional scaling wheel—or cubit meister (on the *Inside CorelDRAW!* floppy disk)—makes it even easier to calculate percentages.

The following list of PowerScript Imaging Centers will help you locate a bureau in your area. If there is not one close by, do not fret; they are all linked together with high-speed modems, so you never have to leave your studio! Colossal will gladly ship your Colossal color prints by overnight mail.

POWERSCRIPT Imaging Centers

CORPORATE HEADQUARTERS
Colossal Graphics, Inc.
437 Emerson Street
Palo Alto, CA 94301
415/328-2264
415/328-0699 (24-hour BBS)

A&E Products
4235 Richmond Avenue
Houston, TX 77027
713/621-0022

Atlanta Blue Print
1025 W. Peachtree Street, NW
Atlanta, GA 30309
404/873-5911

Blair Graphics, Inc.
1740 Stanford Street
Santa Monica, CA 90404
213/829-4621

Blue Print Service Company
149 Second Street
San Francisco, CA 94105
415/495-8700

Carich Reprographics, Inc.
412 S. Harwood Street
Dallas, TX 75201
214/939-0009

National Reprographics, Inc.
44 West 18th Street, 3rd Floor
New York, NY 10011
212/366-7075

Reprographic Plus
176 Main Street
Norwalk, CT 06852
203/847-3839

Reprographic Technologies, Inc.
2865 South Moorland Road
New Berlin, WI 53151
414/796-8162

Riteway Reproductions, Inc.
22 W. Monroe Street
Chicago, IL 60603
312/726-0346

San Jose Blue Print
835 West Julian Street
San Jose, CA 95126
408/295-5770

Triangle Company
314 S. Cincinnati Street
Tulsa, OK 74103
918/628-0400

Triangle Reproductions
2203 Cee Gee
San Antonio, TX 78217

Veenstra Reproductions
850 Grandville Avenue SW
Grand Rapids MI 49503
616/452-1495

Waterfront Reprographics Ltd.
903 Western Avenue
Seattle, WA 98104
206/467-9889

European Imaging Centers

Colossal, LTD
Bournend Business Center
Coref End Road
Bournend, Buckingham, UK
SL8 5AS
628 8509 01

Colossal Trading Company
Cardiff, Wales

No Limits
London, England

The Crawfords Group
London, England

Pronto Prints
London, England

Printronix
London, England

Using Service Bureaus

When picking a service bureau, remember: when you buy cheap, you get cheap. In other words, if you are shopping for Lino output strictly on per-page charges, you are doing yourself (and your clients) a great disservice.

At the risk of infuriating those folks who have plunked down big bucks on a "Mr. Printo" franchise, avoid them—unless they can prove that they are knowledgeable about high-end DTP. The person running the Lino may not know the first thing about PostScript, film densities, or typography. Do not choose bureaus by price alone. Service is what is important.

Be careful of Macintosh-only bureaus. While these folks may know their stuff, they may not be able to help with any Draw-related problems. Familiarity with CorelDRAW! and PCs is more than helpful. When sending files to a Macintosh-only bureau, be sure to click For Mac; otherwise, you will have to remove the very first and last character in the PRN file by editing the file as an ASCII text file (these characters look like a skinny rectangle). If you do not, the file will not print. This can easily be done with Windows Write—just remember to save as text only!

Another convenient way to send files to a Macintosh-only bureau is to export the Draw images in EPS format and import them into a PageMaker document. Since PageMaker converts smoothly from the PC to Mac platforms (and the reverse), this can be a convenient way to include multiple graphics in one file. However, this method should only be used for black-and-white (or monochrome) images; for color separations, print to a file.

Always include a list of the fonts used in each file if you want to use the service bureau's printer-resident fonts. And one more word of caution: Macs do not like PCX bit maps—use a TIFF file instead.

So What Makes a Good Service Bureau?

This one is a tricky question. Due to the nature of the business, service bureaus tend to be hectic places. Time *is* money to these folks. If your bureau spends time with you, making sure that the files you send them print properly, they are saving everyone a lot of grief (and shekels). It is most important for you to have a good line of communication. Don't expect to sit and have tea, but if you can't *talk* to your bureau, you should consider a change.

A good service bureau should provide a number of things, in addition to support. They should have at least the full Adobe font library, so that you do not always have to send your fonts along with your files. Additional font libraries are a bonus, and may be indicative of the shop's commitment to their clients. The bureau should be responsive to your suggestions, and offer answers to your questions.

Once again, it's a good idea to deal with a bureau that is more than just PC-literate. A Mac-only house can be trouble, and in reality, is a dying breed. Savvy bureaus have a PC or two hanging around (along with the latest versions of the most popular programs). In fact, the smart bureaus are running print servers like COPS' PServe or Compumation's BureauMaster on PCs!

You should take a number of heavy-metal hardware issues into consideration. Ask what kind of imagesetter they are using. If you are doing process color separations, look for a Linotype-Hell 330 (or better), Agfa SelectSet, or Scitex Dolev. These boys will deliver the goods—tight register and optimized screens (which lessen the chance of any undesirable moire effects). Lesser machines cannot deliver the quality needed for process work. Be sure to find out what type of color proofing methods they offer; it makes the most sense to get your separations and proofs under one roof.

How serious are they? Even if you are just doing spot color work, you want to know that they are competent. Is their imagesetter calibrated? Do they use a replenishing film processor? Can they guarantee film density (dmax) and halftone dot accuracy? Ask what brand of film and paper they use; if they use Dupont, there's a reason why their per page prices may be a bit more expensive. Quality materials cost more and value is not determined by price alone.

Solving Printing Problems

You may have already run into the horrible reality of a file not printing. To be honest, this does happen, but it is usually not fatal. Although it can be frustrating, especially at deadline, you simply (more or less) tweak the file or the printer setup to work things out. By using the methods covered in this book, you should reduce the likelihood of nonprinting files.

Are You Hooked Up Correctly?

If you are having trouble printing any Draw files at all, check out your printer setup. To begin, make sure that your selected printer matches the default printer. Set the Transmission Retry Time to 600, and set Device Not Selected to 0. You can also try turning Windows Print Manager off. While you may lose the convenience of this feature, it may be necessary if you are short on disk space.

Windows provides a means to monitor what is happening with your PostScript Printer. This mechanism is known as the PostScript Error Handler. You can access this feature by going to Draw's Print Setup dialogue box and clicking Options, and then Advanced. When the Advanced Options dialogue box appears, make sure that Print PostScript Error Information is selected. The error handler report can be used to diagnose a problem file (if you know PostScript programming). Corel's technical support team can interpret the results and suggest solutions to problem files.

However, PostScript clone printers have been known to be rather cranky. If you have one of these devices, you deserve sympathy. True Adobe-licensed PostScript is now cost-competitive with the clones; consider upgrading your printer.

Making Sure Your Files Run

As mentioned throughout the book, try to build streamlined files. Avoid using too many fountain fills, or fountain-filling complex objects. Use Combine, but do not overuse it; try to limit the number of objects combined to twenty in each clump.

Exploit the power of Bezier curves. Reduce the number of nodes in your objects; you will get smoother curves, smaller file sizes, faster printing, and better performance. If you still have problems printing, try using a higher Flatness setting (or try using Auto Increase) in the Print Dialogue box.

When you build your collage, try to keep things clean so that you can easily go back in and adjust things, if need be. Remember, you are actually writing computer programs that run on your printer's internal processor. If you write a bad program, it will not run. You must be able to go in and make sense of what you have created.

Summary

The reason most people purchased Draw was to produce slick-looking print graphics. In this chapter, you have seen how to control Draw's print functions to give the best possible images. In addition, you have learned that the program can be used for far more than just conventional printed imagery. It can be used just as effectively for 35mm slidemaking, serigraphy, and signmaking.

Draw opens doors. Because it works with so many programs and can interface so easily with so many other programs, its possibilities are endless. This chapter has tried to illuminate some of the program's less obvious imaging capabilities and show you how to get those files printed.

Part Four

OLE...Fighting the Bull

CorelPHOTO-PAINT!

CorelCHART!

CorelSHOW!

CorelPHOTO-PAINT!

orelPHOTO-PAINT! is a powerful bit-mapped painting program and photo-retouching tool. It enables you to create art that looks textured and hand-drawn. PostScript art generated through Draw is often too sharp and well-defined to suit a particular job. You can use CorelPHOTO-PAINT! to modify and clean up scans with special effects; create collages; modify palettes; and convert images to 1 bit (black and white), 4 bit (16-color), 8 bit (256-color or grayscale), and 24 bit (16, 777, 216 colors).

CorelPHOTO-PAINT! supports 37 tools and 12 filters. These tools can be used for painting or photo retouching. Some of these photo retouching procedures take days to complete and are very expensive when using conventional darkroom techniques. CorelPHOTO-PAINT! loads and saves files in six formats: BMP, EPS, TGA, TIF, 4-bit PCX, and 24-bit PCX. CorelPHOTO-PAINT! supports *Object Linking and Embedding (OLE)* to enhance your productivity and integrate your work with Draw, Chart, and Show.

CorelPHOTO-PAINT! supports such standard graphic primitives as squares, rectangles, rounded squares and rectangles, polygons, ellipses, and circles. Other standard painting tools include Spraycan, Paint Roller, Paintbrush, Pen, Text, Line, Eraser, Airbrush, Box, and Lasso selections. High end tools include Sharpen, Contrast, Blend, Smear, Magic Wand, and Gradient. See page 22 of the Photo-Paint user's guide for a complete listing of your tools.

The 12 filters also can be used for painting or photo retouching. This chapter uses the Motion Blur, Equalize, and Add Noise filters. Experiment with the other filters on a small image and consult pages 107-124 of the Photo-Paint user's guide for complete descriptions.

Integrating CorelPHOTO-PAINT! and OLE

OLE is a significant new feature of Windows 3.1. You will use OLE in this and the next two chapters, and you need a clear understanding of how it works in order to increase your productivity. OLE's primary purpose is to support compound documents. A compound document can contain text, graphics, or icons that represent data. OLE enables you to embed documents from different formats into one document or to link documents from different formats. For instance, a Draw document can contain a PCX file created in CorelPHOTO-PAINT!. Draw is referred to as the *client* application because it stores the OLE object. CorelPHOTO-PAINT!, which created the object, is called the *server* (see fig. 13.1). Applications which support OLE—such as CorelPHOTO-PAINT!, CHART!, and SHOW!—are referred to as *OLE-aware applications*.

Some OLE aware applications act as client or server; others—such as CorelPHOTO-PAINT!—can function only as a server. An *object* is any encapsulated data that can be displayed and manipulated. A *package* is an embedded icon that contains an object, a file, part of a file, or even a DOS command. Any OLE aware application can create an object which can be embedded (placed inside your Draw file) or linked (the client object remains dynamically linked to the original file) in your Draw file.

Whether you decide to embed or link your scan depends on a number of factors and limitations. You cannot lose track of an embedded object because it is inside your Draw file. An embedded object can only be used in one client application. Use the standard copy and paste if you want to use a graphic in more than one application. A linked object is a pointer to the file name and location on your system. Linked objects can be used in two or more applications. This eliminates the need to copy and paste and saves disk space. A linked object is updated automatically when you make changes to the original file. (You can accidentally break this link by moving the file or renaming it.) Embedded objects are not automatically updated if the original file from which it was copied changes.

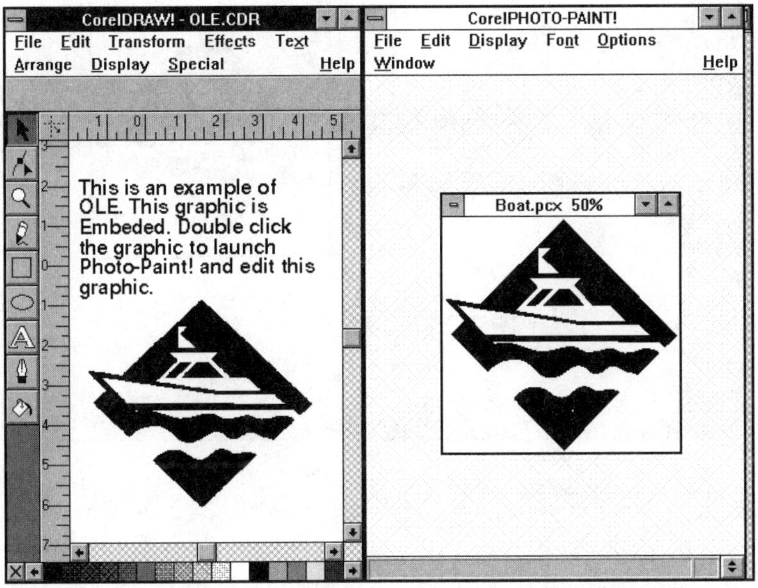

Figure 13.1:
An embedded PCX file.

As you see, neither embedding nor linking is a perfect solution, and Microsoft's implementation of OLE contains some additional limitations. OLE does not support CorelDRAW! objects that contain two-color patterns or full-color patterns, nor does it support CorelCHART! objects that contain fountain fills, bit maps, or vector patterns. Copy and paste to work around this limitation until it's fixed. If you share files in a workgroup environment that contain embedded or linked objects, each of you must have the same OLE-aware applications installed. Refer back to figure 13.1, which illustrates these concepts.

To embed a CorelPHOTO-PAINT! black-and-white PCX file into a Draw job, follow these steps. First create the PCX file in CorelPHOTO-PAINT!, then copy it to the clipboard. In the Draw document, select Paste Special (see fig. 13.2) from the Edit menu. Next choose the CorelPHOTO-PAINT! Picture option in the dialogue box and click the Paste button.

Figure 13.2:

The Paste Special dialogue box.

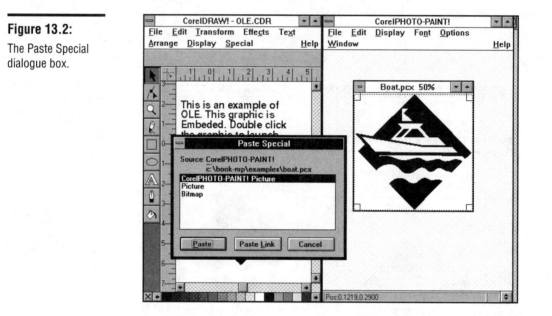

Three days later you decide to make some changes to this PCX file. Open your Draw file and double-click on the PCX file that you embedded from CorelPHOTO-PAINT!. CorelPHOTO-PAINT! is launched and displays your PCX file (see fig. 13.3).

Make your changes in CorelPHOTO-PAINT!, then go to the File menu and select the Exit-Return to CorelDRAW! option. Click the Yes button to update your Draw file (see fig. 13.4). This command closes Paint and updates your modified PCX file in Draw.

Without OLE, this procedure would require more work. You would have to clear your PCX file from Draw, navigate to the Program Manager, launch CorelPHOTO-PAINT!, and load the PCX file. Then you would have to make your changes, copy the modified PCX file to the clipboard, Alt-Tab back to Draw, and paste into Draw.

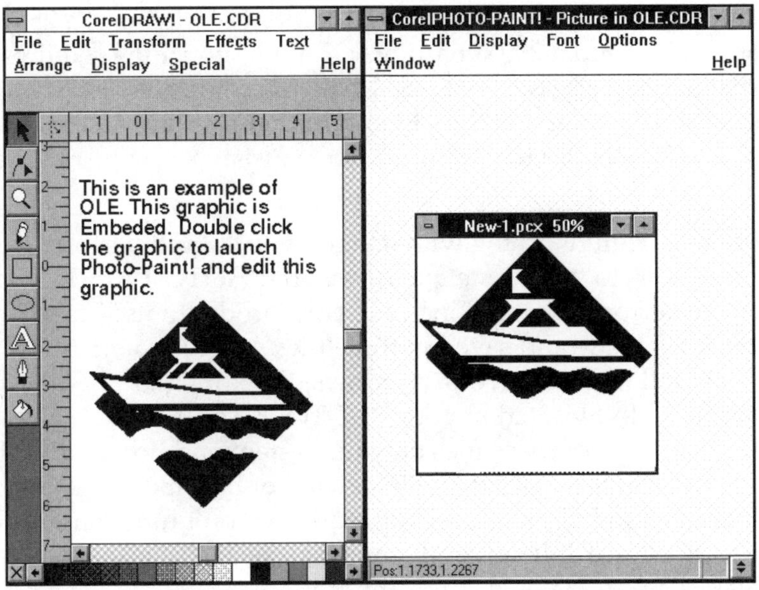

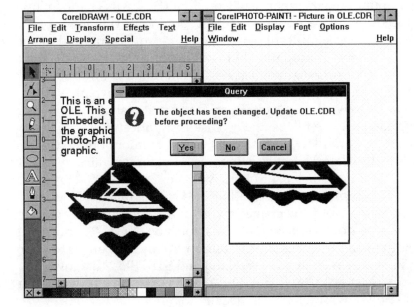

Figure 13.3:
Editing an embedded object using OLE.

Figure 13.4:
Updating your embedded PCX file.

Using CorelPHOTO-PAINT!

Bit-map editing is demanding on your hardware. The minimum system you should use is a 33 MHZ 386, 8M of Memory, a 256 color display, and a 200M hard disk. Photo retouching requires more horsepower: you need a 50 MHZ 486 computer, 300M hard disk, 16M of memory, and a video card that displays at least 15 bits (32,768 colors). More accurate and consistent results require a 24-bit video card.

Before you begin working with images, you should perform a few modifications to your system and to CorelPHOTO-PAINT! to optimize performance and increase your productivity. These changes are made and saved in three files: WIN.INI and SYSTEM.INI located in your Windows directory and CORELPNT.INI located in your PHOTOPNT directory. Maintain current backups of these files on your system and floppy disk. If any of these files are accidentally deleted or become corrupted, your system and all the Corel applications won't function properly. CORELPNT.INI stores all your current settings and desktop display every time you exit the application.

For optimum performance of CorelPHOTO-PAINT!, the following procedures are recommended. You should use Windows 3.1 because of its significant performance improvements and memory management. Thoroughly defragment your hard disk on a regular basis. Make sure that you have a 10M permanent swap file and that FastDisk is enabled. This ensures that you have plenty of memory to work with your images and that disk activity is fast. A permanent swap file using FastDisk is significantly faster than enabling CorelPHOTO-PAINT!'s virtual memory option (more on this feature later) because Windows 3.1 communicates directly with your hard disk controller, bypassing your BIOS. This results in a 25% improvement in loading and saving images. You can display more of your images if you launch the Windows Control Panel and double-click on the Desktop icon. Next, set your border width to one and click the OK button. All these changes to your system are saved in your WIN.INI and SYSTEM.INI. Now you are ready to launch CorelPHOTO-PAINT!. Go to the Options Menu and pull down Preferences (see fig. 13.5).

You first need to configure the At Startup list box. About, New,
Open, and Nothing are your options. Set this option to Open. This
means that every time you start CorelPHOTO-PAINT! it automatically presents you with an Open dialogue box to select the
image you want to work on. You can always change this to suit
your working style. The list box is Units—or units of measure. Set
this to Inches. The Display Help Bar check box enables you to
view context-sensitive help information in the bottom left corner
of the screen. Leave this box checked because it's a great way to
learn about each of the 37 tools.

The Keep Thumbnail Files box saves a separate THB file along
with your regular image. A THB file is a very small rendition of
your image. You access these THB files using the Load a Picture
from Disk dialogue box. When you click the Info button in this
dialogue box, you navigate to the Image Info dialogue box to view
your THB files. Seeing your image before loading it is much easier
and faster than trying to remember what an image looks like from
a cryptic-character file name.

The VGA Palette button is available if you are running Windows
with the standard 16-color driver. This option enables you to

increase the number of grays you see on screen. You should save your work before you use this button because this feature does not work with all video cards. The Monitor Gamma button adjusts the on-screen brightness of your display. To configure your Monitor Gamma, load GAMMA.PCX located in your PHOTOPNT\SAMPLES directory (see fig. 13.6).

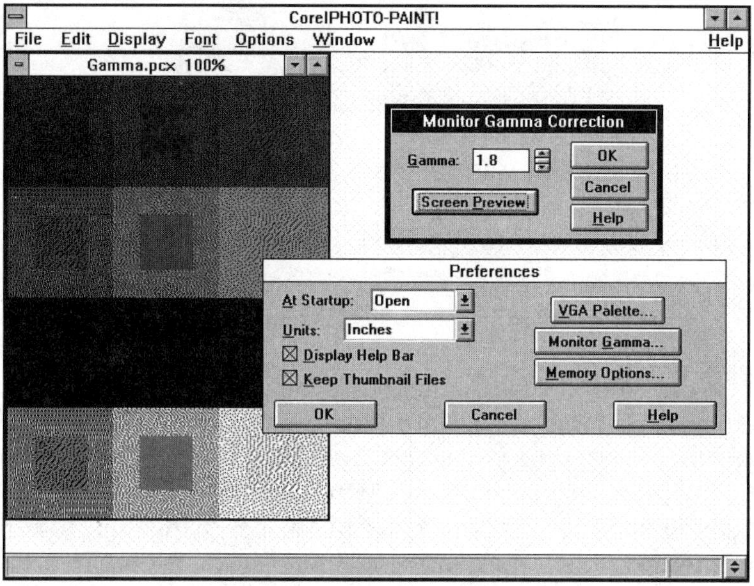

Figure 13.6:

Configuring your Monitor Gamma.

Return to the Preferences screen. Click the Monitor Gamma button and adjust the Gamma numbers which have a range of 1.0 to 2.0. Each time you change this number, click on the Screen Preview button to determine how GAMMA.PCX looks on your monitor. The higher the number, the brighter this picture appears. Adjust the Gamma until 12 solid boxes appear in your image. Click OK when finished. The last options to configure are the Memory Options (see fig. 13.7).

As previously mentioned, editing bit maps and retouching photos is a memory-intensive task. CorelPHOTO-PAINT! consumes memory in the following order: real RAM first, permanent swap file next, and then Virtual Memory. A one-megabyte image re-quires two megabytes of memory to enable you to undo your changes. Many of the supported graphic formats use compression to reduce the storage requirements of an image, therefore, loading a 1M file may decompress the image to a 5M file and require 10M of memory. Virtual memory enables you to use more memory by using your hard disk or RAM drive, but only turn this feature on if you need it to work with a particular image. If your image size does not require virtual memory, turn it off for more speed. Use the Help menu-System Info to monitor available memory.

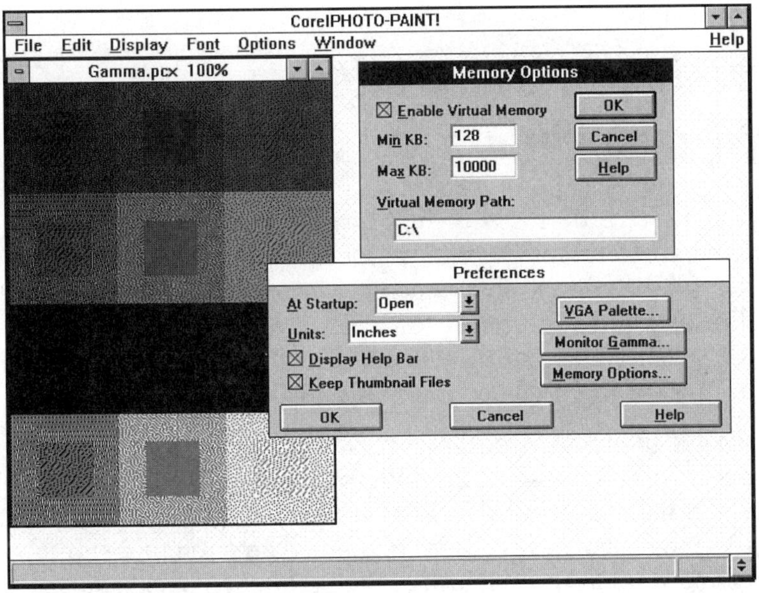

Figure 13.7:

Configuring your memory.

CorelPHOTO-PAINT! will store your image on your hard disk and available RAM if the Enable Virtual Memory option is checked. For now, check the Enable Virtual Memory Box. The Min and Max KB values enable you to control how much virtual memory CorelPHOTO-PAINT! will use. The Virtual Memory Path enables you to specify up to four drives in this text box by separating each one with a semicolon (d:\;c:\). List your fastest drives first. After all your Memory Options are set, click the OK button three times and restart Windows so that your changes will take effect.

The last option you want to activate is in the Display menu. Select the Optimize Display. A check mark appears beside this command when you turn it on. This feature produces a more accurately displayed image as CorelPHOTO-PAINT! adjusts the screen to better simulate the colors in your image. This is particularly helpful when working with 24-bit images on a 256-color display. This concludes your setup procedures. If your system or requirements change, you can always reconfigure CorelPHOTO-PAINT! to suit your needs.

Creating an Illustration for Use in Show

Now you are ready for your first project. Rippin' Surfboards needs a bank loan for expansion. Joe DeLook wants to use Show for the presentation to the bank. He plans to deliver this computer slide show in VGA mode (640×480) using 16 colors and a 33 MHZ 386. This medium will enhance the client's ability to communicate and increase the chances of obtaining the loan.

All the slides in Show require a background scene. This will form the backdrop for a Pie Chart, bulleted lists, and some pictographs. Creating this background in Draw produces an unrealistic image. It looks too sharp and well-defined. Joe wants to use a subtle background that reminds him of the ocean; this background can't overpower the elements on top of it. This is exactly what CorelPHOTO-PAINT! does best.

Before Joe starts the project he conducts research and seeks inspiration. His first stop is the beach. With pencil and paper in hand, he sketches the surf. Next he thumbs through his collection of stock photos searching for surf scenes. He does more sketches and goes to the movies to see the latest surfing movie.

Joe decides to use BACKRND.PCX which you will find on DISK-1 as one of the files on EXAMP-13.ZIP. This image is a 16-color PCX file that measures 640×480. This is exactly what he needs: it is light blue and has perspective. He will perform one modification to this image with the Motion Blur filter.

As an exercise, let's do this modification along with Joe. This filter only works with 24-bit images, so he must convert this image to 24 bits. He will need about 2M of total memory on his system to complete this exercise. If he doesn't have this much memory, he increases the size of his permanent swap file or enables virtual memory before he starts.

Setting Up Your File

Double-click the CorelPHOTO-PAINT! icon in your Program Manager Group	Launches application.
Select Open from the File Menu and double-click on BACKRND.PCX	Opens image at 100% view.
From the Edit Menu, select Convert To 24-bit Color	Your 24-bit image is created as NEW-1.PCX and opens at 100% (see fig. 13.8).
Select Save As from the File Menu and enter BACKRND2.PCX in the File Name box	
Click OK	The Saving Progress Bar appears and your image is saved to disk.
Double-click on the Control Menu of BACKRND.PCX	Closes this image and frees memory.

You now are ready to apply the Motion Blur filter. This effect will give your image a rough and subtle look well-suited for the slide show.

Applying the Motion Blur Filter

Select Filter Motion Blur from the Edit menu	The Motion Blur dialogue box appears.
Click on the arrow located in the top far right corner (see fig. 13.9)	
Set the Speed to 5 and click the Screen Preview button	The Filtering Motion Blur Progress Bar appears and your image is modified.

continues

You can fine tune the Speed value to suit your preference with values from 1 to 50.

Click on the Screen Preview button

When you are satisfied with this effect, click OK

The Filtering Motion Blur Progress Bar appears and the filter is applied.

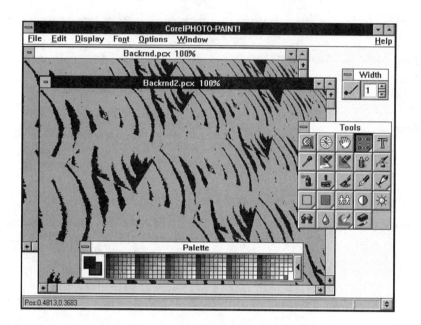

Figure 13.8:

Setting up your file.

Use Ctrl-S to save your modified image. You are almost finished with this procedure. The next step is to reduce the color depth to 4 bits (16 colors) because CorelSHOW! only supports 16 colors.

Converting Your Image

Select Save As from the File Menu

The Save a Picture to Disk Dialogue Box appears (see fig. 13.10).

Enter BACKRND3.PCX in the File Name box

Click on the down arrow in the List Files of Type box

Click on PCX 16 Color/Gray
Click OK

The Saving Progress Bar
appears and your image
is saved and converted to
16 colors.

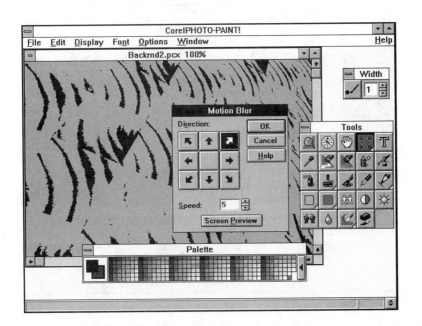

Figure 13.9:

Applying the Motion
Blur filter.

You now have one last step to perform. You have created some
files that you no longer need. Launch the File Manager or MS-
DOS EXE program and delete BACKRND.PCX and
BACKRND2.PCX from your disk.

Photo Retouching a Scan
for Use in CorelDRAW!

In this exercise you will be working with GIRL.TIF, an image
provided by 21st Century Media. This rich selection of high
quality stock photography on CD-ROM suits many projects and is
significantly cheaper than hiring your local photographer. The

images are 300 DPI 24-bit scans that measure 7.82" by 5.00" and occupy 10,557,176 in hard disk space. They are stored on CD-ROM in compressed form. Now you understand why you need a CD-ROM to store 400 of them!

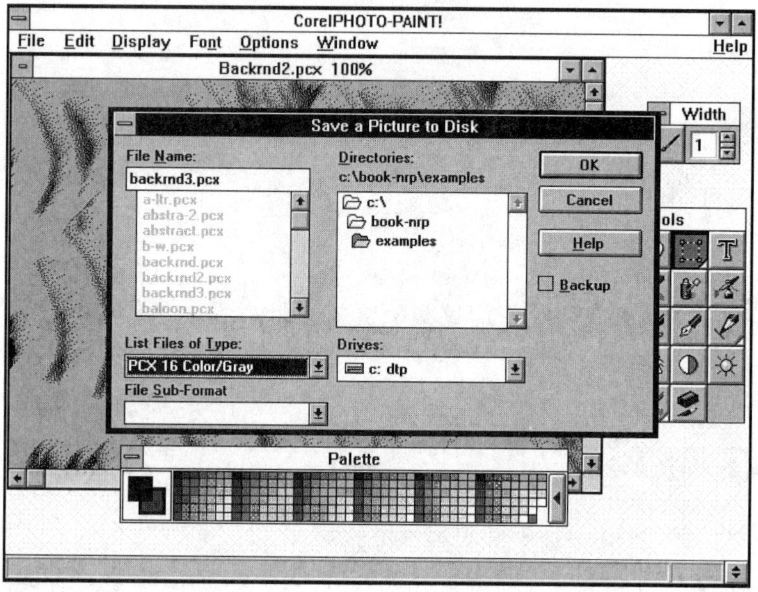

Figure 13.10:

Saving and converting your image.

GIRL.TIF is one of the files in EXAMP-13.ZIP on DISK-1. This image has been resampled (scaled) to a width of 1 inch and a height of 1.46 inches and occupies 392,898 KB in hard disk space. The image was initially saved as an uncompressed TIF after performing a few tests to determine the best method to distribute this file.

GIRL.TIF is 9% smaller (358,308) if saved as a compressed TIF, but loading and subsequent saving the image is about 350% slower than the uncompressed version in Photo-Paint. Importing the compressed TIF in Draw is also 350% slower. The final procedure used PKZIP.EXE (included on bundled DISK-1) to compress the uncompressed and compressed versions of GIRL.TIF. The result-ant archive containing the uncompressed version was 12% smaller than the archive containing the compressed version of GIRL.TIF (Whew!). As you can see, these factors should be considered when transporting and saving your images to best utilize hard disk space and optimize speed.

This exercise only requires about 2M of memory, so if you have virtual memory turned on, you should turn it off. Joe has installed a Pro Designer IIS video card (Orchid Technology), so he sets his video mode to 640 × 480 using 32,768 colors through the Windows Setup program. This video mode is referred to as High Color (15 bit) and uses the Sierra RADMAC chip to produce a more accurate display.

The Pro Designers video driver is optimized for use with Photo-Paint so that screen redraw is 65% faster than using a 256-color driver. The tradeoff with the high color display is that selecting any menu option is slower to use than 256-color mode. An example is the Edit Menu-Filter-Add Noise option. Use a macro program like Windows RECORDER.EXE or keyboard shortcuts to work around this issue.

Joe plans to use this image in a display advertisement for The Navel Base Swimwear Company. The job will be completed in Draw. Before you start this job you'll want to make sure that some variables in your studio don't change while you work. Put tape over the brightness and contrast controls on your monitor to ensure that you don't accidentally change these settings, and make sure that your studio's lighting does not change between work sessions. Both of these procedures will ensure constant and repeatable results while you modify this image.

Open GIRL.TIF and take a close look at this image. Lean forward and backwards to study the color balance. This image is a little flat—the colors look washed out. The color of the sky needs to be bluer and the yellow is not bright enough. You need to pump these up by redistributing other colors. Remember that the perceived color balance of an image is a subjective decision—what you perceive as washed out midtones may look perfect in someone else's eyes. If the midtone colors are brighter, some of the highlights and shadows will change. It's a delicate balance that's best accomplished in small increments.

You also need a point of reference. CorelPHOTO-PAINT! lacks the capability to lock a duplicate of your image to prevent changes

and to use as a point of reference. To work around this, save
GIRL.TIF as GIRL-2.TIF. Open both images and, as illustrated in
figure 13.11, position them next to each other. Perform all of your
modifications on GIRL.TIF, and use GIRL-2.TIF as a point of
reference. You need to view as much of your images as possible,
so hide all your tools, palette, and Width workboxes with Ctrl-A
before you start. Use Ctrl-A to turn them on again.

Figure 13.11:

GIRL.TIF and
duplicate.

Moving Colors Around

Click on the title bar of GIRL.TIF

This ensures that your
modifications apply to
this image and not to
GIRL-2.TIF.

Select the Edit menu-Filter and equalize

The Histogram Equaliza-
tion chart and dialogue
box appear (see fig.
13.12).

*Set the Mid (Midtone) value to 180 and click
the Screen Preview button*

The Filtering Equalize
Progress bar appears
and your changes are
applied.

Click OK   Your modifications are
                                                             applied to GIRL.TIF.

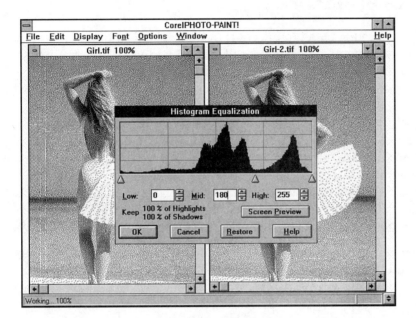

Figure 13.12:

Histogram Equaliza-
tion chart and
dialogue box.

Now is a good time to compare your modified image with your
duplicate. Carefully examine both images. The colors in GIRL.TIF
look richer and darker. This modification also has darkened
some of the shadow areas. Both images should be at 100% view as
indicated on the title bars. It's often helpful to view the entire
image at a zoomed out view. Select the Display menu and the
Zoom To Fit option for both of your images. Lean forward and
backward again and study your modified image and the original
image. If things look good, select your modified image by clicking
on the title bar and save the file using Ctrl-S. Congratulations! You
are a photo retoucher. In one simple procedure you have modified
the color balance of your image. Performing this with conventional darkroom tools would have taken hours and cost hundreds
of dollars.

Modifying a Pie Chart for Use in CorelSHOW!

Joe DeLook created a pie chart in CorelCHART! that needs some enhancements that only CorelPHOTO-PAINT! can make. This exercise requires about 3M of RAM. The chart was exported from Chart as a 256-color PCX file with a size of 640 × 480 (a standard VGA screen) and converted to 16 colors using Paint Shop Pro included on the bundled disks. Open CHT-PIE1.PCX which is found on the EXAMP-13.ZIP file (DISK-1) and make sure that your display menu option is set to 100%. Notice that this chart has a white background so that Joe can drop in some of those neat tiles bundled with CorelPHOTO-PAINT! and apply a filter. You also will notice that CorelPHOTO-PAINT! has converted this image to 256 colors and can't display a 16-color image.

You are going to use the Add Noise filter, so the first thing you need to do is convert this image to 24 bit. From the Edit Menu, select Convert To - 24-bit Color option. Only 5 filters are available for a 256-color image: Brightness/Contrast, color gray map, equalize, poster, and remove spots. Notice that your 24-bit image has been created automatically and pops up to the top. It's best to save this image so that you don't have to start over. Select Save As from the File menu. Name this image CHT-PIE2 and click OK (see fig. 13.13). You don't need your original pie chart anymore so double-click on the control menu of CHT-PIE1.PCX to close it.

The next step is to drop in a Tile pattern in place of the white background. Included on the bundled disks is TILES.ZIP. This archive contains a Windows help file with all of the 26 tiles available. Use this help file to see how your tiles look on screen and when printed. You have other graphics installed on your system that you can use as tiles. Twenty BMP files are located in your CHART\BITMAPS directory and 49 WMF graphics are located in your CHART\VECTORS directory. Use Draw to convert these Vector graphics to bit maps for use as tiles. You also can use the 26 tiles with Draw as Patterns through the Import command.

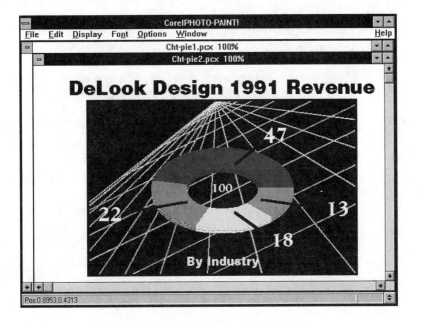

Figure 13.13:
CHT-PIE2.PCX.

Dropping In a Tiled Fill

Select the Tile Pattern Paint Roller Tool From the Tools Palette	The current Tile is displayed in your Palette and the pointer looks like the tool.
Select the Options Menu and Tile Pattern	The Load a Tile Pattern from Disk Dialogue box appears.
Navigate to your PHTOPNT/TILES subdirectory	The 26 PCX tile names are displayed.
Double click on BRICKS.PCX	This tile is displayed in your Palette (see fig. 13.14).
Move the tile fill tool over the white background and click the left mouse button	The white background is replaced with bricks (see fig. 13.15).

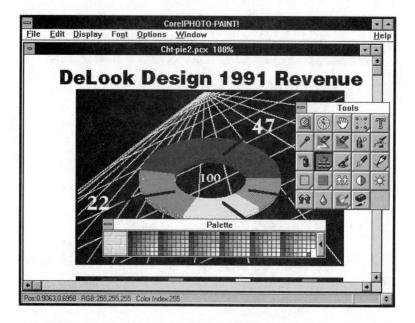

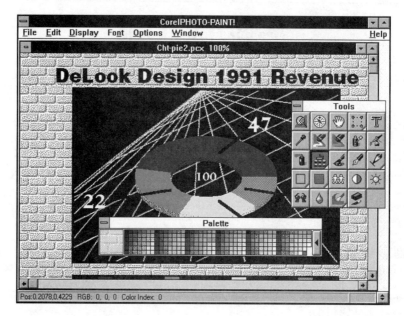

Closely examine your image to locate any areas inside the text where the bricks didn't fill. If you find any, click on the area with the Tile Pattern Paint Roller Tool to apply the brick tile. These bricks really make the chart pop off the page, but they are too consistent. Real bricks look worn and random, so you need to apply the Add Noise filter. This filter scatters the pixels in a random fashion and will produce the result you are after. Run this filter several times on the bricks to produce a random look. Before you apply this filter, save your image again with the File Menu Save option.

Shortcut

Use Ctrl-S to save your work.

Applying the Add Noise Filter

Click on the selection tool	Your cursor changes to this tool.
Click and Drag to define a rectangle of your bricks Make sure that you don't select any text or part of the chart	The selected area displays with a moving rectangle.
Select Filter option from the Edit menu then Add Noise	The Add Noise Dialogue box appears (see fig. 13.16).
Set Variance to 47, Distribution to Flat, and Channel to All	
Click OK	Filter is applied and the selected area looks worn and rough.

Repeat this procedure for all areas in your image that contain the bricks tile. Be careful not to apply the filter to text or your graphic, only to the bricks. When you have completed this step, run this filter again using the lasso tool. The lasso tool selects random areas and helps to ensure that the bricks look natural and random. You also can use the lasso tool to select irregular areas that you couldn't reach with the selection tool. The only difference is that you must set your Variance to 67. Select areas with the lasso tool and run the filter until all the bricks obtain the desired results (see fig. 13.17).

Figure 13.16:

Add Noise dialogue box using the Selection tool.

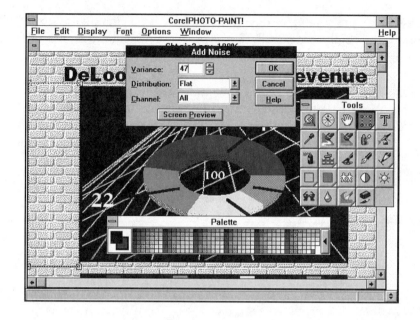

Figure 13.17:

Add Noise dialogue box using the Lasso tool.

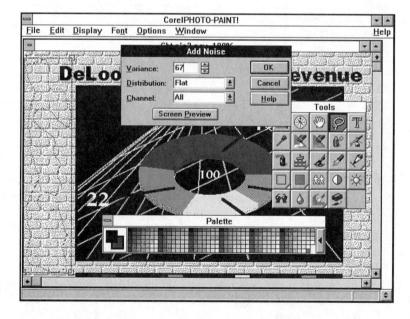

Next you need to convert the chart graphic back to a 16-color image for use in Show. This step ensures that our image file size is as small as possible to save hard disk space, and that it displays as fast as possible in Show. Select Save As from the File Menu. Enter CHT-PIE3 and make sure that the List Files of Type box has the PCX 16-Color/Gray displayed. Click OK to complete this procedure.

The last step involves some house cleaning. Remember that you have the original chart on your disk (CHT-PIE1.PCX), and that you also saved this graphic as a 24-bit image (CHT-PIE2.PCX). You no longer need these two images. Launch the File Manager or MS-DOS.EXE and delete these files.

Summary

CorelPHOTO-PAINT! is a powerful application that requires time and experience to master. This chapter just scratches the surface of CorelPHOTO-PAINT!, but hopefully has provided you with some examples and techniques to shorten the learning curve. The following collection of tips and tricks will make your production faster and more predictable:

- Buried in your CorelPHOTO-PAINT! directory is a rudimentary screen capture program called CAPTURE.EXE. If you already have a screen capture program, delete this file to free up more disk space.

- You can produce some interesting effects by combining two tile fills.

- If your scans are large, experiment with the filters on a small section of your original image.

- Avoid screen redraw whenever possible.

- Plan your moves and learn to click inside the scroll bar to move the image in one large motion rather than a series of small moves.

- For precise alignment, use the cursor keys on your keyboard to nudge the image or selection a pixel at a time.

- Photocopy page 22 of your user's guide and tape this to your monitor as you learn the tools.

- Tape a "cheat sheet" on your monitor that contains frequently used commands. (Wandering around the menus looking for a command causes part of the screen to redraw.)

- Use a macro program like HDC Power Launcher or the Windows recorder to define your own keyboard shortcuts.

- If you set your units of measure to inches, the System Info command still displays the dimensions of your image in pixels. Select Transform from the Edit menu and Area command to view the dimensions of your image in inches.

- Plan your job before you start.

- Work with the smallest image possible and turn off Virtual Memory if your system has enough RAM.

- You live in the imperfect world of color production where what you see rarely matches the printed piece. Never trust your monitor and obtain high quality match prints before you go to press.

- Your goal is to obtain repeatable results. Spend the time and money to produce files to calibrate your system.

- Keep records and samples of all your jobs.

- Use Paint Shop Pro included on the disks to convert graphics to formats supported by CorelPHOTO-PAINT!.

CorelCHART!

Using CorelCHART!

This chapter introduces you to CorelCHART!—a powerful chart-ing program that enables you to quickly and easily create a visual representation of your data. CorelCHART! supports twelve basic chart types: Bar, Line, Area, Pie, Scatter, High/Low/Open/Close, Spectral Maps, Histograms, Table, 3D-Riser, 3D-Scatter, and Pictographs. You can create numerous variations of each chart type. Charts can be exported to the same 17 graphic formats supported by draw; graphics can be imported from the same 16 formats that Draw supports. You can import data in eight differ-ent formats: ASCII-Comma Separated, ASCII-Space Separated, ASCII-Tab Separated Value, DIF, dBase, Excel, Harvard, and Lotus.

Chart is an OLE-aware application that functions as a Server. An important feature enables you to set up a live "conversation" between your spreadsheet or word processor and chart using Windows' Dynamic Data Exchange (DDE) and its Paste Link feature. The next section defines this term and shows you an example.

Dynamic Data Exchange

Dynamic Data Exchange or *DDE* is built into Windows and has been around since version 1 of Windows. Its primary purpose is to seamlessly and transparently transfer data from one Windows application to another. This transfer can be static—such as a DDE script that automatically launches Word For Windows, copies your text and graphics from a ToolBook application, and pastes this data into your letter. The transfer of data can also be a live "conversation" (sometimes referred to as a hot link). For example, as you change numbers in your Word For Windows letter, your pie chart in Chart is automatically updated.

DDE gives you significant benefits. Without DDE in the preceding ToolBook example, you would have to manually select your text and graphics in two separate steps and copy those items to the clipboard. Next, you would have to manually launch Word, open your letter, and paste the text and graphics into your document. Without the services of DDE in the live conversation example, every time your data changes you would have to copy it to the clipboard from Word, Alt-Tab to Chart, clear your old data, and then paste the new data in.

With the services of DDE, as you change the four numbers in the Word document, the Pie Chart is automatically updated to reflect these new values (see fig. 14.1). OLE—discussed in Chapter 13— still relies on the static and live conversation features built into DDE to perform its magic. You can think of DDE as the foundation on which OLE is built; the two features work together to increase your productivity.

Now that you understand how DDE works, you can examine the steps that Joe DeLook used to create the live conversation in figure 14.1. First, Word and Chart are launched and positioned side-by-side (see fig. 14.2). Next, open the letter in Word and the pie chart in Chart. Then select the four numbers in Word and copy them to the clipboard by using Copy in the Edit menu. Activate Chart and select the same four numbers in the By Industry Column in the Data Manager. Next, select Paste Link from the Edit Menu. These four numbers turn blue to indicate that a live conversation has been established. As Joe revises his numbers in Word, this data is updated automatically in Chart.

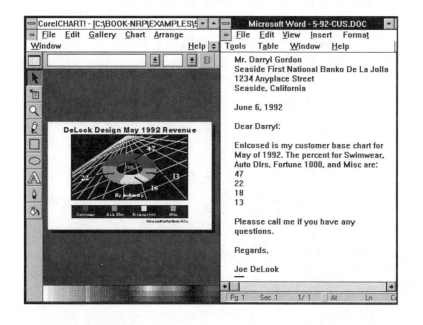

Figure 14.1:
A live conversation (Hot Link).

Figure 14.2:
Chart and Word for Windows.

Joe can now minimize Chart, maximize Word, and finish his letter. The last step is to save both documents and print them. The next time that Joe sends this letter to his banker, the DDE link is established automatically when the pie chart is opened in Chart.

You may have other applications that support this feature installed on your system. If you see Paste Link in the Edit menu, the application should support DDE (and OLE).

Creating a Pie Chart

Joe DeLook must report a profile of his customer base to his banker on a monthly basis. This chart is very similar to the one you used in the Photo-Paint exercise (CHT-PIE1.PCX). A pie chart is the best way to represent the contributions of four types of clients to Joe DeLook's total customer base. His banker requires this data as part of his open-end credit line. Before this chart is created, some planning is involved. Joe pencils out a list of his major client types and the percentage each group represents. His choice of background colors and text must be appropriate for the manner in which he will deliver this chart and for his target audience. This chart will be mailed to the banker as a printed attachment to a cover letter and must be conservative in design.

Creating a Pie Chart

Click File	The File Menu appears.
Click New	The New Gallery appears (see fig. 14.3).
Click on Pie in the Gallery list and select the second thumbnail in the Chart Types	PIE0002.CCH appears below the Chart Types.
Click on the Use Sample Data check box below the Gallery List	Your chart appears as Untitled-1.
Click OK	
Double-click on the Title bar to Maximize your chart	Your chart fills the screen.
Click File	The File Menu appears.
Click Save **As**	The Save Chart dialogue box appears.

In the file name box type **CHT-PIE2.**

In the Directories box, navigate to your working directory.

*In the Description Section, click after
the word series and enter your notes
for this chart.*

Click OK

Your pie chart is saved
and the title bar changes
to CHT-PIE2.CCH

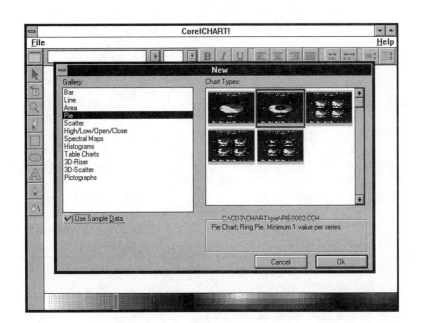

Figure 14.3:
The New Gallery.

Examine your chart and notice that Chart has sample data and
text inserted for you. This enables you to quickly see how your
chart will look when it's finished. Of course, you still have to
change the data and text to suit this job. From now on you will
avoid using menu options and capitalize on one of Chart's neatest
features— the Pop-up menu tool.

The Pop-up Menu Tool

You activate the Pop-up menu tool by clicking on an object, then
clicking the right mouse button. Both clicks are on the same point
of your object. All the appropriate menu options are displayed for
the selected object in a drop-down menu. You can dismiss the

Pop-up menu with a single click of your left mouse button off to the side of the object. This feature saves you numerous trips to the menu bar. In the next exercise you will use this tool to modify your pie chart. It looks a little anemic for Joe's taste, so you will enlarge the hole and make the slices thicker.

Creating a Larger Hole and a Thicker Pie Chart

Click on the yellow slice, then click your right mouse button	The Pie Slice Pop-up menu appears (see fig. 14.4).
Pull down to Hole Size and over to Default	Thumbnails of your options appear, and your hole is enlarged.
Click on the rectangle that your pie chart sits in and click the right mouse button	The Pie Chart Frame Pop-up menu appears.
Pull down to Pie Thickness and over to Major	Thumbnails appear for your selection and your pie chart has thicker slices.

Figure 14.4:

The Pop-up menu for Pie Slice.

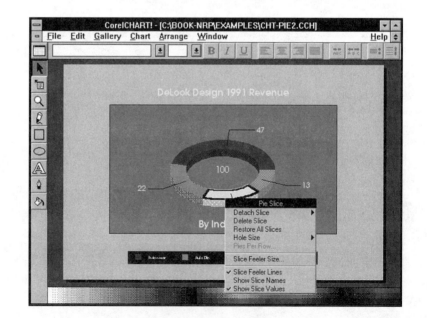

Now is a good time to save your changes with the keyboard shortcut Ctrl-S. The next step is to change the data in your chart. This is accomplished in the Data Manager. The Data Manager is like a mini-spreadsheet composed of cells inside Chart. You enter this mode by clicking on the Data Manager Icon located above the Pick Tool.

Changing Your Text

Click on the Data Manager Icon	The Data Manager Pops Up.
Double-click on the title bar	The Data Manager fills the screen and cell A1 is selected.
Type **DeLook Design 1991 Revenue** *and press Enter*	This text replaces the old text and you move to cell A2.
Click and drag select this text, press Delete, then press Enter	Text is highlighted then deleted. You move to cell A3.
Click and drag select this text, press Delete*, then press Enter*	The text is highlighted and deleted. You move to cell A4, which is empty (see fig. 14.5.)

The Data Manager is easy to work in. As you change cells your modifications are updated. Don't worry about the data in Columns 2, 3, and 4. This data won't appear in your pie chart so there is no reason to delete it. You will continue to work in the Data Manager and modify all your text. You will use the same procedure from your first edits to change cells A6, A7, A8, and A9 to read Swimwear, Auto Dlrs, Fortune 1000, and Misc.—the four major sources of revenue for Joe DeLook. Click on cell A6, type Swimwear, and press Enter to move to cell A7. Continue this procedure until all these cells are changed. The next step is to enter specific data for each of these Groups.

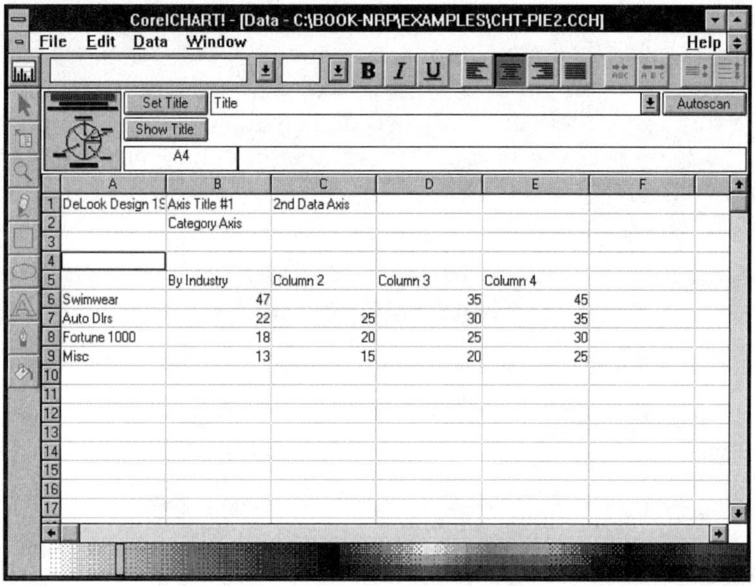

Figure 14.5:

The Data Manager
with Cell A4
selected.

CorelCHART! - [Data - C:\BOOK-NRP\EXAMPLES\CHT-PIE2.CCH]

File   Edit   Data   Window   Help

Set Title   Title

Show Title

A4

	A	B	C	D	E	F
1	DeLook Design 19	Axis Title #1	2nd Data Axis			
2		Category Axis				
3						
4						
5		By Industry	Column 2	Column 3	Column 4	
6	Swimwear	47		35	45	
7	Auto Dlrs	22	25	30	35	
8	Fortune 1000	18	20	25	30	
9	Misc	13	15	20	25	
10						
11						
12						
13						
14						
15						
16						
17						

Entering Your Data

Click on cell B6

The cell number B6
appears and a value
of 25.

Type 47 and press Enter

Your data changes
to 47 and you move
to cell B7.

Type 22 and press Enter

Your data changes
to 22 and you move
to cell B8.

Type 18 and press Enter

Your data changes
to 18 and you move
to cell B9.

Type 13 and press Enter

Your data changes
to 13 and you move to
cell B10 which is empty
(see fig. 14.6).

The last thing you want to do is change cell B5 to read By Industry. Click on cell B5, type this text, and press Enter. You have completed all your data changes so it's time to return to your chart view. Click on the Chart icon located above the grayed-out Pick Tool. Notice that your chart automatically reflects your changes and even includes the total percent of 100 located in the center of your pie chart. If you click on any text in your chart you will notice that the TrueType font Arial is specified and appears in the Font List Box located on your Text Ribbon tool. Arial even appears if you have TrueType turned off and use PostScript fonts and Adobe Type Manager (ATM). Don't worry about this if you are a PostScript user. Windows automatically will substitute Helvetica at print time, and ATM automatically displays Helvetica.

You are almost done with this chart. All you have to do is align the elements. Click on the title text that says DeLook Design 1991 Revenue, then hold down the shift key and click on the border of the rectangle behind your pie chart. Finally, click on the border of the rectangle that contains your four categories. If you click on the wrong element, just click on it again to deselect it. Now that your three elements are selected, go to the Arrange Menu, then Align, and select Align Center Horizontal. The last step is to return to the Arrange Menu and choose Center on Page and the Center Horizontal option. You are finished and your pie chart is in perfect alignment (see fig. 14.7). Use Ctrl-S to save your work.

Figure 14.7:

Your finished Pie Chart.

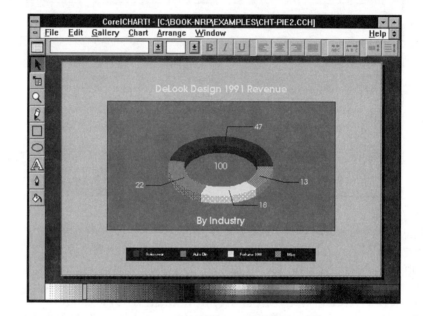

Creating a 3D-Riser Chart

Rippin' Surfboards has planned a sales meeting that needs impact and drama to display the last four months' sales figures for its four divisions. The data for each of the four divisions is to be presented, and the performance of the divisions compared. Joe DeLook has been called on to produce this chart which will serve as a handout. A 3D-Riser Chart is the perfect way to express this data. It is also a dramatic way to present the data, which will help motivate the sales force. Joe starts with the raw data from the client written on a sheet of paper:

Hi, Joe!

Here are the sales numbers for our 4 divisions. I need a really cool chart to motivate the sales staff. I will call you Monday and pick it up. Thanks!—George

Divisions	Gross Sales in $1,000 Increments			
	3/92	4/92	5/92	6/92
North	6K	3K	4K	9K
South	9K	9K	5K	7K
East	12K	11K	5K	9K
West	11K	11K	11K	14K

You already know how to create this chart with dummy text and data from the first exercise. Select 3D-Riser in the Gallery list, and choose the first Chart Type which is 3D0001.CCH. Don't forget to select the Use Sample Data box. Instead of clicking OK, double-click on this Chart's thumbnail to open it with the dummy text and data. When the chart opens, double-click on the title bar to fill your screen with this chart. Go ahead and save this chart as 3D-1.CCH and enter your own notes in the Description section just like you did in the first exercise.

The first stop is the Data Manager to revise the text and enter your data. You will need to refer to the client's sheet to complete these edits. Click on the Data Manager Icon and double-click on the title bar of the Data Manager to fill your screen. Cell A1 should be selected, so type **Rippin' Surfboards Sales Production 1992** and press Enter. Delete the subtitle in cell A2 and the Note text in cell A3.

Entering Your Labels and Titles

Click on cell A6

Type **3/92**

Press Enter

Your label is entered and you move to cell A7 (see fig. 14.8).

continues

Figure 14.8:

The Data Manager with Cell A7 selected.

```
┌─────────────────────────────────────────────────────────────────────────┐
│ ═    CorelCHART! - [Data - C:\BOOK-NRP\EXAMPLES\3D-1.CCH]         ▼ ▲    │
│ ═  File   Edit   Data   Window                              Help  ▲ ♦    │
│ ┌──┐           ┌───────┐ ┌─┐┌────┐┌─┐ B I U  ┌──┐┌──┐┌──┐┌──┐  ┌──┐┌──┐ │
│ └──┘           └───────┘ └─┘└────┘└─┘                                    │
│ ◄   ┌──────────┐ ┌─ Set Title ─┐ Title                      ┌─┐ Autoscan│
│ ▢   │          │ └─ Show Title ─┘                           └─┘         │
│ ◷   │          │ ┌───── A7 ─────┐ Row 2                                 │
│ ○   ├──────────┴───────┬────────┬────────┬────────┬────────┬─────────┤   │
│ ◢      A          B          C          D          E          F        │
│ ◲  1 Rippin Surfboards Axis Title #1 Axis Title #2                      │
│ ▢  2              Axis Title #3 Axis Title #4                           │
│ ○  3                                                                     │
│    4                                                                     │
│ A  5              Column 1   Column 2   Column 3   Column 4             │
│    6 3/92             25         30         35         45               │
│ ♀  7 Row 2            20         25         30         35               │
│ ✋ 8 Row 3            15         20         25         30               │
│    9 Row 4            10         15         20         25               │
│    10                                                                    │
│    11                                                                    │
│    12                                                                    │
│    13                                                                    │
│    14                                                                    │
│    15                                                                    │
│    16                                                                    │
│    17                                                                    │
└─────────────────────────────────────────────────────────────────────────┘
```

Type **4/92** *and press Enter*	
Type **5/92** *and press Enter*	
Type **6/92** *and press Enter*	You are finished labeling your months and cell A10 is selected.
Click on cell B1	
Type **Divisions**	
Press Enter	You have labeled this axis of your chart and moved to cell B2.
Type **Sales in Thousands**	
Press Enter	You have labeled this axis of your chart and moved to cell B3 which is empty.
Click on cell C1	
Type **Months**	
Press Enter	You have labeled this axis of your chart and moved to cell C2.

Type **Sales in Thousands**	
Press Enter	You have labeled this axis of your chart and moved to cell C3 which is empty.
Click on cell B5	
Type **North**	
Press the Tab Key	This division is labeled and you move to cell C5.
To label the other three divisions *type* **South**-Tab, **East**-Tab, and **West**-Tab	The three divisions are labeled and cell F5 is selected,which is empty.

Unfortunately, you can't save your work from the Data Manager, so click on the Chart Icon to return to chart view then use Ctrl-S to save your work. Take a look at your chart. You have changed all the text, labeled the Axis, and inserted titles. You are now going to return to the Data Manager to enter the sales figures.

Entering Your Data

Click on the Data Manager icon to return to the Data Manager	The Data Manager appears and cell F5 is selected.
Click on cell B6	
Type **6** *(see fig. 14.9)*	
Press Enter	Your data is entered and you move to cell B7.
Type **3**	
Press Enter	Your data is entered and you move to cell B8.
Type **4**	
Press Enter	Your data is entered and you move to cell B9.
Type **9**	

continues

Press Enter

Your data is entered and you move to cell B10 which is empty.

Follow this same procedure for the other three divisions using the client's original sheet for your data. After you have entered all your data, return to chart view and save your work. You can see which divisions are consistent and which are not. You also can see how the months compare as a total and by division.

It's also evident that the scale range is too small for your data. All four divisions can do a better job of selling, so we don't want this chart to indicate that they have no room for improvement. To manipulate this, click on one of the numbers in the Sale In Thousands column, then click your right mouse button so that the Pop-up menu tool appears. Pull down to the Scale Range option. The Scale Range dialogue box appears. Click Manual Scale, change the From: number from 2 to 0, and then change the To; number from 14 to 16. Click OK. Your chart looks much better, you now have plenty of room for better sales figures by all the divisions. As you examine the chart, perspective or viewing angle makes it difficult to see all the risers.

Some people think that creating charts is boring, but the developers of CorelCHART! don't. Select the Chart menu and the Preset Viewing Angles then pull down to the Blast-O-Vision view. What a creative name to use! Now your chart fills the screen. We still need to tilt it to improve your view of the risers. You will alter this using a familiar tool From Draw—the 3D View Tool. Select Show 3D View Tool from the Chart Menu. After this tool pops up, click on the 3-D Rotation Button (the one on the far right— see fig. 14.10).

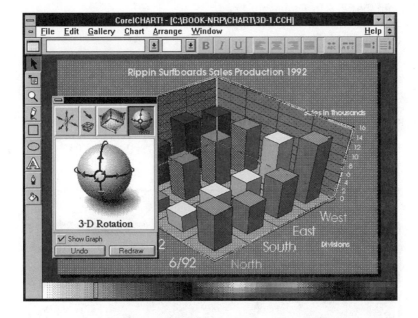

Figure 14.10:
The 3D View Tool—
3-D Rotation

Click and hold down your mouse button on the south red arrow to tilt the chart. The longer you hold down the mouse, the more it tilts. If you go too far, adjust it back with the north red arrow. You will see an outline of your new chart perspective as you make your adjustments. When your chart is rotated properly, click the Redraw button. If you make a mistake, you can click Undo and start over. The final step in the production of your chart is aligning and altering the text.

Modifying and Aligning Your Text

The Month, Division, and Sales in Thousands headings need to be bold so that they stand out.

Click on the heading Month

Shift-click on the heading Division, and the two Sales in Thousand headings	All four text blocks are selected.
Click on the B in the Text Ribbon Tool	Your selected text becomes Bold.

To align the Sales In Thousands headings, click on one, then shift-click on the other

Click **Arrange**

Click **Align** and **Align Center Vertically** *in the fly-out menu*	Both headings are aligned.

To align the Months and Division headings, click on one and shift-click on the other

Click **Arrange**

Click **Align** and **Align Center Vertically** *in the fly-out menu*	Both headings are aligned (see fig. 14.11).

Figure 14.11:

Your completed 3D-Riser Chart.

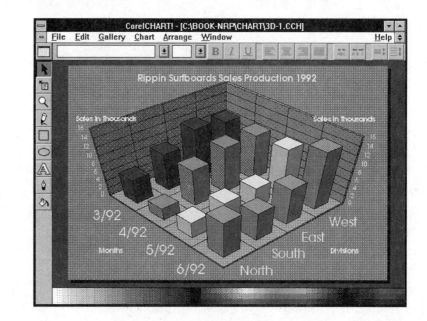

If you need to fine-tune the location of your headings, just drag and drop them into position and repeat the same Arrange procedures. Save your work with Ctrl-S and you have finished the 3D chart.

Creating a Pictograph

Of all the chart types supported, Pictographs are the most visually pleasing and dramatic. Along with this marvelous feature comes the responsibility to keep them simple with plenty of white space. These charts can easily become crowded and hard to read. In this exercise, you will use a familiar tool from your Draw jobs called the Quick Pick Tool (see fig. 14.12).

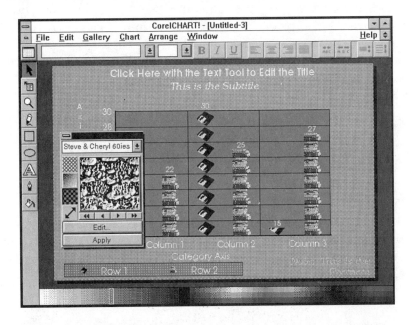

Figure 14.12:

The Quick Pick Tool.

This tool provides a fast way to access hatch patterns, fountain fills, bit-map patterns, and vector graphics. Chart includes 49 Vector graphics in WMF format and 20 bit-mapped graphics in 16-color BMP format accessed with the Quick Pick Tool. You can also use these graphics in Draw. CorelPHOTO-PAINT! provides 26 tiles which are stored as 256-color PCX files in your PHOTOPNT/TILES directory. To use these graphics in Chart, load the PCX tiles into Photo-Paint or Paint Shop Pro included on the bundled disks and save them as a BMP file in your \CHART\BITMAPS directory. Whether you need a 16-color or 256-color bit map will determine which application you use for the conversion. To install these graphics in Chart, click on the Paint Bucket tool and select the Quick Pick Tool (see fig. 14.12). The next step is to click on the bit-map button in the Quick Pick Tool, then click Edit.

The Bitmap Effect dialogue box appears. Click the down arrow in the Picture Name list box and select your new BMP filename. Then edit the other three list boxes. The final step is to click on Save As and give it a long and descriptive name (see fig. 14.13). All these names and related data are saved in a binary file called PICTURES.3FX located in your CHART\EFFECTS directory. WASHES.3FX, VIRGIN.3FX, and SFX.3FX are also located in this same directory and serve the same purpose. Make sure that you have current backups of these four files. If they are ever corrupted or deleted, the Quick Pick Tool won't work properly. A similar conversion procedure can be used to create custom vector graphics for use in Chart. Use Draw to export these graphics as a WMF file to your CHART/VECTORS directory.

Figure 14.13:

Bit-map effect—
Save Effect As
dialogue box.

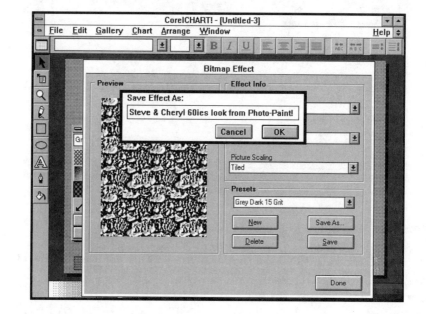

Joe DeLook receives a call from Darryl at his bank. The banker has an important presentation the following week. He needs to illustrate how many male and female customers the bank has. This data must be presented for the last three years to show the increasing number of female customers. Marketing will use this data for a direct mail campaign targeted at female customers. Darryl gives Joe the raw data over the phone and closes the conversation with a plea to make the chart an eye popper for his boss.

This is a good situation for a Pictograph. Select New from the File Menu. Then click on Pictographs in the Gallery list, select the Use Sample Data check box, and click on the third Chart Type. The file name VPIC001.CCH should display in the name section. Press Enter to open this chart. Double-click on the title bar to fill your screen, then save this chart as PICTO-1.CCH. The next step is to change the disk and books graphics to men and women.

Changing Your Graphics

Click on the Paint Bucket tool and drag select the Quick Pick Tool	The Quick Pick Tool appears.
Click on a disk graphic in your chart	All the disks are selected and ready to be changed to men (see fig. 14.14).
Click the vector graphic button in the Quick Pick Tool	A vector graphic appears in the window.
Click the down arrow in the file name list box at the top of this tool	A drop down list WMF graphics appears.
Use the scroll bars to locate BUSI_MAN.WMF, then click on this name	A business man with a briefcase appears in the window (see fig. 14.14).
Click the Apply button	All your disks turn into businessmen as your screen redraws.
Click on a book graphic in your chart	All your book graphics are selected.
Click the down arrow in the file name	

continues

Figure 14.14

The Quick Pick Tool
and Disk Graphic
selected.

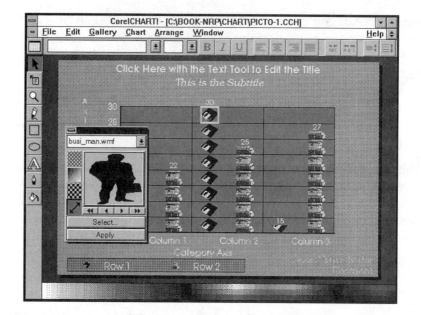

list box of the Quick Pick Tool	
Scroll to FEMWALKS.WMF and click on this name	A walking woman appears in your window.
*Click **A**pply*	All your book graphics are changed to women as the screen redraws.

Take a look at your chart. All your graphics have been automatically changed and scaled. Sometimes when you use the Quick Pick Tool it will lose track of your graphics, and the window display will be empty. If this happens, just click the Select button and navigate to the directory on your system where the BMP and WMF files are stored. You also can use this feature to store BMP or WMF graphics in more than one directory. You are finished using this tool, so click on its control menu to remove it from view. Next save your chart with Ctrl-S. It's time to change your text and data in the Data Manager, so click on the Data Manager icon above the Pick tool.

Changing Your Text

Double-click on the Data Manager Title bar	The Data Manager is enlarged and fills your screen. You have cell A1 selected.
Type **Customer Base by Sex** *Press Enter*	Your chart title is changed and you move to cell A2.
Type **1989 - 1991** *Press Enter*	Your chart subtitle changes and you move to cell A3.
Click and drag across the text that says: "Note: This is a Footnote" *Press Delete* *Press Enter*	Your Footnote text is removed and you move to cell A4, which is empty.
Press Enter twice	You navigate to cell A6.
Type **Male** *Press Enter*	Your legend is changed and you move to cell A7.
Type **Female** *Press Enter*	Your legend is changed and you move to cell A8, which is empty (see fig. 14.15).

If you have worked through the first two exercises in this chapter, changing the rest of your text should be easy. The object is to work in each column and use the Enter key to move to the next cell. Click on cell B1 to start this procedure. Type **Customers in Thousands** in this cell. Next, change cell B2 to Years and the Column 1 text to 1989. Change Cell C5 to 1990, and cell D5 to 1991. Cell D6 should be selected if you have followed the order of these changes. Sometimes it's comforting to take a quick peek at your chart to make sure that you have entered the correct labels. Select the Window Menu and your chart listed as 1. Notice that some of your labels are out of alignment and off the page. You will fix that later. All the text is accurate so return to the Data Manager so that you can change your numbers.

Figure 14.15:

The Data Manager with Cell A8 selected.

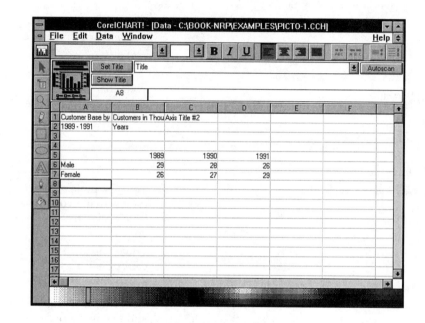

Changing Your Numbers

Cell D6 is selected, so press your left arrow key twice	You move to cell B6 (see fig. 14.16).
*Type **29** and press the down arrow*	Your data is entered and you select cell B7.
*Type **26** and click on cell C6*	Your data is entered and you select cell C6.
*Type **28** and press the down arrow*	Your data is entered and you select cell C7.

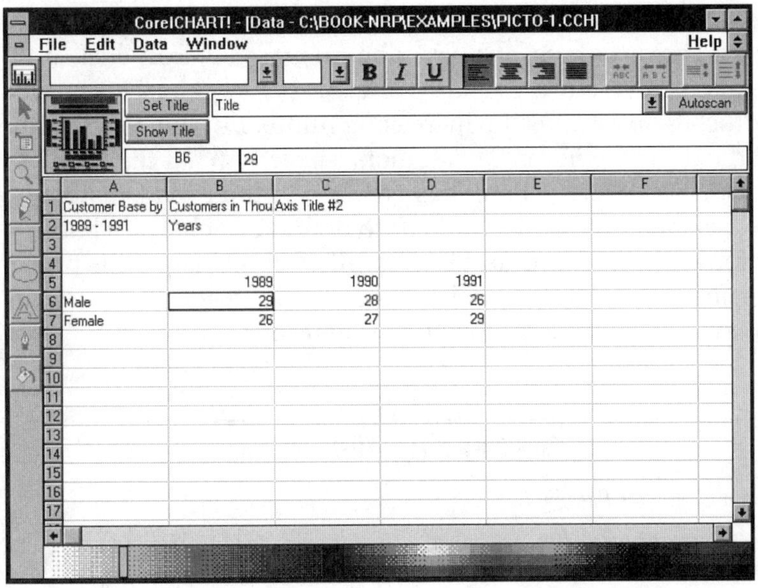

Figure 14.16:
The Data Manager with cell B6 selected.

Type **27** *and click on cell D6*	Your data is entered and you select cell D6.
Type **26** *and press the down arrow*	Your data is entered and you select cell D7.
Type **29** *and press Enter*	Your data is entered and you select cell D8, which is empty.

You have completed all your edits in the Data Manager so return to chart view. Some of your columns are empty, so you need to define the data axis scale. Click on any number next to the Customers in Thousands Column heading. This is a vertical list of numbers. Next click your right mouse button so that the Pop-up menu appears with a label of Data Axis Scale. Click on the scale range option and a dialogue box will appear. Click the Manual Scale box and set From: to 23 and To: to 30. Click OK to change your scale range.

If you would like to view your chart without the distraction of the Toolbar, color palette, and text ribbon, press F9, lean back, and take a look. To return to chart view, press F9 again. This chart graphically illustrates the increasing number of female customers and the decrease in male customers—exactly what the client wants. Of course, the bank has grown and their total customer base has increased. All that's left to do in your chart is change a few font specifications and line up all your labels. In this procedure, Joe DeLook uses Adobe PostScript fonts for all the text. If your system differs, substitute a similar font.

Changing Your Type

Click on Customer Base by Sex

Shift-click on the following text blocks: Customers in Thousands, Years, and Male

Handles appear on your four selected text blocks.

Click on the down arrow in the typeface list box on your text ribbon tool

A drop-down list appears with all your font names displayed.

Scroll down to Helvetica-Black and click on the name (see fig. 14.17)

Your four text boxes change to this font.

Figure 14.17:

Changing your type to Helvetica-Black.

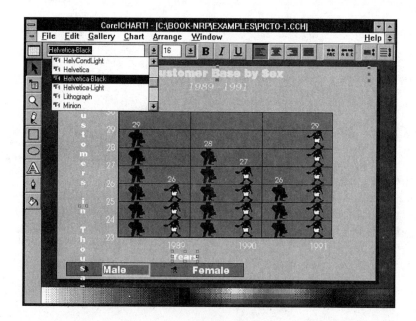

Click on your gray pasteboard surrounding your chart	Deselects your text blocks.
Click on your title text block	Your title has handles and is selected.
Click on the down arrow in the point size list box	A drop-down list box appears with all your sizes.
Scroll down to 28 and click on it	Your text is enlarged and looks more powerful and easier to read.

Your title is hiding the subtitle, so you need to redraw the screen.

Press Ctrl-W	You have forced the screen to redraw, and you can see your subtitle.
Click on your gray pasteboard	Deselects the title.
Click on the "1989-1991" subtitle	
Shift-click on the following text: 1989, 30 in the vertical axis, and 29 on top of the man	Handles appear on your four selected text boxes.
Click on the down arrow in your typeface list box	
Scroll down to Minion and click on it	Your four text boxes change to this font.

Your chart should be easier to read and have more impact after these changes. It has typographical continuity and contrast, all the numbers are set in one serif typeface, and all the text in a dramatic sans serif typeface. The final procedure is to fine-tune and align your text.

The Customers in Thousands label is too large for your chart. Click on this text and specify 10-point type via the point size list box. Next, drag-and-drop this text block so that the last letter (s) is horizontally aligned with the 23 in the data axis scale. The next steps involve roughly positioning your title (Customer Base by Sex) and your subtitle (1989—1991). Click and drag these elements so that they are closer to the body of your chart, and the two lines have more breathing room between them. Don't worry about precise alignment yet; you will do that automatically in the final edits of this chart.

Click on one of the year column headings (1989-1990-1991). Notice that they are set flush right as this button is now selected in the Text Ribbon Tool. Click on the centered text button and all these headings will center in your 3 columns. The last procedure is fine-tuning your elements.

Centering Your Elements

Single click on the border of the legend that says Male-Female at the bottom of the chart

Shift-click on the title, subtitle, years, and the blue-gray rectangle your chart sits on

Handles appear on the five selected items.

Click **Arrange**

Click Center on Page, and Center Horizontal in the fly-out menu (see fig. 14.18)

All your selected elements are centered on the chart.

Click on the vertical text "Customers in Thousands" and drag this into horizontal alignment with the 23 on your Data Axis Scale

Your chart is completed.

Figure 14.18:

Centering your elements.

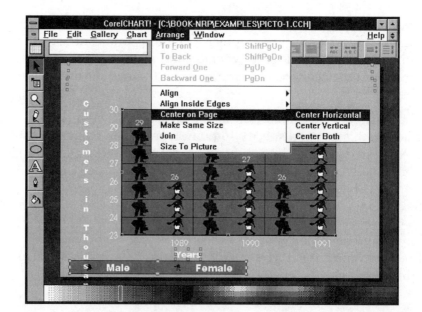

Don't forget to save your latest changes. Press F9, lean back, and study your completed chart. It's dramatic, and it conveys the rising number of women customers in a visually pleasing fashion.

Summary

You have completed this chapter, so it's time to summarize a few key points. Many of the commands you have used do not have keyboard shortcuts. Use the Windows RECORDER.EXE to create your own macros. This will speed up your production by eliminating unnecessary screen redraw and trips to multi-level menu commands. Keep your charts simple and easy to read with large and legible type. Try not to squeeze too much information into one chart. You can always create a second chart to hold the extra data.

Use pleasing and simple colors for all your elements. Before you start your chart, consider how it will be delivered and design the chart with this in mind. Type is harder to read on the screen than on a printed piece, so make it larger. Use graphics only when they help your chart communicate. When editing your chart, try to complete all your changes in the Data Manager—it's much faster than chart view. Work from the top of your chart down and print proofs frequently. Always double-check your chart for accuracy and have a coworker do the same.

CorelSHOW!

orelSHOW! is a remarkable presentation tool that you can use to create screen shows with animation and sound, slide shows, and overheads. Show does not contain any tools to create these presentations, but uses OLE to assemble all the elements. Show functions as an OLE client application and relies on your other Corel applications—or any OLE-aware application installed on your system—to paste or paste link the objects in your presentation.

Show supports 21 transition effects and animations created with Autodesk Animator and Animator Pro (FLC and FLI files). The supported transition effects include such classics as dissolves, wipes, and zooms. The animation files on the floppy disk version of Draw include a computer-like simulation of typing "Welcome" and "The End." Show's support of WAV files enables you to integrate sound in your presentations. If you have the PC Speaker driver distributed by Microsoft, you can use the WAV files included with Windows 3.1 in your presentations. Eight file types can be inserted in your presentation: CCH, CDR, PCX, SHW, BMP, MSP, WAV, and DOC.

Configuring CorelSHOW!

Your CorelSHOW! configuration is saved in CORELSHW.INI located in your COREL\SHOW\ directory. Maintain a current backup of this file on your system and floppy. If this file is ever corrupted or accidentally deleted, Show won't run. If you want to turn off the 3D-look of your dialogue boxes, make a backup of CORELSHW.INI, open it with Notepad or SYSEDIT, and scroll down to the line that reads 3DLook=1. Change the 1 to 0 (zero) and save your changes.

All your screen shows run in standard VGA mode: 640 by 480 using 16 colors. The present version of Show (V3.00 Rev B) runs best using the standard Windows 3.1 VGA driver. You can use Setup to install this driver. If your particular video card and driver don't work properly with Show, edit your WIN.INI so that all your presentations run in small-screen mode. To do this, make a backup of your WIN.INI located in your Windows directory, then open this file with Notepad or SYSEDIT, and scroll down to the section labeled [AAPLAY Animation]. Change the third line in this section from Fullscreen=AAVGA.DLL to Fullscreen=NO. Don't forget to save your changes. The two exercises in this chapter assume that you are running in standard 16-color VGA mode and that all your presentations are full-screen.

Joe will continue to use Adobe PostScript fonts and files from the CorelPHOTO-PAINT! and CorelCHART! chapters (Chapters 13 and 14). If you've jumped ahead in your reading to this chapter, substitute similar fonts and files installed on your system.

Creating a Dog and Pony Show

Joe DeLook receives a call from Statistics Incorporated. They want Joe to prepare 300 charts for their next project. Of course, they would like to drop over in an hour to review Joe's portfolio and see the quality of his work. Like most designers, Joe has a portfolio of his best printed pieces to show prospective clients. In this case, he decides to present some of his chart-specific work through a screen show and the rest of his work in the conventional portfolio review. He plans to let the show run while they visit his studio to present some of his work in a dramatic and unique fashion. This is just the job for CorelSHOW!. To complete this five-slide show exercise, you will need CHT-PIE2.CCH and 3D-1.CCH from Chapter 14, and CHT-PIE1.PCX from Chapter 13. The other necessary animation files are already installed on your system.

Setting Up Your Show

Double-click on the CorelSHOW! icon in your Program Manager Group	Launches Show and the Welcome to CorelSHOW! dialogue box appears (see fig. 15.1).
Click the Start a New Presentation check box and make sure that Options for Presentations reads: Start with 5 Slides Page Settings is 11.00 x 8.25 inches Landscape	These are all default settings.
Click OK	Your show is opened as Presentation1, and you are in slide view.
Click File	
Click Save **As**	The Save Presentation As dialogue box appears.
At File Name, type **SHOW-1.SHW**	
In the Directories box, navigate to your working directory	
In the Keywords box, type **charts Statistics Inc 5/92**	
In the Notes box, type **3 charts for client presentation**	
Click OK	Your show is saved and the title bar reflects your path and SHOW-1.SHW.

Figure 15.1:

The CorelSHOW! dialogue box.

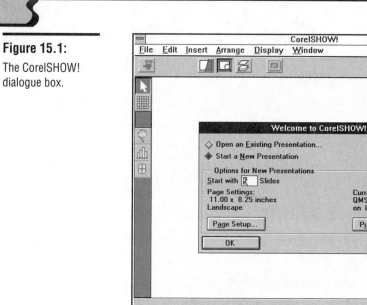

The Right Background

Show has two layers—background and slide—between which you navigate using the two view buttons located below your menu bar. Background view is the button on the left, and slide view is on the right. You also have a Slide Sorter view button. Clicking this button presents a miniature view of all your slides. The first step to create your show is to insert a background. Click on the Background Libraries tool directly below your pick tool on the tool bar.

A dialogue box appears which displays the 25 bundled backgrounds included with Show (see fig. 15.2). Scroll down to the end of the list and click on the third-from-the-last background. This background has perspective and contrasts nicely with the three charts for this show. The selected background is automatically sized and inserted in your show. Click the Done button to close the dialogue box.

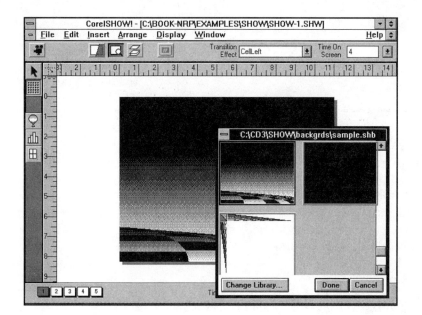

Figure 15.2:
Background
Libraries dialogue
box.

Animation

Now it's time to insert your animation for the opening and closing slides in your show.

Inserting Animation

Click Insert

Click **A**nimation

The Insert Animation dialogue box appears.

Navigate to your COREL\SHOW\FLICS\ directory and double-click on NENWELC.FLI

Your "Welcome" animation is inserted in slide 1 and the Transition Effect list box says Animation. You have 6 slides in your show.

Click on Page Selection button 6 in the bottom left corner of your screen

You navigate to slide 6.

Select the Insert *menu option and* Animation

The Insert Animation dialogue box appears.

continues

Double-click on the file named NENTEED.FLI	Your "The End" animation is inserted in slide 6 and the Transition Effect list box says Animation. You have 7 slides in your show.

Now is a good time to save your work using Ctrl-S. Notice that your Page Selection buttons are numbered up to seven. You don't need that many slides, so click on the Slide Sorter View button. Thumbnail views of all your slides appear. Click on the second slide and press Delete; click on the last slide and press Delete. These two slides are deleted, and your page selection buttons should reflect five slides.

Using OLE in Your Screen Show

You are now ready to use OLE to insert your charts.

Inserting Your Charts

Double-click on slide 2	You navigate to slide view and slide 2 is displayed.
Click **Edit**	
Click **O**mit Background	Your background is hidden.
Click and drag the button in the top left corner of your screen where your horizontal and vertical rulers meet to reset the zero point of your rulers to the top left corner of your page	The zero point changes to this intersection.
Click **D**isplay	
Click **S**nap to Guidelines	A check mark turns it on.
Pull down a horizontal guide to the 1-inch mark on your vertical ruler and another one to the 7-inch mark	Your guides appear.

Shortcut

Omit Background can be toggled by pressing Alt-E-O.

Shortcut

Snap to Guidelines can be toggled by pressing Alt-D-N.

Pull over a vertical guide to the 2-inch tic mark on your horizontal ruler and another one to the 9-inch mark	Your guides appear.
Click Insert	
Click File	The Insert File dialogue box appears (see fig. 15.3).

Shortcut

Insert File can be toggled by pressing Alt-I-F.

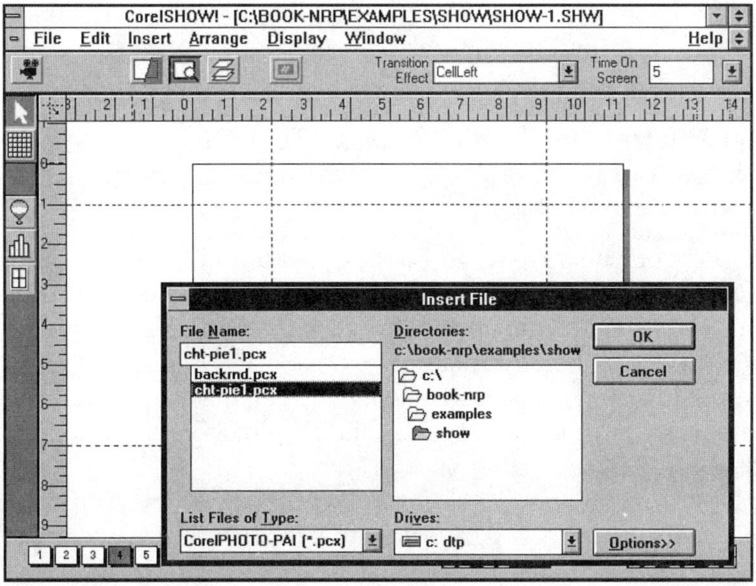

In List Files of Type, click the down arrow key	
Click on the CorelCHART! 3.0 (*.CCH) name	

Navigate to your working directory and click on CHT-PIE2.CCH.

Click OK	Your pointer turns into crosshairs and you return to slide view.
Click and drag to select the area you created with the guides	After a delay, your chart will appear aligned with the guides (see fig. 15.4).
Click Edit	
Click **O**mit Background	Your background appears with your chart on top.

Figure 15.3:

The Insert File dialogue box.

Figure 15.4:

CHT-PIE2.CCH
inserted in your
show.

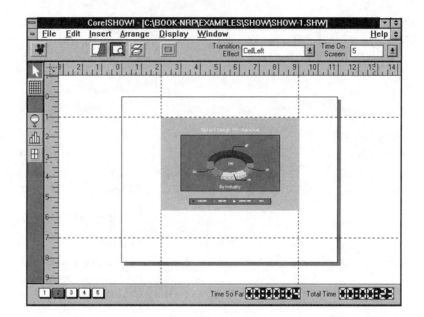

Take a quick peek at how your presentation is progressing. Click the Screen Show button located above the pick tool. (You can stop the presentation at any time by pressing ESC.) The Generating Slides progress bar will display, and the Start the screen show? confirmation box will appear. Click OK to start your show. You will see all your Animations, backgrounds, and chart display, and then you are automatically returned to slide view at the conclusion of your screen show.

Before you leave this slide, change the Time On Screen dialogue box in the top right corner of your screen to 5 by clicking its down arrow, and then clicking on 5.

To insert your next chart, you will follow a procedure similar to the preceding exercise. Click on Page Selection button 3 to move to this slide. Hide the background with the Omit Background command from the Edit menu. Next, choose the File command from the Insert menu and locate 3D-1.CCH. Click and drag to define its size in the same area as slide 2 which you defined with grids. Your 3D-Riser chart should snap into perfect position. To display the background, select the Omit Background command from the Edit menu. The final step in preparing this slide is to set your Time On Screen dialogue box to 5 just like you did with slide 2. Notice the Show Clocks in the bottom right-hand corner of your screen. Time So Far should read 00:00:09, which means your show is 9 seconds long from slide 1 to slide 3. Total Time should read 00:00:19—your entire show is 19 seconds long. The last step is completing slide 4 with OLE and CHT-PIE1.PCX. Click the Page Selection button 4 to move to this slide, and then hide your background with the Edit menu's Omit Background command.

Inserting Your PCX Chart

Click Display

Uncheck **Snap** to Guidelines — Snap to Guidelines is turned off.

Click Insert

Click File — The Insert File dialogue box appears.

Click the down arrow in the List Files of Type dialogue box

Click on CorelPHOTO-PAI (.PCX)*

Navigate to your working directory.

Double-click on CHT-PIE1.PCX — Your pointer turns into crosshairs, and you are returned to slide view.

Click and drag to define the area inside your guides — After a delay, Photo-Paint appears with CHT-PIE1.PCX loaded.

Double-check that you have selected the proper graphic.

In Photo-Paint, click File

Click Exit and Return To — Photo-Paint is closed, and your chart is inserted in slide 4 (see fig. 15.5).

Click and drag the center handle on the right side to resize your chart to fill the area defined by your grids — Your chart is resized to the proper size.

Display your background with the Edit menu's Omit Background option and set your Time On Screen dialogue box to 5. Your completed slide show is 23 seconds long, and you are finished.

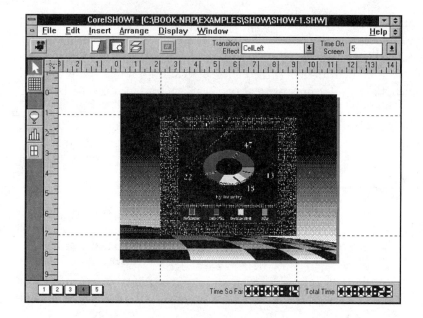

Joe has ten minutes to spare, so he saves his presentation and sets it to run continuously. He selects Presentation Options from the Display Menu. The Presentation Options dialogue box displays. Next he checks both the Automatic Advance to Next Slide check box and the Run Show Continuously Until Escape is Pressed check box. The Generate Slide Show in Advance box is already checked. He then clicks OK. To start this nonstop slide show, Joe uses the shortcut Ctrl-R and clicks OK at the Start the Screen Show? option screen.

Sit back and watch your show. It's dramatic and emotional but not overpowering with unnecessary special effects.

Reviewing Your Work

So far, you have inserted two charts and one PCX graphic in your show using OLE and its paste link feature. Select the Edit menu's Links option. The Link Properties dialogue box appears and lists these three files (see fig. 15.6). Notice the Update—Automatic check box is selected. If you make changes to any of these files, Show automatically updates them in your presentation. You also can use this dialogue box in future presentations to edit these files or reestablish the links if they are accidentally broken. In the next exercise, you will use OLE's embedding feature through the Paste Special command and Paste Link to assemble your show.

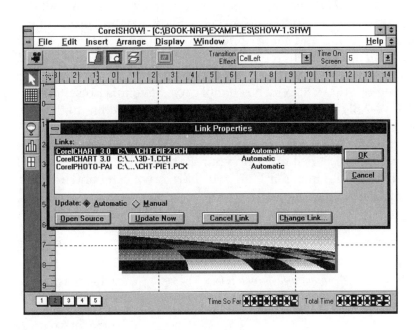

Figure 15.6:
The Link Properties dialogue box.

Creating the Surf Show

As we mentioned in the first exercise using CorelPHOTO-PAINT! (Chapter 13), Joe DeLook has been retained to complete a slide show for Rippin' Surfboards. This presentation will be delivered to their friendly banker as part of an application for a loan. As often happens in the world of design, the client has changed his mind just before production is to begin. Most of the loan presentation will be through conventional printed matter, however, Rippin' Surfboards 1992 sales figures are so much better than 1991, they want to highlight this dramatic growth by including this chart (3D-1.CCH) in the screen show.

Start with the Background

You will need BACKRND3.PCX from Photo-Paint (Chapter 13) and 3D-1.CCH from Chart (Chapter 14). The animation files are already installed on your system. The text for this show will be created in Draw. Double-click on the Show icon in your Program Manager group and set up a new presentation exactly the same way you did in the first exercise. Your Welcome to CorelSHOW! dialogue box should read New Presentation, 5 slides, and a Page Setting of 11.00 x 8.25 inches Landscape. Save this presentation as SHOW-2.SHW and reposition your ruler's zero point to the top left corner of your page. Make sure Snap to Guidelines is not checked in the Display menu. Click and drag a Horizontal guide down to the 1.5 inch mark on your vertical ruler. Drag a vertical guide to the 1.5 inch mark on your horizontal ruler and another one to the 9.5 inch mark.

Inserting Your Background

Click on the background view button below your menu	You move to background view and Background is displayed in the lower left corner of your screen.
Click **Insert**	
Click **File**	The Insert File dialogue box appears.
Click the down arrow in the List Files of Type list box	
Click on CorelPHOTO-PAI (*.PCX)	All your PCX files are displayed in your current directory.
Navigate to your working directory that contains BACKRND3.PCX and double-click on this file name	Your pointer turns into a crosshair.
Click and drag around the border of your page	The loading Progress bar will pop up and your background is inserted.
Click **Arrange**	

Click Fit Object To Page	Your background is automatically re-sized to fill your page (see fig. 15.7).

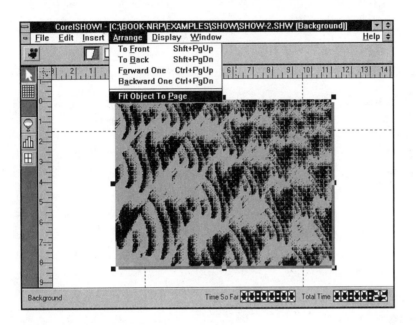

Figure 15.7:
Your inserted background.

Congratulations! You have just embedded your background in the presentation. If you ever need to edit this background, just double-click on it, and OLE will launch Photo-Paint.

Insert Your Animation

The next steps are very similar to the first exercise. You will insert two animations in your show to give it some pizazz. Click on the Slide View button below your menu. Select the Insert Menu's Animation option. Navigate to your COREL\SHOW\FLICS directory and double-click on CPUWELC.FLI. Next, navigate to page 6 of your show with the Page Selection button and insert the second animation file called CPUTEED.FLI.

Your show should have 7 slides, so you need to delete 2 of them. Click on the Slide Sorter button and delete 2 slides so that the first and last slides are animations which display as black rectangles. Now is a good time to save your work through Ctrl-S. Slides 2 and 3 will contain text created in Draw and use OLE to embed these objects in your show.

Embed the Text

The embedded text will be set in Adobe's Helvetica-Black. Substitute a similar font installed on your system. This particular typeface is bold, powerful, and easy to read on the screen. These, by the way, are the traits you should look for when selecting type for your slides.

Embedding Your Text in Slide 2

Double-click on slide 2	You move to slide view, and Page Selection button 2 is gray.
Alt-Tab to Program Manager and double-click on your Draw icon	Draw is launched.
Position your Draw window and your Show window so that they are both visible on your desktop	You are ready to enter text in Draw, and paste in Show.

Click on the title bar of Draw to activate the application.

Enter artistic text that says **"Rippin' Surfboards Inc. PRESENTS."** Each of these four words is on a separate line.

Specify 24-point type in a bold and easy-to-read font like Helvetica-Black and set Justification to Center.

Change the color of this text to yellow with a black 0.003 outline.

Copy it to the clipboard	You are ready to insert your title on page 2.

Click on the title bar of Show to activate the application.

Click **Edit**

Click **O**mit Background	Hides your background, and your guides are visible.
Click **E**dit	
Click Paste **S**pecial	The Paste Special dialogue box appears (see fig. 15.8).
Make sure that CorelDRAW! Graphic is selected and click the Paste button	Your title is embedded through OLE's paste command and appears on your slide.

Shortcut

You can use the keyboard shortcut Alt-E-S to access Paste Special.

Click and drag this text box so that the first line is flush with your horizontal guide.

Use the corner handles to resize the text to fill the area defined by your guides	Your text is aligned with the guides.
Click **E**dit	
Uncheck **O**mit Background	Your background appears with the text block on top.

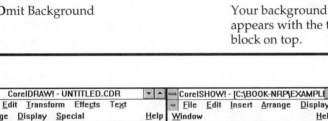

Figure 15.8:

The Paste Special dialogue box.

Notice how your title fills the screen and is easy to read against the blue background. The black outline makes it appear to pop off the background.

The Finishing Touches

Before you leave this slide, you will make two changes to your presentation. Click on the down arrow in the Transition Effect list box, and then click the CurtainOpen effect. Set your Time on Screen list box to 5 seconds. Your Show Clocks should read: Time So Far 00:00:05 and Total Time 00:00:17. Save your work with Ctrl-S and click Page Selection button 3.

Hide your slide 3 background and click on the title bar of Draw to activate it. Your text should still be selected. Edit this text to read "Sales Production 1992" with each of the 3 words on a separate line. Copy this text to the clipboard and activate Show. Use Paste Special to place your text in slide 3 (see fig. 15.9). Resize your text box so that the first line is flush with your horizontal guide, and the text occupies the area defined by your grid. Display your background, set the Transition Effect to CurtainOpen, and change Time On Screen to 5 seconds.

To take a look at your show, click on the Screen Show button and click OK to start the show. You can cancel the show at any time by pressing ESC. Notice how the CurtainOpen effect adds a sense of drama to the presentation and how legible the text is. You have one final slide to complete. Navigate to slide 4 and hide the background so that your guides display. Set your Transition Effect to CurtainOpen and Time On Screen to 5 seconds.

Using Paste Link To Insert a Chart

Inserting Your Chart Using Paste Link

Click Insert

Click File
The Insert File dialogue box appears.

Select CorelCHART! 3.0 (.CCH) in List Files
of Type and locate and select 3D-1.CCH*

Click OK

Your pointer turns into
crosshairs.

*Click and drag inside your guides to define this area
down to the 6.5 inch mark on your vertical ruler.
Watch the whisker to make this procedure more
accurate*

After a delay, your chart
appears inside your
guides (see fig. 15.10).

*Move the chart up if it's not perfectly flush with
your horizontal guide. Use the four corner handles
to fine-tune the size to fill the area defined by your
guides*

Your chart is scaled and
aligned.

Click Edit

Click Omit Background

Your background
displays with your chart
on top.

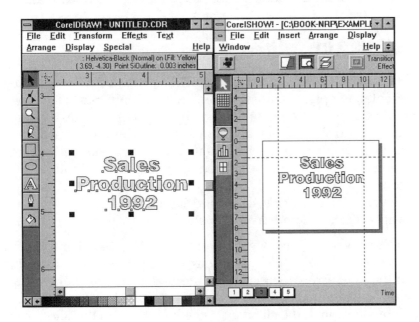

Figure 15.9:

Your slide 3 text
embedded in Show.

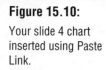

Figure 15.10:

Your slide 4 chart inserted using Paste Link.

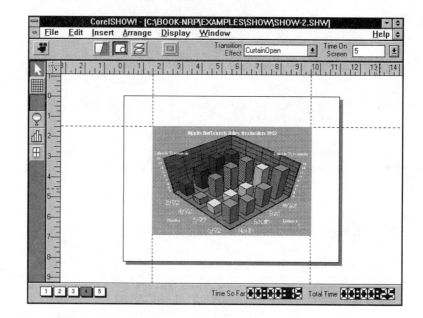

Saving the Show

Your screen show is almost complete. The last step is to set your presentation options and save your show. Rippin' Surfboards will deliver this presentation on Joe's computer. They need the capability to control each slide and move forward and backward. Select the Display menu's Presentation Options. The Presentation Options dialogue box appears (see fig. 15.11). In the Timing section, select Manual Advance to next slide, then select Display pointer on-screen during show, and Generate slide show in advance. Click OK and save your show.

When the Screen Show begins, you can use the space bar to advance to the next slide, the left arrow to go to the previous slide, and the right arrow to navigate to the next slide. The pointer is a valuable tool to highlight the dramatic increase in sales production by division. If the client ever needs changes in this show, you can use OLE to quickly edit your show.

Slides 2 and 3 contain embedded Draw objects. Double-click on this text to launch Draw and perform your edits. Slide 4 contains a linked Chart object. Double-click on the chart to launch Chart and perform your edits. If you need to play your shows on a computer that does not have CorelSHOW! installed but is running Windows 3.0 or later, perform the following procedure. Use the PKZip utility to compress the Corel SHOW! Run-Time player named SHOWRUN.EXE located in your COREL\SHOW\SHOWRUN\ directory. Compress your SHW file also. Some of these files compress up to 90% of their original size. If your show includes any animation sequences, you will have to compress these FLC or FLI files also because they are not included in your SHW file. Move all these files to your target computer and run PKZip to decompress them. Launch the Run-Time Player and double-click on your SHW file to begin your presentation.

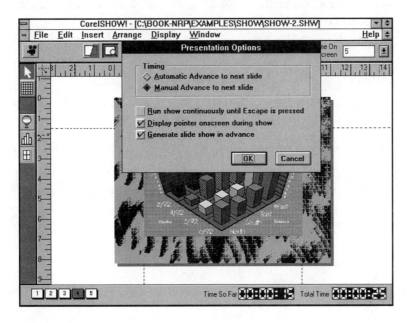

Figure 15.11:

Presentation Options dialogue box.

Summary

Congratulations! You have completed two screen shows. The following tips and tricks are worth keeping in mind:

- Plan your presentations before you start by using thumbnails and printouts of all your elements.

- Define the purpose of your presentation, your target audience, and method of delivery.

- "Grab" the audience and focus attention on your presentation with the opening slide.

- "Close" your presentation in a meaningful way with the last slide.

- Use pleasing colors suited to your target audience.

- Remember that Show only supports 16-color VGA mode, so, whenever possible, try to use pure colors which look better than dithered colors.

- Use animation with restraint to help you communicate—not to show off your collection of "flicks."

- Employ appropriate sound effects for your presentation. Pounding surf would be cool for exercise two in this chapter (Rippin' Surfboards) but a barking dog would not!

- Prepare handouts to both help the viewer follow along and remember your presentation.

- Rehearse your presentation and use coworkers as a test site.

- Keep production notes about your presentations and don't hesitate to remove or improve elements that don't work.

Part Five

Appendixes

Working with Windows

lthough Windows 3.0 was a radical advancement over its predecessors Windows/286 and Windows /386, Windows 3.1 is "only" an incremental improvement over Windows 3.0. Nevertheless, it is an upgrade well worth making: it has many refinements, and far more stability. The fact that the package can be had for as little as $50 (the upgrade fee for registered Windows users) belies an amazing price-to-performance ratio. Considering how inexpensive the software package is, swallowing Windows-increased hardware requirements becomes almost palatable. All kidding aside, Microsoft has done a fabulous job of implementing an unabashedly ambitious software platform. But as you know, there is always room for improvement.

Because CorelDRAW! runs under the Windows environment, it is essential to become comfortable with the Microsoft interface. If you think, "Well, all I use is Draw; I don't need to know Windows," you are selling yourself short. A thorough knowledge of Windows will make you a better Draw user. Although this appendix does not pretend to be the ultimate Windows reference, it can help make your work with Draw—and Windows—more pleasant and productive.

At its simplest, using Windows to your advantage means taking advantage of the mini-programs (like Windows Write and Paintbrush) that come with the package. In addition, you should learn how to navigate the tricky waters of Windows' lesser-known features like Recorder, Character Map, and its built-in screen-capture utility.

Fine-Tuning CORELDRW.INI

The first way to tune up Windows for CorelDRAW! is by editing the CORELDRW.INI file. This file is a plain-vanilla ASCII text file that can be edited with Windows Notepad, Write, or SysEdit. (Be sure to exit CorelDRAW! first.) However, if you use Write, **do not convert CORELDRW.INI to Write format**. The simplest way to edit CORELDRW.INI is to double-click its icon in the File Manager to open up the file in Notepad. You will find CORELDRW.INI in your CORELDRW directory.

As its name implies, CORELDRW.INI is the CorelDRAW! initialization file. Each time Draw is loaded, the program pulls information from the file for configuration purposes. Whenever changes are made to the file, Draw must be reloaded for the changes to take effect.

Editing CORELDRW.INI is not a step to be taken lightly. This is not to say that you should be afraid to touch it, just that you should do so with caution. The best approach is to make a backup copy before editing the file.

There are a number of settings you may want to alter. Table A.1 lists the entries in the [CDrawConfig] section of CORELDRW.INI. A good number of the entries are defined with yes or no (1 or 0) answers, while other entries require variable settings.

Table A.1
CORELDRW.INI [CDrawConfig] Settings

Setting	Option	Default Setting
Applic=x	Directory for CorelDRAW!	C:\CORELDRW\DRAW
ConfigDir=x	Directory for CDCONFIG.SYS	C:\CORELDRW\DRAW
FontsDir=x	Directory for WFN fonts	C:\CORELDRW\DRAW
CorelFiltersDir=x	Directory for filter DLL's	C:\CORELDRW\DRAW
AutoBackupDir=x	Directory for ABK files	C:\CORELDRW\DRAW
AutoBackupMins=x	0 = Disabled, 1 or more = # of minutes	10
BigPalette=x	0 (no) or 1 (yes)	0
BigToolbox=x	0 (no) or 1 (yes)	0
CalligraphicClipboard=x	0 (no) or 1 (yes)	1
ClipboardFountains=x	0 (no) or 1 (yes)	0
CMYKPalette=x	CMYK Palette filename	CORELDRW.PAL
DefaultFont=x,y,z	<Fontname>,<nStyle>, <nPtsize>	FirstFont,1,24
DelayToDraw WhileMoving=x		Delay in milliseconds 500
ExportTextAsCurves=x	0 (no) or 1 (yes)	1
FontRasterizer=x	0 (no) or 1 (yes)	1
INKPalette=x	Ink filename	CORELDRW.IPL
MakeBackup WhenSave=x	0 (no) or 1 (yes)	1
MaxCharsToDraw DuringKern=x		# of characters 25
MaximizeCDraw=x	0 (no) or 1 (yes)	0
OLEConvertObjects ToDraw=x		0 (no) or 1 (yes) 0
OLEServer EmulateMDI=x	0 (no) or 1 (yes)	1

continued

Table A.1
Continued

Setting	Option	Default Setting
PSBitmapFontLimit=x	0 to 250 fonts	8
PSComplexityThreshold =x	# of nodes (20 to 30000)	3000
ShowObjectsWhenMoving =x	0 (no) or 1 (yes)	0
TextOnClpMetafile=x	0 (no) or 1 (yes)	0
WarnBadOrientation=x	0 (no) or 1 (yes)	1
3DLook=x	0 (no) or 1 (yes)	1
SpellLanguage=x	English, French, German, Swedish, Spanish, Italian, Danish, Dutch, Finnish	English
SpellDict=x	Spelling dictionary file	IENM9150.DAT
HyphenateDict=x	Hyphenation dictionary file	HECRP301.DAT
ThesaurusDict=x	Thesaurus dictionary file	COM_THES.DIS

The following sections explain in more detail some of the CORELDRW.INI [CDrawConfig] entries listed in table A.1.

Setting Up Directories

The first five entries under the [CDrawConfig] heading dictate where the various CorelDRAW! program files reside. By default, the Setup routine configures all five entries to point to the C:\CORELDRW\DRAW directory. Of course, your system may be set up differently. You may want to clean up your directory structure so that each entry points to a different subdirectory. The decision is entirely up to you.

The *Applic* or application directory entry should include the following files: CORELDRW.EXE, CORELDRW.INI, USERPROC.TXT, PROLOG.CMP, along with all HLP and PAN files.

The *ConfigDir* or configuration directory entry should contain the following files: CDCONFIG.SYS, CORELDRW.BPT, CORELDRW.DOT, CORELDRW.END, CORELDRW.INK, CORELDRW.IPL, CORELDRW.PAL, and all PAT files.

The *FontsDir* directory entry must include all WFN fonts and symbol libraries.

The *CorelFiltersDir* directory entry is where all of Draw's import and export filters are located. These files can be identified as IMP*.DLL and EXP*.DLL, respectively.

The *AutoBackupDir* directory entry affects where CorelDRAW! stores its AutoBackup ABK files. It is not a problem if you do not have this entry in your file—if it is not specified, ABK files are dumped into the same directory as the CORELDRW.INI file. For performance reasons, do not set this entry to store files on a floppy drive.

Leaving Dictionary Settings Alone

Do not change the default settings for the *SpellDict*, *HyphenateDict*, or *ThesaurusDict* entries. These lines assign the proper spelling, hyphenation, and thesaurus dictionaries, respectively.

Backing Yourself Up

Everyone knows the value of backing up files. CORELDRW.INI gives you a couple of choices about how Draw will automatically back up your files. The *AutoBackupMins* entry can be set for anywhere from 1 to 99 minutes. You can disable the AutoBackup feature by setting this entry to 0. The frequency you decide on depends on your working style and personal preferences. The default setting is 10 minutes.

The *MakeBackupWhenSave* entry has a default setting of 1. By default, then, Draw creates a backup (BAK) file each time you save a previously saved CDR file. This feature can be a lifesaver if you errantly save a job you really wanted to rename. However, to open up disk space, you should check through your files frequently to remove unnecessary BAK files. You can turn off this feature with a setting of 0.

Sizing the Big Toolbox and Big Palette

The *BigPalette* and *BigToolbox* entries control the size of their respective screen representations. You may want to set these options to 1 if you are using a high-resolution video display card (800×600 or 1024×768) with a 14-inch monitor. This will provide a larger, more useable toolbox and palette. With a larger monitor (16-inch or better), both entries should be set to 0. The default setting for both entries is 0.

Controlling the Clipboard

CorelDRAW! provides superior clipboard support with three entries in CORELDRW.INI. The *TextOnClpMetafile* entry controls whether or not text cut or copied to the clipboard is output as text or as (converted-to-curve) objects. Use the default setting of 0 for text as text; use a setting of 1 for text as objects. The *CalligraphicClipboard* default setting of 1 maintains calligraphic outline effects; a setting of 0 ignores the effects. The *ClipboardFountains* default setting of 0 disables high-res radial fountains. However, a setting of 1 should be used only when printing to a PostScript output device.

Locating Palettes

The settings for both the *CMYKPalette* and *INKPalette* entries are reset each time you exit CorelDRAW!. Consequently, any changes you make to either of these settings is overwritten the next time you close Draw with a different palette active.

Specifying a Favorite Font as the Default

You can easily set up CORELDRW.INI so that each time you boot Draw, your favorite font (in your favorite style and size) is the default font. The *DefaultFont* setting conventions of font name, style, size can be set for any font, in sizes from 0.7 to 1440 points. Style is defined with this convention: 1-normal, 2-bold, 4-italic, and 8-bold italic.

Seeing What You Are Doing

Seeing what you are clicking and dragging can be an advantage, but it can be a drag as well. Sometimes just a bounding-box display is sufficient to tell you that an object is moving. With the *ShowObjectsWhenMoving* entry set to its default of 0, the object is not redrawn as it is dragged—an advantage when you are manipulating complex objects or large bitmaps. If you want to see the objects as you move them, set this entry to 1.

The *MaxCharsToDrawDuringKern* entry governs whether or not characters are displayed when kerning with the shape tool. To display interactive kerning, the number of characters being kerned must be equal to or less than the specified number for this entry. The default setting is 25, and *MaxCharsToDrawDuringKern* must be set to at least 10.

With these two entries controlling what is redrawn, you also can control how responsive the redraw is. The *DelayToDraw WhileMoving* entry controls how long you must stop your movements before the object redraws. This setting is extremely fine— you can set it from 1 to 32000 milliseconds. The default is 500.

Organizing Your Workspace

Three settings govern how your CorelDRAW! session is configured for your personal preferences. If you want Draw always to open to a full screen, set *MaximizeCDraw* to 1. The default setting of 0 starts Draw at the default window size.

Are you less than enamored with Draw's dimensional background and controls? Want to use the color scheme—perhaps the classic Black Leather Jacket, Ocean (Joe DeLook's favorite), or even the garish Hotdog Stand—you've specified for the rest of Windows? The default setting of 3DLook=1 makes Draw use the dimensional background, but by setting 3DLook=0, you use the Windows' settings. The default setting is 1.

Perhaps you are working on a project that requires a language other than English. The *SpellLanguage* setting determines which dictionary the Spell Checker users. Draw gives you a wide range of languages. In addition to English, you may choose from Danish, Dutch, Finnish, French, German, Italian, Portuguese, Norwegian, Spanish, or Swedish.

Allowing for Complex Paths

You may need the *PSComplexityThreshold* entry if you have ignored one of the basics of CorelDRAW!, repeated many times in this book: **Keep your paths simple! Delete unnecessary nodes! Easy on the fountain (and other complex) fills!** (You can think of this book as a really fat Strunk and White's *Elements of Grammar*, if you want.)

If a filled path has a value (number of nodes) of more than the number specified in the *PSComplexityThreshold* entry, Draw breaks up the path into simpler paths, without modifying the path's appearance. If you are getting PostScript LimitCheck errors with the default setting of 3000, set the *PSComplexityThreshold* to 200 or so. This entry can be set from 20 to 30,000.

Learning More Bull about OLE

CORELDRW.INI contains two entries that pertain to Object Linking and Embedding (OLE). The first, *OLEConvertObjectsToDraw*, determines whether or not you have full control over linked and embedded objects within Draw. The default setting of 0 does not let you blend, envelope, rotate, skew, or apply perspective to any OLE objects. A setting of 1 converts OLE objects into Draw format, so that they can be manipulated.

The *OLEServerEmulateMDI* entry is a bit less obvious. This setting determines whether or not Draw boots up multiple sessions for multiple OLE edits. The default setting of 1 uses a single Draw session. You can use multiple sessions by changing this option to 0.

Specifying Printer Settings

A few printer options are available to fine-tune your printer specifications. The first, *FontRasterizer*, determines whether Draw uses its internal font rasterizer. The default setting of 1 turns the rasterizer on. Some printers cannot handle the rasterizer; in those cases, turn off the rasterizer with a setting of 0.

The *PSBitmapFontLimit* entry has a default setting of 8, but can be set from 0 to 250. This option controls whether or not Draw creates bit-map printer versions of the fonts you are using. The value specifies the number of bit-map fonts. There are a number of caveats. Basically, the text in question must be untransformed, nonoutlined, and uniformly filled. It must not be a printer resident font. Furthermore, printed character size can be no larger than 75 pixels. You may find bit-map fonts to be worthwhile on low-res laser printers, but on high resolution imagesetters, it is pointless. Low-res printers have far fewer pixels per equivalent type sizes.

The *WarnBadOrientation* entry is a convenience feature. When set to its default of 1, Draw warns you when your printer is set for landscape and you are printing a portrait page (or vice versa). When set to 0, Draw does not give you any fair warning.

Leaving Filter and Color Separation Information Alone

Following the [CDrawConfig] section in CORELDRW.INI is a large number of filter entries [CDrawFilters]. In general, you should not have to touch these settings. You also see a number of settings for color separations [CDrawColorSep]. Once again, you should leave these settings untouched.

Using WFN Fonts

Previous versions of CorelDRAW! used the proprietary WFN font format. By contrast, version 3.0 allows access to TrueType, PostScript Type 1, as well as Corel WFN fonts. You may have created custom WFN fonts with an older version of Draw. If so, you can either use these fonts as they are, or convert them to TrueType or PostScript format with the Ares FontMonger.

In loading order, Draw's internal Font Manager first accesses TrueType, then PostScript (assuming that Adobe Type Manager—ATM—is enabled), and finally, WFN fonts. If you have fonts with the same name in more than one format, the Font Manager uses the first one it finds, and disregards the rest.

The method you use to add fonts depends on the font type you are using. TrueType fonts are added through the Fonts section of the Windows Control Panel. PostScript fonts should be added through the ATM Control Panel.

Adding WFN fonts is not quite as straightforward. However, if you are adding a standard previous-version font, the process is still relatively simple. Just roll down to the [CorelDrwFonts] section of CORELDRW.INI, and delete the semicolon in front of the font you want to access. Then, make sure that that font has been copied into the directory you have specified in the *FontsDir* entry of CORELDRW.INI.

To install a custom WFN font from a previous version of Draw, you must create the font reference line. If you have your old (version 2.x) CORELDRW.INI file around, this isn't too tough. Just copy the reference line from the old file to the appropriate place in the new (version 3.x) file. Not too hard, but the best solution may still be to convert the WFN font to TrueType or PostScript format with FontMonger.

Specifying Printer-Resident Fonts

If you are lucky enough to have a font-loaded hard disk attached to your printer, you might want to make one more change to the [PSResidentFonts] section of CORELDRW.INI. This change has to do with whether Draw uses the printer's fonts or its own. Each font description line ends with a 0, 1, or 3. These numbers refer to the font's printer-residency status. If the line ends in 0, it means that the font is not a printer resident and, consequently, the closest

Draw font is used. A line ending in 1 denotes that the font is one of the "original" LaserWriter fonts (for example, Times Roman or Helvetica). A 3 denotes that the font is one of the "standard 35" fonts found in most Adobe PostScript-licensed laser printers.

If you have a printer-resident font not among the standard 35, you can replace the 0 at the end of its font description line with a 3. This tells Draw to use the printer-resident font rather than the Draw font. Using printer-resident fonts results in faster print times and better type quality because of PostScript Type 1 font hinting. *Font hinting* helps make small type look smoother when printed on a low-resolution laser printer.

In addition to ITC Zapf Dingbats and Symbols fonts, the standard 35 LaserWriter fonts include the following:

ITC Avant Garde Gothic Book

ITC Avant Garde Gothic Book Oblique

ITC Avant Garde Gothic Demi

ITC Avant Garde Gothic Demi Oblique

ITC Bookman Light

ITC Bookman Light Italic

ITC Bookman Demi

ITC Bookman Demi Italic

`Courier`

Courier Oblique

Courier Bold

Courier Bold Oblique

Helvetica

Helvetica Oblique

Helvetica Bold

Helvetica Bold Oblique

Helvetica Condensed

Helvetica Condensed Oblique

Helvetica Condensed Bold

Helvetica Condensed Bold Oblique

New Century Schoolbook Roman

New Century Schoolbook Italic

New Century Schoolbook Bold

New Century Schoolbook Bold Italic

Palatino Roman

Palatino Italic

Palatino Bold

Palatino Bold Italic

Times Roman

Times Italic

Times Bold

Times Bold Italic

ITC Zapf Chancery

Font Mapping from Previous Versions

The last big section in CORELDRW.INI is [CORELDRW20FontMap].
This section determines how version 3.0 opens version 2.x files.
The font map tells Draw how to interpret and assign the font
settings from the previous version's files. Thankfully, this section
should automatically link up all the standard fonts, and even the
bonus fonts included on the CD-ROM.

On the other hand, if you created custom WFN fonts, whether
self-created or converted from other formats, you must set up the
[CORELDRW20FontMap] section to assign the proper 3.0 typefaces.
Otherwise, Draw will not recognize which typeface to use, and
may respond with a "Bad or Missing Font File" message. The
process of assigning 2.x WFN fonts to 3.0 fonts really isn't

impossible, just tedious—especially when you have a large number of custom fonts.

Basically, you must add to the [CORELDRW20FontMap] section a line for each font family you created in version 2.x. This line correlates the 2.x WFN font filename to the 3.0 font name (be it TT, PS, or WFN). The line you add will look something like this:

```
Filename.WFN=FONTname www,bbb,iii,ooo
```

FILENAME.WFN is the 2.x font file. FONTname is the 3.0 font's name (not the 3.0 font's filename). A font's name is usually not the same as the font's filename.

The *www,bbb,iii,ooo* part of this line refers to the space-character width for the normal, bold, italic, and bold-italic version 2.x fonts, respectively. You can determine the space-character width by using the DOS-based WFNSPACE.EXE utility supplied with Draw 3.0. The utility is found in the Draw directory; copy it into the directory in which your 2.x WFN fonts are located. At the DOS prompt, type **WFNSPACE** *fontname*.**WFN**. The program responds with the space-character widths for the font specified by *fontname*.**WFN**. Use this information to complete the font family line you want to insert into the [CORELDRW20FontMap] section.

Using What You Paid For

Throughout this book, you used many of the different programs that came bundled in the Windows 3.1 package. In the chapters on setting type, you saw how easy it was to copy text from Windows Write into the Draw text entry box. In the section on bit maps, you used Windows Paintbrush to create some snazzy bit-mapped images.

The following sections touch on some of Windows' less obvious features. Microsoft's programmers have come up with a couple of great new ideas. By the time you are done with these sections, you will likely be getting some ideas of your own.

Using the Recorder for Ultra-Macros

Windows 3.1 includes a supercharged replacement for Draw's dearly departed (but basically useless) macro function (which disappeared in version 2.0). Get ready for fun, because Microsoft has built a new rollercoaster on the Windows boardwalk, and its name is Recorder.

Recorder is a utility that enables users to register all movements within a screen or window. Try a simple exercise to illustrate how Recorder adds versatility to Draw. This exercise sets up a continuous loop that takes an ellipse, duplicates it, moves it, rotates it, and changes its color. Before you start this exercise, make sure that the Uniform Fill dialogue box is in Process Color/CMYK mode.

A Ghost in the Machine

Click Draw's Minimize button   CorelDRAW! is
                                               minimized to an icon.

In the Windows Program Manager, take the following steps:

Double-click the Accessories icon or window

Double-click the Recorder icon

Click Recorder's Minimize button   Recorder is minimized to
                                               an icon.

Drag the Recorder icon to the bottom   Icon must be at least
of the screen   partially visible while
                                               Draw is running to
                                               perform this exercise.

Double-click the Draw icon   Draw returns to a
                                               full screen.

Click **S**pecial   The Special menu
                                               appears.

Click Preferences   The Preferences
                                               dialogue box
                                               appears.

At Place Duplicate, enter: **0,6 horz**. *and* **1,0 vert**. *picas, points*

Click OK

Click the ellipse tool

Draw an ellipse at the bottom of the page	Make it about 1" high by 0.5" wide.
Click the fill tool	The Fill fly-out menu appears.
Click Uniform Fill	The Uniform Fill dialogue box appears.
Click Process	
At Cyan, enter: **100**	
At Magenta, enter: **100**	
At Yellow, enter: **20**	
At Black, enter: **0**	
Click OK	
Click the outline tool	The Outline fly-out menu appears.
Click the two-point rule	

Now that you have your first ellipse on the page, you are going to use the Record Macro dialogue box (see fig. A.1) to build a continuous loop to duplicate the ellipse and place each duplicate 1 pica above and 6 points to the right of the last. Then scale the duplicate horizontally 110 percent, and fade the color in 2-percent increments for cyan and 4-percent increments for magenta. Because the loop is continuous, you can start the macro and come back later to see what the program has done. During this exercise, be careful not to take the pointer outside the Active Border Tool Box. If you do, Recorder will stop the program each time at the point where you went out.

A Ghost in the Machine pt.2

Click the ellipse	The ellipse is selected.
Double-click the Recorder icon	
Click Macro	The Macro menu appears.
Click Record	The Record Macro dialogue box appears (see fig. A.1).

continues

At Record Macro Name, enter: **Twister**	
At Shortcut Key, enter: **Z**	
At Playback To, click Same Application	
At Playback Speed, click Fast	
Click Continuous Loop	
Click Enable Shortcut Keys	
At Record Mouse, click Everything	
At Relative to, click Window	
Click **Start**	The macro starts recording.
In the Draw Window:	
Click **Edit**	The Edit menu appears.
Click **Duplicate**	The ellipse is duplicated.
Click **Transform**	The Transform menu appears.
Click **Stretch & Mirror**	The Stretch & Mirror dialogue box appears.
Click the up horizontal arrow twice	Registers 110 percent.
Click OK	The ellipse is stretched horizontally 110 percent.
Click the fill tool	The Fill fly-out menu appears.
Click Uniform Fill	The Uniform Fill dialogue box appears.
Click the Cyan down arrow twice	
Click the Magenta down arrow four times	
Click OK	
Click the Recorder icon	The Macro Recording Suspended dialogue box appears. The Save Macro option is already selected.
Click OK	The macro is saved.

Congratulations! You have created your first Recorder macro. Now play it back. Just start it up and watch it do its trick.

Press Ctrl-Z	The macro begins.
To stop the macro, press Ctrl-Break	
To save the macro, go to the Recorder's File menu and select Save **As**	

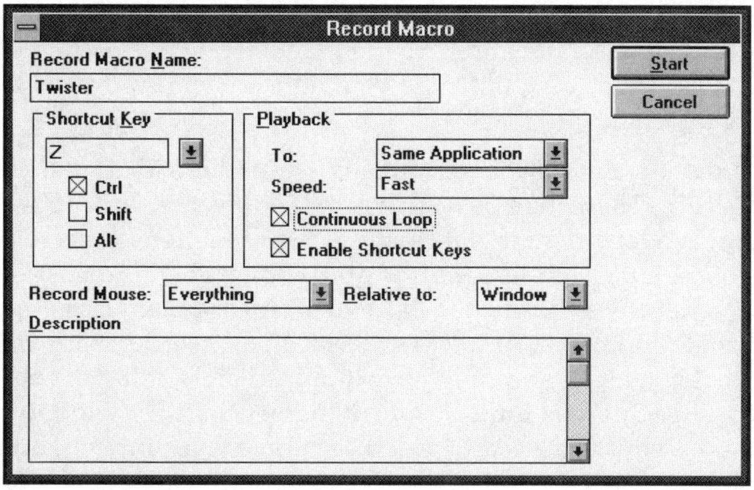

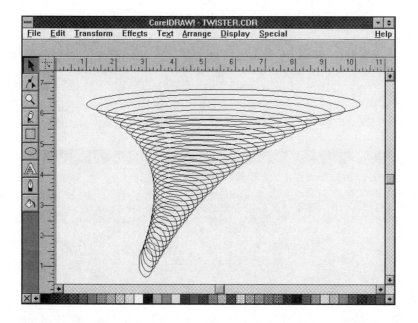

Figure A.1:
The Record Macro dialogue box.

If everything went as planned, you have created a little twister that looks like figure A.2. You hope that it is not headed toward the town of Seaside and your old friend Joe DeLook.

Figure A.2:
Twister.

Now you have seen that Recorder works in a most intriguing manner that deserves some experimentation on your part. The preceding exercise should whet your appetite and start you off in a new direction.

The *Inside CorelDRAW!* disk contains a few macro ideas in the file ICD4.REC. (These macros were created for the standard VGA display mode; different video drivers require different macros.) One of the cutest of these macros drops down and arranges all of Draw's roll-up menus in one fell swoop. All you do is open the macro file and press Alt-J. If you decide that Recorder is for you, and that you always want to have it immediately at hand, you can create a specific icon for it in your Windows Start-Up window. That way, your macros are loaded each time you run a Windows session.

Finding Those Dingbats with Character Map

Remember back in Chapter 3, when you built those playing cards? Perhaps you recall what a pain it was to key in those arcane, unintuitive Alt keystrokes to gain access to high-bit characters. Well, fear not...the Windows Character Map utility makes it easy to find and set those peculiar characters. This nifty little device was introduced in Windows 3.1, although it pays homage to the Mac's Key Caps, and to Norton Desktop's Key Finder. Figure A.3 shows the Windows Character Map window.

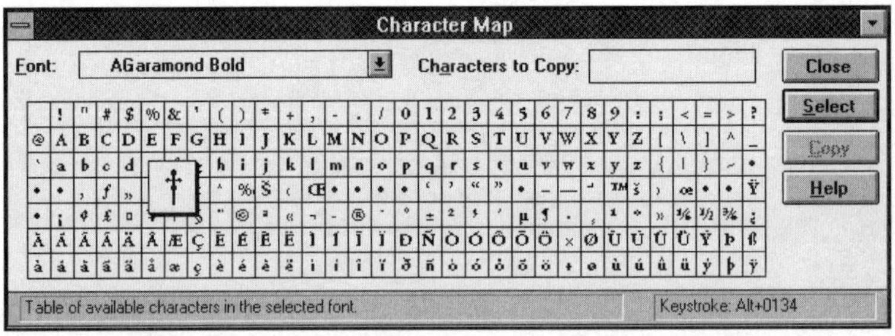

Figure A.3:

Finding a dagger with the Character Map utility.

When you run Character Map, you can quickly identify and select any character in any (TrueType or PostScript Type 1) font you have loaded. You then copy the character to the clipboard and paste it into your application. Once the character has been pasted, you then change the character to the applicable font, and *voila!* You have your special character without having to resort to looking at hard copy or memorizing Alt-key sequences.

If you want to get really slick, you can use a combination of Recorder and Character Map utilities to build a number of mnemonic macros for frequently used special characters. Old-time, code-based typesetters refer to these as *pi calls*.

Capturing Screens with Windows

The folks at Microsoft were very generous when they endowed Windows with a built-in screen capture (or screen grab) utility. This utility is extremely useful in situations where you need to use a screen shot for advertising or documentation.

Capturing screens with Windows is fairly simple, although it lacks the ease and automation found in a dedicated screen capture utility program such as Hotshot. To capture a screen, just press Print Screen or Alt-Print Screen, and presto-chango, the screen is copied to the clipboard. Once the image is in the clipboard, it can be saved in clipboard format or pasted into an appropriate Windows program such as Paintbrush. Be sure to configure Paintbrush's image attributes for your computer's video card resolution (VGA, 640×480; Super VGA, 800×600).

Some Windows programs can accept these clipboard files while others cannot. The author has successfully pasted screen captures into PageMaker using this method.

Take a look at figure A.4, which shows a computer within a computer within a computer. This graphic was produced using the Windows screen capture utility. However, the clipboard image could not be imported into Draw, and Hotshot was ultimately used to get the job done. If the wizards at Corel are looking for a new import filter to build, the Windows Clipboard (CLP) format would be handy.

If you are having trouble capturing screens, there are a few things you can check. The application from which you are copying screens may have its Program Information File (PIF) set for No

Screen Exchange. If this is true, turn the option off, restart the application, and try again. It is possible that the Print Screen or Alt-Print Screen keys are reserved combinations for the application from which you are trying to capture screens. If so, go back to the program's PIF and turn off the Reserve Shortcut Key options. Another item to consider is the program's video mode. Take one more trip back to the PIF and try a higher setting.

Figure A.4:
Captured screens.

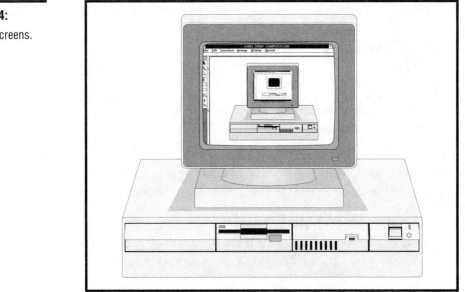

Capturing Screens with CCapture

CorelDRAW! 3.0 includes a crude little screen capture utility of its own. Corel Screen Capture (or CCapture) is an improvement over the built-in Windows screen capture utility, but falls far short of the better screen capture utilities on the market. CCapture offers three screen grab choices. The first choice, PrtScrn, captures the entire Desktop, and does pretty much what the built-in Windows screen capture feature does. The other two choices, Alt+PrtScrn and Alt+Pause, capture just the currently selected window, or the client area of the currently selected windows, respectively.

If you need a large number of screen grabs, get serious and ditch CCapture. To crank out large numbers of screen shots, you need automation, control over image quality, and a choice of file formats. You would do best to look at a commercial package such as Collage.

As with any type of publishing, it is important to determine whether the manufacturer of the program whose screens you are capturing requires permission for publication of their screen images. At the very least, you would be wise to include a disclaimer in the advertisement or in the front pages of any other published work.

Running Windows 3.1 on a Tight Ship

Is your computer underpowered and saddled with a wimpy little hard disk? You are not alone. The first edition of this book was written and illustrated on a lowly 10MHz 286 PC equipped with a meager 20M hard disk. Although this did create some problems, they were more aggravating than insurmountable. In contrast, the last three editions of this book were blasted out of a 386/33 machine (and an even faster box is in the works). Speed does make a difference! Quite frankly, it would be a mean feat (if not an exercise in futility) to attempt to run Windows 3.1 and CorelDRAW! 3.0 on the earlier machine.

It is important to make the most of your system, especially when system resources are limited. People with yesterday's technology must be prudent with their disk space. A couple of megabytes of extra junk on a 330M hard disk is nothing to worry about, but on a 40M hard disk, it could be the factor that causes you to miss your deadline.

Deleting Unnecessary Windows Files

Windows can gobble up lots of valuable disk space if all its options are installed. It is up to you to go back in and delete the files and applications you do not absolutely need.

The best strategy to follow here is to cover yourself. Instead of merely deleting unnecessary files, copy them to floppy disks, and *then* remove them from the hard disk. This way, you can easily restore a file if you need it at a later date—if you finally get that big hard disk. Until then, floppies are easy on the wallet. At less than a dollar per megabyte of storage (for high-density 5 1/4-inch disks), they cost far less than hard disk storage.

For safety's sake, do not remove any Windows files not specifically mentioned in the following sections.

Deleting Leftover TMP Files

If (or when) your system locks up while running Windows, the currently open programs leave behind temporary (TMP) files. These files can accumulate to the point where they take many megabytes of storage. Periodically, delete all TMP files from the TEMP directory where they are stored. Do not do this while Windows is running, or you may delete files currently in use. Exit Windows before deleting the TMP files. If you do not have a separate directory for TMP files, set one up; if you do, your housekeeping chores are less of a hassle.

Deleting Wallpaper Files

You may want to remove the bit-mapped files that Windows refers to as wallpaper. These files are identified by the file extension BMP. Although these files can lend a jazzy look to your Windows desktop, they eat up plenty of space—over 420K (if you have installed over a previous version of Windows). The following wallpaper files are located in your Windows directory:

256COLOR.BMP	ARCHES.BMP
CHITZ.BMP	MARBLE.BMP
TARTAN.BMP	WINLOGO.BMP
WEAVE.BMP	PARTY.BMP
BOXES.BMP	RIBBONS.BMP
PYRAMID.BMP	CHESS.BMP
PAPER.BMP	

Be careful not to delete any BMPs you have created...you may need them! The best strategy is to store your own BMPs (other than those you want to use as wallpaper) in their own directory.

Deleting Game Files

The next group of files that can be eliminated are the two Windows game files, Minesweeper and Solitaire, along with their associated help files. Removing these files nets more than 235K. You may even find yourself becoming more productive by taking these files off your system. Solitaire is known to have addictive qualities. If you have not played it yet, deal yourself a hand before you remove it! These files are fun to have on your system, but feel free to remove them if you need the space. The games and their help files are entitled:

WINMINE.EXE	SOL.EXE
WINMINE.HLP	SOL.HLP

Deleting Unnecessary Help Files

Although Help (HLP) files can be beneficial, they also take up a lot of space. It is perfectly acceptable to run an application file without having its associated HLP file. And because Windows comes with comprehensive documentation, the HLP files are expendable. To this end, you can remove many of the help files from your Windows directory. That is almost a megabyte of space to be saved! For example, you can run quite well with the following HLP files removed:

CALC.HLP	PBRUSH.HLP
CALENDAR.HLP	RECORDER.HLP
CARDFILE.HLP	WRITE.HLP

NOTE

Be sure to use the Windows Control Panel to set desktop wallpaper to None before removing any BMP files.

Deleting Other Applications

The last group of possible files you can delete includes any of a number of Windows application files, along with their help files. It is not recommended that you remove any of these files, but if you need the space, do what you have to do. If you are happy with your communications program, you are probably safe in deleting TERMINAL.EXE. Do you already have a Windows-based word processor like Word for Windows or Ami Professional? Then you can delete WRITE.EXE. Remember that the Windows application files listed here are among the last you should delete to free up additional disk space:

CALC.EXE	TERMINAL.EXE
CALENDAR.EXE	PBRUSH.EXE
CARDFILE.EXE	WRITE.EXE
CLOCK.EXE	

Optimizing Your System for CorelDRAW!

The Microsoft Windows operating environment can be set up in a multitude of ways. Different computer configurations require different arrangements. To get the best performance out of Draw, you should be using a 386 or 486 computer with plenty of RAM, a serious video card, and a large, fast hard disk. If you have a multiple-computer environment, put the fastest machines on the desks of the people doing design and DTP work. Move the slower machines to the desks of those who are doing less processor-intensive tasks such as word processing. This is maximization of resources.

Getting Serious about Video Display Cards

On the subject of video display cards and high-resolution monitors, take heed. Generally, the higher resolution your card and monitor, the longer it takes for the screen to rewrite. You may grow old waiting for that beautiful image. However, faster cards are now on the market. In addition to on-board memory, some of these cards feature graphics processors or coprocessors that can greatly speed things up.

There are scads of display cards on the market, from $50 no name VGA cards, to high-end 24-bit cards that sell for thousands. Do yourself a favor: stick to the brand names. You will save yourself plenty of trouble down the road (like when Windows NT rolls out). You want to be very sure that you can get updated video drivers when you need them.

As of this writing, decent VGA cards can be had for $75, while respectable SuperVGA cards are in the $125 to $200 range. Accelerated cards configured with graphics coprocessors (for Windows) start at around $300. When buying video cards, remember this generalization: the more memory, the more colors, the more cash. You must ask yourself: "What kind of work do I do?" and budget accordingly. If you are creating mostly black-and-white work, a SuperVGA/1024×768 card fits the bill. If you can, spring for an accelerated card: you will appreciate the performance improvement over a vanilla card. For basic layout and design work, you easily can get away with 256 colors. . .just be sure to always specify colors with a swatch book. If you are doing high-end work, such as photo retouching, go for a 24-bit card.

Diamond SpeedStar

Through the production of the fourth edition of this book, a number of video cards were used. The bare minimum configuration for CorelDRAW! 3.0 is a VGA monitor and display card. Most folks are far happier with a display card that supports multiple resolutions. The Diamond SpeedStar display card covers that ground quite nicely. It can switch between VGA, SuperVGA, and 1024×768 resolutions. At the high-res settings, however, only 16 colors are available, because the board is configured with only half a meg of video RAM. The SpeedStar performed reliably when configured with the standard Windows VGA 3.0 driver.

ATI Graphic Vantage

In the midrange, an ATI Graphic Vantage card provides snappy performance. This card uses a graphics coprocessor to expedite screen redraws. The unit tested came configured with 1M of video RAM. VGA, SuperVGA, and 1024×768 resolutions are supported with either 16 or 256 colors. ATI claims that this card runs 11 times faster than unaccelerated SuperVGA cards. The Vantage's big brother, the Graphics Ultra, is even faster. Early versions of ATI's Windows 3.1 driver would not work properly with CorelDRAW! 3.0 in SuperVGA mode, although 1024×768 mode worked fine. If you have an ATI card and are experiencing problems, you may want to give them a call to see whether a new driver has been released.

Radius MultiView 24

At the high end, a Radius MultiView 24 demonstrates what serious 24-bit color is all about. Radius built their reputation in the Mac market, and has brought all their smarts to the PC side with aplomb. The MultiView 24 is an expensive card, but it is a professional tool, not a toy, providing 16.8 million colors at 1024×768. It comes configured with 3 meg of VRAM and 3 graphic coprocessors for the utmost in 24-bit performance. Because the MultiView 24 is a pass-through card, the Diamond SpeedStar card was used to provide VGA capabilities—cabling was a straightforward affair. The pass-through arrangement allows a dual monitor configuration. The Radius card was extremely stable, a joy to behold, and a pleasure to use.

Understanding a Bit More about Monitors

If you decide that you want to run at high-res, consider a monitor larger than 14 inches. Using a 800×600 or 1024×768 driver with a smaller monitor can give you a case of severe eyestrain. To be fair, most video card manufacturers (both ATI and Radius did) supply two sets of drivers for high-res: one with small fonts and one with large fonts. With a small screen, use the large font driver. With a gigantic 20-inch monitor, the small fonts should work just fine.

Buying More RAM

How much RAM should your system have? As much as you can afford. Although Corel recommends a minimum of 2 megabytes, you should really have at least 4M. In general, Windows applications are far happier with gobs of memory, and image editors, like Corel PHOTOFINISH! will use all the memory you can throw at them. With enough RAM, you can turn virtual memory off and reap a speed reward: RAM is far faster than virtual memory. Consequently, if you have plenty of RAM available, you have no need for a Swapfile.

To turn off Swapfile, start with the Windows Control Panel. Click the 386 Enhanced icon, and then click the Virtual Memory button. The dialogue box that appears shows your system's current settings. To alter the settings, click the Change>> button, and then enter your new settings. To turn virtual memory off, go to the Type option and click None, and then click OK. Click Yes at the warning box, and you're on your way.

Most PC clones come equipped to use SIMM RAM chips. You usually find two banks of four SIMM slots each. You must fill complete banks with like chips. Both 1M and 4M SIMM chips are readily available, and 16M SIMM chips are just entering the market. Check your system documentation for the speed and size SIMM chips your machine requires. With two full banks of 4M SIMM chips, you can cook with 32M of fast silicon for about $1,200.

Using SmartDrive

The newest version of Windows SmartDrive—the Windows Disk Cache—runs rings around its predecessor. The previous version was so notoriously slow that it spawned a slew of third-party disk-caching software, such as Hyperdisk and Super PC-Kwik. The third-party houses are now scrambling to hot-rod their products to a higher level of performance. SmartDrive is now a full-blown, well-mannered read/write cache. If you are not using SmartDrive, you are sacrificing performance.

Taking Care of Your Hard Disk

Personal computer hard disk drives are ticking time bombs. People get into a sense of security at the ease with which files can be stored "in the computer." Many folks simply ignore the care and well-being of their hard disks until trouble hits. The following sections describe a couple of practices that can make your hard disk hold more information and run smoother and faster.

Using PKZIP

To fit more files on a hard disk, you can compress files using a utility like PKZIP, discussed in Chapter 11. PKZIP can dramatically reduce the amount of space required to store a file. There is one important caveat: compressed files are not immediately accessible because they must first be uncompressed. Compression is not practical for files needed with any frequency, so use PKZIP with discretion.

Of course, you can use CorelMOSAIC! to compress CDR files (into library files), but you still need a general compression utility. PKZIP fits that bill.

Running CHKDSK

CHKDSK is a DOS utility for analyzing a disk's storage capacity and status. It also can fix lost file clusters that may be wasting space on your computer's hard disk. Every time your system bombs, temporary files are left which, over time, can squander valuable room on your hard disk. Do not confuse these temporary files with the Windows TMP files described earlier. These are temporary files of a different sort.

It is a good idea to run CHKDSK after removing large numbers of files. CHKDSK is another utility that should be run from DOS rather than Windows. By typing **CHKDSK /F** at the DOS command line, you tell DOS to correct any errors CHKDSK discovers. This procedure stores bad files and gives them the CHK extension. After CHKDSK is done, look at and remove any unneeded CHK files. For more information on CHKDSK, refer to a DOS manual.

Running a Disk Optimizer

Running a disk optimizer is especially important on a small hard disk. Disk optimization can encompass a couple of different procedures and requires that you purchase a utility package such as the *Norton Utilities Advanced Edition*.

In general, disk optimization consists of *defragmenting* or repacking your hard disk, along with possibly changing your hard disk's interleave.

Files are stored in 512-byte sectors. When a disk (be it hard or floppy) is new and files are stored for the very first time, they are saved in sequential sectors. As the disk fills up and the files are updated and appended, the files are no longer stored sequentially, and they become fragmented. The File Allocation Table enables DOS to monitor the status of all the sectors on a disk. The more times a disk is used, the more fragmented and less efficient it becomes.

Disk fragmentation is easy to correct by running a disk "defragger," such as Norton's *Speed Disk*. This utility reorganizes the placement of files and directories on a disk, thereby reducing the amount of read-write head movement and increasing the speed with which data can be read off the disk.

Disk interleave can compensate for a computer that does not match the performance of its hard disk. Changing disk interleave can improve disk performance, but it is a tricky procedure best left to hard-core techies.

Summary

Windows is it—at least as far as getting graphics done on the PC platform, that is. Microsoft has provided a rich and diverse repertoire of utility programs with the Windows package, and there is an ever-growing number of Windows applications. But Windows has upped the ante, and it is very demanding of the computers that run it.

As you have seen, you can optimize Windows performance on any platform with a minimum configuration of an 80286 computer with 2M of RAM and a 40M hard disk. To get even better performance in the Windows environment, you need to beef up your platform. For many, a powerful 80386 (or 486) computer, lots of RAM, and a large speedy hard disk have become a necessity. The old computer axiom goes something like, "software sells hardware." In the case of Windows 3.1, this has never been more true.

Beyond the Mouse

ach day brings yet another innovative tool with the promise of mastering the graphical user interface (GUI). Gadgets such as trackballs, touchpads, touchscreens, and other pointing devices seek to win our favor. Many do a fine job for most GUI tasks, but the graphic artist's needs are far more demanding. Zipping from window to window is small potatoes compared to creating complex artwork.

Electronic artists need precision and flexibility. Design concessions based on the limitations of hardware are a sad truth for many artists. Because mice, trackballs, and the like are not conducive to drawing in an intuitive manner, many a work has been compromised. It need not be that way.

An artist should be liberated, not imprisoned, by his tools. Imagine a paintbrush chained to a canvas, or a stick of charcoal wired to a sketch pad—not exactly an artistically stimulating thought. The computer and its peripherals should stimulate artistic creativity.

Throughout the creation of this book, the author experimented with a variety of input devices. Different stages of the production process brought out the good and bad points of each device. This appendix discusses the pros and cons of several input devices with which the author is particularly familiar. Use this information to help make a decision on the best input device for your needs.

The Microsoft Mouse

Without question, and for good reason, the Microsoft Mouse is one of the most popular input devices available today. In the past, Microsoft bundled the mouse with software such as Windows/ 286 or Paintbrush. This made the purchase an attractive package, so truckloads of mice were sold. But there is more than good marketing involved.

The venerable Microsoft Mouse offers a streamlined, ergonomic design. Many consider it the most natural-feeling mouse available today. Microsoft's designers have done a fine job of perfecting the mouse's mechanism and feel. The mouse fits into the palm of your hand, as if (amazing as it may seem) it was designed specifically for the task (and it was).

With a real Microsoft Mouse, you never need to worry about software compatibility, especially when you are running under Windows. In short, if a program uses a graphical interface, it is compatible with the Microsoft Mouse.

No mouse, however, can be considered a tool for serious electronic illustration. Drawing with a mouse is unnatural and cumbersome for most artists. To truly realize your own artistic potential, consider some of the other input devices on the market and save your mouse for backup duty or for non-artistic computing tasks like spreadsheet work.

The IMCS PenMouse

The most unique input device tested was the IMCS PenMouse. This strange-looking creature is best explained as a miniature mouse grafted to a pen-like appendage. Although the IMCS PenMouse is definitely not for everyone, it does hold promise for use in specialized circumstances.

The PenMouse is very conservative in its appetite for workspace, making it worthy of consideration for users with laptops or limited desktop real estate. With a lengthy 9.5-foot cord, the PenMouse has a conveniently long reach. In fact, one of the most pleasant things to do with the device is to mimic a conventional pen. With a pad of paper in your lap, you can use the PenMouse like a normal drawing tool and draw in a relaxed, semi-natural manner.

Although the PenMouse is intended to be held between the middle finger, forefinger, and thumb like a pen, the large angular case is too bulky for some people's liking. Tracing is inconvenient because the PenMouse's base obscures the drawing being traced.

The PenMouse runs flawlessly with Windows 3.1. Because the device uses the standard Microsoft Mouse driver, you do not even need to use Windows Setup to install the PenMouse. Hookup is simple with IMSI's distinctive cable adapter, which couples a mouse bus connection to DB-9 and DB-25 serial ports. The author tried routing the PenMouse through both a mouse port and the more pedestrian DB-25 connection with equally favorable results.

The PenMouse is finicky about the surfaces it is used on. The hard plastic roller does not like the smooth veneer tops of typical office furniture. Taping a piece of paper to the top of the desk or using a mouse pad alleviates the lack of traction. The roller ball is easily removed for cleaning through a hinged plastic door.

In everyday use, the PenMouse is not quite adequate for object-oriented illustration work. It is vague and imprecise when working with tight tolerances. For general Windows work, however, the device operates soundly. Although it is not recommended as your sole input device for artwork, the PenMouse deserves a look if your needs include laptop computing.

The Trackball

The device that first rode to fame in the video game arcade has become commonplace on personal computers all over the world. What is a trackball, you ask? For the uninitiated, think of a trackball as an upside-down mouse. To move the cursor, you roll the orb around. Not quite as much fun as the orb in Woody Allen's *Sleeper*, but quite effective for desktop computing.

In general, trackballs can be an excellent alternative to the mouse. They take up little desk space and, when used for general purpose click-and-drag computing, trackballs perform well. However, when put to the task of freehand drawing, the trackball falls far short. As a drawing tool, it is even less intuitive than the mouse. It is worth noting that although the trackball does not hold up to the task of freehand drawing, it is fairly proficient for node-tweaking chores.

To extol the virtues of one brand of mouse over the other, or to investigate everything from trackballs to touchpads, would be a waste of time. For serious design work, put the mouse, its siblings, and cousins on the shelf.

There is only one serious alternative: the digitizing (or graphic) tablet. Although a mouse may be inexpensive in comparison to a tablet, the mouse can never hope to offer the tablet's drawing precision. With a graphics tablet, freehand drawing becomes a genuine reality, rather than a bad joke. Try a good tablet. The cost differences soon becomes meaningless. The proper tablet should enable the artist to draw in a natural manner rather than in a clumsy tangle of mouse and cord.

All this may invoke the ire of mouse loyalists. But spend some time working with a quality graphics tablet like the ones described in the next section, and you will come to the same conclusion: drawing with a mouse is like painting with a brick.

The Wacom Family of Cordless Digitizers

Among the forefront of digitizing tablet manufacturers, Wacom, Inc. offers high-quality products at reasonable prices. Although there are less expensive graphic tablets on the market, they offer far fewer amenities. For example, all of Wacom's tablets are cordless. That is, there is no cord connecting the stylus (pen) or cursor (puck) with the tablet itself, so the user can hold the pen or puck in the most natural manner possible. Cordlessness alone makes Wacom tablets specialized devices. There are few cordless tablets on the market, and certainly none with the same feel or features.

You can economize by purchasing a smaller (and less expensive) tablet. Wacom offers a full line of digitizing tablets, running from the compact 6"×9" SD-510, to the monster 35"×47" SD-013. For DTP work, a 12"×12" tablet is the largest tablet you will need.

Throughout the production of the four editions of this book, the author had the good fortune to work with a Wacom SD-420 12"×12" digitizing tablet equipped with a cordless pen.

Right out of the box, the tablet was a joy to work with. Everything functioned properly and installation was a simple three-step process. Initially, the author ran the tablet with Windows/286 and was favorably impressed with the digitizer's performance. Windows 3.0 was released the week after the SD-420 arrived. Two days after the release of Windows 3.0, the updated Windows 3.0 mouse driver arrived. The tablet continues to operate flawlessly with Windows 3.1.

Throughout testing, the author ran into only one drawback to the cordless design—it was easy to pick up the pen and forget where he left it. To minimize this problem, Wacom provides a handsome storage case and also offers an attractive desktop pen holder.

In addition to the standard model SD-420, Wacom offers two variations on the same platform, the SD-421L and SD-422L. The SD-421L adds an electrostatic surface, which allows papers to be held to the tablet surface through electrostatic adhesion, avoiding the need for tape. This can be a boon for artists who trace artwork regularly. The SD-422L features a transparent menu that protects heavily used menu sheets from abuse. Although there are no Wacom menus for CorelDRAW! as of this writing, it would not be an insurmountable task to build your own.

The quality-conscious yet budget-minded artist would be wise to look at Wacom's 6"×9" SD-510 as a viable alternative to either a mouse or a full-sized tablet. The SD-510 provides many of the same features as its larger siblings at an affordable price.

The SD-510 is available in two configurations. The SD-510B features a PC Bus Card Controller and is valuable for situations where an extra serial port is not available. This model tablet draws power from the PC's bus, alleviating the need for an external power cord. For computers with an extra serial port but no extra expansion slots, consider the SD-510C, which operates off an RS-232C serial port. Unlike the SD-510B, the SD-510C requires an external power source.

The number of programs that support pressure-sensitivity is on the rise. On the bit-map side, both Image-In-Color and Fractal Design Painter do a fabulous job. In the vector world, Aldus FreeHand's pressure tool is simply wonderful, as is the implementation in Altsys Fontographer. The PC community has finally embraced pressure-sensitivity!

Wacom Inc.
West 115 Century Road
Paramus, NJ 07652
201/265-4226
FAX 201/265-4722

Wacom Technology Corp.
501 S.E. Columbia Shores Blvd.
Vancouver, WA 98661
800-922-6613

Glossary

A

Anamorphic Scaling. Reducing or increasing one dimension (height or width) of an object without doing the same to the other dimension.

Ascender. The part of a lowercase letter that extends above the x-height.

B

Baseline. The implied boundary on which a line of type sits.

Bezier Curves. A mathematical formula for the description of a curve drawn between two anchor points (or nodes, in Corel terms). Each curve has a set of tangent (control) points to delineate the curve's path. The curves were developed in the early 1970s by French mathematician Pierre Bezier.

Bit Map. A dot-by-dot method of rendering images. Common file formats include BMP, GIF, PCX, TGA, and TIFF.

Bleed. The illusion of printing to the edge of the paper. Accomplished by printing on an oversized piece of paper and then trimming to size.

C

Caps. Uppercase or capital letters.

Color Separation. Separating a color original (photograph or illustration) into the four process colors—cyan, magenta, yellow, and black.

Color Trade Shop. A firm that specializes in printing prepress, specifically process color work. Usually employs a combination of traditional stripping techniques along with high-end graphic systems, such as Scitex, DS, Linotype-Hell, or Crosfield.

Comp. Abbreviation for *comprehensive.* The designer's term for a mock-up of a finished job. Used for presentation, rather than production purposes.

Condensed. A narrow version of a font, with a high character-per-line-count. Corel can produce a pseudo-condensed version of any font through the use of anamorphic scaling. Use with caution—readability may be affected. See **Extended.**

Continuous Tone. Refers to an image with a smooth transition in tone, as in original photographs, charcoal drawings, or watercolor paintings. Cannot be rendered through any printing process. See **Halftone**.

D

Decorative. An overdone typeface with a distinctive look. Used mainly for headlines; not normally used for text.

Descender. The part of a lowercase letter that extends below the baseline.

Desktop Publishing (DTP). The use of a personal computer as a system for producing typeset-quality text and graphics. The term was reportedly coined by Aldus chief Paul Brainerd.

Dot Matrix. An inexpensive printer that uses a print head commonly consisting of from 9 to 24 pins. Typically an office printer, a dot-matrix printer does not have high enough resolution to be used for computer graphic work.

DPI. Stands for *dots per inch*. Used in reference to the resolution of an output device or scanner. The higher the device's dpi, the higher the quality of the image.

Dropout (or Knockout) Type. White type that "drops out" of a black or darkly colored background. Often referred to as *reverse type*.

E

Em Dash. A dash approximately as wide as the letter *M* (most often used in text).

En Dash. A dash as wide as the letter *N* (most often used with dates or numbers).

Extended. A wide version of a font. Corel can produce a pseudo-extended version of any font through the use of anamorphic scaling. See **Condensed**.

F

Family. All the fonts of the same typeface in various sizes and weights. Typically includes Roman, italic, bold, and bold-italic.

Flush. A term (as in *flush-right* and *flush-left*) referring to type set with an even margin on either the right or left side. Also commonly referred to as *quad left* or *quad right*, alluding to the metal-type days when such lines were filled out with blanks known as quads.

Font. A set of characters of one typeface, weight, and size. In the hot-metal days, the term referred to a particular font of a particular size and style, such as 10-point Times-Roman. With the advent of digital composition, a font is thought of as the style throughout its complete range of sizes.

H

Hairline. A fine rule of half a point or less.

Halftone. A method of visual trickery used when printing photographs. A halftone image fools the eye into thinking that black and white can produce gray by breaking down the tones into a series of noncontiguous dots. Dark shades are produced by dense patterns of thick dots. Lighter shades are produced by less-dense patterns of smaller dots. Can be produced either photographically or electronically. See **Continuous Tone**.

High-Res. Abbreviation for *high resolution*. Refers to an output device's capability of rendering images at 1270 dpi or higher.

I

Inferior Figures. Small numbers, letters, or special characters set below the baseline.

J

Justified Type. Type set with even left and right margins. High-end composition programs hyphenate and justify (H&J) copy by using both dictionary and algorithm methods.

K

Kerning. Reducing or increasing space between character pairs to compensate for character shape. Some examples of character pairs commonly kerned are *AW*, *LY*, *Te*, and *Ve*.

L

Leading. The amount of space between lines of type. Pronounced "ledding," the term comes from the actual strips of lead placed between lines in the hot-metal era.

Letterspacing. Increasing or decreasing the space between all characters. Current use of the term commonly refers to the act of opening up space, as opposed to *tracking*, which refers to the tightening up of space.

Ligatures. Character pairs, such as *ae, fi, fl, ff, ffi*, and *ffl*, combined to form one character for aesthetic reasons.

Line Length. The column width of a block of type, normally measured in picas.

Low-Res. Abbreviation for *low resolution*. Refers to an output device's limitation of rendering at 400 dpi or less.

O

Oblique. A variation of italic.

Overprinting. Printing over an area that has been printed with a previous color. (The only way to trap with CorelDRAW!.)

Overprint Type. Black or dark-colored type printed over a lighter underlying color, halftone, or light-gray tint.

P

PANTONE Matching System. The printing industry's standard method of mixing inks and describing spot colors.

Pica. The printer's basic unit of measurement. An inch contains approximately 6 picas.

Point. There are 12 points to the pica, approximately 72 to the inch.

Point Size. The measurement used to describe type height. Refers to the approximate distance between the top of the ascenders and the bottom of the descenders.

PostScript. The *de facto* standard page-description language used in laser printers and other output devices. This Adobe Systems product revolutionized the typesetting and graphic art worlds.

Process Color. The process used to produce the illusion of "full-color" printed pages. The image is produced using four printing plates, with one color (cyan, magenta, yellow, or black) on each plate.

R

Ragged. A term (as in *ragged-left* or *ragged-right*) that refers to type set with an uneven margin on one side. Depending on client preference, ragged type can be set with or without hyphenation.

Registration Marks. The bull's-eyes (or cross-hairs) used by printers to align multicolor jobs when stripping negatives.

S

Sans Serif. A typeface without serifs, such as Helvetica.

Script. A typeface rendered with a calligraphic style. Commonly used for wedding invitations.

Serif. A typeface with end strokes, such as Times-Roman.

Service Bureau. A firm that specializes in high-resolution output of PostScript files. Commonly equipped with a combination of imagesetters, color printers, and other proofing equipment.

Set Solid. Type set with a leading equal to the point size. Best used in larger display sizes with all caps.

Small Caps. Type set in all caps smaller than the standard upper-case capital letters of the font. Small caps are drawn to sync with the normal x-height.

Spot Color. Printing with more than one color, but not process. Ink is mixed to attain the precise color.

Spreads and Chokes. Swelling and shrinking negatives to compensate for press variations. Commonly referred to as *trapping*.

Standing Head. A "department head" that identifies a standard feature column in a periodical.

Stripping. The craft of assembling film negatives prior to printing. This art is best left to the professional.

Subscript. Small numbers, letters, or special characters set below the baseline.

Superior Figures. Small numbers, letters, or special characters such as the dollar sign, aligned with (or higher than) the top of the caps.

Superscript. Small numbers, letters, or special characters such as the dollar sign, aligned with (or higher than) the top of the caps.

T

Thumbnail Sketches. These are the first stages of a project. Simple scribbles, often done on whatever paper may be available at the time—including coffee-stained restaurant napkins.

Tracking. Tightening the space between all characters, as opposed to *kerning*, which affects only the space between two characters.

Trapping. Slightly overlapping adjoining colors to prevent gaps when printing.

TrueType. An attempt by Apple and Microsoft to quash the Adobe Type 1 font-format standard. Dead for all intents and purposes on the Mac, its implications on the PC market remain to be seen.

TruMatch. A system for defining process color.

Typography. The craft of designing with type.

U

U&lc. Type set in uppercase and lowercase. Also, an excellent magazine published by the International Typeface Corporation.

V

Vector-Based Art. Drawings based on mathematical equations rather than bit-by-bit representations. This genre of electronic art can be scaled at will, without loss of resolution.

X

X-Height. The height of a lowercase letter *x*. Two typefaces may be the same point size, but have different x-heights.

CorelDRAW! Keyboard Shortcuts

+ (on the numeric keypad). Leaves the original object in place when moving, stretching, mirroring, rotating, or scaling. Also places the duplicate object behind the selected object, without any other actions.

Alt-A. Drops down the Arrange menu.

Alt-Backspace. Accesses the Undo command.

Alt-C. Drops down the Effects menu.

Alt-D. Drops down the Display menu.

Alt-E. Drops down the Edit menu.

Alt-Enter. Accesses the Redo command.

Alt-F. Drops down the File menu.

Alt-S. Drops down the Special menu.

Alt-T. Drops down the Transform menu.

Alt-Tab. Switches between active programs.

Clicking the right mouse button while dragging an object.
Leaves the original object.

Ctrl-1. Accesses the Layers roll-up menu.

Ctrl-2. Accesses the Text roll-up menu.

Ctrl-A. Accesses the Align dialogue box.

Ctrl-B. Accesses the Blend roll-up menu.

Ctrl-C. Combines objects.

Ctrl-D. Duplicates an object.

Ctrl-E. Accesses the Extrude roll-up menu.

Ctrl-Esc. Accesses the Windows Task Manager.

Ctrl-F. Accesses the Fit Text To Path roll-up menu.

Ctrl-G. Groups objects.

Ctrl-Insert. Copies to the clipboard.

Ctrl-J. Accesses the Preferences dialogue box.

Ctrl-K. Breaks apart combined objects.

Ctrl-L. Accesses the Move dialogue box.

Ctrl-N. Accesses the Rotate & Skew dialogue box.

Ctrl-O. Opens an existing CorelDRAW! file.

Ctrl-P. Accesses the Print dialogue box. Press Enter to send the image to the printer.

Ctrl-Q. Accesses the Stretch & Mirror dialogue box.

Ctrl-R. Repeats the last command or function.

Ctrl-S. Saves the current drawing to disk.

Ctrl-T. Accesses the Text dialogue box.

Ctrl-U. Ungroups objects.

Ctrl-V. Converts an object into curves.

Ctrl-X. Quits CorelDRAW!.

Ctrl-Y. Turns the grid on and off.

Ctrl while drawing an ellipse or rectangle. Constructs a perfect circle or square.

Ctrl while moving. Constrains movement to horizontal or vertical.

Ctrl while rotating or skewing. Constrains movement to 15-percent increments.

Ctrl while stretching, scaling, or mirroring. Constrains movement to 100-percent increments.

Ctrl-Z. Aligns text to baseline.

Del. Deletes a selected object or node.

Double-clicking a character node. Accesses the Character Attributes dialogue box.

Double-clicking the page border. Accesses the Page Setup dialogue box.

Double-clicking the ruler. Accesses the Grid Setup dialogue box.

F1. Accesses Help (on active command or dialogue box).

F2. Zooms in.

F3. Zooms out.

F4. Zooms to fit in window.

F5. Enables the pencil tool.

F6. Enables the rectangle tool.

F7. Enables the ellipse tool.

F8. Enables the text tool.

F9. Enables full-screen preview/editing.

F10. Enables the shape tool.

F11. Accesses the Fountain Fill dialogue box.

F12. Accesses the Outline Pen dialogue box.

PgDn. Moves object backward one.

PgUp. Moves object forward one.

Shift-F1. Accesses Help (on selected item).

Shift-F4. Zooms to fit page in window.

Shift-F9. Enables full-color/wireframe editing.

Shift-F11. Accesses the Uniform Fill dialogue box.

Shift-Insert. Pastes the current object from the clipboard.

Shift-PgDn. Moves object to back.

Shift-PgUp. Moves object to front.

Shift-Tab. Selects the previous object.

Shift while drawing. Erases when the mouse moves backward along a curve.

Shift while drawing an ellipse or rectangle. Stretches or scales from the middle of the object.

Spacebar. Toggles between the currently selected tool and the pick tool.

Tab. Selects the next object.

Clip-Art Compendium

This appendix presents a brief list of electronic clip-art vendors. You may recognize some of the names from the collection that accompanies CorelDRAW!. Before you buy any clip art, make sure that you know what you are getting. Feel free to request brochures and samples from the manufacturers.

You will get the most value for your clip-art dollar by installing a CD-ROM drive. Every copy of CorelDRAW! 3.0 includes a bonus CD-ROM disk, which contains thousands upon thousands of clip-art images, from such vendors as ArtRight, Image Club, MicroMaps, One Mile Up, Tech Pool, and Totem. The money you'll spend to install the drive will be far overshadowed by the wealth of high-quality artwork, not to mention the additional fonts!

21st Century Media PhotoDisk

Volume 1 - Business & Industry
Volume 2 - People and Lifestyles
Volume 3 - Backgrounds and Textures

The GIRL.TIF used in the Photo-Paint chapter and supplied on the bundled disks was graciously provided by 21st Century Media. It's part of their PhotoDisk(TM) collection. Each volume contains 408 high quality images on CD-ROM. Every photo is model released and ready for advertising, promotions, newsletters, presentations, and multimedia. These images are scanned from transparencies and provided in low resolution TIFF, PICT (medium resolution), and JPEG High resolution format for the PC/Windows and Macintosh.

PhotoDisk, Inc.
2013 4th Ave., Suite 200
Seattle, WA 98033
800-528-3472

Artbeats

Dimensions Volumes 1 and 2
Natural Images Volume 1
Potpourri Volume 1

Artbeats clip art is distinguished by its professionally rendered backgrounds. These are EPS files that are croppable, scalable, and stretchable. Each collection contains 20 full-page files. All are excellent choices for ad work, packaging, and slides. The images are beautiful and well-constructed.

Artbeats
P.O. Box 20083
San Bernardino, CA 92406
800/444-9392
FAX 714/881-4833

ArtMaker

ArtMaker has a four-volume disk art library that has, all told, over 250 illustrations to round out your collection of 300 dpi PCX files.

You get "An-T-Static" disk storage, a pictorial index guidebook, and the free disk of your choice with your purchase.

> The ArtMaker Company
> 500 N. Claremont Blvd.
> Claremont, CA 91711
> 714/626-8065
> FAX 714/621-1323

ArtRight Image Portfolios

Animals 1
Borders 1
Transportation 1
World Flags
Technology
People

ArtRight produces electronic clip art in the ultimate form for CorelDRAW! users—the native CDR format. Because the artwork comes in the CDR format, you don't wait for the file to import. In addition, the files are constructed clean and lean. Most images are in full color. The automobiles, in particular, are nothing short of stunning. This is the indisputable first choice for Draw users and is included on the CorelDRAW 3.0 CD-ROM disk.

> ArtRight Software Corporation
> Corel Systems Corporation
> 1600 Carling Avenue
> Ottawa, Ontario, Canada K1Z 8R7
> 613/728-8200
> FAX 613/728-9790

Atlas PC EPS Version

This is a versatile, comprehensive collection of maps. It is essential for many business situations. In fact, you may find that this package will pay for itself the first time you use it. It won't quicken your pulse, but it will pay the rent. Included in the package are maps of the USA by state, every US state by county, and maps of the entire world. You will find a nice selection of MicroMaps on the CorelDRAW 3.0 CD-ROM disk.

MicroMaps Software, Inc.
P.O. Box 757
Lambertville, NJ 08530

BBL Typographic

Volume 1—Westminster Abbey
Volume 2—Pontificale of John I
Volume 3—The Golden Bible
Volume 4—St. Mary of Soest
Volume 5—Paris Book of Hours

From the land down under comes a series of well-rendered medieval and renaissance letter forms and ornaments. Each volume contains a full alphabet of initial caps, in addition to decoratives, borders, and other period artworks. More than 70 images per volume. Available in CorelDRAW! Version 1 format.

BBL Typographic
137 Narrow Neck Road
Katoomba, NSW 2780
Australia
011-61-47-826111

Casady & Greene

Vivid Impressions
Special Events

One of the favorite small electronic type foundries, Casady & Greene specializes in calligraphic, classic, and continental-flair typefaces. The company also produces a limited amount of clip art. Special Events is a charming little collection containing Dorothea Casady's "Meow" Cat Alphabet along with a variety of electronic art files suitable for holiday use. Perfect for calendars, lighter newsletters, and so on.

Casady & Greene
P.O. Box 223779
Carmel, CA 93922
800/359-4920 or 408/624-8716
FAX 408/624-7865

Church Mouse Electronic Illustration

Youth Art 1.0 (100 illustrations)
Church Life 1.0 (100 illustrations)
Sports 1.0 (40 illustrations)
Holidays & Seasonal (40 illustrations)
Books of the Bible (15 selected titles)
Demo Disk (includes samples from all five volumes)

As you might guess, these collections are ideal for churches or organizations. Whimsical and "cartoony" renderings in the Youth Art and Sports collections make them appealing and fun. All images are digitized 300 dpi bit maps.

The Church Art Works
875 High Street NE
Salem, OR 97301
503/370-9377
FAX 503/362-5231

Clipables

Clipables: The EPS Graphics Library

Clipables contains more than 1300 professionally drawn black-and-white EPS files. This is a particularly versatile collection, which spans some of the following topics: animals, borders and ornaments, computers and business machines, children, construction, dingbats and symbols, display banners, drop cap toolbox, expressions, famous people, holidays, humor, maps and flags, medical, music, portfolio, sports, and transportation. Fortunately, this extensive library comes with a user's manual featuring a pictorial index that includes every image in the library. Available on disk and CD-ROM. The product is a particularly good value when you consider the excellent cost-per-image ratio.

C.A.R., Inc.
7009 Kingsbury
St. Louis, MO 63130
800/288-7585 or 314/721-6305

Clip-Art Window Shopper (Subscription)

As mentioned in Chapter 11, Adonis Corporation's Clip-Art Window Shopper gives the desktop publisher a way to buy electronic clip art by the piece, rather than the package. A subscription to the service together with a modem lets users download art over phone lines at a moment's notice.

Adonis Corporation
12310 NE 8th Street #150
Bellevue, WA 98005-9832
800/234-9497

Clipatures

Clipatures Volumes 1 and 2

Clipatures offers two collections of EPS artwork targeted specifically for the business user. The collections are populated with lots of people in office settings. Volume 1 includes credit cards, icons, and a good number of business-specific cartoons. Volume 2 includes silhouettes, computers, and airplanes.

Dream Maker Software
7217 Foothill Blvd.
Tujunga, CA 91042
818/353-2297
FAX 818/353-6988

DesignClips—Natural Environment Series

Birds
Fish
Flowers
Fruit
Insects
Invertebrates
Mammals
Reptiles & Amphibians
Trees, Leaves & Plants
Vegetables

A thorough, well-planned library of black-and-white graphic symbols, perfect for use as design elements. For example, the Fish collection includes (from A to D): Albacore, Anchovy, Angelfish, Bandtail Puffer, Barracuda, Bluefin Tuna, Blue Marlin, Bonito, Butteryflyfish, Cod, and Dolphin. Each collection consists of 50 files, along with a comprehensive pictorial index. These images were originally designed as object-oriented art; therefore, the collection is available as EPS files. TIFF and PCX files are also available. LetterSpace is a subsidiary of David Curry Design, a New York-based graphic design firm.

LetterSpace
100 Wooster Street, 2nd Floor
New York, NY 10012
800/933-9095 or 212/226-8766

DeskTop Art/EPS (Subscription)

From Dynamic Graphics, the makers of two of the most popular print clip-art collections—Print Media Service and Clipper—comes DeskTop Art/EPS. Collections are published monthly. Each collection contains approximately 40 images and includes a copy of *Ideas & Images*, a printed design guide with tips and hints for using the images.

Dynamic Graphics, Inc.
6000 N. Forest Park Drive
Peoria, IL 61614-3592
800/255-8800
FAX 309/688-5873

DrawArt Professional

Object-oriented illustrations in GEM format. The collection in-cludes 150 illustrations with subjects including office, sports, and transportation.

Migraph, Inc.
200 S. 333rd (220)
Federal Way, WA 98003
800/223-3729

Enabling Technologies

Clip3D Library
Clip3D Accents
Clip3D Business
Clip3D Fonts
Clip3D Geography
Clip3D Lifestyle

Clip3D Messages
Clip3D People
Clip3D Recreation

Eight volumes of electronic clip art containing 1200 files from the makers of ZING!. Collections are available separately or as a package, in Mac or PC format. On the PC, files are exportable in TIFF, PostScript, Encapsulated PostScript, EPS with TIFF, Illustrator 1.1 EPS, and Illustrator with TIFF formats.

> Enabling Technologies
> 343 South Dearborn, Suite 2000
> Chicago, IL 60604
> 312/427-0408

Federal Clip Art

Federal Clip Art I—A Congress of Artwork
Federal Clip Art II—Areospace Art
Federal Clip Art III—Naval Art
Federal Clip Art—Desert Storm Collection

Serious newspaper publishers along with government and defense contractor DTPers will be very pleased with these four packages. Each collection contains over 170 meticulous illustrations of various military hardware, insignias, and other U.S. government-specific items, including aircraft, missiles, and naval vessels. This is black-and-white EPS art, but packages also include Pantone and CMYK settings for exact government colors. The packages demonstrate an impressive attention to detail. You will find lots of great One Mile Up clip art on the CorelDRAW 3.0 CD-ROM disk.

> One Mile Up, Inc.
> 7011 Evergreen Court
> Annandale, VA 22003
> 703/642-1177
> FAX 703/642-9088

Fine Art Impressions

Fine Art Impressions Art Library

A highly stylized package of hand-created illustrations. The 177 black-and-white detailed illustrations are available in CDR, EPS, CGM (for PC PageMaker users), and GEM (for Ventura Publisher users) formats. Includes *Image Extras* (hardcopy illustrations not found on the disks), *The Designer's Desktop* (a step-by-step layout and design guide), *The Illustrator's Portfolio* (large printed samples of each image), a *Troubleshooting Guide*, and even a full-color three-ring binder to store it all in! Titles in the library include Money & More Money, Making Headlines, Professional Workforce, Borders & Boxes, and Occupational Themes.

> Best Impressions
> 3844 W. Channel Islands Blvd. #234
> Oxnard, CA 93035
> 800/456-4033 or 805/984-9748
> FAX: 805/984-8873

FM Waves

DTPro CD-ROM
15 Graphic Original Portfolios
Graphic News Network (monthly subscription service)

Marketed as "Clip Art With An Attitude," FM Waves offerings come in all flavors: PC or Mac, and EPS or 400 dpi TIFF. DTPro provides a wealth of images on a CD-ROM disk. Graphic Originals contains everything from icons, design elements, and arrows through beautiful fashion pen-and-ink renderings—all done with style. The Graphic News Network is intended for desktop publishers who need timely political cartoons, editorial graphics, and other hard-to-find artwork. Overall, FM Waves provides a formidable wealth of quality images.

FM Waves
70 Derby Alley
San Francisco, CA 94102
800/487-1234

FontHaus Picture Fonts

Set No. 1—Transportation & Travel
Set No. 2—Commerce & Communication

FontHaus calls their Picture Fonts "pictures you wouldn't expect from your keyboard," and that's quite an accurate description. Scalable, PostScript fonts, the first two sets in the series offer nice collections of symbols and borders. You can build your own train set (each car is a character), and create wonderful coupons and advertisements. Borders are created directly from the keyboard, using an old typesetter's trick. FontHaus Picture Fonts are thoughtfully designed, whimsical, and of high quality.

FontHaus, Inc.
15 Perry Street A7
Norwalk, CT 06850
800/942-9110

Image Club

DarkRoom Clip Photography
Digit-Art

DarkRoom Clip Photography is a stock photo library on CD-ROM. This collection consists of over 500 ready-to-use grayscale TIFFs. Subjects include business, lifestyle, sports, and travel. Photos may be used in black and white without paying additional royalties—provided that the photographer is credited. Color photos may be requested for a royalty fee.

Image Club is also known for its massive collection of over 600 PostScript fonts, with an unabashed focus on display faces.

Digit-Art is a collection of 15 volumes of EPS art, available by volume or in combination. The volumes are also available as a complete collection, the ArtRoom CD-ROM, which contains over 2800 images. The work ranges from slick and stylized to fanciful cartoons. The sheer volume of work is impressive.

Image Club Graphics, Inc.
#5, 1902—11th Street S.E.
Calgary, Alberta, Canada T2G 3G2
800/661-9410 or 403/262-8008
FAX 403/261-7013

Images with Impact!

Graphics & Symbols
Business 1
Accents & Borders

Graphics & Symbols covers a broad range of subjects. Ditto for Business 1, which includes people, computers, financial success, and hands at work. Borders 1 contains 270 design elements, including seasonal, geometric, historical, and contemporary designs. These are EPS files.

3G Graphics
11410 N.E. 124th St., Suite 6155
Kirkland, WA 98034
206/367-9321

Innovation Advertising and Design

Ad Art: Logos & Trademarks, Volumes 1 through 8
International Symbols & Icons, Volumes 1 & 2
Flags of the World

Business Symbols Collection
Vinyl Cutter Collection
Safety & Packaging Collection
Recycled Art—Environmentally Safe Clip Art
Ad Art Clip Art for Advertising CD-ROM

Clip art that should be standard issue for those who build advertisements or signage. Ad Art is a superb idea: EPS logos for every company that you can think of! If you have ever spent hours searching out a logo for use in a newspaper ad, you will find this series indispensable. It includes graphics appropriate for businesses that sell or use autos, credit cards, insurance, real estate, and so on. International Symbols & Icons includes over 300 EPS files, perfect for business charts, maps, and packaging. This is bread-and-butter electronic clip art. The CD-ROM package offers exceptional value—everything on one disk!

> Innovation Advertising & Design
> 41 Mansfield Avenue
> Essex Junction, VT 05452
> 800/255-0562 or 802/879-1164

Logo SuperPower

This is not clip art. It is really a set of over 660 electronic EPS design elements developed with logo and publication creation in mind. Design elements can be combined and tweaked for an infinite number of combinations. What formerly took days for an artist to render with pen and ink can be executed in a fraction of the time. An excellent choice for electronic designers who need to crank out logos at a moment's notice.

> Decathlon Corporation
> 4100 Executive Park Drive #16
> Cincinnati, OH 45241
> 800/648-5646 or 513/421-1938

Marble Patterns

Packages 1-5

Looking for a marble pattern for the background of a brochure cover, advertisement, or simply for a design element? Progressive Desktop Publishing offers five packages, available individually or as a set. Each package contains 256-level TIFF files of four different types of marble, including all your favorites: Vermont Verdi Antique (Volume 1), Fior di Pesco Gold (Volume 3), and Mediterranean Black (Volume 5). Professional packages include both 150 and 75 dpi scans. Laser Packages (at half the price) include only 75 dpi scans. A Sample Package is also available.

> Progressive Desktop Publishing
> 13A Park Avenue
> Gaithersburg, MD 20877
> 301/948-3047

Metro ImageBase

Metro, one of the leaders in printed clip art, has published a large body of quality bit-mapped images. Over a dozen collections are available, each consisting of 100 files. Collections include Art Deco, Borders & Boxes, Food, Team Sports, and The Four Seasons. Each collection comes with a printed *ImageIndex* for selecting files. These are 300 dpi PCX or TIFF files.

> Metro ImageBase
> 18623 Ventura Boulevard
> Suite 210
> Tarzana, CA 91356
> 800/525-1552 or 818/881-1997
> FAX 818/881-4557

Moonlight Artworks

PC Set 1 (110 general illustrations)
Holiday PC Set (90 seasonal illustrations)
Logomaster PC Set (195 graphic elements)

Cost-effective choice for those who work with display retail advertising (for example, newspaper ad designers). These sets use EPS files. Additional Moonlight Artworks, Logomaster, and Retail Ad Sets are soon to be released.

> Hired Hand Design
> 3608 Faust Ave.
> Long Beach, CA 90808
> 213/429-2936

NOVA Cube

Pix! Volume 1
Military Art

Pix! includes stylized design elements (line art) over a wide range: anatomy, appliances, buildings, flowers, food, medicine, people, and more. Military Art is "designed to meet the needs of professional military and defense industry users." This collection includes aircraft, equipment, symbols, and weapons. Both Pix! and Military Art are available in EPS format.

> NOVA Cube
> 5600 El Campo
> Ft. Worth, TX 76107
> 817/737-7941

PolyType

Volume 1—Ornaments
Volume 2—Corners

Volume 3—ArtDeco
Volume 4—Images

PolyType images are in font format, so that you access ornaments or objects with your keyboard, rather than by importing a file. Each volume contains 130 images (in 5 fonts). All fonts are supplied in Adobe Type 1 format, along with character outlines in EPS format.

PolyType
P.O. Box 25976
Los Angeles, CA 90025
310/444-9934
800/998-9934

Presentation Task Force

A collection of over 800 files in object-oriented CGM format, from one of the groundbreakers in electronic imagery. As the name implies, these images are perfect for presentation work, including 35mm slides. Almost half the images are color. Subject matter centers on business.

New Vision Technologies, Inc.
Box 5468, Station F
Ottawa, Ontario, Canada K2C 3M1
613/727-8184

ProArt

Multi-Ad Services, Inc., is a 40-year veteran of the print clip-art field. The electronic ProArt collections each contain over 100 files, and topics include holiday, business, sports, food, people, and borders and headings. These are EPS files and are available on floppy disk or CD-ROM.

Multi-Ad Services, Inc.
1720 W. Detweiler Drive
Peoria, IL 61615-1695
800/447-1950 or 309/692-1530
FAX 309/692-5444

Santa Fe Collection

Desktop Publishers in search of Native American and Southwest-
ern art will be pleased by the quality and value of the Santa Fe
Collection. Originally developed on the Macintosh—in MacPaint
format—and now available in PCX format, this is one of the most
complete and affordable genre libraries around. The many designs—including birds, bugs, fish, lizards, and motifs (over
100!)—show care, research, and sensitivity to Native American
culture. An excellent value, especially considering the low cost.
Includes 500 images and 140 borders.

RT Computer Graphics
2257 Calle Cacique
Santa Fe, NM 87505
800/245-7824 or 505/982-1562

Southwest Collection

Volume 1—Borders & Elements
Volume 2—Pottery & Baskets
Volume 3—Rugs & Blankets
Volume 4—Jewelry
Volume 5—Kachina Faces & Garments
Volume 6—Bead Designs
Volume 7—Custom SW Typefaces
Volume 8—Miscellaneous SW Graphics

Extremely detailed, high-end, full-color EPS clip art of the Southwest. Volumes are available individually or as a collection. Files are large. In fact, they are generally 10 to 100 times larger than conventional clip art. Compatible with Illustrator-EPS format (which can be imported into CorelDRAW!). For efficient manipulation, Graphx Associates recommends placing the files into page layout programs, rather than graphics programs (such as Draw), unless color changes are to be made. The sample file they sent weighed in at a staggering 650K!

Graphx Associates
P.O. Box 12811
Tuscon, AZ 85732-2811
800/628-2149 or 602/327-5885

Steven & Associates

Grand Potpourri Volume 1

One thousand images are found in this volume. Topics include architecture, birds, holidays, insects, mythology and fantasy, religion, semiconductors, symbols and signs, and, obviously, many more. All images are 300 dpi PCX files.

Steven & Associates
5205 Kearny Villa Way, #104
San Diego, CA 92123
619/571-5624

The SunShine Graphics Library

Specialists in large and elaborate bit-mapped images, many from the 19th century, some even older. Fabulous collection of intricate borders. All files are in MacPaint format and must be converted to PC/PCX. An interesting source for those with an accessible Mac.

SunShine
Box 4351,
Austin, TX 78765

Tech Pool Studios

The LifeART Human Anatomy Collection

"The best in anatomic exactness and visual clarity." An excellent resource for those involved in medical and legal presentations or publications. Titles in the collection include Cardiovascular, Musculoskeletal, Body Outlines, Reproductive, Special Senses, Dental, Endocrine Glands, Gastrointestinal, Urinary System, Joints, Nervous System, and Regional Anatomy. Over seven megabytes of EPS files. Check out the CorelDRAW 3.0 CD-ROM for a nice selection of TechPool art.

> TechPool Studios
> 1463 Warrensville Center
> Suite 200
> Cleveland, OH 44121
> 216/382-1234

Totem Graphics

Birds
Deluxe Business Images #1
Domestic Animals
Fish
Food
Flowers
Holidays
Insects
Nautical
Sports
Tools & Hardware
Wild Animals
Women

Gorgeous full-color EPS images. You may have seen a number of Totem Graphics' files in the CorelDRAW! Version 3.0 CD-ROM disk. Totem's artists have an excellent feel for wildlife illustration.

The Fish and Insects collections are particularly well executed. Each package includes 96 files and is available in CorelDRAW!, EPSF, and Illustrator formats.

Totem Graphics, Inc.
5109-A Capitol Blvd.
Tumwater, WA 98501
206/352-1851

U-Design Type Foundry

Bill's American Ornaments
Bill's Barnhart Ornaments 3.0
Bill's Classic Ornaments
Bill's DECOrations
Bill's Broadway DECOrations
Bill's Tropical DECOrations
Bill's Modern Diner
Bill's Peculiars
Bill's Printer's Pals
Bill's Victorian Ornaments

Lots of cool stuff from Bill! U-Design specializes in picture fonts with a period feel. These are wonderful decoratives that are most certainly worth owning. All are value-priced, and many come with bonus fonts, such as Bill's Dingbats (which was named by *MacUser Magazine* as one of their favorite 50 shareware products, as well as one of the 200 best products for the Mac). You can download sample U-Design Picture Fonts from CompuServe's DTPFORUM library.

U-Design Type Foundry
270 Farmington Avenue
Hartford, CT 06105
203/278-3648

Visatex Corporation

US Presidents
Hollywood Faces

The US Presidents collection contains portraits of all 41 US presidents. Hollywood Faces contains portraits of 25 movie stars, including Bogart, Brando, Cagney, and Groucho. Manually dithered grayscale PCX format.

> Visatex Corporation
> 1745 Dell Avenue
> Campbell, CA 95008
> 800/PC2-DRAW or 408/866-6562

The Visual Arts—Publishers Resource

"Four styles of art for all styles of pages." The styles referred to are Near Airbrush (similar in look to monochrome photography), Line Art, Enhancers, and Dingbatz. This is an excellent value for the money for everything from advertisements to newsletters and more. Subjects include people, technology, food and leisure, office, and general. Over 10M of EPS art.

> Electronic Pen Ltd.
> 4131 Cimarron Drive
> Clarkston, GA 30021
> 404/296-8623

Yukio Artwork Archives

Historical Aviation Clip Art Collectors Series 1 and 2
30's Poster Art

Aircraft illustrations and rare aviation photographs. Poster Art has 20 original layout and format guides, 20 background and modernistic panels, 8 typeface letter styles, and more. Be sure to specify the required file format.

> Yukio Artwork Archives
> 2025 Federal Avenue, Suite #2
> Los Angeles, CA 90025
> 800/345-3632 or 213/473-5494

Index

Q-R

X-Z

New Riders Puts You on the Cutting Edge of Computer Information!

AUTOCAD

AutoCAD: The Professional Reference $39.95
AutoCAD: Drafting and 3D Design $29.95
AutoCAD: Drafting and 3D Design Disk $14.95
AutoCAD: Drafting and 3D Design
 Instructor's Guide $175.00
AutoCAD 3D Design and Presentation $29.95
AutoCAD for Beginners $19.95
AutoCAD Instructor's Guide $175.00
AutoCAD Reference Guide, 2nd Edition $14.95
AutoCAD Student Workbook $39.95
AutoCAD Windows for Beginners $19.95
Inside AutoCAD, Special Edition $34.95
Inside AutoCAD Release 11, Metric Edition $34.95
Inside AutoCAD Windows $34.95
Maximizing AutoCAD, Volume I:
 Customizing AutoCAD with Macros & Menus $34.95
Maximizing AutoCAD, Volume II:
 Inside AutoLISP $34.95
Managing and Networking AutoCAD $29.95

ENTERPRISE COMPUTING

Enterprise Series: Applications $39.95
Enterprise Series: Connectivity $39.95
Enterprise Series: Operating Systems $39.95

GRAPHICS

CorelDRAW! On Command $19.95
Inside Autodesk Animator $29.95
Inside AutoSketch, 2nd Edition $24.95
Inside CorelDRAW!, 2nd Edition $29.95
Inside CorelDRAW!, 3rd Edition $34.95
Inside Generic CADD $29.95

OPERATING SYSTEMS/NETWORKING/MISC.

Inside CompuServe $29.95
Inside LAN Manager $34.95
Inside Novell NetWare $29.95
Inside OS/2, Release 2.0 .... $34.95
Inside SCO UNIX $29.95
Inside Solaris SunOS $29.95
Inside Windows 3.1 .... $29.95
Managing Novell NetWare $39.95
Maximizing MS-DOS 5 .... $34.95
Maximizing Windows 3 .... $39.95
Maximizing Windows 3.1 .... $39.95
Novell NetWare On Command $19.95
UNIX On Command $19.95
Windows 3.1 Networking $22.95
Windows 3 On Command $19.95
Windows 3.1 On Command $19.95

NEW RIDERS
PUBLISHING

For More Information, Call Toll-Free
1-800-428-5331

You'll Find All You Need To Know About Graphics with Books from New Riders!

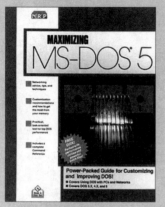

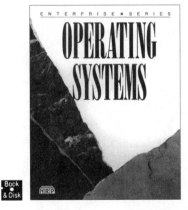